The MAGDALENE *in the* REFORMATION

The

MAGDALENE

in the

REFORMATION

Margaret Arnold

The BELKNAP PRESS *of*

HARVARD UNIVERSITY PRESS

CAMBRIDGE, MASSACHUSETTS

LONDON, ENGLAND

2018

First printing

LIBRARY OF CONGRESS CATALOGING-IN-PUBLICATION DATA

Names: Arnold, Margaret, 1973– author.
Title: The Magdalene in the Reformation / Margaret Arnold.
Description: Cambridge, Massachusetts : The Belknap Press of Harvard
University Press, 2018.
Identifiers: LCCN 2018008137 | ISBN 9780674979994 (hardcover : alk. paper)
Subjects: LCSH: Mary Magdalene, Saint. | Mary Magdalene, Saint—Cult. |
Reformation. | Women in Christianity—Europe—History. | Europe—Church
History—16th century. | Europe—Church history—17th century.
Classification: LCC BS2485 .A76 2018 | DDC 226 / .092–dc23
LC record available at https://lccn.loc.gov/2018008137

For Christopher

Contents

INTRODUCTION A Woman for All Seasons   1

1. The Medieval Magdalene
   Establishing a Cult of Personality   17

2. Teacher of the Dear Apostles
   Lutheran Preaching on Mary Magdalene   43

3. Publish the Coming of the Lord
   Evangelical Magdalenes   71

4. A Most Holy Penitent
   Preaching and Teaching the Magdalene in the Catholic Reformation   95

5. Love Made Her Dare
   The Magdalene among Catholic Women   127

6. These Magdalens
   Diversity in the Reformed Tradition   167

7. Mark This, Ye Despisers of the Weakness of Women
   The Magdalene of the Radical Reformation   201

CONCLUSION An Army of Such Ladies   223

Notes   245
Acknowledgments   291
Index   293

The MAGDALENE *in the* REFORMATION

INTRODUCTION

A Woman for All Seasons

MARY MAGDALENE has always represented a female spirituality as alarming as it is admirable, and never was this more so than during the sixteenth century—the age of reform. Described by name in the New Testament as a woman who supported Christ's ministry, becoming the first to witness his resurrection because she dared to visit his tomb, she had also traditionally been associated with Mary of Bethany, who sat at the feet of Christ while her sister, Martha, tended to the household, and with the penitent prostitute who washed Jesus's feet with her tears. In each of these guises the intensity of her devotion brings both praise and censure, as her courage and audacity are contrasted with social expectations for women and with the actions of men around her. And yet, in the sixteenth century, women across the Christian West eagerly identified themselves with this controversial figure, as they began to encounter her story through the emerging practice of Bible reading in the vernacular. The popularity of this identification reveals a debate over the question of women's divided loyalties, to their families and to their God, as a particular preoccupation of the era's religious reforms. The Magdalene's location, at the disputed intersection of the sacred and the profane, public ministry and private devotion, charged this debate and the larger allied project of interpreting the vocations of all believers, who must be in the world and yet not of it, in the teaching of early modern Catholics and Protestants.

Historical scholarship on the Magdalene has tended to overlook or deny any positive engagement with the saint on the part of Protestant reformers. Much work has been done on her medieval cult, but most authors are content with abrupt conclusions about Protestantism's suppression of devotion to the saints. Katherine Jansen's excellent study of the cult of Mary Magdalene in the Middle Ages concludes with a tantalizing epilogue on the fate of the saint in the period that follows, the era of the Reformation and Counter-Reformation.

1

After describing the rich and diverse spirituality that grew up around the medieval Magdalene, appropriated by male and female Christians in different ways, she sketches a brief outline of the cataclysm for hagiography that was the Reformation. Beginning with the humanist Jacques Lefèvre d'Étaples's debunking of much of her legendary history, Mary's descent from her medieval pedestal is precipitous. As Jansen writes, "Lefèvre's view added fuel to the Protestant fire which burned in readiness to consume the cult of the saints. Luther's distaste for the saints is legendary, as is that of his followers. They made no exception for the *beata peccatrix*."[1]

Likewise, Susan Haskins's art-historical survey of the saint dismisses any possible role Mary Magdalene may have had in the spirituality and teaching of the early reformers. She claims that the Magdalene's specific connection to the sacrament of penance—as well as her intercessory function in Catholic religious practice—made her unacceptable to Protestants, but engages in no discussion of differences among Protestant traditions on such questions as sacramental theology, the use of imagery, and the role of the saints.[2]

The Magdalene's life within the Catholic tradition was not unaffected by the Protestant Reformation, as Jansen notes: "The Protestant assaults, and the Catholic response to them, reshaped the persona of the Magdalen." Larissa Taylor has described the shift in early modern Catholic preaching about the Magdalene as having been made directly in response to Protestantism and the implications of the theology of the priesthood of all believers: "Pre-Reformation preachers, relying on *The Golden Legend*, referred often to Mary Magdalene's preaching in Aix and Marseilles. But increasing concern with order in the sixteenth century and the spectre of women preaching made Catholic preachers more circumspect in describing the role of the Magdalene, and at times this verged on disparagement."[3]

The dignity of her medieval position as teacher of the apostles, *apostola apostolorum*, was replaced by a new focus on the penitent Magdalene, an example for sexual sinners in particular, as she became the patron of countless post-Tridentine religious foundations for reformed prostitutes and the subject of myriad voluptuous depictions in Baroque art. Haskins acknowledges the Magdalene's deployment in Counter-Reformation polemics and programs: "Mary Magdalen's role as exemplar and intercessor brought her into the argument as a prime propaganda weapon against Lutheran tenets, and to uphold the Tridentine doctrine of merit." She does not, however, explore the problematic truth that it was, as we shall see, the *same saint* who was being used to uphold and teach those Lutheran tenets, particularly the assertion of justification by faith alone and the priesthood of all believers.[4]

Some studies have begun to address this lacuna. David M. Whitford has suggested that the Magdalene was central to the changes brought by the Reformation not because of her disappearance in Protestant preaching, but precisely because of her continued presence in sermons in both Catholic and Protestant communities, sermons that commented on each other. He writes,

> But what happened to her story following Reformation critiques of medieval preaching and medieval understandings of the care of souls? Mary Magdalene's story is an ideal lens through which to view these changes because first . . . it fits the model of medieval preaching nearly exactly. Second, because of the popularity of her story, there is ample evidence to examine from both before and after the implementation of the Reformation. Third, Mary Magdalene's life story was criticized directly during the sixteenth century thus allowing us to weigh the general critique of sermons and the specific critique of the composite Mary Magdalene.[5]

Patricia Badir's *The Maudlin Impression: English Literary Images of Mary Magdalene, 1550–1700,* looks at poetry and plays both Catholic and Protestant and manages to correct some of the misleading portrait of a disappearing Magdalene. While her study is limited to English literature, it confirms that the Magdalene continued to feature prominently in the tradition of Passion devotion and in the construction of religious identity on all sides of the confessional divide into the eighteenth century.[6]

Joan Kelly has famously asked, sparking the work of a generation of scholars of women's studies and early modern history, "Did women have a Renaissance?" One could similarly ask, "Did Mary Magdalene have a Reformation?" This book proposes to examine the two parts of this question. First, what was the fate of Mary Magdalene in Protestant teaching and devotional life? Was there really no exception made, even by reformers deeply suspicious of medieval piety, for a biblical saint engaged in so evangelical a task as divinely instructed preaching of the Word of God? Did she really drop out of sight, past a distant confessional horizon, or were parts of her medieval legend taken up by pastors counseling Protestant congregations and by women arguing for their right to speak as apostles? And if the Catholic response was shaped by the threat of a new application of her example to early Protestant laity, and to women in particular, how exactly was the Magdalene's image reformed in the church's teaching, and how did believers react to the various presentations of "the favorite saint of the Counter-Reformation"?[7]

Saints and Sanctity

Early modern religious culture emerged, in Europe and the Americas, from a dialogical relationship between Catholic and Protestant communities. Biblical saints continued to be important models for Catholics *and* for Protestants; among those saints, Mary Magdalene was central to the development of core theologies and institutions of both Catholic and Protestant reform. The recent interest in the role of saints in the Reformation era is part of a wider look at the complex process of confessionalization, the development of faith identities and cultures in societies that had become religiously divided. Studies of confessionalization examine popular piety, liturgy and preaching, education, and the arts in order to understand how Catholics and Protestants defined their confessional identities in opposition to each other during the late sixteenth and seventeenth centuries. Through this process, the models of religious and devotional life available to women were adapted and transformed according to the needs and goals of individuals, groups, and institutions.[8]

The early reformers engaged the cult of the saints: Martin Luther discussed the benefits of such piety for some Christians and warned his colleagues against an utter dismissal of this aspect of religious life. He sought not to remove the saints from view altogether, but to correct believers' relationship to them, promoting the study of the lives of saints from scripture and from the early centuries of the church, commending them as examples of faith rather than as supernatural intercessors. Luther's pastors followed his guidance, especially in the case of Mary Magdalene. Evangelical leaders fashioned a new piety around those saints whose lives and testimony were in accord with the theological program of the Reformation. The stories of the saints were published in books of martyrs and included in liturgy and preaching. Far from being ignored in the Protestant tradition, the saints of the Bible provided evangelical theologians and preachers with irresistible models for their congregations: familiar, time-honored stories of men and women reacting to the presence and instruction of Christ, offering cautionary tales at need, but also examples of faith and obedience to imitate.[9]

Reassessments of saints in the Reformation have led to other unexpected discoveries, including the practice of writing saints' lives that existed among humanists, a group long associated with the rejection of medieval piety. In fact, rather than suppressing or ignoring the tradition of the saints, some humanist authors wrote about saints to advance their programs of religious reform and innovation. A particular focus of saints' biographies produced in fifteenth-century Germany, for example, was the bishops who had converted the region in late antiquity. This backward look was intended to reenergize the church, to return to its original mission. Some of this evangelical zeal would fuel the German Reformation, where it found expression in further adaptations of the tradition, emphasizing those saints who had professed and taught the faith from the beginning, the Magdalene among them.[10]

These shifts involved not only new relationships to traditional saints but also explorations of the saintly life as it was being demonstrated in the age of reform. The lives of Catholic holy women, as documented by their male confessors, shaped the image of female sanctity presented to their contemporaries. In a culture particularly concerned to ensure and promote orthodoxy in the face of Protestant threats, Counter-Reformation definitions and redefinitions of sainthood were closely linked to the project of regulating popular piety and suppressing heresy. Yet the genre of saints' lives was not a simple tool for the promulgation of a single model of holiness. The diversity of lives recorded, including significant numbers of laywomen hailed for their sanctity, exposes a greater degree of resistance to the Catholic Reformation's restrictions on women than was previously understood.[11]

While early modern Catholic and Protestant attitudes toward sanctity and sainthood have been the object of scholarly interest, there has not been a comparative study of the different confessions' uses of the Magdalene tradition as they emerged in relation to each other and which takes particular account of the Protestant articulations of Mary's story. Adding Protestant narratives to Magdalene scholarship does more than correct the common misconception that all saints fell out of favor during the Reformation. Without an examination of both Catholic and Protestant developments within Magdalene interpretation as they developed in parallel, the picture of the

Counter-Reformation identity of the saint is incomplete. A thorough investigation of the Protestant discussions of Mary Magdalene as a female lay preacher, an interpretation known to Catholic theologians and explicitly cited and disputed by them, casts new light on the Catholic turn to emphasizing the penitent Magdalene, a sexual sinner redeemed by asceticism and incorporation into the sacramental system. This study provides a more complex picture of Protestant attitudes toward the saints while informing existing work on the Magdalene of the Counter-Reformation, helping the movement's "favorite saint" to be understood more fully in the polemical context of the era.

Women in the Age of Reform

The question of Mary Magdalene's place in the Reformation is inextricably linked to the interpretation of the Reformation's effects on women. The different readings of such a prototypical woman contribute to our understanding of how *woman,* as a category, was constructed in the early modern period and how women gave form to their own self-understanding as people of faith. One of the chief difficulties in understanding early modern women is the dearth of texts by women as compared to the record of male authorship. The accounts that do survive tend to belong to the lives of elite women, those few who were literate and able to have their work published, or those who were so prominent, socially and politically, that their actions and words were noted by contemporaries and historians. Among those whose writing survives, we find evidence for the continued possibility of pastoral ministry for women, while—except in the traditions that emerged from the Radical Reformation—sacramental and preaching roles were denied them.[12]

Natalie Zemon Davis has undertaken a systematic study of the era's social developments, and in her groundbreaking essay on the French Reformation, "City Women and Religious Change," she asks direct questions about the effect of the Reformation for women, what it meant to them, how they participated in its different movements, and how it changed the status of women in society: "Did the Reformation have a distinctive appeal for women? If so, what was it and to what kinds of women? What did Protestant women do to bring about religious change? And what innovations did the Reformation effect in the lives of women of different social classes?" Davis's analysis of the urban merchant and artisan classes finds that these women were already accustomed

to a high degree of independence in business and were becoming more educated and literate. Such women embraced the opportunity that Protestantism
offered to read scripture, debate theology, and even—at the beginning of the
movement—to preach.[13]

After the initial freedom that proved so attractive, a reassertion of clerical
authority by Protestant leaders in subsequent decades reduced the possibilities for women's public ministry and enforced a hierarchical marriage and
family structure, with the result being that women's status in Protestantism
remained "unequal."[14] Still unequal, but perhaps less limited, options existed
on the Catholic side: the avowed religious life, closed to Protestants, continued to offer vital vocations and leadership roles for Catholic women. Similarly,
models of specifically female holiness—such as the Magdalene—remained
available in Catholic culture, while Protestant women achieved a measure of
spiritual equality only by transcending their femininity. As Christians, all believers were equal before God, yet this did not translate into changes in gender
roles in the secular sphere. Davis concludes that while both Catholicism and
Protestantism contributed to the modernity that would ultimately recognize
gender equality, neither of their early modern incarnations advanced women's
rights in their essential character or through concrete acts of social reform.
In fact, according to this reading, the Reformation served to remove some of
the more positive female images and practices inherited from the medieval
tradition and hastened to stifle any potential freedom that may have been
promised by the movement's revolutionary first years.

This narrative arc, moving from an initial openness toward lay and female
ministry to an increasing clerical domination of new church structures, can
be found in numerous subsequent studies of the effect of the Reformation
on women.[15]

Lyndal Roper's analysis of the German Reformation exposes inherent contradictions between evangelical theology and the Lutheran Reformation's
teaching on women and the family; she asks, "How could a religion which
began by exulting in the prophetic talents poured out upon daughters as well
as upon sons come to view women almost exclusively as wives, whose sphere
it was to be subordinate to their husbands and instructed by their preachers?"
Roper evaluates the relationship between the reform movements and women
as "deeply ambiguous," but goes on to characterize the Magisterial Reformation as largely constricting for women, both at the practical level and in terms

of the Protestant religious imagination that developed. Nor was this effect tangential to the Reformation as a whole. Roper finds the conservative stance on gender that was adopted by the reformers to be central to the success and identity of their movement.[16]

Merry Wiesner-Hanks's study of conditions for women in early modern Europe confirms the male reformers' conservatism while seeking to reveal the ways women found to avoid the limitations placed upon them. "Religious traditions were used by men as buttresses for male authority in all realms of life, not simply religion," she notes. "Nevertheless, it was the language of religious texts, and the examples of pious women who preceded them, which were used most often by women to subvert or directly oppose male directives." Like Davis, Wiesner-Hanks finds most of the opportunity for that subversion at the initial stages of the Reformation era, in the first decade following a community's embrace of reform and before the institutionalization of the movement. She describes the domestic religious roles that would have been available to the majority of women: prayer and the instruction of children, communal worship, and some possibilities for charitable work. An alternative to domestic life remained open for Catholic women. Wiesner-Hanks outlines nuns' participation in the mission drives of the Counter-Reformation, and notes the tension that existed between the manifest benefits of women's efforts in this direction and the Counter-Reformation's expressed ideal of strict enclosure for women's orders, an ideal that ultimately reduced the sphere of an "active apostolate" for religious women to "the instruction of girls, and that only within the convent." Thus Catholic women's religious activity, like that of Protestant women, was often defined by a domestic orientation, whether the home was a communal or a marital one. In Elizabethan England, Wiesner-Hanks points out, that very domesticity could provide a haven when the practice of Catholicism was outlawed for those with public legal identities— men and single women—thus leaving a loophole for married women, who often exercised remarkable religious leadership.[17]

Susan Karant-Nunn evaluates the institutions that formed the framework for domestic life, looking at the social changes to marriage and the family as they affected women. Her work helps to explain the mechanisms by which the Reformation's initial promise of freedom was qualified for women. The focus on the virtues of Christian marriage in early modern Catholic and Protestant preaching and teaching described a fixed sphere for women's activity: in the home, subject to their husbands' authority. Changes to marriage and family life brought increased attention and expectations for women, and additional demands were placed on them with the Reformation's reduction of the family to the nuclear unit, which removed social institutions—monastic orders, confraternities—that had provided quasi-familial relationships. With these changes, Karant-Nunn notes, "immediate families were thrown back upon their own resources." While the status of the women who became pastor's wives was elevated above that of the late medieval priest's concubine, these women were also under pressure to serve as paragons of Christian marriage, mothering, and household management. For both Catholics and Protestants, preaching and wedding liturgies delivered a message of wifely subordination and relegation to a domestic role.[18]

In tandem with this work in social history, Karant-Nunn has collaborated with Wiesner-Hanks to trace the theoretical sources of the Reformation's attitude toward women. In their analysis of Luther's own pronouncements about women, Karant-Nunn and Wiesner-Hanks examine polemical and pastoral texts, as well as Luther's interactions with the women in his life as documented in letters. They find him providing both "conservation and inno- vation," though with an emphasis on the former. For Luther's conservative thought, they point to his acceptance of the Aristotelian understanding of women as physically and intellectually inferior, a claim that was used in sup- port of the existing social hierarchy. More innovative was Luther's embrace of a humanist emphasis on romantic love within companionate marriage, an expectation that presumes a responsive partner both physically and intel- lectually. Karant-Nunn and Wiesner-Hanks conclude, however, that Luther was, on balance, "a force for tradition rather than an innovator." Their focus is on the reformer's teaching about women as belonging in the home; they do not explore instances of his commendations of women's public religious testimony, which were frequently expressed in discussions of female saints. Here, attending to Luther's interpretation of the Magdalene can inform our understanding of his theological anthropology, shedding light on his reading of the role of women and of all believers in confessing the faith.[19]

The reform movements produced a chaotic era whose divisions affected women, often adversely. For those in areas dominated by Protestants, or by open conflict between different confessions, women were vulnerable to the resulting violence and social disruption. In the Catholic south of Europe, where open conflict was less common, women were instead subjected to the oppressive forces of the Inquisition.[20]

What happened when women chose to join the religious communities that were most persecuted and whose theologies tended to isolate them most from nonmembers—that is, the movements of the Radical Reformation? Davis's original inquiry into whether religious freedom and women's freedom were allied or opposed could be tested by examining the experience of women in these reform traditions that claimed the greatest degree of spiritual liberation and rejection of social norms. Such a question touches directly on the interpretation of the Magdalene among the communities of the Radical Reformation, on whether her role as evangelist, as teacher of the teachers of the church, would be taken up as a model for the laity and for women in particular.[21]

The study of early modern women and religion continues to be animated by Davis's formative questions even as her conclusions about the Reformation's effect have been nuanced or even challenged. Current scholarship has pushed the exploration of women's experience ever further beyond the small circle of exceptional women in an attempt to gain access to the operative worldviews and motivations, as well as the actions and recorded testimony, of more ordinary women in the early modern period. Constructing such a detailed and rich portrait makes broad conclusions more difficult. The present study of the early modern Magdalene will attend to the variety of options on offer and also look for insights into why particular interpretations were chosen and what might have made them convincing or popular in different communities.[22]

Members of each of the different faith traditions that emerged from the age of reform considered Mary Magdalene an ideal for women and for people of faith in general. Exploring the shifts in her identity will lead us to the heart of the debate over women in early modern religion. The Protestant Reformation's effects on women were ambiguous: the potential equality embedded in the evangelical theology of the priesthood of all believers was balanced by the loss of the mystical and saintly patterns of female holiness that had existed in the medieval church. The Protestant reformers' promotion of domestic life as the only vocation open to women denied them the option of public ministry, either as prophetic witnesses in society or as leaders within a women's religious order. Those who did protest against this limitation, or whose martyrdom opened a brief window for public testimony, stand as the few exceptions to that narrative. Perhaps the signal development in women's religious history has been to begin writing the stories of the unexceptional women and to devise means of accounting for their work and witness. Those women who did *not* protest but who accepted and perpetuated the model of a female domestic vocation also served as active participants in shaping the culture of the Reformation; as Kirsi Stjerna has observed, "The movement(s) flourished and endured from roots that were both male and female: the product not just of the male theologians but of women who as daughters, sisters, spouses, mothers, widows and as believers espoused the new faith and 'taught' it and 'preached' it in their own domains, so participating concretely in the new Protestant mission." Women made decisions in the home about what feasts and fasts to observe, which businesses to patronize, which stories to tell and songs to sing, how to educate their children, and which saintly models to follow as Christian women. All of these decisions contributed to the successful establishment—or rejection—of different religious movements during the centuries that followed Luther's initial reform.[23]

Sources on Sixteenth-Century Women

In studying the spiritual lives of those who may not have been able to write about themselves, it is helpful to look at the texts they knew, and at the many different ways in which they would have encountered them. Literate women (by far the minority) were able to read the Bible for themselves, in Latin or in the vernacular. More common would have been hearing the Bible read and discussed in church or at home, singing psalms and other hymns, and seeing illustrations of biblical stories in religious art and popular media. The sixteenth century marked an increase in women's access to the Bible, newly available in vernacular translation and in comparatively affordable print editions that made their way into homes and schools. But even illiterate women experienced preaching, liturgy, and visual culture that had a new focus on the individual's ability to appropriate the Gospel message and convey it to others.

Surviving sermons can provide a means of understanding what theologies, images, discipline, and practices were being conveyed to congregations. The emergence of Protestant devotion to Mary Magdalene can be found in collections of sermons published as guides or even as stock homilies for use by unprepared or poorly educated clergy. They provide evidence of the identity of the saint that was being taught to ordinary members of congregations. Sermon collections can be especially useful in that they demonstrate not only a widely approved and popular range of images as they were heard in parishes but also teaching tools for the clergy as they themselves learned how to preach an evangelical message. Many Protestant communities, including Lutherans, continued to observe Mary Magdalene's traditional feast day of July 22, and so preached on texts related to her on that day, as well as on Easter Sunday, when she features in the resurrection narrative. Congregations, and the priests and pastors who ministered to them, were influenced as well by a milieu that could include other kinds of spiritual reading, visual imagery, music, and worship, both in church and in the home. Sermons were received within the wider context of scripture study, devotional literature, and religious art, all of which helped shape the diverse adaptations of different elements of the Magdalene tradition in the early modern period.[24]

An investigation of sixteenth-century preaching about the Magdalene raises the question of preaching itself. The Magdalene, the first witness of the resurrection, had been used as a model for male preachers during the Middle Ages. Her role in the Gospels caused theologians of the Reformation era, both Catholic and Protestant, to debate the possibility of preaching by nonclergy and even by women. Preaching by the laity had been explicitly banned by canon law as part of the suppression of the Cathars and Waldensians, medieval sects that were condemned as heretical in part because they had promoted female preaching and lay religious leadership. Sixteenth-century reformers reopened the question as part of their attack on clerical authority. Luther's Bible translation used the words "preaching" and "preacher" to describe activities that ordinary men and women were instructed by God and Christ to undertake; in the medieval Latin Bible, the roles God gave to laypeople had been translated with words for more ordinary communication: "talking" or "speaker." The open debate over who was authorized to preach is paralleled by a question of how to evaluate the speech and work of early modern women. Can conversation and letter writing, offers of hospitality and other public support of the church, prophetic utterance or mystical visions, and the testimony of female martyrs from the scaffold be considered preaching? Were these activities ever understood as kinds of preaching by early modern women or their audiences? In exploring these questions it will be useful to keep in mind two of the main functions of preaching: converting an audience to faith in the Gospel and conveying the authoritative teaching of the church from a publicly acknowledged office. As they considered the nature of preaching and who might do it, early modern authors tended to distinguish or emphasize these two functions according to their different understandings of the vocation of the believer and the relationship between the clergy and the laity. These differences would affect the kinds of roles that early modern women were encouraged in or denied, as well as the roles that they envisioned and sought for themselves.

THIS ACCOUNT of Mary Magdalene begins with the development of the Magdalene cult through the period of the early church and the Middle Ages, with a focus on the late medieval background to the Reformation era. The late medieval author Christine de Pizan's employment of the Magdalene in the literary debate over the status of women foreshadowed the way in which Protestants would appeal to the resurrection narrative in their arguments for female preaching. The popularity of Passion plays, in which the Magdalene featured as a central character, confirms that her active role in scripture and worship was also engaging the piety of illiterate audiences, right up to the eve of the Reformation. The "three Marys" controversy of 1519, over the Magdalene's composite identity, shows the concern of humanist scholars to correct inaccuracies that had developed in the Bible and in church tradition over the centuries; the opposition's counterarguments reveal the continued loyalty felt to the saint and the stakes involved in potential changes to devotional practice.

We then turn to the theology and preaching about the Magdalene that emerged from the Wittenberg reform movement. Luther's preaching on the resurrection narrative in the Gospel of John included an extended discussion of Mary's vigil at the tomb. He praised her tears, commending her ardent devotion to Christ and her eager announcing of the news of the resurrection as examples for all Christians, and especially for preachers. Luther's preaching on the Magdalene was interpreted in the sermons written by his colleagues and students. I include examples of several sermons and hymns on Mary Magdalene by Luther's most influential followers; their work was published and republished through the century, reaching audiences through public worship as well as private reading and home devotion.

Prominent women of the Reformation, including the early evangelical authors Argula von Grumbach and Katharina Schütz Zell, laid confident claim to the title and legacy of the Magdalene. The characterization of English Protestant martyr Anne Askew as a figure comparable to the Magdalene was formative for Protestant female spirituality as it was published in one of the most popular works of early Protestant martyrology, John Foxe's *Book of Martyrs*. French reformer Marie Dentière's 1539 treatise proclaimed women's right to preach using the example of the Magdalene, provoking Catholic preacher François Le Picart to respond with his own sermon, published two years later, that explicitly denounced "Lutherans" who used scriptural figures to claim that women had the right to speak in public.

Le Picart was not alone in reacting to the use of Mary Magdalene in defense of female preaching. His fellow Catholic churchmen addressed the vexing question of her role as the first witness of the resurrection, as well as the issue of her personal history. Catholic teaching on the Magdalene was shaped by preachers, church administrators, poets, visual artists, and popular devotional authors such as François de Sales. While a variety of interpretations of the saint were still available, the predominant focus was on her conversion from sexual sin to a piety of extreme penitence and devotion to the sacraments.

The environment of Magdalene piety these authors created was inhabited by early modern Catholic women who responded to its possibilities and limitations with new Magdalenes of their own. Catholic women made use of the Magdalene in devotional practices and liturgies in Magdalene houses, founded for reformed prostitutes, and other convents associated with the saint; they made or commissioned artwork that adapted the Magdalene legend; and, above all, women such as Teresa of Avila developed theologies to discern their own vocations through reflection on Mary Magdalene's different identities. These images and practices are examined in tension with the messages about the saint that women received from their male colleagues. Particularly interesting is the question of gendered appropriation: was the sexualized Magdalene, so appealing to male authors and patrons both within and outside the ecclesiastical hierarchy, equally compelling as a focus for women's own piety and self-understanding? Marguerite de Navarre and other royal women who served as regents offer fascinating examples of public figures who pondered the Magdalene's identity, engaging both nascent projects of reform and traditional institutions from positions of significant social responsibility.

The religious climate of the Catholic Reformation influenced much in the culture of the Calvinist Reformed tradition as it defined itself in opposition to Catholicism. The theological roots of the Reformed Magdalene reveal Calvin's ambivalent relationship to her as she is described in the Bible. Calvin took up Lefèvre d'Étaples's deconstruction of Mary's legend and therefore restricted himself to discussing the figure identified by name in the Gospels as Mary Magdalene. Though he acknowledged some positive elements in her character, he used his commentary on the Gospel of John's Passion narrative to argue vigorously against women's public preaching, refusing to admit that Mary Magdalene was anything but an exception in this regard while criticizing her sentimental behavior and general unsuitability for discipleship. Unlike in the case of Luther, however, Calvin's followers did not all adopt his image of the Magdalene. Other Reformed authors' writing and piety reveal the extent to which even some of his closest colleagues departed from his inter-pretation, seeking to redeem the long-beloved saint for devotional use and theological teaching.

Though a variety of interpretation can be found in Reformed communities, it was the Protestants of the Radical Reformation traditions who diverged most from one another in their uses of the Magdalene. Many radical reform-ers asserted comparisons to the Magdalene that made claims about women's public role in the church, but they did so in ways that ranged from extreme circumspection to bold embrace. The most tentative references to the Mag-dalene's character come in Anabaptist martyr narratives. These recorded testimonies contain scores of scripture passages, but only a few briefly men-tion her as a model of faithful dedication to Christ above all else—even above the duty to family. Her example was used by these imprisoned men and women, often mothers and fathers leaving young children, to encourage each other as they prepared for a holy death. At the other end of the spectrum were the founders of Quakerism, Margaret Fell and George Fox, who invoked Mary Magdalene as the foremost among other female scriptural prophets to establish a theological foundation for women's leadership in the Society of Friends. Here we can find compelling evidence that even those traditions that do not acknowledge sainthood apart from the lives of ordinary believers still interpreted the Magdalene's legacy and derived spiritual authority in doing so.

Finally, we look ahead to the nineteenth century, when the exegeti-cal interpretation of Lefèvre d'Étaples was officially recognized by the

Catholic Church, which thereafter promulgated a severely curtailed cult of Mary Magdalene limited to her scriptural identity. Was it then the modern period, rather than the Reformation era, that witnessed the decline of the influence of the diverse Magdalene heritage? On the contrary, the tradition of the *apostola apostolorum* was seized upon anew by the emerging feminist movement among African American Baptist activists arguing for women's right to public testimony, leadership, and recognition. The so-called resurgence in interest in the saint in the twentieth and twenty-first centuries is really the continuity of a legacy that has persisted in the work and words of women and men from the early church to the present day.

By surveying the testimony of voices from across the early modern period's religious divisions, I hope to show that there is wider evidence for what Patricia Badir has called the "lively early modern history of Mary Magdalene . . . a figure whose embeddings in the medieval imagination help us to think across the rupture between old and new forms."[25] The images of holiness, of spiritual purpose and identity available to both women and men, Catholic and Protestant, were shaped by the enduring appeal of the Magdalene tradition, and by her role in the religious controversies of the Reformation era. The adaptation of ancient traditions into vigorous new forms expressed profound theological understanding and commitment, demonstrating the seriousness with which reformers of all the traditions that emerged from the sixteenth century took the project of discerning and living according to God's will. The Magdalenes they produced, whether daring preachers, devout contemplatives, or both as circumstances demanded, reveal the deepest hopes of their authors for a renewed church and a life of integrity.

CHAPTER ONE

The Medieval Magdalene
Establishing a Cult of Personality

WANTING TO HEAR THE NEWS of the resurrection from its first witness, the disciples plead, "Dic nobis Maria" (Speak to us, Mary). This formula appeared in medieval Passion liturgies and dramas and was echoed in a hymn for Easter Sunday by sixteenth-century Lutheran hymn writer Nicolaus Herman: "Speak to us, Mary. Ah, Mary, tell us without shyness, whom you met on the road."[1] Through such references the images of Mary Magdalene's medieval cult were carried into the era of the Reformation by preachers and authors eager to transform one of the central figures of popular piety into an exemplar of evangelical theology. The medieval tradition included many different understandings of who the Magdalene was, but it is possible to identify the key themes that came to inform early modern dialogues about her character and activity.

The Magdalene had developed a rich legend over the course of fifteen hundred years of the Christian tradition—particularly rich given the lack of descriptive material about her in the New Testament. A woman named Mary Magdalene appears in all four Gospels. She was a Galilean follower of Jesus, whom he had healed of seven demons and who thereafter supported his ministry (Luke 8:1–3). She was present at the Crucifixion (Matt. 27:55–56; Mark 15:40; John 19:25) and witnessed the resurrection, when she was instructed to tell the other disciples what had taken place (Matt. 28:1–10; Mark 16:1–10; Luke 24:1–12; John 20:1–18). But that is all that the canonical Gospels record of her.

With the important role she has in the Easter narrative, as the first witness and preacher of the resurrection, theologians were naturally inclined to muse on her identity: Who was this figure, a woman with such unusual prominence, and why had she been chosen for this task from among all of Jesus's early followers? The need to explain her character, to fill the enigmatic void left by those scant scriptural verses, produced myriad elaborations of her life both before and after her encounter with Christ on the road. Over the centuries Mary was made to speak not only her good news but also her whole story, a chronicle of sin and redemption that contains within it humanity's fall and salvation. Her progress from sinner to penitent, from prodigal to ascetic, from witness to missionary, describes the arc of the church's founding narrative. The varying emphases that can be found in different versions of her story point to the preoccupations of those who gave her voice, to the questions that interested, inspired, and infuriated them.

Her legend was shaped by the preachers and authors who used the Magdalene legend in orthodox and unorthodox ways to direct the piety of their audiences, as well as by the many women who saw themselves as descendants of Mary Magdalene. While devotion to the Virgin Mary was always central to popular piety, her almost supernatural status made her a somewhat presumptuous model for claims about one's own spiritual life. Mary Magdalene, on the other hand, offered the hopeful example of an ordinary woman, even one with a sinful past, who had renounced the flesh for contemplation and pious attachment to Christ. The different features of her story permitted women from many walks of life, whether married or celibate, to find points of comparison with their own experiences and aspirations. The various interpretations of her role proved useful in women's descriptions of their vocations, allowing both spirited defenses of public ministry and postures of humility in which women retreated into silent adoration. Both the active and contemplative modes of the Magdalene's identity were each seen as important forms of witness or testimony in the Christian narrative of salvation.[2]

The list of medieval women who identified themselves in some way with Mary Magdalene reads like a survey of medieval female mysticism, including Bridget of Sweden, Catherine of Siena, Christina of Markyate, Hadewijch, Ivetta of Huy, Margaret of Cortona, Marguerite Porete, Margery Kempe, and Mechthild of Magdeburg. Emerging from the almost too fertile climate of Magdalene piety, a debate over the authority of her long-established legend broke at the opening of the sixteenth century. The contradictions that Mary Magdalene's multiform identity had held in creative tension through the medieval period resurfaced with the reform debates of the early modern era, exposing a question at the heart of Christian theology: What is the place of the human person—sexual and sinful—in the divine plan?[3]

The multiplicity of Magdalenes available to believers in the Middle Ages is not an incidental feature of her tradition, but helps explain her popularity over that long and complex era, as well as her adaptability to the changes of the Reformation era. Helen Meredith Garth describes the medieval Magdalene as a woman of extremes, suited to an age of extremes: great sin caused by the temptation of great delight in the world, and great penitence that fostered great love for God and compassion for Christ's suffering. But among the different medieval interpretations of Mary Magdalene, three were most prominent and influential: the patron of sinners and contemplatives; a figure of symbolic identification for the church as a whole and for individuals; and the first preacher of the Gospel. We will now turn to examine the ways in which these interpretive categories were used by the men and women of the medieval church.[4]

The Development of the Medieval Cult

Scholars of late antiquity have traced the role of Mary Magdalene in the early centuries of Christian tradition, including her significant presence in the Gnostic Gospels, a collection of writings about Christ that were rejected by the ecumenical councils as they established the canon of texts that were included in the Bible. Although some strains of the Gnostic Magdalene would endure in later histories, most of her identity in that movement was lost with the suppression of texts such as The Gospel of Mary.[5]

The chief influence on the saint as she developed in medieval piety was Pope Gregory the Great's creation of a composite of three biblical women in a sermon from 591. Not content to leave so important a figure with the brief outline she receives in the canonical Gospels, Gregory chose the most orthodox possible method for fleshing out her personal history. Rather than invent a past, he simply identified her with two other characters in the New Testament: the sinful woman who washes Christ's feet with her tears and is forgiven her sins (Luke 7:36–50), and Mary of Bethany, sister of Martha and Lazarus, who is praised for her attention to Christ's preaching, even at the expense of her household duties (Luke 10:38–42). The conflation of these three women, and sometimes others, would become ubiquitous throughout the medieval tradition, and the explanations of how one woman could have been so notoriously debased yet passionately devout, sinful and yet the chosen messenger of the resurrection, would occupy countless sermons, scripture commentaries, dramas, and mystical works.[6]

Renditions of her story came to follow a common pattern. She had been the privileged and beautiful daughter of a wealthy landowning family in Galilee, in a town called Magdala. Engaged to the young man who would become John the Evangelist, her wedding at Cana was the stage for Jesus's first miracle, and also of her undoing: John is converted to discipleship and abandons the marriage immediately. Frustrated, she succumbs to the temptations of the flesh and the powers of her own attractions, and gives herself to sensual pleasure and promiscuity. At the urging of her sister Martha, Mary finally heeds Jesus's preaching, making a dramatic confession of her sins at the house of Simon the Pharisee, in the scene where she weeps over Christ's feet and anoints him. After that she becomes his devoted disciple, even to the point of irritating the now perhaps regretful Martha, who would like some assistance with the housework, but Mary's attentive contemplation is rewarded as being "the better part." Finally, she remains faithful to Christ when the other disciples have fled in fear during the Passion and witnesses not only his suffering and death but his rising again as well. Thus is an abject sinner selected to bring the news of the resurrection to the rest of Christ's followers.

The medieval legend did not conclude there, however. Speculation grew as to the activities of the disciples after the end of the Gospel stories. Most older accounts have her traveling to Ephesus and dying there. By the ninth century a different history had taken shape, first appearing in a biography long attributed to a scholar at Charlemagne's court, Rabanus Maurus. In this legend, which achieved wide popularity in the west, Mary, Martha, and Lazarus are expelled from Jerusalem by opponents of the Jesus movement; they journey to the south of France, where they begin preaching to pagans. Mary converts a king by a series of miracles, allowing him and his barren queen to produce a child and saving the mother and baby from a disaster at sea. Following these triumphs, Mary retires to a life of ascetic solitude in the mountains outside Aix-en-Provence, where for the rest of her life she is daily elevated by angels to be nourished on heavenly music and the Eucharist, her only food. Her relics (and the rapidly accumulating stories of their miraculous works) were claimed by churches in Marseilles, the reputed site of her preaching and burial, and Vézelay Abbey in Burgundy, where they were supposed to have been brought to keep them from Muslim invaders in the ninth century. The first official record at Vézelay specifying the Magdalene as the abbey's patron dates from 1050; papal recognition of Vézelay as the site of her relics was granted in 1058. The northern monastery experienced a corresponding surge in power and influence in the twelfth century. By 1279, however, the shrine of Mary Magdalene at Sainte-Baume, near Aix-en-Provence, had staged an official "discovery" of the relics with the approval of Pope Martin IV, canceling Vézelay's claim. Thereafter, the Abbey of Vézelay went into a decline, while the Provençal shrine, overseen by the Dominican Order, increased in prominence. Her tradition thus developed, supported by local expressions of piety, nurturing regional senses of spiritual identity. At the same time, Mary Magdalene's cult provided economic and political benefits and was used to define and defend particular brands of monasticism.[7]

The Magdalene as Ascetic Contemplative

This sketch of Mary's legend displays the principal themes of her cult: her great compassion for Christ in his suffering, born of his own forgiveness for her sins as well as of feminine affection with which the faithful could identify; her association with the contemplative life; and her preaching of the good news of Christ's resurrection, in her role as *apostola apostolorum,* which was carried on beyond the time and place of his death. According to the account attributed to Rabanus Maurus, "She preached to unbelievers and strengthened believers . . . she was an example of conversion to sinners, a certain home of remission to penitents, a figure of compassion to the faithful and to all Christian people a proof of divine mercy. . . . There was in the countenance of both Mary Magdalene and Martha a beauty to be venerated, honor in habits, and most swift grace for persuading in words. There was scarcely or never anyone found who returned unbelieving, or without weeping, from their preaching."[8] That which gave force to the preaching of both Mary and Martha was their relationship with Christ, who had stayed in their home and loved them and their brother as friends.

This intimacy was expanded on in yet another identification of Mary Magdalene with a scriptural figure, the bride in the Song of Songs, a work of erotic poetry that became one of the most popular texts for allegorical and devotional interpretation in the Middle Ages. Mary Magdalene's imagined speeches were often couched in the romantic language of the Song of Songs, giving theologians and preachers a means to express and recommend a deep devotion to the person of Christ. This devotion was linked to participation in the sacramental system of the church, with the bride and Mary Magdalene seen as symbols of the church itself and models for the individual's encounter with God. Entry into the life of the church was compared to a marriage: sacraments were the physical consummations of the verbal pledges made by the penitent seeking union with the divine. The author of the legend attributed to Rabanus Maurus inserts a Song of Songs reference in the Mary / Martha comparison story, as part of Mary's self-description; "I sit in the shadow of my beloved, and the fruit of his lips is sweet to my taste."[9]

Modern scholars suggest that the text is not by Rabanus, but more likely of Cistercian authorship, based on similarities to texts by the founder of the Cistercian movement, Bernard of Clairvaux, including Bernard's *Commentary on the Song of Songs*. The positive features of Mary Magdalene's identity in this text became influential in her tradition. Loyal and loving, she is favorably compared with the disciples who abandon Christ in the Passion. The theme of human and divine love was central to Cistercian piety. For the Cistercians, charity was the "aim and intention of all speech," as David Mycoff has noted, and it was the Magdalene's affection for Christ that found necessary expression in her public speech, as in the speech of those inspired by her example. The Cistercian focus on God's loving grace in the story of the sinful woman of Luke 7 is an early exploration of the nature of salvation, which would be debated in interpretations of this text throughout late medieval and early modern preaching.[10]

The contemplative form of monasticism practiced by Cistercians found support in the opposition between Mary and her sister Martha. The biblical account of the two sisters affirms the medieval separation of the contemplative from the active life, and the emphasis on a rigorous distinction between the two vocations is clear: "The contemplative life of that sweet lover of Christ, dearly loved by him and worthy to be named with reverence, the blessed Mary Magdalene; the active life of her glorious sister, the servant of Christ, Martha."[11]

The Cistercians' adaptation of the Magdalene in forming their identity and spirituality led to similar efforts by other monastic orders. The British

Franciscan, Nicholas Bozon, writing in the late thirteenth and early fourteenth centuries, produced an exploration of Mary Magdalene's life as a redeemed penitent whose intimacy with Christ provides comfort and assurance for the sinner: "For this [reason] have I put it in the vernacular / In order to comfort the repentant / Through her who was a sinner— / So that despair may wound no heart." The accessible message of solace reflects the program of the new mendicant order, oriented toward the laity rather than the otherworldly cloister. Her story would have reminded Franciscans of their founder's own youth; St. Francis had been born into a wealthy family in Assisi and was converted in the midst of youthful excess. The Magdalene is converted by Christ's preaching, which gives Bozon an opportunity to recommend to his listeners that they attend sermons as well, building an audience for the Franciscan preaching order.[12]

A late medieval chronicle of the saint, from fourteenth-century Florence, presents the concerns of its place and time as clearly as do the Cistercian and Franciscan legends; here the context is the city, with its dangerous corruption. The author contends that moral standards had been very high in the first century and compares sinners of the early Christian era to promiscuous women of fourteenth-century Italy, claiming that the modern women are much worse: "I have thought many times of the women of today, seeing their graceless carriage, that had they lived in the time of the Magdalen, they would have been called more than sinners. . . . Certain I am that the Magdalen did not uncover her bosom as they do." The scene of Mary Magdalene as the jilted bride at Cana gives him an opportunity to evoke a social situation that would have resonated with his readers: an urban, upper-class wedding banquet. The familiar setting is peopled with a family and its friends as the author links numerous scriptural stories and characters together, making the Gospel events seem like nothing so much as the saga of a large and influential Florentine clan. After Mary receives forgiveness at the house of Simon the Pharisee, she resembles a fourteenth-century flagellant, attempting to take revenge on her body for her sinful past, scratching her face, tearing her hair, and stripping naked to beat herself bloody. Just as Mary becomes a contemplative ascetic, Martha busies herself with performing the charitable works of a more active order, like a fourteenth-century Italian confraternity member, taking the poor and sick into her home and going out to care for them. By the time she poses her fateful question comparing the two vocations, then,

Martha is really asking Christ if Mary should be involved in these civic works of charity, not pleading for help with mere housekeeping.[13]

Vernacular lives of the saints were aimed at lay and female audiences who could find themselves in stories recounted with immediacy and heightened emotion. Mary's responses or soliloquies on the events of the Passion provided a script for the ordinary penitent to enact during Passion Week, calling forth a sense of the believer's own culpability in the death of Christ, shock at the insult to the divine majesty, and deep compassion for Christ's suffering.[14]

Anne Thayer has examined the role of identification with Mary Magdalene in preaching on the sacrament of penance in the late medieval and early Reformation eras; she writes, "Different sermon collections present the ideal penitent, often exemplified by Mary Magdalene, differently. Some stress her deeds of satisfaction, some her contrition; others portray her as making a powerful confession. These portraits convey varying expectations to hearers being urged to penitence." The saint's prominence in sermons on penitence was owing to her centrality in one of the texts most often used in defending the theology of the penitential system, Luke 7. The story clearly shows Christ bestowing forgiveness of sins and pronouncing absolution; therefore the Magdalene was "the saint most frequently cited" as a model that all penitents should adopt. But which of her actions were the salutary ones—her tears and service, or her internal sorrow and decision to seek Christ's pardon?[15]

A thirteenth-century sermon for the Feast of the Magdalene by the Franciscan theologian, Bonaventure, titled "Such Love," claims that "Mary Magdalene, then, is shown us as our model for repentance." Bonaventure portrays her as the one who loved Christ more than anyone else did. Amid its Franciscan concern for repentance, the sermon, like the Cistercian life of the Magdalene, includes many comparisons of her love to that described in the Song of Songs. Bonaventure encourages all Christians to imitate the Magdalene's affective piety, and to have "such love" for Christ.[16]

Later medieval authors of sermon collections continued to present the emotional contrition of the Magdalene as exemplary. Johannes von Werden, in his 1494 *Sermones dormi secure de sanctis*, praises Mary's tears, saying that many weep over other things, but too few weep sufficiently over their sins. In Paratus's 1492 *Sermones parati de tempore et de sanctis*, he points to her eagerness in confession, as she hastens to the house of Simon the Pharisee immediately upon Jesus's arrival, without waiting.[17]

In addition to describing the attitude of her confession, preachers addressed themselves to the question of how it affected her forgiveness. Some stressed Mary Magdalene's contrition and God's grace, while others emphasized the works of satisfaction in which her contrition was expressed. Johannes Herolt, the German author of a collection published in 1494, makes his position clear: "Mary Magdalene exemplifies those who 'through penal works fulfill the satisfactions for their sins'" and therefore do not have to go through Purgatory. In his Sermon 27, Herolt lists the parts of her body (eyes, hair, mouth) with which she has sinned against God, and which she then uses to perform the satisfaction for her sins. It is up to her to correct the choices that have corrupted her body by forcibly turning each part to its proper use.[18]

Italian preacher Robert Caracciolo's 1472 collection of penitential sermons describes a spiritual transaction between the merciful Christ and the devout sinner that anticipates the encounter the believer will have with her own confessor. He portrays Jesus's "sweet" kindness to the sinner, and gives the woman an imagined, passionate confession, to which Jesus responds with the standard formula of absolution. The enacting of a sacramental scene familiar to the audience would have served to support the practice, guiding the penitent's experience and reinforcing the role of the priest with the comparison to Christ.[19]

A similar rehearsal of confessional practice can be seen in an altarpiece by the fifteenth-century Flemish artist Dieric Bouts, *Christ in the House of Simon the Pharisee*. In keeping with the generally heightened interest in penitential spirituality toward the end of the Middle Ages, Mary Magdalene's role as the penitent sinner of Luke 7 was increasingly the subject of depiction in the visual arts. Bouts's painting shows the repentant Magdalene with an emphasis on her humility, grief for her sins evident in her face. Within the composition, she is placed directly under the sign of absolution made by Christ's fingers, as a sinner would be in receiving the sacrament of penance.[20]

Mary Magdalene functioned as the model for fifteenth-century artists such as Bouts as they worked to illustrate the doctrine of the penitential system, emphasizing its urgency for contemporary believers. Artists exploited the poignant contrast between her abject contrition and her sumptuous clothing as a woman of luxury. In early sixteenth-century works such as Hendrik Dowerman's *Magdalena* from Kalkar, and in the reliquary bust displayed in Albrecht von Brandenburg's Moritzburgkapelle, also known as the

Maria-Magdalenenkapelle, in Halle, she is dressed as a wealthy contemporary woman in the latest fashion.[21]

The Magdalene's identity as exemplary sinner and ideal penitent points to the paradox of her gender in the role she played in medieval spirituality. Hers is an emphatically gendered sin and salvation: her preconversion state is conveyed by voluptuousness, while her penance is burnished by feminine tears and blushing modesty. The medieval church rejected a public preaching or teaching ministry for women, while at the same time adopting the sexualized Magdalene as a model for male preachers. Just as sinfulness disqualified her and other women from leadership roles in the church, it served to encourage those who could preach—men—by assuring them that God chose sinners to spread the Gospel. More widely hopeful was the message that Mary Magdalene's works of penance were effective, for herself and others, in achieving a reunion with God for those compromised, as she was, by sinful acts and inclinations.[22]

Given her role as model penitent—and especially her sexual sin, combined with the theme of powerful conversion and reform—another role for the Magdalene came naturally: she was made the patroness of convents and homes for reformed prostitutes, beginning in the twelfth century. The first prostitution reform campaign was initiated in France around 1100. The movement reached a peak of enthusiasm in Italy during the thirteenth and fourteenth centuries, following Pope Gregory IX's bull endorsing the foundation of "repenties," with a majority of new convents founded during that time being either explicitly Magdalene houses or other kinds of convents that also took the Magdalene as their patroness.[23]

Just as her penitence was occasioned and shaped by her identity as a woman guilty of sexual sin, the Magdalene's gender also contributed to her character as a contemplative and to how other women identified with that model. The self-destruction of her body, of female beauty and fertility, was presented as the ideal of women's spirituality, erasing the marks of the Fall: the temptation and subsequent punishment of Eve with pain in childbearing. Catherine of Siena's biographer, Raymond of Capua, dwelled on the Magdalene's fasting as her most exemplary feature for the severely ascetic Catherine. Even where no explicit comparison to Mary Magdalene was made, biographers of medieval holy women drew on her legend for their construction of sanctity, establishing her as paradigmatic for female holiness. St. Colette of Corbie's *Vie*, written in approximately 1447 by her confessor, Pierre de Vaux, uses this ploy to excuse the unusual vocation of his subject. Colette was a very politically involved abbess, leading a reform of her order; her public power was noted as dangerous, even as it was identified as apostolic during her lifetime. In creating her biography, Pierre emphasizes her asceticism, her "abundance of tears," and calls her an "apostle." All of these elements of the Magdalene's character would have been well known and meaningful to his Burgundian readers, in the region where one of her major shrines, Vézelay, was located. The House of Burgundy claimed its lineage from the king and queen who had been miraculously aided by Mary Magdalene in her legend. This was the paradoxical utility of the Magdalene, a malleable figure who was both sinful and redeemed, self-denying and powerful. She, and those who claimed her as patron, relied not on her own strength or position but on her connection to Christ. This strategy would be adopted to authorize many institutions and individuals for reform and innovation in the medieval church.[24]

The First Christian: Mary Magdalene in Relation to Church and Self

The Magdalene served, for many scriptural interpreters and theologians, as a symbolic figure for the church itself, expressing its need for reform. In times when the church engaged in self-criticism, such as the twelfth century, the Magdalene provided a ready image of a contrite figure, much loved by Christ despite her sinful character, and able to be turned to the divine purpose once she had been converted from error. Her equation with a sinful but redeemable human institution had been made by figures from Augustine to Rupert of Deutz and Odo of Cluny, who included a reference to the meaning of Magdala (strong tower) as representing the church.[25]

The identification of Mary Magdalene with the institution of the church presented interesting challenges given Mary's character as a woman—and an especially sinful one at that. The very fact of her public preaching constituted a problem, for it contradicted Paul's instructions about female silence in 1 Corinthians 14. But her disputed position could prove helpful, as in the case of the mendicant orders' appeal to the Magdalene as a model for preaching, to serve their reform efforts. Identifying publicly with the humble status of her gender helped set them apart from the established religious authority,

Peter's church, that they sought to criticize, allowing them to shelter behind a nonthreatening posture of female submission.[26]

The Magdalene's role as a symbol of the church was ambiguous; her gender lent both positive and negative associations to the image. She could be embraced as a representation of female meekness, or criticized as a representation of female unruliness and potential disorder (or even heresy). Luci Halliwell and Beverly Mayne Kienzle have noted the conflict between the church represented by Mary Magdalene, passionately devoted but potentially ungovernable, and the church represented by Peter, a figure of ecclesiastical authority and doctrinal orthodoxy. This conflict was played out in stock scenes of medieval religious drama in which the jubilant and effusive Mary is shouted down by a stern Peter lest the church be founded on the untrustworthy chatter of women.[27]

A necessary transformation was achieved by the ultimate subjection of her character to the leadership of the male disciples. Medieval plays actively exploited the potential conflict between Mary Magdalene and male saints, including Peter, to achieve dramatic tension and to present the birth of an authoritative church. The late medieval English Wakefield / Towneley Mystery Plays, for example, have St. Paul present at Mary Magdalene's announcement of the resurrection and rebuking her for speaking publicly, refusing to believe based on a woman's testimony. The plays describe a narrative of reform from the very beginnings of the Christian tradition, with heretical or unreliable elements in the church, personified by the Magdalene, being conformed to orthodox teaching.[28]

Less divisive than her speech, Mary's sorrow at the tomb was praised and often compared favorably in Passion plays with the desertion of the other followers of Jesus, encouraging audience members to imitate her. Jean Michel's *Mystère de la Passion,* for example, from the end of the fifteenth century, describes her in terms his audience would have identified with their own context. He portrays the saint of late antiquity as a fifteenth-century chatelaine with courtly lovers, and Lazarus as her noble brother, a knight hunting with falcons. Just as Michel adapted his character to French social structures and culture, the English Digby Mysteries, also from the last half of the fifteenth century, tell the story of the Magdalene in ways suited to the local audience. The plays were produced in a coastal area, and the text emphasizes the sea voyage of the Magdalene, using a mariner's vocabulary. The tavern in which the Magdalene is tempted in the beginning of the play resembles a late medieval English public house. Not only the setting but the treatment of character in the plays also encourages viewers' identification with the events and experience of the Passion. In *Mary Magdalene,* the focus is on the Magdalene herself; Christ has moved to the background as the object of her first-person observation. The interpretation of the Magdalene can be seen to be in transition here, from a collective symbol of the whole church to a figure with whom audience members are encouraged to identify as individuals.[29]

A new theology of lay piety was needed to accommodate economic and social developments at the close of the Middle Ages. Among the expanded possibilities for women's piety were devotional and secular roles described with notable respect in the Digby *Mary Magdalene.* Unlike much other medieval drama, the play refrains from mockery at Mary Magdalene's expense, indicating a local climate of civility between clergy and holy women. The play also departs from convention by having Mary Magdalene pay for passage alone (without Maximin and Lazarus) on a ship bound for Marseilles, after being told by Christ to become an "apostylesse." The uniqueness of this journey to France, made without her traditional companions, makes the Digby Magdalene into a new kind of dramatic hero; the solitary heroic journeys of medieval literature are more usually undertaken by male protagonists. Even within the outlines of an ordinary, laywoman's life, the Digby play offers innovation, with its depiction of companionate marriage between the king and queen of Marseilles, a relationship that is given saintly approval by Mary Magdalene's support. In bringing together previously disparate or conflicted groups, such as the established authorities of the church and idiosyncratic mystics (or husbands and wives!), the Digby Magdalene is able to accomplish a reunion of warring opposites represented by her own character since the days of the early church.[30]

The saint's unifying role, assisting believers to cross boundaries between clergy and laity, sacred and profane, and even male and female, is supported by the visual record of the medieval church. The Magdalene first appeared in depictions of Gospel events, and those continued to be the most common instances of her appearance in religious art. By the late Middle Ages, her role in Passion imagery was often that of an intermediary figure, drawing the viewer into a sense of immediate participation in the scene. In Jan Van Eyck's *The Crucifixion: The Last Judgment* (1430), for example, the Magdalene serves as a focal point, kneeling and praying in the same stance as the viewer would, dressed in expensive finery suggesting her worldly attachments. One can identify more with her than with the Virgin Mary, whose extreme grief doubles her over and thus hides her face from the viewer. Similarly, in Rogier van der Weyden's *Deposition* (1435), Mary Magdalene is the figure toward which the composition points. She is not at its center, however, which contains the arms of Christ and the Virgin Mary, but at its periphery, again, at the intersection of the dramatic plane with the viewer's world. As with her physical location, her affect underscores her accessibility: her eyes are open while she prays. The artist creates a greater connection with her than with the dead Christ or with his mother, who looks dead herself from grief and is therefore distanced from viewers, who are directed to approach this supernatural trauma in the Magdalene's attitude of watchful prayer.[31]

The imitative piety fostered by religious drama and images can be observed in self-identification with the Magdalene in the writing of late medieval women. The Italian holy woman known as Blessed Battista typified the period's focus on compassion for Christ's suffering by suggesting an association between herself and Mary Magdalene. Her 1488 treatise *I Dolori Mentali di Gesù* tells of how a vision of Christ prompted her toward an emotional, unregulated devotion that conformed to the model of the Magdalene: "Christ tells [Battista] that the Magdalen 'loved me without order and without measure. So too, without order and without measure was her sorrow.'" The pattern of a woman's conversation with Christ, as Battista experiences in her vision, takes its precedent from Christ's dialogues with Mary Magdalene and the other women with whom she is linked in scripture, so that both the content of piety and the form of spiritual discourse are determined by the image of the Magdalene.[32]

One very prominent example of this kind of internal dialogue, with the author in the role of Mary Magdalene contemplating Christ's suffering, is found in the writing of the English mystic Margery Kempe. This identification was used to authorize Kempe's own sometimes publicly suspect mystical experiences. The connection serves both to lift Kempe from the world to the level of desired intimacy with Christ and to bring him close to her in a loving mutuality. Kempe writes, "I wish I was as worthy to be worthy of thy love as Mary Magdalene was." In her vision of the Passion she stands in the place of the Magdalene, and Christ addresses her, telling her that he does indeed love her in the same way as he loved the original Mary. The comparison is not solely flattering, however. Kempe excuses herself for the apparent presumption of such a parallel, recording her own history of temptation by the same sins as had lured Mary Magdalene to her fall. Margery's love of fine clothes and her pride in her status as a businesswoman represent the luxury associated with the Magdalene's wealth and position, and an adulterous relationship in Margery's past reveals the same capacity for sensuality that formed such a vivid part of medieval legends of the saint.[33]

Despite such sinful histories, both women receive similar graces as rewards for their compassion: Margery hears heavenly music, just as the Magdalene does in the account in the popular thirteenth-century collection of saints' lives, the *Golden Legend*. Both women are described as regaining virginal purity after their conversions, which they express through the adoption of white clothing. Likewise, both were blamed for the same spiritual faults. Though instructed by the Virgin Mary in a vision that she must weep like Mary Magdalene, Margery was publicly rebuked for overly lachrymose mourning, an ironic repetition of a criticism directed at the saint herself in liturgical Passion dramas of the period.[34]

Though not without the problematic associations of sin and female hysteria, the ultimate effect of Kempe's identification with Mary Magdalene is the authorization of her visions and her public testimony. In one vision, Christ himself declares, "I am in you and you are in me and those that hear you hear the voice of God." Margery, like the Magdalene, had been commanded by the incarnate God to speak on his behalf before his church.[35]

The First Missionary: The Magdalene as Preacher of the Resurrection

The Magdalene's scriptural role as first witness of the resurrection was used to support the preaching ministry of those, both male and female, who identified with her. This function is evident in the Magdalene legends produced by monastic orders whose mission included preaching. In the Cistercian account of her life, her divinely authorized preaching receives particular emphasis: she is both "the evangelist of the resurrection" and "the apostle of his ascension to the apostles." The Magdalene is included in a group of apostles who gather just before the Ascension for a meal with Christ, who commands them all to preach. The account of the Ascension that follows even gives her priority among the apostles, as her status is equated with that of John the Baptist: "And standing with the apostles at the ascension, as though pointing with her finger to the ascending host, she showed that she was equal to John the Baptist in being more than a prophet."[36]

The legend includes her ascetic sojourn in the desert, so that alongside the presence of a call to preach, the Cistercian Magdalene is deeply committed to contemplative withdrawal and can only consider a public ministry as part of the expression of her interior life. The text discusses her reluctance to leave silent prayer in order to preach and stresses the importance of an attitude of contemplation for true preaching: "So from time to time she left the joys of contemplation and preached to the unbelievers or confirmed believers in the faith. . . . For her lips spoke from the fullness of her heart, and because of this all her preaching was a true exercise of divine contemplation."[37]

A German life of the saint from the fourteenth or fifteenth century, a manuscript now known as the *Nürnberger Maria Magdalena-Legende III*, emphasizes another incarnation of monastic preaching in its Magdalene piety—in this case, the culture of the Dominican Order, which had adopted the saint as its patron in 1297. The theological basis for the association had been developed by Pope Gregory X, who had commended the mendicant orders as exemplifying the virtues of both Mary and Martha, both contemplation and action. The Nuremburg legend "describes Mary Magdalene as a Dominican nun, that is to say, as a preacheress; she loves the order and calls the Dominicans her brothers." Here her relationship to the preaching and teaching vocation is less ambiguous; the Dominican Magdalene does not express the Cistercian saint's scruples about leaving her contemplative life. "Then I became a preacheress [*predigerin*] and apostless [*appostolerin*]," she declares confidently. A fourteenth-century sermon by the Italian Dominican, Giovanni da San Gemignano, demonstrates the extent to which his order saw itself practicing an active preaching ministry in harmony with a contemplative vocation rather than in tension with it. He understood the Magdalene herself as able to represent both ways of life: "The Magdalene selected the best life for herself because sometimes, as it were, she was active and she ministered to him . . . she was also a contemplative, as it were, when she was meditating, listening to his words. This was an admirable life made best through the exercise of both lives."[38]

Nicholas Bozon's Franciscan account is similarly positive in its treatment of her preaching and her suitability as an evangelist. Bozon makes an unusual addition to the typical presentation of the story, contradicting an assertion in the Cistercian legend that the Magdalene had not believed the resurrection at first. He claims that even as she approached the tomb on Easter morning, she had faith that Christ would rise again, as he had told her he would: "But from that which she had heard— / That he would rise again— / She took comfort to herself." After the Ascension she and her family go to Marseilles, where she preaches to a house of pagans. Bozon stresses the Magdalene's eloquence, derived from her intimacy with Christ:

> The Magdalene there took her stand,
> And nobly preached to them
> About the truth of our Faith.
> And many marveled
> That any woman knew how to speak so
> That her words so pierced their hearts,
> From which many received devotion
> And contrition for their sins.
> It was no wonder that spoke so well
> That mouth which formerly touched
> The feet of him who is the font
> All full of grace and wisdom.[39]

Indeed, her words mimic the actions and gain the force of Christ's own life: piercing the hearts of her listeners as the events of the Gospel had pierced the Virgin Mary's soul, her mouth like a baptismal font, issuing forth the living water of rebirth.

Though individual forms of monasticism and their understandings of preaching are reflected in the Magdalenes that emerged from those orders, the popular tradition of the saint's life also featured significant emphasis on her preaching and its theological implications. Jacobus de Voragine's thirteenth-century *Golden Legend* constitutes a synthesis of much of the lore about the saints that had developed over the preceding thousand years. *The Golden Legend* was likely produced originally as a resource for Dominican preachers, but quickly became a popular and widely accessible devotional work. In

Jacobus's narrative, the vividness of Mary Magdalene's initial proclamation to the disciples on Easter morning is repeated in her preaching at Marseilles, where she demonstrates her rhetorical capability: "She came forward, her manner calm and her face serene, and with well-chosen words called them away from the cult of idols and preached Christ fervidly to them." Establishing boundaries for this persuasive power, Jacobus confirms her subservience to Rome. The fraught relationship between Mary Magdalene, the apostle to the apostles, and Peter, the first among the apostles, is here explored in terms of a deft negotiation. When challenged by the infertile Provençal governor, "Do you think you can defend the faith you preach?" she responds with confidence but is careful to ground her authority in the primacy of Peter and the Roman church: "'I am ready indeed to defend it,' she replied, 'because my faith is strengthened by the daily miracles and preaching of my teacher Peter, who presides in Rome!'"[40]

The Magdalene's power and efficacy could be accessed by the faithful at her pilgrimage sites, Marseilles and Vézelay. A series of lives emphasized her career in Marseilles; these narratives were likely used as part of practices associated with pilgrimages to Santiago de Compostela and the stop on the pilgrimage route at the site sacred to the Magdalene cult in the south of France. In a manuscript from the late fourteenth to early fifteenth centuries, the saint is described as preaching to many at Marseilles, including fellow evangelists who are labeled "her disciples.": "They came to the Port of Marseilles and went outside the boat and found the Magdalene and all her disciples who preached to a great multitude of people. And they cast themselves at her feet and said to her, 'O blessed Magdalene, your God whom you loved and whom you preach."[41]

The saint's special love for Christ also authorizes her preaching in the legend produced in late medieval Italian Florence. The author, like Bozon, includes moments of special knowledge for Mary Magdalene. He muses that she had become aware, before anyone else, that Christ was the Son of God. The revelation comes in a moment of domestic bliss shared with her siblings and Christ; in reaction, Mary Magdalene says, "as Peter said on the Mount: 'Master, let us make here three tabernacles,'" a reference to Peter's enthusiastic response at the Transfiguration. In this episode of the ongoing competition between Mary Magdalene and Peter, Mary comes out the winner. The reference to the Transfiguration reminds the reader that Peter had foolishly misinterpreted a clear manifestation of Christ's divinity, trying to comprehend revelation by confining it within a human framework. But Mary is able to understand the sacredness of the even most mundane moments in Jesus's life. In effect she uses Peter's words to humiliate him and the other obtuse, male disciples, for Christ is already recognized as divine and housed within a tabernacle, given the hospitality she and her family offer him in their own home. Not only do Mary and her family receive a kind of private Transfiguration, but the Virgin Mary and the Magdalene are given permission by Christ to come to the Last Supper and to be among the first to receive the Sacrament from him, which the author defends by arguing for the two women's position as apostles and as carriers, each in her way, of the Word of God. "And why should it not be so, and why not as meet or more for her and the Magdalen as for the disciples? Was she not the apostle and guardian of the Gospel?"[42]

Mary's insight into Christ's identity comes from her intimacy with him, from the closeness of the relationship he has with her and her family. This knowledge gives her a license to preach, which she begins to do even before the resurrection and Christ's explicit command that she proclaim the Gospel. She speaks publicly to the people of her territory, the serfs her family had renounced as part of their embrace of holy poverty; her "sweet speech" converts them. The author effuses about her worldly judgment and her spiritual graces, and concludes with a literary comparison between the Magdalene and Christ himself, echoing the final words of the Gospel of John:

> Oh, most prudent Magdalen! . . . there was never a realm in this world that thou wast not capable of ruling, both in judgment and discretion; . . . the good Lord restored thee through His great mercy, and made of thee an example to women in the Church, as He did of Paul to men; and if thou hadst had disciples, and they had written down thy deeds and all thy sayings, and the gentle nature of thy person, and thy sweet talk of Christ and His doctrine, they would have filled more volumes of books than one could count.[43]

Medieval interpretations of the Magdalene, intended to shape piety, can thus be seen taking their audiences in different directions according to the goals of their authors and communities. They all emphasized her preaching, but in ways that served specific ecclesiastical programs and theological orientations. Secular discussions of the Magdalene's life would also adapt her identity as a preacher in the context of the literary dialogues of emerging humanist scholarship.

The Magdalene became an exemplar for women's speech and conduct in the late medieval debate over the status of women, the *querelle des femmes*. Christine de Pizan's *The Book of the City of Ladies,* from the early fifteenth century, uses the life of the Magdalene to refute misogynistic claims of women's essential inferiority. Pizan notes the scriptural record of divine favor on women, approving the feminine character and granting them authority to preach. On the criticisms of female weeping, she points to Christ's compassion for the weeping of Mary Magdalene and Martha over their brother, Lazarus, and for the penitent tears of Luke 7's sinful woman: "What special favors has God bestowed on women because of their tears! He did not despise the tears of Mary Magdalene, but accepted them and forgave her sins, and through the merits of those tears she is in glory in heaven." And on her opponents' denigration of women's speech, she counters, "If women's language had been so blameworthy and of such small authority, as some men argue, our Lord Jesus Christ would never have deigned to wish that so worthy a mystery as His most gracious resurrection be first announced to a woman, just as He commended the blessed Magdalene, to whom He first appeared on Easter, to report and announce it to His apostles and to Peter. Blessed God, may you be praised, who, among the other infinite boons and favors which you have bestowed upon the feminine sex, desired that women carry such lofty and worthy news."[44]

The *querelle des femmes* was one skirmish in a long history of debates over women's position in society and in the church. Pizan engages this history by mentioning Peter in particular among the apostles and noting his debt to the Magdalene for the news of the resurrection. She thus makes reference to the long-standing tensions in the relationship between Peter and Mary Magdalene, representative of two sides of the Christian tradition: the one as orthodox authority and the other as divinely inspired prophet.[45]

The threat represented by the Magdalene was that she was too closely attached to Christ's humanity, and too inspired by fierce emotion, for orthodoxy. Many interpreters found Christ himself addressing this potential problem, when he reveals himself to Mary in the garden on Easter Sunday but warns her not to touch him, as he has not yet ascended to the father. This passage was used by medieval theologians to argue for the inappropriateness of Mary's attitude toward Christ after his resurrection: the rejection signaled an end to their previous easy intimacy and a rebuke to her temerity in speaking. Illustrations of this scene were among the most popular images featuring the saint, the *Noli me tangere* genre. Another common image of late medieval art suggested the possibility of renewing the intimacy between the Magdalene and Christ following his death and resurrection, but in a different mode. Late medieval portraits of the dead Christ make pointed reference to his body as the Eucharistic Host. Would viewers of these images have seen Mary Magdalene, coming to prepare Christ's body, to have been figuratively performing the Eucharistic liturgy, establishing a priest's familiar contact with the elements? Just such a liturgical role was alluded to in the Cistercian legend, which features the saint not only preaching but also acting as a priest in carrying out Christ's instruction to communicate the news of the resurrection: "Just as Eve in Paradise had once given her husband a poisoned draught to drink, so now the Magdalen presented to the apostles the chalice of eternal life." And as a logical consequence of her preaching ministry, a late

FIG 1.1 Anonymous, *Mary Magdalene Preaching in Marseilles,* 1451. Fresco, Chapelle Saint-Érige d'Auron, France. Photo: Hervé Champollion / akg-images.

fourteenth-century account of the saint, in Pietro de' Natali's influential *Catalogus sanctorum*, describes her not only converting the pagans of Marseilles but also baptizing them.[46]

A few images from medieval art explore this clerical identification for the saint, displaying a Magdalene daring in her embrace of male roles, such as those of public preacher or priest. There is a unique image in a stained glass window from Klagenfurt, Austria, from 1170 showing Mary Magdalene dressed in priest's vestments (alb, chasuble, stole), holding her customary ointment jar but also a thurible. Where the depiction of the conversion of Marseilles in the windows at the Chartres Cathedral shows only Bishop Maximin preaching, the fresco cycle in the chapel at the Church of Saint-Étienne de Tinée, in Auron, showing the life of Mary Magdalene, portrays her preaching to the people of Marseilles. In such a position of leadership, however, she is still a relatively accessible character in whom viewers can see themselves. Contrast her figure, the same size as the others in the Auron frescoes, with the ubiquitous medieval Madonna of Mercy image, a supernatural protector who towers over miniature men and women, sheltering them from God's wrath beneath the folds of her cloak. Perhaps the Magdalene's nearest equivalent among the saints of the church was the professedly unsupernatural John the Baptist, with whom she had been compared in the Cistercian life. Lucas Moser's altarpiece (c. 1431) for the side altar of the Kirche St. Maria Magdalena in Tiefenbronn, Germany, shows the legendary boat journey to France; Mary Magdalene is pointing, as in the traditional portraits of John the Baptist, another association of her own preaching ministry with his model of inspired prophetic witness. Both the Magdalene and John the Baptist were figures of repentance, intense asceticism, and profound insight into Christ's identity and mission, expressed in public testimony that challenged the prevailing religious authorities.[47]

Controversy

Mary Magdalene's story follows the arc of the Gospel narrative, from the first prophetic call to repentance made by a desert ascetic, through a compassionate journeying alongside Christ in his work and suffering, to the triumphant preaching of the resurrection. She represented penitent sinners and new converts, as well as powerful evangelists; in her was seen the life of the church, the bride of Christ, and the struggle of the individual toward God, ultimately sur-

FIG 1.2 Lucas Moser, *Altar of Magdalene* (wings closed), 1431. Tempera on parchment on top of wood. Photo: Erich Lessing / Art Resource, NY.

rendering in awestruck contemplation. She is both self-effacing and bold, the creator of her own cloister and yet somehow still a fallen pleasure seeker. She had been associated with conflicting impulses within the human character in part because of the multiple identities she had been assigned by the tradition since Gregory the Great. In the early sixteenth century, humanist scholars would seek to undo that complex tangle of scriptural characters and emerged with three separate women, characterized only as they are in the biblical text.

The French humanist and biblical scholar Jacques Lefèvre d'Étaples argued in a treatise published in 1517 that the scriptural record supported no connection between the penitent sinner of Luke 7, Mary the sister of Martha and Lazarus, and the woman from whom Christ had expelled seven demons. This last was the only woman truly associated with the name of Magdalene and was the witness of the Crucifixion and resurrection. Several scholars leapt to the defense of the traditional, composite Magdalene. Most prominent among them, the bishop of Rochester, John Fisher, published a tract in 1519 refuting Lefèvre d'Étaples's thesis, despite Fisher's own humanist and even possibly evangelical leanings. Fisher's arguments were themselves based on conclusions drawn from scripture, and on the authority of church tradition reaching back to the patristic period. He warned against the potential dangers of Lefèvre d'Étaples's reliance on scripture alone on the question of the Magdalene's identity—thus, already by 1519 we find her at the center of one of the crucial debates of the Reformation, the claim of *sola Scriptura*.[48]

Fisher's friend Thomas More advised combining the two figures of Mary and Martha within oneself, engaging by turns in both study and public life, though definitely asserting Mary's contemplation as the "better part." A decade after the initial controversy More would return to Mary's medieval legend to advance the contemplative, penitent Magdalene in a counterreform dialogue against Luther.[49]

The most renowned humanist, Desiderius Erasmus, maintained an ambiguous position, attempting to distance himself from the controversy by maintaining that the Magdalene's value for piety, in her multiple roles, was more important than separating them into an accurate series of figures. His earlier *In Praise of Folly* (1509), however, had arguably associated Mary Magdalene with Lady Folly, lampooning a sterile contemplation as the inevitable product of women's education; indeed, many later sixteenth-century editions rendered his "Moriae" (folly) as "Mariae," suggesting less reverence for the saint on the part of Erasmus or his editors than Fisher and More evinced.[50]

Teresa Coletti and Sheila Porrer argue that the humanists who favored separating the three Marys did so to guard the purity of Mary of Bethany, representative of the contemplative life, and to keep the sinful woman of Luke 7 from any connection with the first public proclamation of the resurrection.

Lefèvre d'Étaples's own professed motive for distinguishing the different women was, in part, the impropriety of a sinner maintaining so intimate a relation with Christ; "Mary the sister of Martha was not that public sinner, but holy, pure and a virgin, which is what I prefer to believe." Perhaps it was, in fact, the late medieval fascination with elaborating the details of the Magdalene's worldly life and its many temptations that finally provoked scholars to distinguish this most voluptuous of sinners from the friend and preacher of Christ. The medieval church had attempted to resolve the question of the Magdalene, of why this woman was chosen for so great a role. Her complex legend developed over centuries, adding layers of imaginative explanations about character and circumstances, wealth and sex, love and persuasion, holding in tension what is ultimately inexplicable: how a fallen humanity pursues a divine purpose. With the coming of the age of reform, the medieval solution eventually failed: for many of those desiring the purification of the church, so sinful a saint simply could not fill so crucial a place.[51]

For those who defended the composite Magdalene tradition in the age of reform, how would they argue for the continued importance of each feature of her legend? How would her sin affect her status as preacher? For the reformers who maintained her as central to evangelical narratives, how would they adapt her image and deploy it in the service of the new teaching? For those others who minimized her place in the story, on what terms would they deny her apostolic role?

In addition to the scholarly controversy and the theological programs of various reformers, Magdalene piety of the early sixteenth century was influenced by changes for women both Catholic and Protestant, as they interacted with the programs of the midcentury Council of Trent or as they discerned new lay vocations in evangelical congregations.

For its part, the Catholic Church asserted the traditional legend of the Magdalene against the claims of reformers beginning with Lefèvre d'Étaples. But the saint's legendary preaching would become problematic given the dangers opened up by evangelical uses of Mary Magdalene as a figure of divinely empowered lay ministry. With the attempts to conform convents more closely to official policy, the Catholic Church itself began to find the *apostola apostolorum* an undesirable champion and sought to emphasize instead the other features of her character: the abject contrition of the penitent, the converted wanton made compassionate lover of Christ, and the visionary ascetic.

On the Protestant side, the leaders of new church communities addressed a fundamental question raised by the doctrine of the priesthood of all believers: just who was authorized to preach in congregations modeling themselves on an early church, a church undeniably founded by the testimony of a woman. Scholarship on the cult of the Magdalene has not always recognized this history, especially when it has been obscured by assumptions about the Protestant Reformation's attitude toward the saints.

CHAPTER TWO

Teacher of the Dear Apostles

Lutheran Preaching on Mary Magdalene

JUST AS THEIR medieval forebears had, sixteenth-century Lutherans identified themselves with Mary Magdalene in their self-descriptions as sinners, as
the faithful community of the Word of God, and as preachers. The Magdalene
was advanced in public discourse on the question of lay and female preaching
and vocation within the church from the very beginnings of the Reformation, and continued to be so through the development of Protestant cultural
identity in the sixteenth and seventeenth centuries. Even where her role was
not interpreted so radically, Mary Magdalene remained at the heart of the
Gospel accounts of Christ's Passion, and therefore could not be ignored by
scholars and preachers.

The principal project of Reformation theologians and pastors was the reinterpretation of biblical texts to express the evangelical Gospel: the message of
justification by faith alone. In his analysis of the scripture passages in which
the Magdalene figures, Martin Luther established the model that would be followed by the church leaders in his community of influence. Luther accepted
the Magdalene's composite identity; though he emphasized her roles as the
penitent sinner and as witness of the resurrection, he continued to speak of
all three figures traditionally identified with her, recasting each of them in
an evangelical mold. He read the story of the sinful woman in Luke 7 as a
parable of Christ's absolution producing gratitude in the sinner. His account
of the confrontation between Mary and Martha described Mary's devotion
to God's Word above all things as paradigmatic for the faithful. And most
positively, Luther held her up as an example of devotion to Christ, and of
faithful, evangelical testimony, in his readings of the Passion and resurrection narratives. In contrast to the presentation of Eve in his *Lectures on
Genesis,* whose "substitution of the devil's word for the word of God" serves

as a kind of perverted preaching to Adam, Mary Magdalene speaks the news of the resurrection as she is commanded to by Christ and by angels; that the disciples in the different Gospel accounts fail in various ways to believe her message is no fault of her own. Luther's sermon series on the Johannine Passion narrative, delivered in 1528–1529, included an extended discussion of Mary's vigil at the tomb, praising her tears. Luther commended her ardent love for Christ and her eager announcing of the news of the resurrection as patterns for all Christians, and especially preachers, to follow. The use of a woman as a model for faithful preaching inevitably raised questions in the nascent reform movement about the role of women, and of laypersons in general, in the church.[1]

Luther's teaching on the different aspects of Mary Magdalene's identity was taken up in his colleagues' and followers' postils—volumes of sermons published as aids for preachers. Many of these collections, especially those of Luther's most well-known pupils, were republished in numerous editions, reaching a wide audience and becoming influential teaching tools and reference works that shaped the preaching heard in churches around the growing Lutheran world.

The teaching role of the pastor and of his sermons in Protestant culture was "to propagate norms among the laity."[2] Thus, in the preached treatments of the resurrection narrative, as well as of the other biblical texts in which she appears, Mary Magdalene was presented as a normative model for ordinary Christians, male and female, lay and ordained. She became the model Lutheran: experiencing the gracious work of Christ who forgives her sins and overcomes death on her behalf, and then herself giving witness with confident and bold faith.

Luther's own record of teaching on Mary Magdalene has not been systematically explored. He discussed her frequently in his academic lectures and writing, and his treatments there are often the source for the interpretations to be found in the preaching of his students. Further evidence for his reading of the saint can be found in his sermons on texts related to her, falling roughly into three categories: preaching on the Sunday before July 22, when her traditional feast day was observed; on the Feast of the Assumption of the Virgin Mary; and sermons for Easter Sunday, on the text from the Gospel of John.

The evangelical church's liturgical calendar continued the medieval tradition of the reading appointed for the Feast of the Magdalene: Luke

7:36–50, the account of the penitent sinner who washes Jesus's feet with her tears, then dries them with her hair and anoints them with precious oil. Likewise, since the seventh century, the Gospel for the observation of the Assumption of the Virgin Mary had been Luke 10:38–42, the comparison between the contemplative Mary and the industrious Martha, stemming from a connection made between the quiet devotion of Mary of Bethany in this text and the character of the Virgin Mary, said to ponder the events of her son's life "in her heart" (Luke 2:19). Both the sinful woman and Mary of Bethany had been identified with Mary Magdalene by Gregory the Great, and Luther chose to retain this association even after its recent controversial debunking by the French humanist scholar Jacques Lefèvre d'Étaples.[3]

One aspect of the medieval Magdalene tradition Luther rejected as false: the identification of Mary Magdalene as the bride in the wedding at Cana, subsequently abandoned by her husband when he became the disciple John the Evangelist. Maintaining this association would have meant undermining the importance of Christ's first miracle having been performed at a wedding, a fact that Luther wished to interpret as indicating divine approval for the married life. If Mary Magdalene's life of sin had been the result of the Cana nuptials gone wrong, an aborted wedding would not have served Luther's agenda of divine support for the institution of marriage. Thus we see Luther carefully crafting an evangelical identity for the Magdalene, retaining those elements of the tradition that could be engaged in service of the reforming Gospel and leaving aside those that might counter his arguments.[4]

The resurrection narrative in the Gospel of John served as the lectionary reading for the highest festival of the church year, Easter Sunday, but the Feast of the Magdalene and, to a certain extent, the Assumption of Mary, also remained in the Lutheran liturgical calendar, and the different aspects of her identity therefore continued to be celebrated as part of Lutheran spiritual formation. Several of the most prominent authors of sermon collections, Anton Corvinus, Johann Habermann, and Johann Spangenberg, as well as the renowned hymn writer Nicolaus Herman, spent significant time exploring aspects of her role, repeating and developing Luther's teaching on the saint. The retention of these Magdalene texts in the worship and preaching of the Lutheran Church guaranteed that her story would continue to be told; the ubiquity of Mary Magdalene in Lutheran sermons established her as a central character in the evangelical project of scripture interpretation and theological reform. Her composite identity gave Luther and his followers the opportunity to provide scriptural foundations for the core reform doctrines of justification by grace alone and the nature and implications of a priesthood of all believers.[5]

The Sinful Woman of Luke 7

In his exposition of Luke's account of the sinful woman in the house of Simon the Pharisee, Luther constructed an evangelical reading of a story that had traditionally been used in support of the sacrament of penance. Medieval preachers had emphasized the grievous nature of the woman's sexual sin and saw her abject kneeling as an appropriate work of penitence, duly rewarded with Christ's absolution. Just as she is the prototypical sinner, so is she the model of repentance, as a fifteenth-century sermon collection claimed: "God has set up before us a model . . . that we, who are sinners, take an example from her, as she separated herself from sins, that we too do the same; and as she repented of her sins, that we also allow ourselves to be sorry for our sins." The sermon tells the story of her fall and then her action in washing Christ's feet. The author emphasizes her actions as the cause of her redemption, "And, in truth, I tell you, many sins have been forgiven her, because she has great love." The account of her life from then on includes a brief acknowledgment that she witnessed the Crucifixion and resurrection. No mention is made of her role in preaching about Christ's rising, though her legendary ascetic retreat to the desert is given considerable space. When asked to identify herself on the point of death, she confesses merely that she was "Mary, the public sinner."[6]

In considering Luther's adaptation of this tradition it is important to be attentive to the influence of his particular circumstances and audience in shaping Luther's use of the Magdalene, as well as that of his colleagues. Luther's theology was famously determined by controversies with his theological opponents, but certain scholars have also noted how much of his thought and approach were formed by pastoral situations in which he found himself called on for advice and authoritative pronouncements. Luther was attempting both to reform the medieval church in order to return to the model of early church practice and to minister to believers whose immersion in the medieval cultural legacy made them vulnerable to attacks of conscience. Throughout his career, he demonstrated a keen awareness of the need to modulate his tone and even his doctrine in the achievement of his evangelical goals.[7]

The Magdalene of Luke 7 had been a feature of Luther's arguments against the system of penitential works and the necessity of priestly absolution since the earliest years of his protests against indulgences. She featured in the *Acta Augustana,* his defense against the censures issued by Cardinal Cajetan at the hearing held in 1518 in Augsburg, a work in which Luther developed his theology of justification using scriptural evidence.[8] For Luther, Mary's absolution is an example of what faith receives in grace, not a reward for groveling: "So says St. Augustine on John: join the word to the element, and make the sacrament, not because one does, but because one believes. Behold, Baptism washes, not because one does it, but because one believes in the washing. Thence He absolved Mary, saying: Your faith has saved you [*Fides tua te salvam fecit*], go in peace."[9]

His exposition of the text in the *Sermon on Two Kinds of Righteousness,* a theological treatise also produced during the period 1518–1519, reveals the Magdalene's personification, for Luther, of the radical humility that seeks and expects no reward, but only mercy:

> Consider the story in Luke 7[:36–50], where Simon the leper, pretending to be in the form of God and perching on his own righteousness, was arrogantly judging and despising Mary Magdalene, seeing in her the form of a servant. . . . Simon the leper is now nothing but a sinner. He who seemed to himself so righteous sits divested of the glory of the form of God, humiliated in the form of a servant, willy-nilly. On the other hand, Christ honors Mary with the form of God and elevates her above Simon, saying: "She has anointed my feet and kissed them. She has wet my feet with her tears and wiped them with her hair." How great were the merits which neither she nor Simon saw. Her faults are remembered no more. Christ ignored the form of servitude in her whom he has exalted with the form of sovereignty. Mary is nothing but righteous, elevated into the glory of the form of God, etc.[10]

Mary Magdalene is Luther's paradigmatic sinner, at once condemned and saved. She is elevated to the status of Christ because she claims no status for herself, making no appeal to her own merits because she knows that she has none. She thus gains the only kind of righteousness truly possible for the Christian: that with which Christ clothes the passive recipient.

The same reinterpretation of Luke 7 is presented in Luther's published sermon collections, where the Magdalene is a model for an evangelical kind of contrition, one that has been separated from any consideration of merit based on works of penance.[11] In a 1527 collection of homilies for feast days, his notes on that Gospel passage read, "The hypocrites and works saints write that such signs or works bring righteousness, but Christ says: your faith has saved you."[12] An important distinction in the new theology of absolution makes it clear that forgiveness is not earned, but that gratitude could create a joyful response in the believer. Thus, the evangelical reading of Luke 7 does not portray Mary's great self-humiliation as so impressing Christ that he forgives her, but rather his generosity summons her great love. In a book of sermons from 1544 intended for delivery in the home, her "great love" is the appropriate fruit of a graciously bestowed forgiveness, a beautiful gesture denoting her humble awareness of both her own unworthiness and Christ's great mercy.[13] In a sermon on John 4 from the same collection, Mary Magdalene is still being used—near the end of Luther's preaching career, just as at its beginning—to assert the worthlessness of works. She stands in the list of great exemplars of justification by faith alone. "Then thus speaks Paul: 'We hold that man through faith and not through the work of the Law is made righteous.' And the Prophet Habbakuk says: 'The righteous shall live by his faith.' And Christ says to Mary that her sins are forgiven: 'Go, your faith has saved you.'" (Gehe hin, dein glaub hat dir geholffen.)[14] Faith in the Gospel, not the loving deeds that only follow from faith, is proposed as Mary's path to salvation.

The Magdalene interpretations made by Luther's followers echoed the theological themes and language that their mentor had used. Especially in publishing sermon collections and preaching manuals, which were marketed as reliable guides to orthodox, evangelical teaching, authors sought to ensure that they were providing sound exemplars by hewing closely to Luther's pronouncements. One of the earliest such manuals published by one of Luther's colleagues was Johann Bugenhagen's 1524 *Postillatio*, a collection of notes on the texts for each Sunday. Bugenhagen was Luther's close associate and the pastor of St. Mary's Church in Wittenberg. For several of the Sundays in the *Postillatio*, Bugenhagen simply refers the reader to Luther's own sermon on the text, showing how strongly he trusted in his friend's teaching. Bugen-hagen's sermon notes for the Feast of the Magdalene present the penitent, foot-washing Magdalene of Luke 7 as an example of true repentance and salvation by faith. Another of Luther's initial supporters was Urbanus Rhe-gius, who began to write and minister on behalf of the evangelical cause in 1521 in Augsburg, eventually becoming the superintendent of evangelical clergy in Lüneberg, where his supervisory role led him to produce a preach-ing manual, published in 1535–1536. As part of the book's goal of theological education for a recently converted population, Rhegius addressed many of the areas of religious life that Luther sought to reform, with sections on how to speak "properly," "carefully," or "circumspectly" about such sensitive topics as fasting, human traditions, the cult of the saints, and images, including a section explaining the new theology of confession. There he refers to Luke 7, offering a close application of the story to the contemporary congrega-tion and its practices of piety. The Magdalene's absolution is an encouraging example for Christians that every absolution is spoken to believers directly, from Christ, when spoken by their pastor: "People [under the papacy] were persuaded that sins were remitted by the act of confessing and their own con-trition. The merits of Christ were scarcely considered. . . . Christ gave to his church the keys to the kingdom of Heaven and commits them to ministers of the Word. . . . We ought to believe firmly, therefore, in the absolution, no less than if Christ himself would visibly absolve us just as he absolved Mary Magdalene." The faithful were assured that they continued to be absolved from their sins, but were directed toward a new understanding of how that freedom was achieved and what it meant.[15]

As Luther had taught, the emphasis on Christ's action gives new meaning to the Magdalene's washing of Christ's feet: she tends to Christ out of love and gratitude for what he has already done for her, not as a propitiation for her sins. This interpretation was elaborated in a collection of instructional sermons for children and youth published by Johann Spangenberg in 1544. Luther's close associate and supporter, Spangenberg had served as evangelical pastor of Nordhausen since 1524, going on to become church superinten-dent in Mansfeld County in 1546. Having been a schoolteacher in Stolberg before his ordination, he applied his talents to religious education, founding a school at Nordhausen and producing curriculum materials, including the preaching manual.[16]

Spangenberg's sermon for the Feast of the Magdalene expresses an evangelical theology of confession and absolution, organized around a series of questions in the standard formula of catechesis. He gives an introduction to the different kinds of possible sinners: unrepentant sinners, hypocrites, and the penitent, of which the sinful woman of Luke 7, whom "some" connect with the Magdalene, is the model.[17] She is not merely a model for particularly sinful sexual miscreants, nor even for women as such, though he acknowledges "lust" as the character of her sinful past. Rather, Spangenberg uses the story to emphasize the universality of the sinful condition, noting in several places that Christ came for "poor sinners [*die armen Sünder vnd Sünderinnen*], male and female [*Man vnd weib*]." He urges his students to do as she does: "We should learn from this example, how it must happen that we will attain forgiveness of sins from God." (Wil uns mit diesem ihrem Exempel leren wie die müssen geschickt sein die bey Gott vergebung der Sünden erlangen wollen.) Once students imitate her faith, they will demonstrate it in acts of love and compassion like hers. Spangenberg very clearly lays out the evangelical order of contrition, then faith that Christ forgives sins, and "lastly [*Zu letzt*]," the works of gratitude. The sermon firmly refutes a suggestion that Mary's action might have played some role in securing her forgiveness: "How could a human work achieve forgiveness of sins, which pertains to God alone?" (Wie kan ein menschlich werck vergebung der sunden erlangen / das alleine Gotte gebürt.) Spangenberg asserts, however, that so great a faith "is not idle or without works, but rather extends itself through love." (Darüber ist solcher glaube auch nicht müssig odder wercklos sondern breitet sich aus durch die liebe.) He thus warns his young audience against the possibility of an overemphasis on unmerited forgiveness, an interpretation Luther and his colleagues combated as leading to lawlessness. For Spangenberg's pupils, the Magdalene is thus the paradigmatic believer: one who knows herself to be sinful, and responds appropriately. As he notes, citing 1 John 1:8, "If we say we have no sin, we deceive ourselves." All are therefore sinners like the Magdalene; all must seek her steadfast faith, which is then expressed in service of God and the neighbor.[18]

This kind of theological instruction, identifying believers with the sinful woman, took place not only in sermons but throughout the worship service in prayer and in song. The hymn author Nicolaus Herman was the cantor in Joachimsthal, in northwest Bohemia, and another early supporter of Luther's reform program.[19] His collection of hymns for the church year, published in 1560, includes two hymns for the Feast of the Magdalene. Notably, the hymn Herman had written for Easter Sunday, describing the Magdalene's visit to the tomb, is reprinted just before the hymns for her feast day, indicating that the liturgy for her feast may also have included an observance of her role in the resurrection narrative. The first hymn for the Luke 7 text creates a similar connection between the sinner of the story and the contemporary worshipper, with a first-person speech that places the words of the woman's desire to care for Jesus in the mouth of the singer. The hymn concludes with an admonition to imitate her piety: "You sinful men and women / learn from this penitent woman / how God admits so graciously / the penance done / in faith and improves it."[20] A second hymn for the same occasion emphasizes the part of the Luke 7 story in which Jesus offers Simon the Pharisee a parable about two debtors, one of whom is forgiven a much greater debt and who therefore feels more gratitude to the creditor. Herman describes Mary's love as great *because* she has been forgiven much; like Luther he inverts the cause and effect relationship from the medieval interpretation of this passage, asserting the evangelical order of forgiveness followed by the fruit of faith: "For her love toward me is great, / Because [*Drumb*] she is being loosed from many sins. / However, one who is not forgiven much, / That one also loves so much the less."[21]

Christopher Brown has established the catechetical relationship between hymns such as Herman's and preaching. The symbiosis between the two served to create a coherent message in worship and to promulgate the lessons taught at church in the home and workplace, creating a powerful vehicle for the evangelical Gospel. A parallel interpretation of the text does, in fact, appear in the sermon for Mary Magdalene's feast in the sermon collection published in 1565 by Herman's colleague in Joachimsthal, the pastor Johannes Mathesius. Mathesius, like Herman, presents a consistent reiteration of Luther's teaching on this passage; both preaching and song would have reinforced each other in conveying an evangelical reading of the text that was both memorable and theologically rigorous.[22]

Unusually among evangelical interpretations, Mathesius's introduction of Mary Magdalene describes her as an upper-class woman, a "pious *Schloss-frau*," in what he admits is a reference to her medieval legend. He notes that she was among the women who supported Christ and his disciples from their means, subtly connecting her with the wealthy female patrons of his own congregation, on whose support he depended in a confessionally divided area. He also pauses to recall the events of Easter morning, when to Mary Magdalene "the Lord first appeared after his resurrection on Easter day, and commanded her to preach and declare his joyous resurrection to his beloved disciples and brothers." He acknowledges the identification of this Magdalene with the sinful woman of Luke 7 (and with Mary of Bethany) and that the tradition associates this text with the Magdalene's feast. Claiming that he does not wish to dispute the point, he suggests that these figures were, in fact, three separate women but proposes to examine the text for its intrinsic value. Placing some distance between the identities of prostitute and patroness was likely a wise choice, given Mathesius's audience of noblewomen. Serving a similar purpose, and also innovative among Lutheran interpretations, is Mathesius's focus on the Magdalene as praiseworthy for her recognition of Christ as a true preacher, especially in comparison to the inadequate reception given to him by Simon the Pharisee. The emphasis is not only on her self-awareness as a contrite sinner; she is also insightful about Christ's identity and reveres him as the Word incarnate. In this she provides an admirable model for women as discerning supporters of the true mission and message of the church, perhaps in a context in which men fail to welcome the new teaching. Such a model would have been reassuring to women such as Mathesius's parishioner Margarethe von Hassenstein, whose husband Felix remained loyal to the Catholic Church.[23]

More conventionally, Mathesius goes on to describe how the Magdalene honors Christ in gratitude for the forgiveness of her sins. As Luther often had, Mathesius lists her among other sinners selected by God for great service: Paul and David. Again like Luther, Mathesius insists that her love is a "fruit of faith" rather than the cause of her redemption. In concert with the other evangelical interpreters of this passage, Mathesius uses Christ's statement to the woman, that her faith has saved her, to establish that justification is based on faith alone, not works.[24]

That assertion was still being made two generations after the beginning of Luther's reform. Johann Habermann's very popular 1575 *Postilla* contains a long exposition of the story. Even at sixty years' remove from Luther's attack on indulgences, Habermann was still dealing with the legacy of medieval piety. He was superintendent of Naumburg-Zeitz, a diocese that had been

FIG 2.1 Lucas Cranach the Elder, *Mary Magdalene*, c.1525. Oil on panel. Walters Art Museum, Baltimore, USA. Photo: Bridgeman Images.

forcibly reformed when Saxon Elector Johann Friedrich installed the evangelical Nicholas von Amsdorf as bishop in 1541. The area had passed back into
Catholic hands during the Schmalkaldic War in 1546–1547, then reverted to
the control of the Saxon princes in 1564, with the death of the last Catholic
bishop. When Habermann began his tenure in the region in 1576, it had thus
experienced religious upheaval for more than thirty years, and firm teaching
on evangelical identity must have been among his chief tasks.[25]

Habermann begins his treatment of the Magdalene by parsing the saint's
tradition, distinguishing between those parts that he will continue to observe
and those elements that are to be rejected. He notes that he is accepting Gregory the Great's identification of the three scriptural Marys, as Luther had. He
briefly addresses the legends that have accrued around her cult, her travels
to Marseilles and conversion of the pagans, remarkably, allowing that they
"may well be" true. His own sermon focuses, however, on a consideration of
the biblical texts.[26] He describes how the sinful woman hears the preaching
of Christ and becomes convinced of her sin, fearful of death and hellfire.
She brings the ointment, bathes Christ's feet with it, and dries them with her
hair, "which is a sign of great love" and of faith, "for the love is a fruit of faith
[*die liebe ist eine frucht des glaubens*]." The preaching of the Gospel, Habermann urges, should affect us in the same way, causing repentance, love, and
a new obedience as the expression of faith. He insists that shame, regret,
and penitence are not enough; one must have faith in the grace of Christ
who mercifully forgives sins, as the Magdalene's story also shows. Believers
should learn from this that all are sinners, in need of grace, and should repent,
confessing their sins. Christians are saved by grace, not works, to contradict
the false teaching of the pope, as can be seen from Christ's words: "Your faith
has saved you." Habermann points out that Christ does *not* say "Your love has
saved you." (Und er saget nicht, Deine liebe hat dir geholffen.) The love is
gratitude for the forgiveness and, again, its "fruit"; it does not produce the forgiveness. The importance for evangelical theology of Jesus's story about the
two debtors here becomes evident. Jesus asks the Pharisee who loves the
merciful creditor more; the question and answer establish, for Habermann,
that love is created in response to mercy. This is true, he affirms, for the sinful
woman and in his own congregation. Lastly, Habermann claims that right faith
"never [*nimmermehr*]" comes without bringing love, manifested in deeds and
obedience to God's commands. Like Spangenberg, with his impetuous young

pupils, Habermann is concerned to prevent anarchic abuses of evangelical freedom. The Luke 7 text both extends the promise and sets the limits on the theology of justification by faith alone.[27]

Mary and Martha

The story of Martha and Mary from Luke 10 continued to be read during one of the few remaining festivals of the Virgin Mary in evangelical worship. This practice allowed another feature of Mary Magdalene's traditional identity, that of the pious contemplative, to shape the devotional life of the saint in the preaching of Luther and some of his followers. Although the Feast of the Assumption was not observed by most Lutherans after the first generation of the Reformation, it was a feature of the piety of confessionally divided cities, such as Augsburg. For Luther, the text became another opportunity to reassert the importance of faith over works. The "better part" taken by Mary is listening to the Word incarnate, and this is commended to all Christians as beneficial, in comparison to the human activity of Martha. In contrasting Martha with Mary as a law / Gospel paradigm, Luther was returning to the teaching of early church theologians such as Clement of Alexandria, Cyril of Alexandria, and Origen, as well as Augustine, who had read Mary's contemplation and Martha's action as two parts of the same life rather than as two opposed ways of life.[28]

Luther's 1523 sermon for the Feast of the Assumption explicitly rejects the medieval readings of Martha and Mary as representing an opposition between the active and the contemplative life—the laity versus cloistered monks and nuns: "We can dismiss what has been said until now about the active and the contemplative life. . . . I would cover up their words and let them be unknown." Luther redresses the traditional inequality between religious and secular vocations and, indeed, the separation of them into two distinct estates. He seeks to embrace Martha's work as an example of industry in the pursuit of one's secular calling, but to remove the anxiety associated with a valuation of works as meritorious. "It is in our nature . . . not to be satisfied with faith, but to require works as well. We should be active, but we should not worry." Mary's contemplation, on the other hand, is praised as part of constructing an evangelical distinction between faith and works: "All people's works are transitory things; there is nothing except the word of God and faith.

The word remains eternally, and is steadfast against the devil, death, and hell." Mary's work is shown to be no work at all, but the passive attitude of trust in God's spoken promises. In the sermon for the same festival from the previous year, Luther had said, "For I wish to have no work but the work of Mary, which is faith, that you believe in the Word [*dann ich wil kain werck haben dann das werck Marie, das ist den glauben, das du gelaubest an das wort*]."[29]

A 1531 sermon further refines the new definition of contemplation. It is not to be confused with the kind of esoteric speculation on the nature of God that Luther associated with medieval theologians and universities; instead, contemplation is to remain simply listening to the Word itself: "My doctrine and preaching cannot be obtained in all of the books. . . . For this would I do, and him only would I hear, and I will sit with Mary at his feet, then I will also learn what was taught by Christ about faith. That is necessary for us, what we Christians have each to believe seriously."[30] Mary, in her humble simplicity, provides the example for faithful Christians with her meek posture and in her direct reception of the bare Word. It is not necessary to be a doctor of theology but only to do as anyone may, even an unschooled woman. This praise of Mary's simple faith stands within Luther's larger theology, which prefers a childlike dependence on God to the idea of faith as an intellectual quest.[31]

Luther's followers also adopted his interpretation of the comparison between Mary and Martha as they taught evangelical congregations about the new theology of vocation: how to incorporate contemplation into the life of the laity and how to understand the sacredness of being active in the world. Because the Mary and Martha text was attached to a feast no longer celebrated in most Lutheran communities but mostly in those with a divided confessional affiliation, there are fewer records of preaching on this story in Lutheran sermon collections. Johann Spangenberg's manual for children's homilies gives us an example of one of these sermons. In answering Martha's plea for some help with the housework, Christ responds, "Mary has chosen a good part, and it shall not be taken from her." In Spangenberg's reading, she has a "good" part, but not the "better" one actually stated in Luke's Gospel. Here we can see a preacher taking license with the scriptures, as Luther himself had advised, in order to deliver the message of the Gospel clearly and emphatically. Like Luther, Spangenberg did not wish to diminish the work of Martha as a worldly good, important in the secular kingdom, but only to indicate its irrelevance in God's kingdom.[32] He asks what men have made of the two lives represented by Mary and Martha and describes how, under monasticism, Mary's contemplative life was held up as the holy one and the physical labor of Martha was seen as less worthy. What kind of predicament does this create for the majority, who must endure in their lot in life? "So must all worldly business, handicraft, townspeople and peasants be lost?" Spangenberg asks. "What will become of them?"[33] He contends, following Luther's 1523 sermon on this text, that it is not Martha's *work* that is being rebuked or rejected but the false meaning attached to it. The emphasis is on Christ's statement that Mary's choice is the one thing needful, that God's Word is what is necessary to bring us to eternal life; physical works are good, but not necessary in relation to salvation. "Your work is certainly useful and good, but Mary's work alone is necessary. Your work is fleeting, Mary's work (namely, to hear God's Word) is eternal and brings the hearer at last to that place where the Word sits in its essence, at the right [hand] of God in eternal life."[34] In his concluding summary of this text, Spangenberg writes, "That works do not make us righteous before God, but rather sitting at the feet of Christ and hearing His Word—that justifies and makes holy."[35]

This story was thus used by Luther and subsequent preachers of reform to argue for a rejection of the medieval hierarchy of different ways of life, which had elevated the celibacy of the cloister over the domestic and mercantile existence of the laity. In Lutheran preaching, Mary Magdalene was brought back from her retreat into a hermit's cell and relocated in the hurly-burly of the mundane. Sitting at the feet of Jesus—as she and all other Christians are commanded to do—does not represent a turning away from the duties of this life but a devotion to the Word as it pierces through the cacophony of market place and nursery, workshop and battlefield. Rather than counseling the faithful to imitate her example by preferring religious vows to marriage and children, Lutheran pastors could hold the Magdalene up as a figure for ordinary believers in listening to the Gospel even as they attended to their daily tasks.

The Resurrection Narrative

The Gospel of John's resurrection narrative served as the Gospel text for the Easter Sunday morning service, and Luther therefore preached on it almost every year in which he wrote an Easter sermon. On occasion he also expanded his treatment of the passage during the week following Easter Sunday, as in 1530, when his preaching for Thursday featured a sermon dedicated particularly to the Magdalene's role as the first witness of the resurrection. Luther's preaching career contains at least eleven preserved sermons on this text, a substantial record of evidence about the way in which he strove to interpret this story for his congregation and colleagues.

There are two principal themes of Luther's work with John 20:1–18. The first is Mary Magdalene's character as an ordinary sinner, comparable to male prophets and disciples of both the Old and New Testaments who were chosen, despite their failings, to reveal and serve the Gospel. This trope was common throughout Luther's work; in the 1525 treatise *Against the Heavenly Prophets,* Mary is counted alongside male sinners Peter and Paul, who became saints by the means of grace alone, and in the *Lectures on Genesis,* in the early 1540s, Luther declared, "sin was aroused in Manasseh, but for grace and salvation, and similarly also in the case of Peter, Paul, and the Magdalene." This marked a significant shift away from the tradition of medieval liturgical drama that mocked Mary Magdalene in comparison to the authoritative Peter. In the Easter preaching, Luther explicitly described a spiritual equality of all sinners, as in the sermon for Easter Sunday 1530, where Luther himself, along with Peter and Mary Magdalene, are all likewise sinful until Christ calls them to new life on Easter. In the sermon for the following Thursday, everyone—Peter and Paul, Mary Magdalene, Luther, and his listeners—"are all brothers alike and there is utterly no difference between persons [*so sind sie alle bruder zu gleich und ist gar kein unterscheid unter den personen*]." This point is also emphasized in a 1526 collection of Luther's sermons, in a discussion of the relative merit of different scriptural figures, when Luther acknowledges that Peter would, of course, have done a greater work than the thief crucified with Jesus, and that Mary, the mother of God, performed a greater work than the sinful Magdalene, yet all are made brothers with Christ, and there is to be no distinction of persons.[36]

It may be that Luther's frequent comparisons of the Magdalene to Peter, in addition to being a reassurance for all Christians that they are equally recipients of grace, also served the purpose of undermining the traditional primacy of Peter among the saints and thus provided a subtle attack on papal authority.[37] In a 1524 sermon, Luther imagines an indignant Peter appealing to God: "Mary had seven demons. If Peter said: Mary cannot be equal to me, God would respond: how much more has actually been given to the Magdalene, than to you. Here he works for the whole day with no effect."[38] Peter's plea and God's response refer to the Parable of the Workers in the Vineyard (Matt. 20:1–16), in which those who had worked for a full day are paid as much as those who were hired at dusk. The evangelical emphasis on unmerited grace is made while, at the same time, Peter is portrayed as ungrateful and petty.

God's championing of the sinful Magdalene or the latecomers in the parable seems, on the face of it, unreasonable and enigmatic. The very ordinariness of Mary Magdalene, a mere sinner, demonstrates another of Luther's favorite themes, the foolishness of the Gospel: God's rejection or inversion of worldly wisdom, power, and status. Luther often notes the strangeness of the Lord's resurrection being announced first to and by mere women, and ignorant ones at that; in a 1528 sermon collection, Christ's revelations to the non-Jewish woman at the well (John 4:1–26) and to Mary Magdalene confound the established order. In the sermon for Easter Monday, in the 1544 collection of Luther's sermons made by one of his close colleagues, Caspar Cruciger, Luther speaks of the women, led by the Magdalene, who were so unknowing as to go to the empty tomb to minister to a dead body. He dramatically claims for them the title of preacher. "Now these madwomen and fools become the first to whom Christ reveals His resurrection, and He makes the same into preacheresses and witnesses." (Noch werden diese Tolen und Nerrin die ersten, den Christus seine Aufferstehung offenbaret und zu Predigerin und zeugen der selben mache.)[39] An Easter week sermon from 1529 also draws attention to the astounding fact of Christ's first post-resurrection appearance to a woman. The emphasis on the weakness of Mary and the other women at the tomb is coupled ironically with an acknowledgment of the "excellent, unconquerable strength" of these women once they are sustained by grace.[40] The contrast is offered not to establish the nature of women as weak (an undisputed characterization in the sixteenth century), but to point to the weakness of all Christians before the receipt of grace, and to the contrast with their power and freedom in Christ.[41] The paradoxical coexistence of pitiable weakness and magnificent strength within the same person considered from two different perspectives is one of Luther's most common tropes about Christ's incarnation, in which the Lord of creation is born a helpless infant, and suffers an ignoble death. That Luther's emphasis is not on Mary's special frailty as a woman is also argued by his failure to take up a common trope of the medieval Magdalene tradition. John 20:17, in which the newly risen Jesus tells Mary, "Do not hold onto me," had been long interpreted as a condemnation of Mary's carnality.[42] The passage was read by Luther, however, only as an indication that the earliest witnesses of the resurrection did not understand the nature of the risen Christ. He even develops a passage of imagined dialogue in which Jesus rejects the idea that Mary's touch was itself inappropriate. "I am not concerned by your touch," Luther has the risen Christ tell Mary, "but what does concern Me is what you think about My resurrection, namely, that you should believe that through it I have entered a different existence."[43]

The second theme of the Easter preaching is Luther's praise of the Magdalene as an example of faithful devotion to Christ by her zeal in going early to the tomb and her patient mourning there when others had left or stayed away.[44] In her ardent seeking of the Word incarnate, and in her divinely ordained mission to strengthen the disciples with the message of their newfound brotherhood with Christ, she is held up as a model for all Christians, and particularly for preachers: "Oh, that we also should have such a heart" [O das wir auch ein solch hertz solten haben], Luther laments, in referring to the depth of her love and grief. In his preaching on John 20 from 1529, Luther gives an extended discussion of her passionate fidelity: "Thus Mary is a fine, beautiful image and an outstanding example of all those who cling to Christ so that their heart is set aflame with pure, genuine love for Christ. . . . And the evangelist has so carefully noted all of this in order to present an example to the whole world, so that we who preach or hear it may also gain such longing, love, and ardor for the Lord Christ in accordance with her example. . . . This example of Mary puts us all to shame."[45] As we have already seen, Luther proclaims that John 20 shows Christ appointing Mary Magdalene to be the first preacher of the Gospel. In the 1530 Easter Thursday sermon, Luther writes, "Christ makes of her a preacheress, that she must be a mistress and teacher of the dear apostles [macht ein predigerin aus yhr, das sie mus eine Meisterin und lererin der lieben Aposteln sein]." Similarly, in his Easter Monday sermon preached before the Duke of Saxony in 1538, Luther has Christ telling Mary, "Go forth and become a preacheress and declare this (as I say to you) before my dear brothers." (Gehe hin und werde eine Predigerin und verkuendige dis [so ich dir sage] weiter Meinen lieben Bruedern.) In these references Luther uses the female form for the role of Mary and the other women at the resurrection; he is not invoking them allegorically, as symbols of faithfulness meant only for imitation by male clergy. These are emphatically women, whose very humble reality makes them models for the believers sitting before the Wittenberg pulpit.[46]

Providing a foundation for these discussions of the Magdalene as a preacher, Luther elsewhere insists on her identity, among other men and women in the New Testament, as a disciple.[47] In the context of a 1529 sermon directed against the authority and power of priests in the papal system, Luther advances a theology of the priesthood of all believers, using the women's integration among the disciples as proof:

> Discover that the disciples are not only the apostles, but all those who believe in Christ. Luke in Acts, chapter 9 [says], "There were disciples at Lydda," etc. In this word all are comprehended, so this teaching makes them blush, because women are mentioned by name, etc. And without doubt the women, Mary Magdalene, Martha, Johanna, were at the supper, and went with Him freely, who went together at Passover and on Easter. He does not speak of apostles, of priests, but of disciples, whereupon you should observe this. . . . Just as the name of Christians and disciples is common to all, men and women, so remains this text for our community also.[48]

This sermon, written five years after the German Peasants' War and the emergence of radical reformers such as Thomas Münzer, argues against the claim that Luther, when confronted by the threat of insurgent, unauthorized preachers, abandoned his early theology of the priesthood of all believers in favor of a more traditional understanding of the division between clergy and laity.[49] Timothy Wengert has proposed that the theology of the priesthood of all believers as it is commonly understood today was, in fact, a seventeenth-century construction by the Pietist theologian Philipp Jakob Spener. According to Wengert, what Luther really intended by applying the terms for priests and pastors (Luther never actually uses the phrase "priesthood of all believers") to all Christians was a largely negative statement. The assertion that Luther makes in the early 1520s—that "We are all priests"—meant, according to Wengert's reading, merely that no one person could be elevated by the pope over any other in a spiritual hierarchy. The clergy is an identification only of office among Christians, who are all equally members of the spiritual estate. In *A Treatise on the New Testament* (1520), for example, Luther describes Christian men and women as "priests and priestesses."[50] Thus, Luther can call scriptural women—such as Mary Magdalene and the others at the tomb— "priestesses" without meaning that all women thereby gain the authority of a public, ecclesial office. Wengert concedes, though, that Luther's theology of universal Christian priesthood is not *only* a negative one; a positive duty attaches to each believer at need, to minister the Gospel one to another, and even to do so publicly, in an emergency. This returns us to the role played by the Magdalene at the resurrection. Wengert writes, "Those called to the public office of ministry have *no more to say or do* in our vocations than Mary Magdalene."[51] And *no less,* as Luther's praise of Mary's faithfulness at the tomb and in her proclamation afterward attest. While Luther certainly did not intend to open the office of the pastorate to women, the scriptural ministry of women had become an argument against the medieval theology of the priesthood, and the choice of Mary Magdalene to be the first preacher of the resurrection served Luther's aim of promoting active evangelism by the laity.

Luther's discussion of the Magdalene's preaching is consistent with his more general considerations of female and lay preaching. His early polemical treatise against the sacramental theology of the Catholic Church, *The Misuse of the Mass* (1521), deals with the question of the nature of the priesthood as Luther understood it: "This is a spiritual priesthood, held in common by all Christians, through which we are all priests with Christ. . . . Thus it follows that the priesthood in the New Testament is equally in all Christians, in the spirit alone without any roles or masks, as Paul says in Gal. 5 [3:28]: 'In Christ Jesus there is neither Jew nor Gentile, neither male nor female, neither master nor servant; for you are all one in Christ.'" These are the kinds of pronouncements that had suggested the possibility of female preaching and lay preaching in general. The dangers associated with that possibility were already evident to Luther in 1521 and led to cautious and careful treatments of the question. He had authored this treatise during his time of hiding in the Wartburg Castle from the death sentence issued by Holy Roman Emperor Charles V at the Edict of Worms, after Luther refused to submit to papal authority. During this period his fellow reformers in Wittenberg, led by Andreas Bodenstein von Karlstadt and Philipp Melanchthon, had moved toward abolishing the Mass as a misinterpretation of Christ's institution: if all believers were priests, then there was no need for one person to offer the Mass as a sacrifice on behalf of others. Luther wanted to encourage his colleagues without inspiring anarchy, and so his treatise contains both revolutionary theology and a deliberately measured tone. He therefore follows his claims about the common spiritual priesthood with arguments that seek to place authoritative limits on the filling of the public preaching office: "We readily admit that not many of you are to preach at the same time, although all have the power to do so."[52] He specifically addresses the provocative question of public female speech and the texts marshaled against it, apparently already raised by his opponents:

> Now, however, the papists quote to us the saying of Paul (I Cor. 14[:34]): "The women should keep silence in the church; it is not becoming for a woman to preach. A woman is not permitted to preach, but she should be subordinate and obedient." They argue from this that preaching cannot be common to all Christians because women are excluded. . . . Paul forbids women to preach in the congregation where men are present who are skilled in speaking, so that respect and discipline may be maintained; because it is much more fitting and proper for a man to speak, a man is also more skilled at it. Paul did not forbid this out of his own devices, but appealed to the law, which says that women are to be subject [Gen. 3:16] . . . How could Paul otherwise have singlehandedly resisted the Holy Spirit, who promised in Joel [2:28]: "And your daughters shall prophesy." Moreover, we read in Acts 4 [21:8–9]: "Philip had four unmarried daughters, who all prophesied." . . . Paul himself in I Cor. 11[:5] instructs the women to pray and prophesy with covered heads. Therefore order, discipline, and respect demand that women keep silent when men speak; but if no man were to preach, then it would be necessary for the women to preach.[53]

Luther is obviously attentive to the scriptural examples of female preaching, such as that of Mary Magdalene. Without denying the value of these figures or the veracity and divine inspiration of their messages, he is at pains to prevent exposing his movement to ridicule and his new pastors to subversion of their authority. The spiritual equality before God that Luther found between the Magdalene, Peter, and Paul is upheld, but the divinely established temporal authority of husband and father, teacher and pastor remains firmly in place, dictating who may hold the public office of preacher.[54]

A more positive discussion comes in a treatise from the same year, but this time it is addressed *To the Christian Nobility of the German Nation*, encouraging laymen, the secular princes and rulers of Germany, to consider themselves as divinely authorized to intervene in ecclesiastical affairs to further the Reformation. Luther writes,

> To put it still more clearly: suppose a group of earnest Christian laymen were taken prisoner and set down in a desert without an episcopally ordained priest among them. And suppose they were to come to a common mind there and then in the desert and elect one of their number, whether he were married or not, and charge him to baptize, say mass, pronounce absolution, and preach the gospel. Such a man would be as truly a priest as though he had been ordained by all the bishops and popes in the world. That is why in cases of necessity anyone can baptize and give absolution. This would be impossible if we were not all priests.[55]

This goes further than asserting only that no one shall be set over another in absolute spiritual authority, such as the pope claimed. It is the common potential of priesthood, specifically the power of delivering Christ's Word to the neighbor, that gives *anyone* the power of assuming the office for a given community. Luther's argument goes on to classify both men and women as priests and priestesses in this way.

When examining the case of female preaching by itself, however, separated from the question of the laity as a whole, Luther's position is more conservative. He discusses the injunction to silence among other problems of congregational organization in his *Lectures on 1 Timothy* from 1528, concluding that women may speak only where there is no man in authority over them—that is, in the case of unmarried women in their own homes. He again mentions the daughters of Philip from Acts 21 as examples of such unmarried women but maintains that the possibility explored in 1 Corinthians 14, of women teaching publicly, "has now perished," except in the absence of a male teacher, even though he might "wish it were still in effect, but it causes great strife."[56]

Questions of the local situation and audience, then, had an influence on the force and direction of Luther's rhetoric about the openness of the preaching office. When he is defending his reform movement against accusations and trying to forestall abuses or avoid quagmires, he is careful to reinforce established authorities. When a revolutionary challenge to traditional authority and a proclamation of evangelical freedom are called for, however, he seizes on examples that are both powerful and perilous in the liberty they suggest.

Though Luther did praise the Magdalene herself as a "preacheress," he weighed the biblical examples of female testimony against the potential turmoil to be caused in the nascent reform movement by such a challenge to pastoral authority, and he advised against allowing women to preach publicly. Some of his followers, in their preaching on the resurrection narrative, went further than Luther in exploring the possibility of public religious speech for women. The particular contexts and aims of their work, emphasizing education and perseverance in the faith for second- and even third-generation Protestants, may have allowed for a different acknowledgment of women's roles as the new church matured and developed.

Spangenberg's teaching sermons offer a clear exposition of the potential controversy suggested by the prominent activity of women in the resurrection story. After recounting the events of Easter morning, he pauses to wonder whether the female witnesses were, indeed, being given the work of priests in being instructed to spread the news that Christ was risen. He states of the women's role, repeating Luther's language, "Here He makes them into preacheresses / She must be the mistress and teacher of the Apostles." (Da macht er sy zur Predigerinnen / Sy müs der Apostel Maisterin und Lererin sein.) Of the group of women as a whole, he asks, "Does Christ make these women into preachers? Freely Christ the high priest himself makes these women into priests and preachers." ("Macht Christus dise weiber zü Predigern? Freylich / Christus der Hohe priester weihet dise weiber selbst zü Priestern und Predigern.")[57] In answering that they were being given a priestly office, he notes, as Luther had, that one can find other examples of women fulfilling prophetic vocations in Scripture: Hannah in Luke 2 and the daughters of Philip in Acts 21. He then addresses the apparent conflict with Paul's injunction of silence for women in church, from 1 Corinthians 14:34–35: "Saint Paul's meaning is not that women should not teach and confess Christ, but rather he wants that in Christian community it should be done in an orderly manner.

Where men can fulfill the teaching office, there women should keep silence. Where, however, no man is able to preach, why should a woman not be authorized [*gestattet*] to teach? Women must, as Christians, baptize in need, thus they also must preach [*Predigen*] at need, not through their own merit, but rather through the death and resurrection of Christ."[58] Given that male preaching also derived its authority not from an individual's merit but from Christ's death and resurrection, and that the Reformation was an era in which communities were encouraged to find preachers of the evangelical Gospel if that Gospel was not being preached by the established, local church, this represents a significant encouragement to women's teaching and preaching, in theory even if seldom in practice.

Spangenberg was drawing on the work of his contemporary, Anton Corvinus, who had taken up the same contradictory texts at the end of his sermon for Easter Sunday in his 1539 preaching manual.[59] Corvinus had been influential in the progress of the Reformation in northern Germany, through his published sermon collections and in writing church orders—sets of instructions for worship and various other aspects of church life. Part of his work in developing the church orders was the removal of material about the saints from the liturgy.[60] Corvinus advised that the saints, such as the Virgin Mary, be honored and studied as models of faith but not venerated as supernatural, intercessory figures. He had written, "'It is just that Mary is praised, extolled, and commended as a blessed child of God, and put forward as an example of justifying faith for all Christians, but let her remain a creature,' and do not place her over Christ."[61] Consistent with this approach, his treatment of the Magdalene in his sermon for Easter Sunday focuses on the application of her example to ordinary men and women. In describing the preaching of the angel who gives the good news to Mary Magdalene, Mary the mother of James, and Salome, he writes, "Note that the women here should do a priestly office. [A marginal note printed as part of the text here reads, "We are all priests."] Who had sanctified them as priests? John the Baptist? No, but rather God through His Son and our high priest, Christ. Whoever believes in Christ, and receives the Holy Spirit through His Word, that one is among those of whom Peter had spoken (1 Peter 21). God grants it to man or woman."[62] Following Luther, Corvinus uses the active ministry of the women to affirm the evangelical doctrine of the priesthood of all believers, though his emphasis seems to go further toward the legitimation of the women's preaching than Luther had. Corvinus offers the same examples Spangenberg would use, Hannah and the daughters of Philip, and to make the same evaluation of 1 Corinthians 14, that women ought to keep silent if a man is correctly fulfilling the preaching office, but a woman may be authorized to preach if there is no male preacher performing the duty. He concludes, "We all together, women and men, must confess that we are born again to a living hope through the resurrection of Christ from the dead."[63]

The confession of faith was at the heart of Corvinus's own vocation and that of the female ruler of his region, Elisabeth von Braunschweig-Lüneburg, whom both he and Spangenberg clearly viewed as a colleague in ministry. As regent, she introduced the Reformation in her territory following her husband's death in 1540, collaborating with Corvinus on a Protestant Church order for Calenberg-Göttingen issued in 1542. One of Spangenberg's catechetical sermon collections had been dedicated to her. Corvinus provided an introduction to Elisabeth's own pamphlet, A Christian Open Letter, which she wrote to encourage her subjects to persist in their faith despite religious strife and to help form them in evangelical belief. Their work faced significant opposition from Elisabeth's Catholic relatives and even from her son, who eventually broke with his mother and reconverted to Catholicism. Corvinus staunchly resisted compromising and restricting the new faith despite political pressure from the Holy Roman Empire, for which he was imprisoned for three years, dying from ill-treatment shortly after his release. As the Reformation came under threat from religious and secular opponents during Luther's lifetime and after his death, the necessity of fostering brave and faithful testimony from all of its adherents, male and female, was surely apparent. The powerful story of Christ's call to the Magdalene could not be ignored.[64]

LUTHER'S FOLLOWERS drew on his own innovative legacy of preaching and writing about Mary Magdalene in order to teach evangelical theologies of justification and the priesthood of all believers. They, in turn, developed interpretations they considered faithful to his teaching and appropriate to their own circumstances, recasting medieval theology and practice but preserving the centrality of the Magdalene and her associated texts. The activity of Christ, as opposed to the passive reception of the sinner, was presented as the orthodox understanding of the story of the woman in Luke 7. The penitent's good works follow upon faith in Christ's forgiveness—indeed they must follow, to prevent a dangerous reading of the passage as promoting anarchy—but they have no part in effecting salvation. In the comparison between Mary and Martha, the medieval elevation of the contemplative life was replaced with an assertion of devotion to the Word as the duty and delight of every believer, even as Martha's worldly work was given new appreciation. In preaching on these passages, Luther's followers tended to follow the interpretations of their mentor almost to the letter.

It is in the interpretation of the Magdalene's role in the resurrection narrative that Luther's colleagues expand most on the reformer's writing, demonstrating a greater license in considering women as potential preachers in the contemporary church. The shift between Luther's assertion that women should now speak only within the home and his followers' greater readiness to justify some female preaching may be accounted for, in part, by noting the later authors' location as preachers to already Protestant congregations. In this context they did not face the challenge of defending a brand-new movement against the ridicule of opponents, but were attempting to instruct the laity in its evangelical responsibility of confessing the Gospel promises to one another and to equip the faithful to endure and triumph over persecution. Neither Anton Corvinus nor Johann Spangenberg felt it necessary to add Luther's qualification that would restrict the teaching and confession of women to the private, domestic circle. The young boys and girls listening to Spangenberg's catechetical sermons, for example, or the parents using them for instruction in the home, would have heard the urgency of the need for the true Gospel to be preached and taught despite all obstacles, by whoever could speak the Word.

The Lutheran theology of the priesthood of all believers, clearly preached by Luther and his followers using the examples of Mary Magdalene and other scriptural women, laid a foundation within Protestantism for the public ministry of women. The discussion of women's preaching in the case of need, from Corvinus and Spangenberg's sermons, argues that evangelical liberty for women and the laity lasted well beyond the first few years of the movement. These popular preaching guides, grounded in Luther's teaching and expanding upon it with his approval, place the assurance of the forgiveness of sins above the restrictions of gender or social position. Indeed, while the younger Luther was concerned to prevent chaos in his new churches by warning against women's preaching, the next generation gives evidence of lessening anxiety on this question and greater appreciation for the role of women in defending reform as it came under increasing attack. This recognition acknowledged female preaching as lying at the heart of the Gospel and the birth of the church, alongside that of men, though women were certainly not being encouraged or permitted to serve as pastors in the sixteenth-century church. The equality of opportunity may have needed centuries more, but the equality of the message, in the authority it grants to any faithful speaker, made that full equality, if not inevitable, at the very least a tantalizing promise.

CHAPTER THREE

Publish the Coming of the Lord

Evangelical Magdalenes

PROTESTANT WOMEN of the Reformation that Martin Luther had begun laid claim to the title and legacy of the Magdalene. We have seen how common a practice was the identification of holy women with the saint in medieval piety. The assumption of modern scholars has often been that this model would have been rejected by Protestants eager to do away with Catholic veneration of saints. An examination of the work of women authors, however, reveals the Magdalene as an essential tool in the construction of a Protestant, female, religious subjectivity. The roles she was given place her at the center of the reform movement's theological preoccupations: the doctrine of the priesthood of all believers and the transformation of medieval spirituality into new forms of lay piety.[1]

Luther's teaching on the priesthood of all believers raised immediate questions about the liberties and duties of an evangelical laity. If not only the clergy but all Christians were endowed with the authority to forgive sins that Christ gives to Peter in Matthew 16, if all believers were instructed to testify the promise of salvation to their neighbors in the Great Commission of Matthew 28, what did that mean for each person's ability to teach and preach in church, home, and community?[2] Some claimed that women were empowered by this doctrine to preach publicly, just as men did. Authors making this argument referred to several women in scripture to assert the legitimacy of female preaching; the Magdalene was their most important precedent. For example, Marie Dentière, in her 1539 treatise addressed to Marguerite of Navarre, offered Christ's appearance to Mary Magdalene after the resurrection, with his instruction that she bring the news to the disciples, as justification for the women of Dentière's own era to bear the Gospel to the contemporary church.

This chapter will explore the production of texts by female authors such as Dentière, and their reception and influence in their immediate contexts, Catholic and Protestant alike. While Dentière argued broadly for women's equal right to preach the Gospel, Katharina Schütz Zell, wife of the Strasbourg Lutheran pastor Matthäus Zell, appealed to the example of the Magdalene on a much more personal and particular occasion. As she gave her husband's funeral oration in 1548, Zell compared herself to the first preacher of the Gospel in order to defend and excuse her temerity in offering her own public speech. Dentière's boldness contrasts with Zell's posture of humility to demonstrate the versatility of the Magdalene as a model for different kinds of self-understanding and argument.[3]

The application of Mary Magdalene as example was not confined to female authors. Men used her image to describe and praise women around them, holding them up as paradigmatic for the evangelical believer in society. John Bale, in his *Elucidation,* printed with Anne Askew's description of her interrogation and torture, compares this Protestant martyr to Mary Magdalene and the other women who followed Christ for her resistance to clerical tyranny and her material support of the church. This characterization, though not a self-identification, is perhaps all the more important as it comes in one of the most published works of early Protestant martyrology, a popular genre celebrating the deeds of martyrs. Because of her prominence in these publications, Askew continued, throughout the first centuries of the Church of England, to have considerable spiritual authority. In Ireland, an early provost of Trinity College Dublin credited no less a person than Elizabeth I, with imitation of the anointing at Bethany through the act of promoting Protestant religious instruction, in part through the act of founding the college itself. In all of these examples, authority to preach and teach is granted by comparing the female subject to the Magdalene, as one with an intimate connection to Christ, the incarnate Word of God. That authority was strengthened by the special exigency of need: when the Word was not being properly taught and defended, in situations of persecution or confessional strife, it was the duty of female believers to bear public witness to the Gospel. The tradition of contrasting Mary Magdalene and the other women at the tomb with the fearful male disciples becomes particularly important, therefore, as a justification for women's ministry in situations of inadequate clerical leadership. Such situations were identified with increasing frequency

FIG 3.1 The Master of the Magdalene Legend, *Saint Mary Magdalene Preaching,*
c. 1500–1520. Oil on panel. Photo: John G. Johnson Collection, 1917 (cat. 402). Philadelphia Museum of Art / Art Resource, NY.

in the early years of the Reformation, as communities agitated for evangelical preachers and religious freedom.[4]

Thus we see an ongoing life of the Magdalene in Protestant spiritual circles, though it was not limited to her role as evangelist. The themes we traced through the Middle Ages, of compassionate witness to Christ's suffering and valuing contemplation over activity (especially domestic activity), can also be found in the writing of Protestant women. Women working within and at the margins of emerging Protestant traditions shaped a new model of the contemplative life, one that would be led outside the context of a cloister. This model was not merely a passive devotion to husbands and fathers as the instruments of divine authority. Just as the history of avowed religious women is infinitely more complex than the ostensible model of absolute obedience and retreat from the world, so the records of Protestant wives and mothers tell of a vocation worked out amid the competing claims of loves and burdens. Women celebrated a piety of marriage and family, as Zell eulogized her beloved husband, but they also observed their own ambivalence about the demands of practical responsibilities that took time away from prayer.

Grappling with the Magdalene's multiple identities—of sister, sinner, and saint—gave women a language with which to chronicle their own experiences of formation in faith as new Protestant communities took shape in the sixteenth century. Nor was the phenomenon a briefly lingering relic of a traditional culture, whose effects could be seen to wane as the Reformation's changes took increasing hold over the generations. Exploration of these Magdalene themes continued to inform Protestant spiritual writing through the close of the seventeenth century. During that period in England, M. Marsin published a defense of women in the church that made very similar arguments to those of Dentière. Marsin used the examples of scriptural women, including those at the tomb in the resurrection narrative, as part of a theological argument for public female preaching within the Reformed tradition. And in Austria, the Lutheran spiritual writer Catharina Regina von Greiffenberg wrote about the anointing at Bethany, identifying with Mary's gesture and equating it to present-day speech and writing in Christ's honor. In the Netherlands, the renowned biblical scholar Anna Maria van Schurman adopted the "better part" of Mary to describe and legitimize her intellectual work. This brief survey indicates that the Magdalene was advanced in public discourse in support of female preaching, devotion, and leadership within the church from the very beginnings of the Protestant Reformation and continued to be so through early modern Protestant history.[5]

Argula von Grumbach

The first woman to publish in support of Luther's reform was the German noblewoman Argula von Grumbach (1492–1568). Her eight pamphlets, authored in 1523–1524, were part of an initial spate of lay religious writing that was largely silenced following the 1525 German Peasants' War, as the Reformation became more focused on the founding of a new, evangelical, clergy. The early pamphlet movement offered women both possibilities and challenges. The huge market for writing by Luther and about his new ideas allowed even women to publish and participate in the debate. Female authors had to justify their entry into the fray, however, and they used the examples of scriptural women to establish a holy precedent.[6] One of those explanatory self-images was that of Mary Magdalene, to whom Christ had spoken. In Argula's open letter in 1523 to the theologians of the University of Ingolstadt she writes,

> I beseech and request a reply from you if you consider that I am in error, though I am not aware of it. For Jerome was not ashamed of writing a great deal to women, to Blesilla, for example, to Paula, to Eustochium and so on. Yes, and Christ himself, he who is the only teacher of us all, was not ashamed to preach to Mary Magdalene, and to the young woman at the well. I do not flinch from appearing before you, from listening to you, from discussing with you. For by the grace of God I, too, can ask questions, hear answers and read in German.[7]

Here, both scripture and the early church are invoked, reflecting the common desire of the reformers to reorder the present-day church according to the pattern established in the first decades and centuries of the church, aiming at a more authentic Christianity. The texts to which Argula appeals provide examples of spiritual communication between men and women. The Reformation's emphasis on vernacular Bible translation and theological writing made such conversations possible for laywomen, not ordinarily educated in Latin, in a way they had not been since late antiquity. Another feature of Luther's new theology, that of the believer's direct relationship to Christ alone in salvation, provides Argula with an equalizing argument. If Christ is "the only teacher of us all," then men and women alike receive the same teaching and are equally prepared to understand and confess the Gospel. With this justification, she proposes in this treatise that she will write to the local nobility and lecture to them, acting in the place of the university faculty, whose teaching role this would otherwise be, because the university is not offering correct (that is, evangelical) teaching on the Gospel. In doing so she makes another allusion to the Magdalene, in this case in her guise as Mary of Bethany, who had preferred listening at Jesus's feet to any other occupation: "I am prepared to write to [the local nobility] in this vein, since, because of other business, they have no leisure to sit down and read for themselves. Although there is nothing more needful than the word of God, as the Lord says in Luke 10: 'That is the best part—to listen to the word of God.'"[8]

The inadequacy of male leadership, which provided Argula with a need to write publicly, is attested to by a comparison between the contemporary nobility, busying themselves like Martha with worldly concerns, and the devoutly studious Mary. Putting herself, a laywoman, in the traditional place of Mary of Bethany, Argula paradoxically negotiates an active, public role for herself as a teacher of men in secular authority by comparing herself to the traditional patroness of cloistered contemplatives. It is interesting to note that for her temerity Argula was labeled a whore by one of her pamphleteer-opponents; the term was, admittedly, a common epithet for women in rhetorical diatribes, but nevertheless introduces into the debate another element of the Magdalene's legendary character. Interesting also is the frontispiece to the first edition of her open letter, which features an image of Argula standing with an open book before a group of men, a visual echo of medieval portraits of Mary Magdalene as doctor of the church. In her own self-awareness and in the perception of her by her contemporaries, Argula was positioned in reference to the multiple identities of the Magdalene: sinful penitent, devout contemplative, and preacher.[9]

Katharina Schütz Zell

Both supporters and detractors of women's public speech made such comparisons between contemporary women and scriptural figures, as connections to the early church were common among the Reformation's self-reflections.[10]

The sixteenth-century Lutheran historian Johannes Kessler claimed that prominent female evangelicals, such as Argula von Grumbach and Katharina Schütz Zell (1498–1562), wife of the Strasbourg pastor Matthäus Zell, should be compared to the prophetic women of the Old and New Testaments, including Anna, Deborah and Hulda, and the daughters of Phillip.[11] Unlike Argula, whose public career lasted only for the short span of the pamphlet war, Katharina Zell published work throughout her life.

Defending herself in this unusual role, Zell appeals to what would become a standard justification for lay and female public testimony in the Reformation, one we have already seen from Argula: the absence of correct teaching from the appointed authorities. Zell writes, "I have no doubts whatsoever about what I am doing or about my beliefs, and I am not frightened to speak up. Why did his [Lutheran theologian Ludwig Rabus's] brothers and other preachers not speak up? In that case I would not have been allowed to do so. I watched them for a long time to see whether they would do something—had they done so I would have remained quiet, as is appropriate for a poor woman, and would have left the talking to others." Despite her remarkably public profile (or perhaps because of it), Zell maintains a humble, self-effacing posture, excusing her speech and writing on various grounds. In her correspondence with Ludwig Rabus, she is careful to state that all her activity is authorized and even suggested by her husband. Despite that claim of reticence, however, what is evident from Zell's argument is that she considers herself entitled to evaluate the actions of the religious leaders around her, assessing them in relation to a new, evangelical standard she has internalized, and then speaking out when she finds them falling short of that standard. This is the work of the priesthood of all believers, the freedom and duty of conscience advocated by Luther.[12]

One of the ways in which Zell excuses herself in this work is through a self-identification with Mary Magdalene, one that seems to deny her own agency in the act of evangelizing. In the funeral oration she delivered for her husband in 1548, Zell compares herself to the Magdalene as one who preaches publicly and announces the good news, not on her own initiative, but because of Christ's call to her.[13] Zell writes, "I ask you not to take it wrongly and not to be irritated with me for what I am doing, as if I now wanted to place myself in the office of preachers and apostles: not at all! But it is only as the dear Mary Magdalene without any prior thought became an apostle and was charged by the Lord Himself to tell His disciples that the Christ was risen."[14] She is not guilty of aspiring to an inappropriate office or position nor even of having wanted or planned to speak out at all, but her mandate to testify comes from Christ himself. By deflecting attention from herself as the actor, and proclaiming Christ as the true messenger as well as the content of the message, Zell's words gain the authority of the Magdalene's transparent act of witness: not a calculated speech or prepared sermon, but simply a faithful account of what God has done.

In addition to expressing her own connection to the saint, Zell also holds up Mary Magdalene as an exemplar for her audience in their devotional lives. In her 1532 exposition of the Lord's Prayer (published in 1558), Zell identifies the tears of Peter and of the Magdalene as representing the ideal posture toward God. She prays that she and her readers will not be like Judas, "but weep over our sin with Peter and Mary Magdalene, to repent and gain great love [*sonder unser sünd beweinen mit Petro unnd Maria Madalena zur buss tretten unnd vil lieb gewinnen*]." In a letter of comfort (written on St. Mary Magdalene's Day, 1524) to the persecuted evangelical community of Kentzingen, Zell compares the town's mourning women, whose husbands had been killed in conflicts with local authorities, to the bride in the Song of Songs, a figure often connected to the Magdalene in the medieval tradition. Identification with Mary Magdalene, a figure at once reviled for infamous behavior and yet favored with a particular intimacy with Christ, held a special power for women facing difficult circumstances, including Zell herself. The image of a woman vulnerable and imperiled but still beloved and useful to God can be found at the core of Zell's self-understanding, and it helped guide her private contemplation as well as her public activity as a builder of the body of Christ, as a "church mother." Like Argula von Grumbach, Zell understood herself and her place in religious reform partly in terms of a return to the model of the early church, called to follow the Magdalene as a founding apostle of the new church.[15]

Marie Dentière

Zell was not the only wife of an evangelical pastor to use Mary Magdalene as justification for her own work and for public, female, religious witness. As clerical marriage became a part of reform programs, pastors' wives in the emerging traditions of the Reformation had to forge new roles for themselves. They held responsibilities as models of marriage, motherhood, and faith within their communities; especially in the early years of the movement, they had to define the scope and limits of their leadership. In these early years of change and new possibilities for women, Marie Dentière (1495–1561) sought to establish herself as an activist and theological innovator. Dentière had been an Augustinian nun converted by the evangelical movement in France; she later fled to Strasbourg, where she married a former priest. After his death, she married the evangelical pastor Antoine Froment, and they worked in Geneva's Reformed community alongside its leaders, Guillaume Farel and John Calvin. From that base, she engaged in a project similar to that of Argula von Grumbach, when she wrote to the local nobility advocating for religious reform. Writing to the evangelically minded Marguerite of Navarre, Dentière composed what is essentially a sermon presented in letter form, using the rhetorical techniques and conventions of letter-writing to argue the need for church reform.[16]

Dentière begins by excuse her boldness in approaching this subject at all, addressing the Bible's injunction to women's silence from 1 Timothy 2 in her prefatory remarks to Marguerite. She defines her activity as the private, personal communication of one woman to another, rather than as public preaching: "Even though we are not permitted to preach in congregations and churches, we are not forbidden to write and admonish one another in all charity." Her claim raises interesting questions about the interpretation of "silence," arguing for a strictly literal reading that liberated women's words in the age of printing: while they might remain silent within the context of worship services, women could make themselves heard through letter writing and even published texts that would, in effect, "speak" to the church.[17]

Dentière's letter was, in fact, published in 1539 as a treatise, the *Epistle to Marguerite de Navarre*. It contains a defense of public, female preaching, in which the author cites the Magdalene as an example of women being called to preach by Christ:

> What woman was a greater preacher than the Samaritan woman, who was not ashamed to preach Jesus and his word, confessing him openly before everyone, as soon as she heard Jesus say that we must adore God in spirit and truth? Who can boast of having had the first manifestation of the great mystery of the resurrection of Jesus, if not Mary

Magdalene, from whom he had thrown out seven devils, and the other women, to whom, rather than to men, he had earlier declared himself through his angel and commanded them to tell, preach, and declare it to others?[18]

Here the reader may note that Dentière, whose circle in France included Jacques Lefèvre D'Étaples, limits the identity of the saint to the roles specifically associated with Mary Magdalene by name in the Gospels. Like Katharina Zell, Dentière invoked other scriptural women beyond the Samaritan woman: Deborah, Moses's mother, the Queen of Sheba, Ruth, Sarah and Rebecca, the Virgin Mary, and her cousin Elizabeth are all mentioned in the "Defense of Women" section of the *Epistle*. The treatise engages in the ongoing *querelle des femmes* tradition in which a catalog of virtuous women was offered as proof against misogynistic arguments. Dentière also draws on the convention of comparing the male and female disciples, which we saw depicted in the medieval Passion plays. She asks, "Why has it been necessary to criticize women so much, seeing that no woman ever sold or betrayed Jesus, but a man named Judas?" Addressing a more recent question of women in the church, the text features a sympathetic reading of the Waldensians, a late medieval heretical movement that included prophetic female preachers who used the Magdalene as their justification; the surviving Waldensian communities joined the Reformation in the sixteenth century.[19]

Dentière's arguments in the *Epistle* provoked strong reactions from her male contemporaries. The Catholic preacher François Le Picart (active 1530–1556) interpreted Mary Magdalene as a weak woman, used by God to show up the arrogance of men. In a sermon published in 1541, possibly responding to Dentière's treatise published only two years earlier, Le Picart explicitly denounces "Lutherans" (a term of abuse for early Protestants in France at that time, and so not necessarily a reference to German authors) who use scriptural figures to claim that women have the right to speak in public. His sermon offers the Samaritan woman, who had been named in parallel with the Magdalene by Dentière, as an example of one such figure who had, in his interpretation, been wrongly used.[20] An equally confrontational encounter occurred on the evangelical side, between Calvin and Dentière. In 1546 she challenged him about the wearing of long robes, and a reference to the conflict is found in one of his letters to Farel from that year. Calvin's account is clearly dismissive of women's participation in public religious discourse:

> Froment's wife came here recently; in all the taverns, at almost all the street corners, she began to harangue against long garments. When she knew that it had gotten back to me, she excused herself, laughing, and said that either we were dressed indecently, with great offense to the church, or that you [Farel] taught in error when you said that false prophets could be recognized by their long garments. . . . Feeling pressured, she complained about our tyranny, that it was no longer permitted for just anyone to chatter on about anything at all. I treated the woman as I should have.[21]

Dentière's response, as recorded by Calvin, indicates a shift we have also observed in Germany, between the relative freedom of the early reform movement, in which women and other lay authors, "just anyone," could contribute to reform debates, and the more strictly clerical leadership that evolved as the Reformation took hold.

Anne Askew and Her Biographers

One means of gaining entry into reform debates was through the testimony of martyrdom. In England, Anne Askew (1521–1546) was tortured and executed in 1546 for holding Protestant theological views on the Lord's Supper and the interpretation of scripture, during the reign of the Catholic Mary I. The literate daughter of a landowner, Askew wrote an autobiography, *The Examinations of Anne Askew,* which was published with her martyrdom narrative by the reformer John Bale during his exile in the Lutheran territory of Cleves. Bale's *Elucidation* adds introductory material and commentary to Askew's text; he compares her and other gentlewomen involved in the Reformation to Mary Magdalene for material support of the church, defiance of ecclesiastical tyranny, and proclamation of the Gospel. In the first edition of Askew's *Examinations* (1546), Bale's introduction also draws a parallel between Askew and the scriptural figure of Lydia (Acts 16:14), as well as between Askew and female martyrs of the early church, including Blandina and Cecilia. In Askew's narrative, when she is asked why she disobeys the injunction to silence in 1 Timothy, she assumes a very humble posture, only replying that the inquisitor should "find no fault in poor women." Bale provides more theological grounding, however, listing examples from the Bible and from the early church of women whose scriptural learning and testimony were approved by God, among them arguing that "the women which gave knowledge to his disciples that he was risen from death to life, discomfited not he, but solaced them with his most glorious appearance." In Bale's reading, not only was Christ not ashamed to talk to women including the Magdalene (as Argula von Grumbach had noted), but he desired to give them comfort and to authorize their speech. By implication, then, Askew's own speech is defended as pleasing to Christ.[22]

Bale's celebration of a female martyr of the new church influenced the emerging English tradition of martyrology through the work of Bale's friend John Foxe. Though Askew does not herself mention Mary Magdalene, the details of her life as provided by Bale and Foxe might well have suggested an association with the saint for readers. Askew had been forced to marry the fiancé of her dead sister Martha, plunging the spiritually minded Anne into the life of domesticity represented in the Christian tradition by Martha, the sister of Lazarus and Mary of Bethany. It was a domestic situation from which Askew fled in order to pursue her spiritual life, a desertion of duty that finds no condemnation in either Bale's or Foxe's accounts. Edith Wilks Dolnikowski has analyzed the legacy of religious women as they appeared in Foxe's *Acts and Monuments of the Church*, in which Askew's text (with Bale's commentary) found a prominent place, and notes Foxe's praise for Askew's decision: "Foxe defined the parameters of women as role models for the reformed church. Though clearly lacking clerical authority, Foxe suggested that women . . . could contribute to the mission of the church as teachers, theologians, and evangelists in addition to performing their traditional duties. . . . His open commendation of women who stepped out of the private sphere of home and family to proclaim their faith, even at the risk of ridicule or martyrdom, underscores his conviction that public testimony is a vital component of Christian life, regardless of gender."[23]

Foxe mentions the Magdalene herself, the original model for the preference of faith over domestic duty, a handful of times in his *Acts and Monuments*. She is presented alongside David and Peter as an example of a great sinner redeemed by God. Foxe defends her insight into Christ's true nature, listing among the false claims of the Catholic Church that Mary Magdalene "did not know Christ to be God, before his resurrection." In a letter of spiritual comfort written by M. Philpot to John Careless, presented in Foxe's 1563 edition, Mary Magdalene's washing of Christ's feet is associated with the remission of her "sevenfold sins," drawing on the medieval tradition that equated her seven demons with the seven deadly sins. The tradition is reimagined for Protestant readers, who are to know that such sorrow for sin, as experienced also by the Virgin Mary and by Peter, is an assurance from God of our election: "it is the earnest penny of eternal consolation." And in a letter from William Tyms to his sister, meant to encourage her in the faith, the Magdalene is linked directly with Askew's contemporary example: "Also I do remember Mary Magdalene, how faithful she was, for she was the first that preached the resurrection of Christ. Remember the blessed martyr Anne Askew in our time, and follow her example of constancy."[24]

Elizabeth I

Foxe's sovereign, Elizabeth I (1533–1603), was herself occasionally characterized as a follower of the Magdalene's example, despite her more frequent identification as a virginal monarch. In Elizabeth's case, the association with the Magdalene consisted more of a series of passing references rather than an enduring program of self-definition. These references attest the Magdalene's cultural currency as a touchstone for women, a kind of shorthand for the justification of their public roles. Jane Eade has noted that common elements of Elizabeth's own iconography—vivid red hair and luxurious pearls—were shared with the visual tradition of the Magdalene, and likewise represented a paradoxical intersection of femininity and power, marked by tantalizing sexual renunciation. In a public speech made as queen, Elizabeth claimed Mary of Bethany's spiritually derived authority, stating, "I hope the better part is mine." Earlier, as a princess during the brief reign of her Protestant brother, Edward VI, Elizabeth had made a translation of Marguerite of Navarre's *A Godly Meditation of the Christian Soul* that was published by John Bale in 1548, with an illustration of Elizabeth as Mary Magdalene. The woodcut image shows the young princess kneeling at the feet of the risen Christ. Rather than making the gesture that had warned the Magdalene against touching him in the traditional compositions of the noli me tangere scene, Christ here points upward, indicating that Mary must rise and broadcast the news of the resurrection. Elizabeth's mission is underscored by the fact that she is shown holding a book. Whether the book represents the evangelical Gospel or the princess's translation, the message is clear: Christ directs her to offer the words she carries to God and others. This public duty, and the identification that supported it, appeared again in Thomas Bentley's 1582 *The Monument of Matrones,* an anthology of English women's devotional activity that praises Elizabeth as the patron of true religion; she calls Christ "Rabboni," using the form of address that the Magdalene used in the resurrection scene.[25]

The identification between Elizabeth and the Magdalene was not confined to the earliest generations of the English Reformation, but persisted long into the era of Reformed English piety. In a seventeenth-century sermon, George Ashe, the provost of Trinity College Dublin, made a comparison with a similarly evangelical message. When Elizabeth herself became queen, she held the role of Defender of the Faith and was responsible for shepherding the ongoing reformation of the Church of England. In 1694, Ashe reflected on Elizabeth's founding of the college a century before by comparing her work with the anointing at Bethany. The provost celebrates the queen as nurturing the living body of Christ, the church, through the establishment of a university for educating Protestant clergy and defending against the threat of Catholicism:

> A Princess the most eminent for Piety, Learning, Chastity, and Happy Government that ever blessed these Kingdoms, having enlightened our neighbouring Nation with the brightness of the Reformation, . . . *She pour'd this Box of Pretious Ointment upon the Head* or Capital of our Kingdom, whence it might stream or descend to the most distant parts, and refresh the whole with its most excellent *savour;* She laid in here such lasting supplies of Piety and Literature. . . . We and all who benefited by this Auspicious Foundation, must ever gratefully join with our Blessed Saviour in my Text, *Verily we say unto you, wheresoever the Gospel* (whose Holy Doctrine we have here suck'd in, and to the understanding and declaring of which we have been here train'd up and educated) *shall be preach'd* by any of us *in the whole world, there also this, that this Woman has done* for us, *shall be told as a memorial of her.*[26]

Elizabeth's legacy is assured, and her contribution properly remembered, because of the worthiness of her actions—as worthy of celebration as those of the Magdalene before her.

These examples involve a public association between the saint and the woman at the center of a fragile religious settlement, and thus argue for the perceived legitimacy—and safety—of such a comparison. If Elizabeth could be likened to Mary Magdalene, at first as the exemplar of a Protestant-educated princess and later as the Defender of the Faith, it must have been a comparison suggesting only praise and appropriate behavior, carrying so little residue of the saint's sinful origins as to be inoffensive, and offering no provocation to those wishing to distance themselves from any association with Catholicism.

Catharina Regina von Greiffenberg

Protestant women continued to identify themselves with Mary Magdalene into the seventeenth century, as can be seen in the work of the mystic and spiritual writer Catharina Regina von Greiffenberg (1633–1694). Born to a Lutheran noble family in Catholic Austria, Greiffenberg wrote as part of a dwindling religious minority, in part with the forlorn hope of converting her peers, including the Habsburg emperor. Her major work, *Meditations on the Incarnation, Passion, and Death of Jesus Christ,* celebrated women's active roles in the scriptures, including those of Elizabeth, Mary of Clopas, Mary Magdalene, the Virgin Mary, and the anonymous female followers at Golgotha and at the tomb. She also entered into the traditional comparison between the faith of women and men, proposing women's faith as greater by using as example the women who remained steadfastly at the tomb while the male disciples stayed away out of fear.[27]

The meditation on the anointing at Bethany shows Jesus defending the actions of the woman who had ministered to him with costly oil. Greiffenberg claims that he was thereby championing all women, arguing that his attitude was proved by the fact of the incarnation itself, by Christ's being born of a woman, and by the choice to live and die in their company:

The panacean seed of women did not reject women, refusing to be served by them. Since He dignified them by His own being, made flesh of a woman, He therefore also found them worthy to witness His death. He wanted to begin His life emerging from this sex and to end it in their company. He knew that He had caressed and pressed the ardor of love into them and granted fidelity to them in particular. Thus He meant to enjoy the noble fruit of this tree that His right hand had planted and to receive the sweet perfume of the love of this true-hearted refresher before His suffering, bitter as gall. Thus He testified that He respected not strength but gentleness and that He cared more for the inward ardor of love than the outward pretense of holiness from good works.[28]

Greiffenberg's language echoes that of Christine de Pizan, seeking to advance the status of women by noting that women were manifestly acceptable to the incarnate Christ. That argument is then neatly turned to serve the author's devotional aim: because particular women were beloved of Jesus, then all women are so loved, and therefore all women will wish to participate, through identification and imitation, in the actions that formed the sacred intimacy between Christ and his female followers. She yearns "that this blissful anointing had been granted to me! . . . let the jar of my life be broken for Thy sake at whatever moment it may please Thee." The Magdalene's original sacrifice of her means to purchase expensive perfume and put it to such prodigal use is subtly compared to Christ's death on the cross by making it an existential spending of the whole self, a breaking open of her own life. In meditating on the anointing, Greiffenberg can both describe care for Christ and pattern her life on his self-sacrifice. This then becomes a radical asceticism, as she moves toward a rejection of the world, herself taking up Christ's words to Peter, who had sought to prevent Jesus from facing suffering and death: "Get you behind me, you bitter worldly pleasure . . . for you are the materials from which the jar of vanity was blown!" She prays instead to be attached only to Christ, to become "enflamed" with passion for God alone.[29]

The image of the Magdalene was not as purely positive as that of the Virgin Mary, and Greiffenberg addresses this feature of any identification with the prostitute-saint. She asks the logical question of Mary Magdalene and herself: "But, righteous God, how shall praise from the mouth of a sinner please Thee?" Mary is credited by the tradition with two anointments, after all, coming at two different points in her relationship with Christ: both the dramatic act of conversion made by the repentant sinner (Luke 7) and the gesture of intimacy made by a devoted disciple to signal the movement toward the Passion in the final days of Jesus's life (Matt. 26:6–13; Mark 14:3–9; John 12:2–9). Greiffenberg's meditation ponders the unity of motivation behind those two events. She finds the impulse to penitence perpetually within herself, so that the loving follower of Christ remains always the sinful woman, freshly aware of her need for forgiveness. This sense of the believer's predicament, at once both justified and sinning, is an expression of Greiffenberg's inheritance of the Lutheran theological legacy of *simul iustus et peccator:* "Oh, let me shed the angelic balm of tears of repentance before Thee, like Mary, and cast off the adamantine jar of my heart so that I am not eternally cast out." Confession and repentance are acts that the faithful Christian must take up anew each day, experiencing both the peril of her soul and the relief of Christ's assurance of pardon.[30]

The appropriate affect of penitence, as demonstrated by the Magdalene, is sorrowful tears. Greiffenberg dwells on this expression of gratitude for divine forgiveness and grief over the suffering that achieved it. She discusses the weeping of women, with reference to the sisters of Lazarus (Mary Magdalene and Martha), as a laudable sign of love for Christ: "Should not the agony of Him who helped to relieve the agony of many be lamented? Oh, yes! It is most right to sorrow over Him who relieved the sorrow of so many. . . . Thus these women very rightly and ardently bewailed Him, crying the most passionate tears." She describes the compassion of Mary Magdalene and the other women gathered at the foot of the cross, a sympathy so complete that they are wounded in the same way as the nails wound Christ, their eyes bleeding tears, cut by his crown of thorns, embracing the cross as Christ's arms are stretched upon it, feeling every blow. Not all strands of the Reformation would embrace the affective piety Greiffenberg praises here. The exploration of the value of female tears in Lutheran writing of the seventeenth century constitutes not only a survival of the earlier convention of hymning the Magdalene's compassion but also a rebuttal of more recent criticism of religious emotion as unnecessary and effeminate.[31]

In addition to defending the scriptural women's weeping as a traditionally female attribute to be commended to all Christians, Greiffenberg notes that Jesus's female followers also acted in ways that were considered inappropriate for women but argues that they were, in fact, praiseworthy in this as well. She writes of the female disciples' great loyalty in following Christ, even to the point of neglecting their domestic and family duties, as Mary of Bethany had, and encourages her contemporaries to do the same at need: "No land should be too far away and no home too dear to follow our dearest Jesus. . . . To follow Jesus, many [of these women] must have abandoned their husbands, children, friends and relatives, and also their household and housekeeping for a few days and perhaps did not leave them all that well provided for and instead in danger of unpleasant occurrences. . . . We choose that good portion: Christ. It shall not be taken from us." We have seen Protestant female authors adopting postures of humility to excuse their public writing, as in the cases of Argula von Grumbach and Katharina Schütz Zell; they only emerged from home and hearth reluctantly, because of a special need. This passage in *Meditations* is notable for making no such excuses, explicitly rejecting women's domestic duties as less important than discipleship. Far from employing tactics of equivocation here, Greiffenberg proclaims that women reading the Bible should feel confident that their devotion will find the same divine approval that Mary's did.[32]

Greiffenberg dismisses the Magdalene's legacy as a sexual sinner with similar boldness. In discussing the women witnessing the Passion, she echoes the language of the late medieval preachers of penitence, who had pointed to the hope provided to the ordinary believer by the example of the Magdalene, a notorious sinner pardoned and uplifted by grace: "The Holy Spirit suffered these women, especially the sinner and penitent Mary Magdalene, to be named by the Evangelist here as well as later in describing the Resurrection so that no sinner, man or woman, would despair of the grace of God and true repentance. If she is deemed worthy of the true love of Jesus and of touching His sacrosanct body living and dead with her mouth, hands and hair, she who had once given her body over to the most unclean sins, then no one who truly repents should lose heart in the midst of sin." She also employs the identification of Mary Magdalene as the woman cured of seven demons, continuing in the Lutheran tradition that engages all of the different Magdalene roles in order to offer the comfort of the Gospel to despairing sinners.[33] On the question of Mary Magdalene's particular sinfulness as a woman and as an individual, Greiffenberg ultimately concludes that it is irrelevant when measured against the overwhelming grace of Christ, who calls her from her former life into one of proclaiming the promise of forgiveness to all:

The trusty recorder, the Holy Spirit, . . . cannot extol and praise these enough, even those of the greatest sinners, men and women alike. He certainly mentioned the discipleship and constancy of Mary Magdalene and of the other women who loved Jesus. How He lauds their presence and persistence, not only in living and suffering, but also in death and at the sepulcher of Christ. . . . This happens because poor womenfolk, on account of being completely despised and defamed by most men, seek and find their honor in the apologia of the Holy Spirit. And why ask in the end about the disgrace of people who have God himself eulogizing them? If it is God who takes care of our honor, we are thus free from care.[34]

Here is an instance of the Lutheran theology of salvation by grace alone making possible the claims of women's equal worth before God, and Luther's language of Christian liberty speaking to the needs of women in the church. God makes every believer honorable by exchanging divine righteousness for human sin, freeing Christians from slavery to the law, in Luther's classic formulation. God offers this promise universally, for all of creation and humanity afflicted by original sin, but also, particularly, for the besetting sins of each individual and for the sins plaguing societies, such as the unequal treatment of women. According to the terms of *sola gratia,* neither the specific sins nor the individual works of believers can effect condemnation or salvation. The focus of Mary Magdalene's story becomes Christ's election of her, with her personal unworthiness merely taken as a given, as it would be for anyone, rather than being described as a pathetic spectacle of the redemption of the almost irredeemable.[35]

Protestant Vocations

Protestant women thus adapted the Magdalene tradition to express their commitments to justification by grace alone and to describe their own vocations, including both contemplation and public proclamation of the Gospel—whether it was called preaching or denied that title. For the two centuries that followed the beginning of the Reformation, women and their male apologists continued to refer to the Magdalene as an inspiring example, either as the guiding pattern for a whole life or as a potent proof text used in combination with other arguments.

Like Dentière, Greiffenberg, and Zell, the seventeenth-century English author known as M. Marsin (active 1694–1701) used the example of Christ's first revelation of the resurrection to women as proof of a divine endorsement of women's public ministry. Marsin is believed to be the pseudonym of a female author, a woman evidently of independent means who produced fifteen theological tracts on women's religious roles, writing on the margins of the Reformed tradition in England. Her work advocates for women's ministry and education and appears aimed at a common, rather than an aristocratic, audience.[36] She describes the women at the tomb as disciples given an evangelical mandate: "The Lord made women the Publishers of the Messiah's first coming." As Dentière had, Marsin praises the Waldensians as having honored the Magdalene's example by permitting women to preach. She does adopt the posture of humility that we have seen from Katharina Schütz Zell and Argula von Grumbach, in which Christ's use of women as messengers serves to shame men neglectful of their own duty or simply underscores divine power by comparison. In *The Near Approach of Christ's Kingdom,* Marsin writes, "God has made choice of so weak an instrument [so that] his power might the more eminently appear therein." In *Two Remarkable Females of Womankind,* she again echoes the language of the other writers we have surveyed—in particular, Greiffenberg—in noting Christ's associations with women from his birth until his death: "As the Lord came by a Woman, so after he arose, he appeared first to the Women." From this Marsin goes on to encourage other women to imitate the testimony of those first witnesses of the resurrection. Indeed, such imitation is not an exceptional virtue reserved for a few; because of this precedent, it has become the duty of women: "O ye women! Be sound in your Duty; now the word is given according to promise, that at the time of the end, Knowledge should be increased. That you may prepare for, and Publish the coming of the Lord."[37]

Debate over how to define the duty of women drew on another facet of the Magdalene tradition. The German-Dutch scholar, poet, and artist Anna Maria van Schurman (1607–1678) offered a defense of the unusual project of serious female scholarship. As the theological foundation for her work, she compared herself to Mary of Bethany, sitting at the Lord's feet and taking the "better part." Van Schurman was a distinguished linguist, taught by her father, a man who favored education for girls; she wrote a treatise advocating women's education, *Regarding the Fitness of the Female Mind for the Study of the Arts and Sciences* (1641). Raised in Cologne, she lived for most of her adult life in Utrecht. Though a member of the Reformed tradition, her theological context was broad: she corresponded with Marie de Gournay, who used the Magdalene to argue for women's right to preach in Catholic France, and she was associated with the Labadist movement, a forerunner of German Pietism.[38]

In her autobiography *Eukleria: Or Choosing the Better Part,* Van Schurman proclaims that by engaging in intellectual contemplation of the wonders of the created world and the revealed Word, she is doing "the one thing necessary." She acknowledges that her chosen life has involved sacrifice, separating herself from the family and social position, the "bourgeois proprieties" she would have known if she had followed a more conventional woman's path, and she emphasizes self-denial as the heart of Christianity, the key to intimacy with Christ. For Van Schurman, that intimacy can be achieved by the individual, whether at home or at work, without the cloistered seclusion it had once implied. She writes of having experienced "being taught by the master directly." Where the medieval church had associated the fruits of Mary's devotion with the rewards of the contemplative life, the same text now serves Van Schurman's secular scholarship, supporting a Protestant argument for a worldly vocation offered to the glory of God. Rather than escaping from the home into the convent, Van Schurman escaped from the home into the world, precisely because the immediacy of her connection to God made conformity to religious institutions unnecessary.[39]

Scholarship was one avenue of pursuing devotion to God; a more common expression was mysticism. Anna Trapnel (active 1642–1660), the seventeenth-century English Reformed mystic and Fifth Monarchist, published an account of prophetic visions she experienced in 1654 during an eleven-day period in which she fasted almost completely, miraculously sustained by only small amounts of bread and beer. Other Protestant women shared the practice of extreme fasting as a mark of female sanctity, including Trapnel's friend and fellow Fifth Monarchist Sarah Wight (in her case, up to seventy-six days), and the Dutchwoman Eve Fliegen (fifteen years), following the model established by the Magdalene's legendary asceticism in France. Religious *inedia* is thus another feature of the Magdalene's medieval legacy that persisted in Protestant circles and was used to express an evangelical sense of radical reliance on the Word of God.[40]

Trapnel's account of her visions, *The Cry of a Stone*, includes this description: "I, not relishing the discourse [an argument with friends], had a mind to walk in the Garden by myself, and so I did a while; wherein the Lord gave me much of his loving-welcome, and kinde salutations."[41] It is unclear whether Trapnel here describes a real escape outdoors to shrug off a brief unhappiness, or whether she intends a purely figurative meditation, but the use of garden imagery invokes a rich group of associations. A garden suggests both Eden and the fertile landscape of the Song of Songs, but also the mutual discovery of Mary Magdalene and Jesus in the garden before the empty tomb, where he famously gave her so transformative a "kinde salutation," calling her by name, that she recognized him to be the risen Lord. Authors such as Trapnel gained license for their public speech and writing from their special intimacy with Christ, expressed by the marriage metaphor even in a Protestant religious culture that ostensibly denied women the legal marriage to Christ so prominent in the vocation of Catholic nuns.[42]

The issues at stake in Protestant women's reinterpretations of the Magdalene, for both public ministry and private contemplation, can be seen in the adoption of language from the Song of Songs. The image of mystical marriage provided a metaphor for the believer's relationship to God. Many of these women used marriage imagery, in which they identified themselves as the bride in the Song of Songs, to describe an equality before God not available to them in their own society and church. The Magdalene tradition—which included identifications with the bride, as well as with the contemplative, Mary of Bethany, and with the woman who was the first to greet and proclaim the resurrected Christ—provided a supple model for circumventing the restrictions on women's speech and activity.[43]

THESE CONTINUITIES from the medieval Magdalene tradition—of mystical marriage with Christ, contemplation, and a divine command to preach— point to a more complex evolution for Protestant women's spirituality than has often been assumed. Protestant women did not simply move from the silence of the convent to the enforced submission of the household.[44] They participated in the development of Protestant religious culture, negotiating their roles by adapting images that had always spoken to the concerns of women of faith. Stories of the saints had provided the foundations of medieval spirituality, the rock upon which the church was built. Every word and command of Christ to the apostles was counted over and sifted for implications and instructions they might carry for believers and, especially, for the clergy. And, as we saw in the medieval period, the life of Mary Magdalene had also formed a paradigm for both women and men, religious and lay alike, though the question of her femininity had posed challenges for consideration of her identity as a model for imitation. From the early sixteenth century through the end of the seventeenth, we have seen Protestant women drawing on and reshaping the remnants of medieval tradition. As they responded to the new, evangelical theology, they brought the legacy of Magdalene piety with them and adapted it according to the goals of their respective reform programs and their individual vocations.

Some features of the medieval Magdalene vanished altogether in Protestant circles, such as the legendary description of her preaching career in southern France. Nor did the abject recitation of her sexual sins find expression among Protestant female authors. Where her sinful nature is mentioned, it is spoken of alongside the universally sinful character of humanity as the burden Christ overcomes for all, not as a particularly grievous stain on which one should dwell. The salacious details of the Magdalene's early history were not a popular focus for late medieval women who had identified themselves with the saint, and this trend continued among the women of the Lutheran and Calvinist Reformations. The sensuous harlot would find early modern incarnations, but not here.[45]

The feature of the Magdalene most often appealed to by early Protestant women was her role as witness of the resurrection, the disciple who was called upon, even though a woman, to preach the Gospel message to the other followers of Christ. From Argula von Grumbach in the heady days of the pamphlet wars, through Katharina Schütz Zell and Marie Dentière, to Catharina von Greiffenberg, the sheer fact of a woman's having been chosen for so prominent a place in the Christian story required a response from those who would set that story as the pattern for their lives.

The Magdalene had been the first witness of the resurrection, according to the reading of Luther and his colleagues, because of her intimate relationship to Christ, attested to by her coming to the tomb in the darkness of the early morning, when the male disciples remained away out of fear. This intimacy, claimed as a particular province of women, defines the character of contemplation in the work of the early modern Protestant women we have surveyed. Katharina Zell's prayer was formed in parallel with the exemplary penitence of Christ's beloved friends, Peter and Mary Magdalene. Elizabeth I was compared to the contemplative Magdalene, becoming a paragon of Protestant education, both as student and patron. Catharina Regina von Greiffenberg described the compassion for Christ that was engendered by her overwhelming sense of his loving work on her behalf. Anna Maria van Schurman wrote of her intellectual contemplation as a complete submission before God, arising from and leading toward the love of God.

Such self-identifications with the Magdalene served to permit (or even demand) outward expressions of the interior transformations they describe. Authors experienced an intimacy with Christ in meditation on his suffering and in study of his revealed Word, and understood themselves to be thereby authorized—just as Mary Magdalene was authorized by her relationship with Christ—to speak and write publicly. Female authors acknowledged that this call to public testimony often moved them away from the domestic sphere and its duties, and they used the story of the Magdalene to defend themselves as obedient to the Word of God above all else. Here we can observe the long tradition of Magdalene interpretation being adapted for evangelical use. But these early Protestant women were not simply clinging to a positive model from the legacy of late medieval popular piety. They were formed by the preaching and teaching of the evangelical congregations to which they belonged, and by their interactions with Protestant and humanist intellectual circles. The women who lived and worked at the beginning of the Reformation era, Argula von Grumbach, Katharina Schütz Zell, Marie Dentière, and Anne Askew, can only be understood as participants in the larger movement, as parishioners, as readers, and as wives and colleagues, helping to construct Protestant theology in conversation with Martin Luther and other leaders (and opponents) of religious reform.

CHAPTER FOUR

A Most Holy Penitent

Preaching and Teaching the Magdalene in the Catholic Reformation

WE HAVE SEEN that Mary Magdalene was taken up by authors both male and female in the Protestant Reformation as a symbol of the new theology of justification by grace alone, as an ideal of an evangelical kind of contemplation, and as a model for preachers, with an emphasis on the universal responsibility of the confession of faith for a priesthood of all believers. As members of the Catholic Church engaged with the ideas of reform, interpretation of the Magdalene's identity became an important marker of theological orientation. Scholars of early modern Catholicism have observed a shift in the Catholic cult of the Magdalene toward an increased focus on her penitence, a turn that served the teaching of the Council of Trent (1545–1563), the church's programmatic effort to respond to the Protestant Reformation and renew itself as an institution.

The council's approach was twofold: for the clergy there were moral reforms and innovations in education and mission, and for the laity the council reinforced the need for informed participation in the sacramental system in order to obtain salvation. The complex figure of the Magdalene stood at the intersection of both of these initiatives, embodying the ideals of reform and rededication. With the emphasis on the Magdalene's penitence came even greater interest in the sin that caused it: the saint's sexual licentiousness was the frequent subject of moralizing sermons and of visual art, where her condemned sensuality was in full view, offered up for the delectation of audiences in fevered oratory and in the eroticism of Baroque portraiture. This shift begs the question, to what extent did this turning toward a Magdalene as penitent sexual sinner mean a turning away from her as preacher? Did the Counter-Reformation's use of the Magdalene tradition focus so exclusively on her conversion from sexual sin to penitential piety that her preaching ministry was obscured? And if this did happen, was it consciously done in reaction to Protestant appropriations of the preaching Magdalene, or did it simply arise in answer to internal pastoral and theological concerns?[1]

To explore these questions, we will first investigate the character of the Magdalene that emerged from the teaching and testimony of Catholic male authors in the sixteenth and seventeenth centuries. In many cases, those men held significant positions of religious and secular authority, as high-ranking clergy, renowned preachers and widely published authors, or powerful rulers and patrons. In other cases, the voices and images represented here are those of poet-priests or barely respectable painters, whose works nonetheless contributed to the portrait of the Magdalene that was available for public consumption and personal devotion. More than half of the audience for that portrait was female. Examining the Catholic Magdalene that was shaped by male authors, artists, and patrons allows us to understand the figure that early modern women received when they heard sermons, read books, and viewed (or posed for) paintings, all of which necessarily conveyed an interpretation of women's spiritual identity and experience.[2]

By her very nature, Mary Magdalene was an image of womanhood. Having given in to sensuality in her youth, she represented the sex that was thought to be more prone to physical temptation in general. In addition to the contrition and repentance encouraged for all women, Mary Magdalene was also interpreted in this era as a particular example for religious women, continuing the traditional association of Mary of Bethany with the contemplative life. Religious life for women was another area the Council of Trent sought to reform: there was an effort to enforce strict enclosure in convents, aimed at ending the experiments with lay monastic communities, such as the Beguines, that had developed in the late Middle Ages. Alongside the changes advocated for nuns came a renewed focus on clerical celibacy and moral purity, both responses to Protestant attacks on immorality in the church and the society it fostered. The Magdalene's sorrow over her sinful past became, in the sixteenth and seventeenth centuries, an agonized sense of guilt for sexual crimes, and it was to serve, in the words of Catholic preachers, as a special model for the reform of prostitutes.[3]

With attention focused on these parts of the medieval heritage, what became of the Magdalene as the first preacher of the resurrection? While the penitent and the contemplative Magdalenes were undeniably emphasized in programmatic efforts on a large scale, such as campaigns against prostitution or in favor of participation in the Sacrament of Penance, other aspects of the Magdalene's history were still employed in specific contexts to sustain female religious institutions and women's spirituality. The cardinal of Milan, Federico Borromeo, for example, encouraged devotion to the Magdalene, including her testimony on Easter morning, as part of his support of nuns' musical composition and performance. And in England, the Jesuit poet Robert Southwell developed an extended allegorical interpretation of the Magdalene's experience to counsel and encourage Catholics under Protestant rule. The church hierarchy at the Council of Trent sought to represent the tradition as authoritative and coherent, yet local leaders approached individual situations pragmatically. Although the rhetoric of orthodoxy was a significant theme in the discourse of the Counter-Reformation, it should not be mistaken for a homogeneous religious climate. Even in studying the aspirations that the church sketched for itself, we must recognize the pluralism of imagery that was created for believers' consideration and devotion.[4]

Scripture and Preaching

In the sixteenth century a profound devotion to the Magdalene was shaped and supported by the preaching that ordinary believers heard in their parish churches on Sundays, at festivals, and during special preaching series organized for civic purposes, such as communal prayer and repentance during a time of plague or war. Catholic preachers used the same biblical texts as did the Protestant reformers, primarily Luke 7 and 10, and John 20, though they continued to work from the Latin Vulgate, following the directives of the Council of Trent. The program established by the council represented an effort to conform what had been a diversity of local practices and movements in the late medieval church to the centralized teachings of the Catholic curia. The council's decrees included a ban on individual interpretation of the scriptures, which meant that most Catholics experienced the stories of the Magdalene through some form of mediation rather than as a text they were encouraged to read for themselves. The council did take steps, however, to ensure that the church's preachers and teachers were literate and educated—at least, in theory, passing on the orthodox doctrine of the faith.[5]

As in the Middle Ages, the Magdalene's role as sinner and penitent was offered as an example by preachers for women and men in their congregations. The salutary fruits of penitence, commended to potential converts and believers alike, were directly tied to the penitent's intention and measure of self-loathing. The following examples, by authors of considerable influence and popular appeal in areas where Protestant reforms were being actively combated, and from sermon collections republished during the sixteenth century, survey the Magdalene interpretations of Catholic preaching in German-speaking regions.[6]

In preaching on the text for Mary Magdalene's feast, Luke 7:35–42, Catholic authors were renewing a medieval interpretation that had long supported the theology of the Sacrament of Penance, emphasizing the importance of the sinful woman's penitence and acts of love. Cardinal Cajetan had affirmed this interpretation against Martin Luther's reading in his 1532 *De fide et operibus contra Lutheranos:* "In Luke 7[:50], Christ said to the sinful woman, 'Your faith has saved you.' But he also said about her: 'Many sins are forgiven her, because she has loved much' [7:47]. In this text the conjunction 'because' shows that love is the proximate cause of the forgiveness of sins, that is, 'because she has loved.' Faith is the cause inchoately, but charity is the cause completing the forgiveness of sins." One of the most prominent opponents of Luther's teaching was the renowned Jesuit theologian Peter Canisius, who founded schools in Germany to train anti-Protestant missionaries. Beginning in 1559, Canisius served as cathedral preacher in confessionally divided Augsburg, with a mandate to correct evangelical teaching that had spread in the city. Canisius put the Magdalene before his audience as an exemplar of penitence who offers "not words nor language, but works and true love [*nec verbo aut lingua, sed opere & veritate diligens*]" that are the means of reconciliation to God in Christ. In Canisius's reading, the Magdalene's story demonstrates conclusively that Christ has the power to forgive sins. She in turn displays the ideal spiritual progression in response to Christ's mercy: not the verbal testimony encouraged by Protestants, but work that embodies the three virtues of faith, penitence, and charity.[7]

She is the perfect penitent, because her sin is so egregious; as the vicar general of the Augustinian Order in Germany, Johann Hoffmeister, observed, she did not merely sin as other women do, "but this woman exceeded the others in the commission of sins [*sed haec mulier in perpetratione peccatorum excedebat alias*]."[8] Hoffmeister had been prior of the Augustinian cloister at Colmar, a city that, though officially Catholic during his tenure in the first half of the sixteenth century, included a significant evangelical population; the community became legally biconfessional in the 1570s. Hoffmeister was intimately involved with the earliest response to Luther's movement, corresponding with many of Luther's own circle and participating in discussions about the means of justification at the Regensburg Colloquy in 1546. He shared Luther's desire for reform of the church, but believed that reform only extended to bringing practice in line with Catholic teaching, improving preaching and spiritual care to prevent people from leaving the church, and himself opposed Luther in print. Like Canisius, Hoffmeister affirmed that the Magdalene's penitence "indeed produced truly penitent works" (Hic produnt se vera verae poenitentiae opera.) All Christians therefore needed to seek the same "remedy of penitence" [*remedia poenitentiae*].[9] He admitted that the interpretation of this text caused much controversy over the nature of justification, whether by faith alone or also by the works of love produced by faith, and condemned this as "foolish to dispute."[10]

Hoffmeister's mentor, Friedrich Nausea, the bishop of Vienna, had been the author of the earliest published collections of sermons that combated Luther's theology, in the mid-1520s.[11] Along with Johannes Eck and Johannes Cochlaeus, Nausea debated evangelical theologians at the Colloquy of Worms in 1540. Nausea's sermon on Luke 7 claimed that the Magdalene was saved *because* of her great love, and proposing this love, expressed in works of penance and charity, as the means of salvation for his audience. "Before all, keep yourselves in continually in mutual charity, because charity works against a multitude of sins, for the fervor of love is a spiritual fire, and sins are consumed by penance."[12]

Throughout sixteenth century, the rhetorical work went on. The auxiliary bishop of Bamberg, Jakob Feucht, had been trained at Ingolstadt, the faculty with which Argula von Grumbach had sought to enter into theological dialogue. Feucht published numerous sermon collections during the 1570s that aimed both to purify and to defend the teachings of the church in the face of local opposition, in particular from Lutheran schoolteachers in his region.[13] His sermon for the Magdalene's feast dwells at length on the extraordinary depths of her sinfulness. She is again presented as a teaching example: the penitent must share her attitude of profound contrition, and must then make confession to a priest, just as the Magdalene has done to Christ himself. Feucht reminds his audience that priests are the only ones to whom God has granted the power to bind and loose sins. She has been forgiven because she performed the works of the Sacrament of Penance and not "as the new Christians foolishly babble: that faith alone is needful and sufficient to obtain forgiveness of sins and holiness."[14]

The Magdalene's identity as a performer of good works connects her penitence with her presence at the tomb on Easter Sunday. Johann Hoffmeister's sermon for that festival characterizes her bringing scented oil for the anointing of Christ's body by saying "that she has done a good work for him [*das sie ein güt Werck an jhm gethon hab*]." Hoffmeister offers a glowing evaluation of the Magdalene and the other women who went to the tomb that morning. He praises them as "honest, pious women" [*Haec honestae ac piae mulieres*] who had supported the work of Christ and the disciples from their substance. It is, he acknowledges, "a great thing, and worthy of much admiration [*Magna res est & admiratione dignissima*]" that these women show great faithfulness in going to the tomb, and for that reason "are the first witnesses [*primi testes sunt*]," after the angels, of the resurrection.[15]

In discussing the resurrection narrative that formed the Gospel text for Easter Sunday, many preachers saw the need to justify Christ's use of the Magdalene as the first witness of his rising from death. Hoffmeister's Easter Sunday sermon also noted that the Virgin Mary and Elizabeth had been the first to recognize that the Savior had come into the world. The saint's role was thus part of the unfolding of the plan for cosmic redemption that arced from Eve's disobedience through Mary's submission; Mary Magdalene's evangelism was emphatically not a precedent for ordinary women in the life of the church. Friedrich Nausea is adamant on this point, making a sharp distinction between the miraculously favored saint of legend and the prospects for women to lead the contemporary church. He gives the Magdalene the title *apostola apostolorum* and speaks of her missionary work in France with the saints Maximin and Lazarus, but cautions that she was given this role because of her great love. Her preaching is "a singular privilege," he warns, "not without much fruit, as Paul otherwise forbids, however, that women preach or teach publicly [*illi singulari priuilegio . . . nec sine summo fructu, quum tamen*

alioqui Paulus nolit, vt mulier publicitus aut praedicat aut doceat]." Another early
opponent of Luther's reforms, the Cologne Franciscan Antonius Broickwy
von Königstein, published a sermon for Easter Sunday in 1530; he quotes
Jerome in explaining why the news of Christ's resurrection would have been
delivered by a woman. The resurrection was "spoken and announced to the
apostles by women; because by a woman death was announced, so through
a woman life was resurrected." (Mulieribus dicitur vt annuncient apostolis,
quia per mulierem mors annunciata est, per mulierem vita resurgens.)[16]

One of the most interesting discussions of the figure of the Magdalene
comes in the sermons of Georg Witzel, a priest who had converted to Luther's
teaching in the early years of the Reformation, then apostasized and returned
to an idiosyncratic Catholicism during the 1530s—he continued to promote
worship in the vernacular, and he rejected papal primacy. Witzel took up the
perhaps unenviable task of preaching renewed loyalty to the Catholic faith
in Luther's birthplace, Eisleben. Witzel's sermons reflect both his experience
of Luther's teaching about Mary Magdalene and his concern to promote a
reunification of the church. He claims that Mary Magdalene and the other
women who receive the news of the resurrection are preachers, and he uses
the Magdalene's title of apostle to the apostles. In setting the scene at the empty
tomb, though, he notes that the angels' garments are described with a word
for priests' vestments, identifying them with clergy preaching the news of the
resurrection and giving the women a secondary status by implication. In his
sermon for Mary Magdalene's feast day he again combines strains of both
evangelical and Catholic theology, describing the Magdalene's guilt over sexual sins, then comparing her to other women who dared to ask something of
Christ, such as the woman with a hemorrhage and the Canaanite woman. On
the question of justification, Witzel is ambiguous. He praises the Magdalene's
tears in terms that connect her sorrow with her salvation: "O saving water
of tears, water of life, water that extinguishes death forever." (O salutarem
aquam lachrymarum, aquam vitae, aquam mortem aeternam extinguentet.)
Good works, he states, are the fruit of penitence, and they please God. Sins
are remitted through grace, however; nothing else is demanded.[17]

The contrast between the Catholic preachers' emphasis on penitence and
the preaching she took up in Protestant interpretations suggests that the character of witness to the resurrection diverged for the two communities. The
Protestant form of witness became an active testimony, associated with the

verbal confession of faith central to evangelical theology. The Magdalene's witness in the Catholic tradition, on the other hand, was more inwardly focused, a process of self-awareness producing a sense of the sinner's desperate need for Christ, a need that could only be overcome using the sacraments. Even in the resurrection narratives, Protestants focused on the saint's message for the apostles, while the Catholic interest remained on the gravity of the Magdalene's sin and the earnestness of her contrite love.

Women and the Reforms of the Council of Trent

Both Catholic and Protestant preachers worked within the context of an evolving confessional culture and institutional identity, which would have significant implications for women. Women were among the chief objects for the Council of Trent's reform and increased control. One of the goals set by the Counter-Reformation, in its answer to Protestant reformers' claims about the moral corruption of the church, was that of eliminating nuns' worldliness and the damaging sexual scandals resulting from lax convent discipline. The decrees of the council, subsequently affirmed by the 1566 papal bull *Circa pastoralis,* formally established enclosure for all women's religious communities, essentially attempting to force all professed women to take the formal vows of nuns. In part, the increased attention to nuns' conduct was determined by an economic concern. The aristocracy and merchant classes in the sixteenth century faced the prospect of dowry inflation, which they combated by placing up to 20 percent of upper-class women in religious orders to protect their honor, keeping them unmarried and thus reserving a smaller pool of marriageable women for whom wealthy suitors would have to compete. Keeping a priority on sexual purity became an important element of social and economic order.[18]

The well-regulated ideal established at Trent for religious women was celibacy and cloistered seclusion, but the realities that were negotiated across Europe and the Americas included versions of that option, as well as a range of vocations that integrated activity into the contemplative life. Enforcement of Trent's enclosure decrees varied widely, with the process often resisted by nuns and their powerful families. Family, economic, and political connections were maintained by cloistered nuns, with power and patronage exercised within and without the cloister's walls. Outside the cloister, informal associations of women dedicated to charitable and teaching work remained, escaping external control because of low public profiles or humble spiritual claims, and because their charitable work proved vital to communities' survival in difficult economic conditions. Those communities that did move toward enclosure often desired it as a more prestigious vocation that would attract wealthier patrons and committed members. Women's commitment to organized religious life is demonstrated by their participation in, and agitation for, the convent system; it was women who founded the overwhelming majority of new convents in the seventeenth century.[19]

Many of the new orders that had arisen during a vigorous period of experimentation at the beginning of the sixteenth century were suppressed or forced to become cloistered societies, such as the French Visitandines. The Milanese Ursulines, however, were allowed to leave their convents to teach in the catechetical program Archbishop Carlo Borromeo had set up in that region. The Daughters of Charity had similar freedom to do important nursing work in France under Vincent de Paul, though in order to maintain this they had to adopt a strategy of taking simple, temporary vows rather than formal ones, and to accept a lower legal status than that of full nuns. This diversity of approaches to women's religious orders was worked out in response to local needs and social pressures. The treatment of nuns was affected by the church's program for countering or preventing Protestant gains in Europe and beyond, both in the public assertion of stricter enclosure and in the pragmatic reliance on women for important tasks such as charitable work and teaching.[20]

One of the projects undertaken in response to the Protestant threat was the reform of education, in which the education of women was necessarily, if problematically, included. Understanding the Counter-Reformation's attitude toward education as part of its response to the challenge of Protestantism points to the importance of educating women for the survival of Catholicism, so that they would be able to educate their children as good Catholics, a crucial goal in areas where Protestants were making a lot of headway. The church clearly understood the need to involve women and the laity in the project of religious education, both in their natural roles as parents and in their vocations as nuns or members of confraternities who ministered to vulnerable members of society: children, but also the sick, the dying, and the poor. The Parisian Ladies of Charity, for example, were expected to provide basic religious instruction to the sick whom they visited. The directions for how they were to do this even gave them some latitude in conveying correct doctrine. After following a given question and answer formula, the visiting sister could improvise, and "say something of the grandeur and majesty of God, of the care that he has for all his creatures, etc."[21]

And yet the very need that called women toward teaching the faith involved a danger, for this came perilously close to the Reformation's own justification for its encouragement of women's education: the evangelical goal of confessing the faith, especially by teaching the Gospel to one's children.[22] St. Paul's prohibition on women's speech and teaching, which was being so closely parsed in the Protestant communities, was thus a focus of fierce debate on the Catholic side as well. The Catholic polemicist S. Hosias, in his 1561 *De expresso dei verbo,* condemned heretic women for abandoning their spinning wheels, an example of the common tactic of directing women to their domestic duties instead of to theological thought or instruction. Anabaptist martyrs would warn each other against exactly this attack from their Catholic jailers. In reality, there was a contradiction between such pronouncements about Catholic reform and the complexities of local practice. The apparent institutional hostility to lay leadership in education and mission was less a ruling premise than it was a political and ideological posture, exercised when it was advantageous to do so but, at other times, downplayed as the need arose. It is important to keep in mind the disjuncture between rhetoric and reality, particularly on this question of women and education, where investigations of Catholic practice reveal female and lay teaching being tolerated or encouraged, even as the principle of their role in catechesis was dismissed or derided. On this question, as on many others, the spirit of Catholic reform was not a single, unified, and coherent program but rather a broad collection of vigorous movements and visionary experiments, sharing some common characteristics but also containing, as a whole, many conflicting ideals and strategies.[23]

Mary Magdalene and Women's Education

Catholic texts on women's education are then of special interest for an investigation of the role women themselves were expected to take in teaching. This was a popular genre during the sixteenth and seventeenth centuries on both sides of the confessional divide, and Catholic and Protestant authors drew on the life of Mary Magdalene in her various incarnations for an exemplar of different facets of female education and teaching. The lives of the saints were an important part of religious education in the Counter-Reformation. According to the decrees of the Council of Trent, "Through the saints, the miracles of God and salutary examples are set before the eyes of the faithful, so that they may fashion their own life and conduct in imitation of the saints and be moved to adore and love God and to cultivate piety." Putting the instruction into practice, Archbishop Carlo Borromeo of Milan recommended, for example, that fathers read aloud in the evening to their families from saints' lives, thus encouraging the use of the saints as part of the education of girls, no matter what other possibilities for learning they may have had.[24]

Two treatises, published in the period immediately after Luther's initial agitation for reform, were influential in forming later attitudes to women's education in Counter-Reformation Catholicism; Mary Magdalene plays a paradigmatic role in both. Their authors' status in relation to Luther's movement would have given their opinions credibility: Desiderius Erasmus was Europe's most renowned humanist scholar and Luther's polemical opponent in the debate over good works in salvation, and Erasmus's protégé, Juan Luis de Vives, had been the tutor of Mary I, who restored England to Catholicism during her eight-year reign. In Erasmus's brief text "The Abbot and the Learned Woman," written in 1520, the education of women is explored through the figure of Mary Magdalene. Women's education is praised in the form of the witty and lettered Magdalene surrogate, Magdalia, who easily defeats the corrupt and foolish monk, Antonius, in debate. Erasmus approved of a humanist education for upper-class women, such as the daughters of his friend Thomas More. Yet Erasmus did not challenge the subjection of women to their husbands' authority in marriage, and the possibility of an education did not permit a woman to go beyond the goal of fulfilling her traditional role of wife and mother.[25] Magdalia asserts women's need for competence in her domestic responsibilities as her fundamental claim to higher education:

ANTONIUS: Distaff and spindle are the proper equipment for women.
MAGDALIA: Isn't it a wife's business to manage the household and raise the children?

ANTONIUS: It is.

MAGDALIA: Do you think she can manage so big a job without
wisdom?[26]

The chief aim of women's education for the Catholic tradition is supported
by Erasmus's statements that women should be educated in order to raise
children. He repeats the claim as woman's paramount duty in his treatise on
"The Christian Widow" (1529).[27]

Juan Luis de Vives's *De institutione de feminae christianae* (1523) expands
on the question of women's proper education and offers advice to the parents of young girls as well as to women on how to conduct themselves in
marriage and widowhood. In Vives's account, particular aspects of Mary
Magdalene's traditional, composite identity are highlighted in the models
presented for women, while others are rejected, depending on how they
suited his theory of women's education. Vives affirms the prohibitions
of 1 Corinthians 14 and 1 Timothy 2 on women's public speech. Women's
education is not to promote public speaking, but rather to foster the
moral life: "Her whole motivation for learning should be to live a more
upright life, and she should be careful in her judgment. . . . She will always
remember and bear in mind that it was not without reason that Saint Paul
forbade women the faculty of teaching or speaking in church and that
they should be subject to men and silently learn what it behooves her to
learn." A woman's judgment is good, for Vives, if it leads her to complete
submission to a man who will guide her correctly, after the pattern of Mary's
sitting at the feet of Christ. The chapter "On the Solitude of the Virgin"
discusses the ideal pursuits of young women: "Mary Magdalen, sitting at
the feet of the Lord listening to his words, did not enjoy the contemplation of heavenly things only at that moment but while she was reading,
listening, or praying. Not only should I wish my ideal young woman to
do this, but any other woman, for in many passages in this book we give
instructions to women in general." The instruction she receives from her
male guide, whether Christ, her father, or her eventual husband, will shape
her conduct even after she gets up again and goes about her other duties.
A father reading Vives's text is assured that his daughter will so thoroughly
internalize the correct teaching that he need not worry about her even
when he is not present.[28]

To guard against any potentially improper activity, Vives counsels his female readers to prefer silence to speech of almost any kind. He praises the Virgin Mary's reticence in the chapter, "How She Will Behave in Public": "Tell me, how many words of Mary do you find in the whole story of the four Gospels?" The passage goes on to list all of the important events in the life of the mother of Christ—the Annunciation, the Visitation, the Adoration of the Magi, the Presentation at the Temple—at which she says little or nothing. Even at the Crucifixion, when one might have expected a display of extreme emotion, she utters no protest; indeed, she manifests no need whatsoever: "At the cross, she was entirely speechless; she asked nothing of her Son—to whom he would leave her, or what his dying wishes were—because she had learned not to speak in public. Imitate her, virgins and all women, imitate this woman of few words, but of remarkable wisdom." The long discussion of Mary's passive silence stands in contrast to the complete absence, in Vives's work, of any praise of Mary Magdalene's active, scriptural role in testifying to the resurrection.[29]

Also absent is any consideration of the legendary aspects of the Magdalene's *apostola apostolorum* tradition, such as her preaching in southern France. The reform of the cult of the saints was one of the concerns shared by Luther and humanist scholars who remained within the Catholic Church. Vives was a humanist colleague and sometime collaborator of Erasmus's; as such, he would have known about Jacques Lefèvre d'Étaples's recent work in asserting the separate identities of the three Marys and the debunking of the nonscriptural elements of her cult.[30] Yet in *De institutione*, published in 1523—only four years after the controversy—Vives uses the name Mary Magdalene to refer to Mary of Bethany. Indeed, aside from a short discussion of the Magdalene's judicious choice of perfume (therefore associating her with the penitent woman of Luke 7, as well), Vives writes exclusively about the Magdalene in the character of Mary of Bethany. He explores the Mary-Martha pericope to distinguish married women from single women, in their relationship to God: "The wife is pleasing to the Lord but through the intermediacy of her husband, because she is anxious to please her husband, whom God placed over her. The unmarried woman and the widow are pleasing to God without a man and without an intermediary, as it were. Their thoughts are as different as the activities of Martha and Mary were different, not through opposition but in degree, as the thoughts of an unmarried woman are more elevated than those of a married woman."[31]

Vives affirms the medieval assessment of the celibate life as more valuable than the secular life of marriage and family. After married life has ended, however, in the case of widowhood, women are again offered the possibility of a retreat from worldly responsibilities to pursue divine contemplation. He advocates a serene attitude for widows: "Peace of mind is what elevates us to colloquies with the divine, as it did with Mary Magdalen, who put aside worldly things and sat at the Lord's feet, intent on his words. For that reason, she received Christ's praise, that she had chosen the best part, and it would not be taken away from her." Even in the humanist context in which Vives worked, he, like Luther, found the different faces of the Magdalene too useful to his pedagogical program to be cast aside. Yet Vives's preference for the traditional interpretation of the Mary-Martha comparison, as establishing a hierarchy in which chaste contemplation trumps the prosaic duties of husband and children, clearly marks him out as theologically opposed to the evangelical readings of Mary Magdalene.[32]

Vives's text rejects all learning for women that would overstep the bounds of their traditional roles as either submissive wives or cloistered nuns. In this dangerous era of vernacular reading, women's access to texts must be strictly limited to books that will not provide confusion or temptation. Any application of what reading they are permitted, in speech that might contradict a husband or father at home, much less emerge in a public confession of faith, is out of the question. A woman's education takes place in the private sphere of the home or convent, and it prepares her for life there.[33]

The Reform of Prostitutes

One form of women's education with more public repercussions became a particular focus of Counter-Reformation efforts. The reform of prostitutes was a part of the church's response to Protestant attacks on Catholic moral failures, as well as an attempt to address the societal threats of venereal disease and undermining of the family. There was growing concern with the problem of prostitution in cities across Italy in the sixteenth and seventeenth centuries. A genre of popular literature was developed to address the crisis, a pamphlet and poster campaign that supported the work of Magdalene houses for converting and reforming prostitutes. The pamphlets were likely read aloud, broadening their audience beyond the still relatively small literate population, while the moralizing broadsheets were displayed in taverns, workshops, and homes.[34]

As Rachel Geschwind has shown, Mary Magdalene was the most popular saint subject in Italian antiprostitution booklets from 1570 to 1670, with their topic universally being her conversion. Cover illustrations for these publications, such as that for Marco Rossiglio's *Conversion of the Magdalene* (1611), typically portray her nude, referring to her sexual history. The Magdalene served as a bridging figure between secular and sacred, it was hoped, to lead sinners directly from the one to the other. Taken together, the pamphlets and posters offered positive and negative reinforcement of the desired moral lesson: the booklets described a role model to which prostitutes could aspire in Mary Magdalene, while the posters showed examples of what happened— disease and a lonely death—to those who persisted in sin.[35]

Devotional Writing

With their direction to women to study and emulate the Magdalene's example, the works aimed at converting prostitutes trod the line between polemic and devotional literature, a genre that grew dramatically with the increase in literacy during the sixteenth and seventeenth centuries. Catholic devotional literature and practice supported the assertions made from the pulpit and the textbook. The positive embrace of the Magdalene in popular piety was shaped and sustained by these instructive texts, which permitted a measure of theological education for women within the safety of the home or convent.

Again, the rhetoric of confessionally divided regions demonstrates how the Magdalene was interpreted by Catholic authors as part of their response to Protestant theology. In increasingly Protestant Geneva, the Catholic bishop François de Sales wrote the enormously influential *Introduction to the Devout Life*, in which he offered advice on making a good confession, drawing on the Magdalene as the example of ideal penitence. Adopting the conventional comparison of the Magdalene to the male disciples, in his correspondence Sales had noted that Mary Magdalene's conversion was perfect, while St. Peter was allowed to stumble in sin after his calling, as when he discouraged Christ from martyrdom or abandoned Christ during the Passion. Indeed, Mary's contrition was so complete that it seemed, according to Sales, to erase the consequences of her sin even before Christ proclaimed her forgiven. In

Chapter 29, "Of Detraction," Sales warns his readers not to judge others as sinners, even if they appear to be so, because they may be similarly pure: "Simon the Leper called Magdalen a sinner, because she had been so long before; yet he lied, for she was then no longer a sinner, but a most holy penitent, and therefore our Savior took her cause into his most holy protection." In contrast to the evangelical readings of this text, where her grateful love is the product of Christ's unmerited forgiveness of her sins, here it is the Magdalene's own praiseworthy attitude of hatred and regret for her sins that gains Christ's approval and therefore assures her salvation. Chapter 19, "How to Make a General Confession," makes clear how exactly the remission of sin is obtained: "So sin is shameful only in the committing; but being converted into confession and repentance, it becomes both honourable and wholesome. Contrition and confession are so beautiful and so fragrant that they efface the ugliness and disperse the ill savour of sin. Simon the leper said that the Magdalen was a sinner; but our Saviour said she was not so, and spoke of nothing but the ointment she poured out, and of the greatness of her love." Christ does not so much pronounce absolution as acknowledge what Mary has already become.[36]

The Magdalene's active participation in her own salvation is to be the model for Sales's readers, albeit with modifications for a realistic approach to self-improvement. As Chapter 8.2, "Of the Means to Make This Second Purgation," instructs, "We must, then . . . increase our contrition and repentance as much as possible, that it may extend to the least belonging of our sin. St. Mary Magdalen, in her conversion, so utterly lost the taste for sin, and for the pleasure she had taken in it, that she never more thought of it." Readers must not forget, however, that the Magdalene presents an exalted model, an example of "perfect purgation," like that of St. Paul; ordinary sinners should not expect this for themselves, but should rather think of a more gradual process, over a lifetime of prayer and self-discipline. In a letter to married laywoman Madame Brûlart, Sales called on another aspect of the Magdalene's traditional identity to counsel a humble persistence in virtue on a small scale: "Let us go by land, since the high sea is overwhelming and makes us seasick. Let us stay at our Lord's feet, like Mary Magdalene, whose feast we are celebrating, and practice those ordinary virtues suited to our littleness." It is a versatile saint indeed who can represent both sublime perfection and a becoming modesty of aim and achievement.[37]

Other authors of the period followed Sales's pattern, encouraging imitation of the Magdalene's penitence and love. Charles Vialart was the superior
general of a convent founded in Paris by Henry III in 1587 as a movement of
Cistercian reform in the midst of the Wars of Religion. Vialart himself engaged
in anti-Protestant rhetoric as well as devotional works. His *Tableau de la Magdelaine en l'état de parfaite amante de Jésus* (1628) describes the Magdalene as
an example of a loving intimacy with Christ. Vialart addresses Mary Magdalene in a prologue, noting that she is a complex character but declaring that
he has decided to celebrate her great love. He discusses the virtue of love in
society, looking at the treatment of this subject by classical authors. Vialart
then looks at the love of Jesus, the perfect love; Mary Magdalene was the
recipient of that love, second in honor only to the Virgin Mary.[38] He affirms
the legendary tradition about her early life, claiming that she had every
worldly advantage and power, from wealth and position to physical charm.
He also continues the convention of comparing the Magdalene favorably to
the male disciples. In a section titled "The love of the Magdalene was more
perfect than that of the Apostles," he contrasts the men who were recruited
by Jesus (and needed to be convinced with speech and miracles) with Mary
Magdalene, who sought Jesus out in the house of Simon on her own initiative, because of her great love. The apostles abandoned Jesus at the Passion,
clinging to each other in relative safety, but the Magdalene accompanied Jesus
courageously through danger and death, even to the solitude of the tomb.[39]

Such devotion is rewarded with the graces of intimacy. The apostles are
not permitted to wash Jesus's feet at the Last Supper, but the Magdalene had
already done so, and for it she is praised and promised eternal renown. As
Vialart writes, addressing Christ, "It is she, whom you first spoke to, after you
left the tomb, her name is the first that your sacred mouth pronounced, you
gave her the first commission that you delivered, which was to announce to
your Apostles your glory and your resurrection."[40] Vialart stresses that the
saint was selected for this prestigious role because of love—both Christ's
love for her and hers for him, making the choice appropriate. Far from the
ordinary sinner of Protestant interpretation, whom God puts to work for his
purposes as he might anyone, Mary Magdalene's extraordinary affection for
Christ nominated her, of all men and women, to carry the message of salvation. If Protestants were empowered by the Magdalene's story to confess the
faith boldly among their neighbors, Vialart encouraged his fellow Catholics

to imitate the saint's great love, and so become more worthy of God's love and favor in return.

Evidence for the appeal of this imitative Magdalene piety can be found in the devotional lives of religious orders and the families who supported them. The records of the Carmelite Order supply evidence of the extent to which laymen also venerated the contemplative Magdalene. These documents describe the generosity of a M. Le Camus, benefactor of a Carmelite convent for the sake of his daughter, who was a nun there. In 1668 he paid for church decoration, including the Chapel of the Magdalene, the place where he himself chose to be buried.[41] In addition to the Carmelites, the Jesuit Order benefited from the special devotion to the Magdalene of one M. le capitaine Béreur: "The reverend fathers of the Company of Jesus also regarded him as their benefactor: he had a chapel built in their church in the honor of St. Magdalene, whom he, and all his family, venerated with a particular devotion."[42]

Jesuit devotion to the Magdalene can be traced directly to the order's founder and the spiritual practices he established to equip its members to combat the spread of Protestant ideas. The resurrection appearance to the Magdalene is one of the recommended subjects for meditation in Ignatius of Loyola's *Spiritual Exercises*. In the third apparition, Ignatius does include the commandment to her and the other women at the tomb, to "announce the resurrection of the Lord to the other disciples." This is not connected to any action the exertant might perform other than in contemplation, but the fifth apparition describes Christ giving the disciples Communion when he appears to them at Emmaus, making a sacramental interpretation of the scripture's account of a shared meal. The disciples then told the others "how they had recognized him in the Communion." The illustrations of the resurrection appearances commissioned at Ignatius's request by the Jesuit artist Jerome Nadal made clear connections between the Gospel stories and the contemporary church's rituals. Nadal's 1594 companion to the lectionary, *Adnotationes et Meditationes in Evangelia,* was an influential resource for Catholic worship and meditation. The image of the apparition to the Magdalene shows Christ gesturing to Mary, refusing her touch. The depiction of the meal at Emmaus has Christ distributing bread directly into the mouth of a disciple, as a priest would distribute the Host. Catholic readings of the resurrection narratives, in devotional texts and in the visual images that accompanied and supported them, instructed the faithful to seek Christ in penitence, confession, and the Eucharist rather than in personal proclamation of the Gospel.[43]

Baroque Art

Supporting the messages received from the pulpit and from educational and devotional texts, the principal theme of Mary Magdalene's representation in Catholic visual art was that of the penitent sinner.[44] To an extent, this represents a continuity of part of the tradition. As we have seen, Mary Magdalene's popularity as a saint can be traced to her accessibility for ordinary people who could relate to her as a fellow sinner beloved by God. Ingrid Maisch has claimed, though, that this penitential emphasis marks a decisive shift from the medieval character of her visual identity, with a new concentration of focus on her sinful nature for its titillating provocation, rather than as a means to the end of her salvation. The increased consideration of the Magdalene's sexuality in visual art may be explained partly by developments in anatomical and psychological realism that had emerged in the Italian Renaissance. The figure itself had become a subject for consideration, and its depiction a means of conveying emotion and character. A schematic icon can make a powerful intercessor symbolically present, but it takes a portrait to captivate viewers with a human narrative of conflicted love. The Magdalene functioned as a symbol of the chief intellectual and spiritual preoccupations of the age: she became a symbol of human frailty and the transience of worldly pleasure, and the flight from such temptation into the fevered, ecstatic spirituality that characterized the Baroque era. Where other saints from the medieval canon might have continued to offer more static models of supernatural purity, the Magdalene's story contained an inherent tension between this world and the next. More than most holy figures, she had experienced intense temptation and vice. Just as intense were the manifestations of her conversion: tortured weeping, a bride's desire for the person of Christ, and punishing asceticism. Hers was a dynamic narrative suited to the era of Ignatian spirituality, of a culture of piety that encouraged elaborate visualizations of scriptural scenes and rigorous self-examination, all focused on the work of turning one's life in the right direction.[45]

The fascination with the Magdalene's role as sinner and penitent was not merely a fluctuation in the religious currency of the intellectual and cultural elites. The message was delivered by preachers across the Catholic world, from Europe to the Americas, and applied to real women as well as painted figures.[46] In 1539 the Capuchin preacher Bernardino Ochino delivered a sermon on the subject of the penitent Magdalene and the reformed prostitutes of Padua. In colonial Mexico, Alonso Franco y Ortega wrote of a Father Pedro y Urrutia, whose vivid preaching on confession caused a woman to come forward who, "like another Mary Magdalene, recognized her ugliness and sins." The ugliness to be recognized was an inward quality, however. The beauty and sensuality of the Magdalene functioned as a proof of the sinfulness of the prostitute, and therefore as a testament to the worthy motives behind her conversion; if she were truly unattractive, turning from her trade would have seemed like making a virtue of necessity. This distinction was also applied to ordinary women, as Sara Matthews-Grieco has found: "In Rome, for example, the Charity of Saint Jerome had precise standards for admission to the convents it directed: 'We will give admission neither to the infirm nor to those encumbered with old age, since the art of sinning has abandoned them, and not they the art.'" The fruits of penitence, commended to potential converts and believers alike, were directly tied to the penitent's intention and measure of self-sacrifice, with potentially disastrous results for those who did not reform. Visual warnings were illustrated in permanent iconographic programs in prominent locations within churches and other religious buildings. The Scuola di San Rocco, a confraternity house in Venice, for example, had a particular mission to syphilis patients and former prostitutes. The house's portrait of Mary Magdalene depicts heavenly relief of suffering as the fruit of conversion, promising the only escape possible for those so afflicted by the consequences of prostitution that they were beyond any recovery in this world.[47]

Given such dire consequences for sin, the potential benefits of penitence must then be advertised as still more desirable than a life of indulgence. The results of the Magdalene's conversion are displayed in an early sixteenth-century Flemish painting that shows the saint later in life. In the painting, she reads a prayer book; a lute and sheet music for a popular love song have been put away but remain in sight, signaling her past but showing that she has set such worldly pleasures aside.[48] A pair of paintings from the same region and approximate date, *Christ Speaking with a Woman* and *Lady with a Lute*, show Mary Magdalene before and just after her conversion, as a wealthy Flemish

FIG 4.1 Titian, *The Magdalen*, 1533. Oil on canvas. Photo: Galleria Palatina, Palazzo Pitti, Florence / Nimatallah / Art Resource, NY.

woman.[49] In the panel that shows her inside a house, she is surrounded by the attributes of luxury: gambling games, a lute, rich clothes, and a bed, though an ointment jar prefigures her future as Christ's anointer. The other panel has the same woman sitting outside, now humbled, at Christ's feet; this scene would have been the view from the open door in the interior where the preconversion Magdalene was still among her secular temptations, thus suggesting the moment at which she contemplated her repentance and conversion.[50]

Although clearly the penitence of early modern Magdalenes expressed the interests of the Church and artists of the period, it was also the product of patrons' urging, as can be seen by the history of one of the most influential of Magdalene images, Titian's *Mary Magdalene* (1531–1535). The painting was commissioned in 1531 by Federico Gonzaga, who requested that the artist make her "as lachrymose as possible." Spawning a long line of imitations, Titian's image duly focuses on the contrite expression of the tearful saint, while still permitting viewers an enticing glimpse of her naked body through its miraculous clothing of hair.[51]

This tension between the convert and the coquette remained a feature of her visual identity over the course of the following century. The Baroque era witnessed a Magdalene who oscillated between a truly abject penitent and a sinner still tantalizingly caught up in the enjoyment of her own destruction.[52] The saint's association with the sinful woman of Luke 7 together with her legendary background of sensual abandonment made her the perfect choice for a central role in the visual culture of penitence and in the church's efforts to reform the morality of church and society.[53]

That effort is evident in Caravaggio's the *Penitent Magdalene* (1596–1597), which depicts a very young Magdalene at the moment when she turns from a worldly life really only just begun; the emphasis here is not on beauty or worldliness but on a realistic, puffy-eyed contrition. Her jewelry is cast aside and broken on the floor beside her, her expensive perfume ready to be taken up to anoint Christ's feet in the house of Simon the Pharisee. The emotional focus of the painting is a sensitive exposition of her inward state, not an enjoyment of the voluptuousness of her sin.[54] Indeed, so purely penitent is this Magdalene that scholars have claimed it as the source for a seventeenth-century Lenten sermon by Francesco Panigarola, indicating that while art often illustrated sermons, it could also inspire preaching. Following an Ignatian model of visual reenactment of the scriptural story, Panigarola preached about the very moment of Mary Magdalene's conversion, as shown in the painting: "sacred fear overwhelms . . . a fear that is the basis of all that is good . . . let us take as our example the Magdalene . . . casting down her necklaces and jewels, shaking out her tresses, violently wringing her hands, she trembled and declared, 'O Floor why don't you open up, why don't you swallow me? O Bed, you have witnessed so many of my evil deeds, why don't

FIG 4.2 Caravaggio, *Mary Magdalen*, 1597. Oil on canvas. Photo: Galleria Doria Pamphilj, Rome / Alinari / Art Resource, NY.

you smother me?' Now she could not even bear to look at the walls of her house which concealed and surrounded her lascivious acts."[55]

Alongside this strain of unsexualized Magdalene imagery, focused on her contemplative life after her conversion, portrayals of the dissolute path of the woman who would only later become the saint were far more common in visual art. The appealing ambiguity of the sinner-saint was so dynamic that it crossed cultural lines, appearing even in Protestant England in secular paintings that capitalized on the power of her religious identity. Though Protestant regions did produce art that expressed their theology, the dominance of Italy through the Renaissance and Baroque periods as the origin and arbiter of cultivated style meant that a considerable amount of Catholic imagery continued to circulate in the Protestant world. Post-Restoration English images of the Magdalene dwelled voluptuously on her sinful, sensual past. The source for these works was often Titian's *Magdalene*, well known in England through prints.[56] Though we have noted the Magdalene's tearful affect in that painting as its original emphasis, the eroticism of her nude form, just revealed beneath its covering of hair, arguably came to be the more famous—or infamous—aspect of the image. What Titian had suggested, others would strip bare. In Peter Paul Rubens's *Christ and the Repentant Sinners* (c. 1620) the Magdalene is most emphatically a sinner: naked (even though the painting depicts her after her conversion, in the Easter morning scene), prostrate, abased, an unvarnished natural in a Baroque world schooled in artifice and discipline yet yearning to transcend them.[57] Based on these continental models, Mary Magdalene became the fashionable ideal for English court portraiture, especially that of royal mistresses. Peter Lely's *The Penitent Magdalene (Countess of Castlemaine, Lady Jenkinson)* (1660) and *Louise de Kéroualle, Duchess of Portsmouth as Mary Magdalene* (1670) and Sir Godfrey Kneller's *Elizabeth Villiers, Countess of Orkney* (1698) all depict their subjects as not-quite-penitent sensualists, with the cascading hair and loose draperies of the saint's traditional iconography.[58]

The Magdalene in Music and Poetry

Part of her traditional iconography included an association of music and dancing with the Magdalene, both before and after her conversion. Before her conversion they were among the temptations of the world; afterward they would be taken up again in a new way, purified and sanctified as angelic song. In the legendary retreat of Mary Magdalene to the mountain grotto near Sainte-Baume at the end of her life, she was lifted to heaven by angels every day, hearing chants from the heavenly host. These angels also play instruments in an altarpiece by the Master of the Magdalene Legend (c. 1520). Still more frequently, though, music and dancing were shown among the activities of the sinful life that Mary Magdalene enjoyed before her conversion. A group of paintings of the saint by the Master of the Female Half-Lengths depicts the Magdalene as a lute player.[59] An engraving by Lucas van Leyden from 1519 portrays the Magdalene engaged in worldly pleasures, including playing music and dancing, as a contrast to her later activity of preaching, shown in another section of the composition.[60] As source material for these images, Passion plays such as the Donaueschingen Passion Play (c. 1480), Jean Michel's *Mystère de la Passion* (1486), and the Frankfurt Passion Play (1493) all incorporated scenes of Mary Magdalene dancing during her sinful youth. Two surviving dance pieces from the early modern period titled *La Magdalena,* by Pierre Attaingnant (1530) and Marc'Antonio del Pifaro (1546), are the kind of *basse* dance that she performs in the plays and in Leyden's engraving.[61]

The Magdalene herself appears as a character in the very kinds of secular songs she was supposed to have enjoyed. Her preconversion life was explored in a song published in 1515, "Maugré dangier," in which the sinful Magdalene mourns a lost lover in terms that foreshadow her mourning for Christ:

Despite her hesitation, Magdalene will display herself gloriously,
Whether these accursed spiteful men like it or not.
The Castle of Magdalon is a real paradise,
Such good comfort does not belong to a low-born woman.

"I am in pain and sorrow for my lover;
I cannot endure my sorrowful heart.
Away all care, sadness and all its supports!
In love I am very passionate and quick."

A noble heart, which feels pain in love
And which, in spite of these enemies, takes pleasure
Should be placed beyond sorrow and affliction.
There is no danger, for comfort drives them out.

"I am sure and certain of my own pleasure;
I have goods enough in a charming lodging;
And my beautiful body is much in demand by many people;
So I call myself sovereign over all other women."

"I shall make a fountain of my two eyes.
And of my head, whence all my pleasure springs,
I shall have it cut off, if I do not see my lover;
Wherefore I die of a sovereign love."[62]

The song alludes to an opposition—between sinful and saved humanity, between old and new creation—in the Christian salvation narrative, in which the Magdalene figures as a new Eve, reversing, in the arc of her own life, the story of the Fall. The "paradise" of the first verse, the home where she begins on a sinful path, is a false paradise, suggesting, by contrast, the garden where Mary Magdalene will later discover the risen Christ. Her pain in losing a lover is "unendurable" here, and yet she admits that it is, in fact, easily chased away by worldly comforts, in ironic parallel to the truly unendurable pain she will suffer as she witnesses the Crucifixion of her spiritual bridegroom. She weeps prodigiously, as always, but here her tears are frivolous, finding no worthy object. An audience familiar with her late medieval cult would have compared this early manifestation of a sympathetic, emotional nature to its mature flowering after her meeting with Christ, when it becomes an expression of the deepest compassion, her tears anointing the body of God incarnate. The earthly love and human soul she had mistakenly thought "sovereign" will be laid at the feet of her true sovereign, whom she will lose, only to gain an eternal communion with him after death.

Songs about the Magdalene could refer to real women, too, though in doing so artists took care to emphasize her praiseworthy qualities as a feminine ideal. Another popular song, the very one whose music was shown set aside in the Flemish painting of the reading Magdalene, had been altered and used in the composition of a poem, "Tous nobles coeurs venez voir Magdalene," written for Madeleine de la Tour d'Auvergne, on the occasion of her marriage to Lorenzo II de' Medici in 1518.[63] The text invokes the noble Madeleine's saintly namesake as a wealthy and cultured woman at the height of her powers:

All noble hearts come to see Magdalene
In her chateau, full of happiness;
Her noble heart has, through love, proclaimed
"I would spread worldly glory everywhere."[64]

The poem connects Madeleine with the preconversion Magdalene, though not critically this time, celebrating her beauty, position, and generosity rather than condemning her. The Magdalene's personality is defined by an exuberant love, which leads her to the overindulgence of her sensual desires, but her great love is ultimately that which will save her when it finds its true object in Christ.

The loss of and promised reunion with Christ is the subject of much of the more explicitly religious verse that features Mary Magdalene. A late sixteenth-century poem by Cardinal Robert Bellarmine expressed this in Neoplatonic terms, as the divine approach to humanity, creating longing to renew the damaged *imago Dei* within: "Father of the supreme light, / When you look at the Magdalene, / You generate flames of love, / Melting the ice within her heart." Henry Constable's *Spiritual Sonnets* (1594) explored a similar theme of reunion, the only way to overcome the Magdalene's grief at her sexual sins. Shame and regret at her former life of promiscuity continue to affect her even after the Crucifixion; it is contrition, as much as mourning, that produces her weeping at the tomb. She longs for death, so that she might be in perfect union with Christ.[65] Constable's imagery provides an interesting contrast to Luther's famous metaphor of the soul clothed with divine grace:

> My body is the garment of my spright
> while as the day time of my life doth last:
> when death shall bring the night of my delight
> my soul, unclothed, shall rest from labours past:
> and clasped in the arms of God, enjoy
> by sweet conjunction, everlasting joy.[66]

Where, for Luther, the sinful soul is only made acceptable to God when it is covered with the beautiful, borrowed cloak of Christ's righteousness, this Catholic Magdalene sheds the ugly garments of her fleshly existence after death, when her naked soul is finally united with God. Luther's theology hews to an Augustinian model of sin as located in the will, not in the body. Constable displays a more Neoplatonic dichotomy between physical and spiritual existence; the flesh must be escaped, transcended, in order for the soul to achieve unity with the divine.

The Jesuit Robert Southwell's popular and influential prose work *Marie Magdalens Funeral Teares* (1591) exemplifies this theme of the Magdalene's longing for Christ. The absence and loss explored is certainly that of all Christians in confronting the death of Christ, but Patricia Badir has argued that Southwell engages this grief in a particular context, interpreting the experience of English Catholics under Protestant rule.[67] The text is organized around a female character who represents the religious life of an entire community; Mary Magdalene herself is a shrine desecrated by Protestants, part of the whole environment of faith that Southwell and the rest of the Catholic community have been denied: "Though I have been robbed of the Saint . . . I will at the least have care of the shrine, which though it be spoiled of the most sovereign Host, yet shall it be the altar where I will daily sacrifice my heart and offer up my tears."[68] Given this sense of disruption and loss, Mary Magdalene's direct encounters with Christ, her personal memories of him, are enviable.[69] Yet even a fulfilling experience of connection with the divine is complicated by the altered conditions under which she now exists. After she tells the disciples of her meeting with the risen Christ, she admits that she is unchanged, or even more miserable, having had this brief taste of what she cannot possess: "I am nothing different from that I was . . . in having taken a taste of the highest delight, that the knowledge and want of it might drown me in the deepest misery." Her extreme sorrow precludes the new life Christ's resurrection is supposed to bring; rather than experiencing the renewal of Christian life—the washing of baptism—instead, she merely drowns.[70]

Paul Cefalu contends that Southwell's work typifies increased interest in the Gospel of John's resurrection narrative in early modern English treatments of the Magdalene. John's Gospel was important for many prominent reformers, including Martin Luther and John Calvin, with its themes of the revelation of God through hearing the Word rather than by seeing. The Magdalene in the Johannine narrative recognizes the risen Christ only by hearing him speak her name. Yet her response to that call in Southwell's work is not the same as it was for Luther. The emphasis here remains on the depth of Mary's mourning, an emotion understandable before she finds that Christ has risen, but now she also experiences it afterward, when even the medieval tradition had supposed her to be transported by joy and a zeal to communicate the good news. In this new reading the Magdalene is not a transformed evangelist, not the inspired preacher who would go on to convert Marseilles. Instead of moving forward to speak the news of the resurrection across the Mediterranean world, she returns obsessively to the tomb, where she dreams only of embracing Christ once more. An ideal Catholic, she devotedly refuses any substitute, even the word of the Gospel, for the Host she continues to seek.[71]

The contrast between the experience of the Magdalene here and the preaching she took up in Protestant interpretations confirms that the character of witness to the resurrection diverged for the two communities. The Protestant form of witness was an active testimony, associated with the confession of faith central to evangelical theology. The Magdalene's witness in the Catholic tradition, on the other hand, became a more passive observation and a sense of the presence of Christ, defined by an internal feeling of awe and a need to overcome Christ's absence using the sacraments. In the resurrection narratives, Protestants focused on the saint's message for the apostles, while the Catholic interest, in the arts as in preaching, remained on the noli me tangere scene, with its explanation of the necessity of approaching Christ in a new way.

The English Catholic community produced Magdalenes that addressed the needs of their context of persecution and discontinuity. Less conflicted, more vocal Magdalenes can be found, however, in epic poetry from seventeenth-century France and Germany. In France, the Magdalene's *apostola apostolorum* role persisted in the work of several poets, including the Capuchin Remi de Beauvais. Remi's seven-hundred-page *La Magdeleine* (1617) emphasizes her legendary preaching career, drawing on the medieval tradition from the *Golden Legend*. The poem identifies the Magdalene's great love as her motivation for speaking, and is careful to maintain the hierarchy of the contemplative life over the active.[72] Still, Remi's description is remarkably comfortable with her evangelical role: "Take up your evangelical word! / Proclaim! Rejoin the apostolic troop! / Preach! Raise your voice! Teach Salvation!" He has her sister Martha praise Mary's intellect and eloquence.[73] Thomas Carr has argued that Remi wrote the poem as a devotional manual for his noble patroness, Marie de Longueval, presenting the saint—as François de Sales had—as an exceptional figure, not as an example for imitation except within the context of home and family. Remi's context, of encouraging a wealthy female patron of the church with the example of the Magdalene, was interestingly similar to that of the Lutheran pastor Johannes Mathesius, whom we saw praising the saint in such language before an audience that included the local noblewomen who supported his ministry.[74]

Secular women's lives were also the aim of a long devotional poem by the seventeenth-century German Jesuit, Friedrich Spee. The poem (1640) was published in his *Güldenes Tugend-Buch,* a book of advice for women on how to live a spiritual life outside the cloister, amid the cares and responsibilities of the home. The attempt to form a domestic spirituality for married women can be read as part of the Counter-Reformation's response to Protestantism. Protestant theologians and pastors, beginning with Luther and continuing through the seventeenth century, had addressed the spiritual lives of married persons; Catholic teachers, such as Remi and Spee, deliberately sought to engage the household as an important site of religious formation, in addition to the convent and the abbey.[75]

Echoing medieval monastics' self-identifications with the Magdalene, Spee described the soul's longing for God as a desire to imitate the faithfulness of the saint, in order to achieve the intimacy she had with Christ: "Before your cross, by day and by year / Will I sit with Magdalene." After the Passion, "The weeping Magdalene" is shown mourning devoutly at the tomb—again, the place where the author would like to be. The images presented of the saint are largely positive; she is a model for emulation rather than an object lesson in the need for repentance. Any reference to her sinfulness is made only in passing; the focus is on her love for Christ. Spee maintains the Magdalene's connection with Mary of Bethany and the "better part" she chose, and with the bride from the Song of Songs. His example of a truly regretful sinner is not the loyal Mary Magdalene but instead Peter, who deserted Christ in his time of greatest need.[76]

These positive evaluations of the Magdalene mark a continuity from the medieval tradition in that this female saint could provide a model for spirituality through her devotion to Christ. The discontinuity emerges when she is assessed as a model for public teaching. The Dominicans of the late Middle Ages had explicitly claimed her teaching and preaching role for themselves by making her their patron saint, but the monks of the Counter-Reformation needed to adopt a different strategy. Agustin de la Madre de Dios, a Mexican Carmelite writing around 1650, acknowledged that the primary association of his order's patroness—also Mary Magdalene—was with contemplation. By the mid-seventeenth century, a monastic order linked to the Magdalene had to argue that it was appropriate for its monks to take a role in the Catholic Church's great mission efforts: "Our sacred religion, having determined the character of the Carmelite institute and found that its principal employment is the greater part that Mary Magdalene chose for herself and was so much approved by Christ, left for the other sacred religions this apostolic employment [missions], although even in doing so not omitting the pious occupation of winning souls to Christ when and in the manner that it can be done without losing the [souls] of its sons."[77] If men of the Carmelite Order wished to follow an active vocation, they needed to renegotiate the prevailing interpretation of both their order and their patron saint, contending that evangelism could still be carried out with integrity even by those to whom tradition assigned a contemplative life. The same question would be faced by women with a similar missionary impulse, as we shall see.

THIS ASSESSMENT of Counter-Reformation piety reveals those elements that survived, and those that were lost or rejected, from the previous cult of the Magdalene. The associations of the saint with Mary of Bethany and with the penitent woman of Luke 7 both persisted and were used in new ways according to the needs of the contemporary church. The better part of Mary continued to reinforce teaching about the contemplative life, while the penitence of the sinful woman was given increasing attention as an example of properly abject contrition and amendment of life for prostitutes, in countering Protestant attacks on Catholic morality.[78]

Mary Magdalene was understood as a witness to Christ's Passion and resurrection, though the concern was with how she herself was affected by compassion for what she saw rather than with Christ's command that she spread the Gospel to others. For those in a context of persecution, such as English Catholics, the focus was on her grief at the loss of Christ and the encouragement of the faithful to find him in new ways. For continental Catholic authors such as François de Sales, Ignatius of Loyola, and Charles Vialart, the Magdalene's great love for Christ was emphasized as a means of guiding their readers' devotional lives according to orthodox teaching, away from dangerous interpretations. The character of witness Catholic audiences were encouraged to embrace is an internal transformation of experience shaped by love. An insight born of sorrow is the wellspring of the Magdalene's testimony to others, the foundation of her speech. When she does speak in the early modern Catholic tradition, as she still did in French and German poetry, God's command that she deliver the message of salvation is not a mandate for the ordinary reader, as it is for Protestant preachers, but the emphasis remains her own emotional state and the passionate, interior encounter with the divine that cannot help but break forth in some outward manifestation.

In Chapter 5 we will turn to Catholic women's embrace of the Counter-Reformation Magdalene and how their sense of themselves and their relationship to God was formed by the preaching and teaching they heard, saw, and read about the saint. Were the fears about Protestant arguments for lay preaching shared by women as well as men? Or did the character of the new Magdalene cause women to set her aside in frustration as an undesirable model for their vocations? To what extent did the more active, medieval Magdalene persist in women's devotion, continuing to capture the imaginations and imitation of religious women in Catholic countries in the sixteenth and seventeenth centuries?

CHAPTER FIVE

Love Made Her Dare

The Magdalene among
Catholic Women

EARLY MODERN CATHOLIC WOMEN, both lay and religious, took up the subject of the Magdalene, writing about her life and expressing their devotion in prayer, music, and visual art. In this chapter, the themes and practices they engaged will be examined in tension with the images of the saint that women received from male authors. Male authors, and preachers in particular, were often the interpreters of biblical texts for women, who were not encouraged, as Protestant women were, to read scripture for themselves. The Council of Trent's prohibition on individual scripture interpretation had a particular effect on women; as Belinda Jack has observed, "Protestant and Catholic women found themselves in rather different reading contexts."[1] Catholic women's attempts to defend their theological study using the Magdalene's example could prove dangerous, incurring mockery, suspicion and institutional discipline, as we will see. Nevertheless, Catholic women did engage the Magdalene of the Bible directly, and wrote about her in ways that were influenced by the tradition and by their male contemporaries but also contained innovative adaptations of the saint for women's changing circumstances. We have observed the appeal of a sexualized Magdalene to male authors, audiences, and patrons, both within and outside of the ecclesiastical hierarchy. To what extent where these same images appropriated, altered, or dismissed by their female colleagues, neighbors, wives, and queens? Within the writing, artistic patronage, and recorded lives of sixteenth- and seventeenth-century Catholic women, we will find both wholehearted embraces of the penitent, contemplative Magdalene and rejections of that identity as an unhelpful model, as well as attempts to keep a more active, vocal Magdalene alive.

The opposition between active and contemplative vocations was exposed and critiqued by early modern women themselves as they struggled to shape their own vocations and those of the women and men around them. Examinations of their writing and practice reveal the importance of mystical, contemplative spirituality for those with active vocations, and the vivid sense of a call to action among contemplatives.[2] In addition, it must be remembered that the Counter-Reformation emphasis on the sacredness of celibacy appealed to both men and women seeking a holy life.[3] The saintly models that women used to defend and sustain their vocations embraced the celibate ideal and, in turn, influenced the spirituality of their male colleagues.[4] While those models emerged from the culture of the Counter-Reformation, and to some extent aimed at refuting Protestant attacks, the polemics of opposing Martin Luther and his colleagues were more often the work of male clergy, while women's writing was generally more concerned with, and shaped by, internal goals and debates—the struggle to pursue a vocation, whether in the convent or the world, with integrity.[5]

Religious Women: "Mary and Martha Walk Together"

The age of reform was a period of religious investigation and discovery. Women responded to the creative ferment of the spiritual life of the era and fostered it with innovations of their own. New institutions and mission drives were founded and supported by women, just as female authors and artists produced images to shape the piety that undergirded these efforts. The Council of Trent's decrees attempted to regulate the institutions and imagery that affected religious women, producing a complex environment in which women often had to contend with restrictions on their activity even as they were encouraged to intense devotion. As they faced new circumstances that challenged previous understandings of the religious life, early modern Catholic women adapted the Magdalene tradition to create relevant models of female sanctity and vocation. The legacy of the medieval Magdalene as a model for contemplatives and mystics remained influential, especially for women in religious orders. The themes we have observed in medieval Magdalene piety, of a spousal intimacy with Christ, exemplary contemplation, and ascetic penitence, can be found activating the vocations of early modern women as well.

The paradox of a radical commitment to God's will combined with an absolute obedience to the human institutions of the church preoccupied one of the greatest spiritual authors of early modern Catholicism, Teresa of Avila. Despite a consuming interior life, Teresa was active in the management and expansion of her order, accomplishing an astonishing amount of travel and writing for a woman often subject to debilitating spiritual and physical crises.[6] Her own experience therefore necessitated a reconciliation of the demands of the world and of the spirit. Teresa was aware of an existing opposition between the two vocations within convents, between the lay sisters who did the practical tasks of cleaning, cooking, and other care of the community, and the choir sisters who were supposed to give their time to prayer. Teresa describes how this hierarchy of vocations had fostered a sense of competition: "I believe that when those of the active life see the contemplative favored a little, they think there is nothing else to the contemplative's life than receiving favors."[7] The division of roles between those devoted to prayer and those performing the physical labor of the community seems to have led to resentment among the nuns who felt burdened with practical cares.[8] The opposition between active and contemplative vocations within the convent mirrors a larger conflict in early modern Catholicism, between religious orders dedicated to the active life, such as the Jesuits, and to the contemplative life, such as the Carmelites. This conflict was not a simple institutional difference, but a fundamental inquiry about the divided nature of the believer who must be in the world and yet not of it. Teresa characterized the antagonism as an internal struggle within the individual, who must combine attention to daily tasks with more esoteric spiritual pursuits. "It seemed to her [Teresa writes of herself in the second person] that there was, in a certain way, a division in her soul. . . . She complained of that part of the soul, as Martha complained of Mary, and sometimes pointed out that it was there always enjoying that quietude at its own pleasure while leaving her in the midst of so many trials and occupations that she could not keep it company." And yet the path of the contemplative was not all joy and quietude, but a severe and challenging labor of its own. Teresa writes of the "great penances" performed by the Magdalene, likening them to the hunger and suffering for God of Elijah, St. Francis, and St. Dominic. Despite her own predilection for ascetic withdrawal, manifested in fasting, periods of bodily incapacitation, and divine visions, she marvels at the Magdalene's experience of God as something surely overwhelming: "I at times wonder what the feeling of the saints must have been. What must St. Paul and the Magdalene and others like them have undergone, in whom this fire of the love of God had grown so intense?" Between the intensity of contemplation and the demands of daily life, then, lies the space Teresa must negotiate for herself and her nuns, and she does so by exploring the relationship between Mary and Martha.[9]

One of her most common approaches is to assert a communion between them, to be achieved within each individual. The description of how this happens comes from her own experience, as presented in the *Spiritual Testimonies*: "The will is completely occupied in God, and sees it lacks the power to be engaged in any other work. The other two faculties are free for business and works of service of God. In sum, Mary and Martha walk together."[10] Likewise, in *The Way of Perfection* she writes, "This is a great favor for those to whom the Lord grants it: the active and the contemplative lives are joined. . . . Thus Martha and Mary walk together." And in her *Meditations on the Song of Songs*, it is explained that the soul is always able to withdraw in contemplation, even during active ministry: "Martha and Mary never fail to work almost together when the soul is in this state. For in the active—and seemingly exterior—work the soul is working interiorly." In the *Interior Castle*, she addresses the potential objections of those who might not see this tandem work as possible or desirable: "You will make two objections: one, that He said that Mary had chosen the better part. The answer is that she had already performed the task of Martha, pleasing the Lord by washing His feet and drying them with her hair." Where medieval monastic theology had often valued the contemplative over the active, Teresa proclaims an equality between them as vital roles that must coexist within the individual and at the communal level.[11]

Part of establishing parity between Mary and Martha lies in correcting the prevailing hierarchy of roles by emphasizing Martha's importance. In considering what Martha must have felt when Christ praised Mary, Teresa sides sympathetically with the more industrious sister:

I sometimes remember the complaint of that holy woman, Martha. She did not complain only about her sister, rather, I hold it is certain that her greatest sorrow was the thought that You, Lord, did not feel sad about the trial she was undergoing and didn't care whether she was with you or not. Perhaps she thought You didn't have as much love for her as for her sister. . . . Love made her dare to ask why You weren't concerned . . . for love alone is what gives value to all things; a kind of love so great that nothing hinders it is the one thing necessary.[12]

Martha's physical care for Christ is thus shown to emerge from a love that exists in parallel to Mary's, so that *both* women do "the one thing necessary." Teresa demonstrates just how necessary Martha's part is with subtle humor. Issuing instructions for her fellow nuns about how to combine the vocations of contemplation and service, she writes of the need for Martha's practical work: "This is what I want us to strive for, my Sisters; and let us desire and be occupied in prayer not for the sake of our enjoyment but so as to have this strength to serve. . . . Believe me, Martha and Mary must join together in order to show hospitality to the Lord and have Him always present and not host Him badly by failing to give Him something to eat. How would Mary, always seated at His feet, provide Him with food if her sister did not help her?"[13]

Religious communities must be organized to provide for material needs as Martha did: "St. Martha was a saint, even though they do not say she was contemplative. . . . If she had been enraptured like the Magdalene, there wouldn't have been anyone to give food to the divine Guest. Well, think of this congregation as the home of St. Martha and that there must be people for every task."[14] Proper stewardship of both spiritual and tangible resources marks the right ordering of both the convent and the soul. Those who might think themselves above menial tasks are sharply rebuked: "There is a small lack of humility in wanting to raise the soul up before the Lord raises it, in not being content to meditate on something so valuable, and in wanting to be Mary before having worked with Martha."[15]

This emphasis on Martha's importance is not only an acknowledgment of the necessity of doing the business of life competently; it marks a theological stance. For Teresa, the believer must not only receive from God, but must give to God, in the form of service to Christ in the neighbor. We have seen this interpretation, in which the two sides of religious life represented by Mary and Martha must be joined in the individual Christian, since Augustine. The idea that passive reception of God's grace must be paired with the active response of loving the neighbor is also characteristic of Luther's theology, a correspondence noted by the Inquisition in its investigations of Teresa's reform movement.[16] Teresa echoed Luther's assertion that the Christian can do nothing to prepare for grace, this time discussing the Magdalene's worldly life before her conversion. God comes to sinners in the midst of life, not only to those who have already made dramatic renunciations of the world and the flesh: "Seeking God would be very costly if we could not do so until we were dead to the world. The Magdalene was not dead to the world when she found him, nor was the Samaritan woman or the Canaanite woman."[17] The faithful do not go seeking God in their own righteousness but accept salvation gratefully when it finds them.

Teresa's attempt to reconcile the gratitude of the believer with the response of service, the contemplative with the active, is not easy or static. At times the urgency of human need seems to push contemplation into the background, as an almost self-indulgent preoccupation that must be set aside in order to take up important work in the world. Teresa affirms the ultimate primacy of the "best part" of Mary, however, in describing the true loyalty of the soul, even as it busies itself with external works. "In the prayer of quiet the soul didn't desire to move or stir, rejoicing in that holy idleness of Mary; and in this prayer it can also be Martha in such a way that it is as though engaged in both the active and contemplative life together. It tends to works of charity and to business affairs that have to do with its state of life and to reading; although it isn't master of itself completely. And it understands clearly that the best part of the soul is somewhere else." In this way the mystic can pursue the Magdalene's intimacy with the divine while in the midst of assuming Martha's responsibilities. At other times Teresa is able to focus exclusively on Mary's contemplation, setting aside exterior demands in order to welcome Christ more completely: "Since she believed that this Lord truly entered her poor home, she freed herself from all exterior things when it was possible and entered to be with Him. . . . She considered she was at His feet and wept with the Magdalene, no more nor less than if she were seeing Him with her bodily eyes in the house of the Pharisee."[18]

The attraction of that intimate contact with Christ is, for Teresa, evident in her descriptions of the visions that she experienced. As she summarizes them, "The Lord almost always showed Himself to me as risen. . . . Sometimes He appeared on the cross or in the garden," though it is unclear from Teresa's text whether the garden here is the Gethsemane of the Passion or the garden where the Magdalene encountered Christ on Easter morning. Intimacy is earned by the perseverance of having endured as witness to Christ's suffering, when others might have departed. Teresa uses the Magdalene's faithfulness as an admonition to her peers, to persist in contemplation of the most harrowing passages of Christ's life: "Whoever doesn't want to use a little effort now to recollect at least the sense of sight and look at this Lord within herself . . . would have been much less able to stay at the foot of the cross with the Magdalene, who saw His death with her own eyes." The reward of such steadfastness becomes clear. A detailed account of her sense of Christ's presence alludes to Mary Magdalene's meeting with the newly risen Christ, from John 20: "It seemed to me that Christ was at my side—I saw that it was He, in my opinion, Who was speaking to me. Since I was completely unaware that there could be a vision like this one, it greatly frightened me in the beginning; I did nothing but weep. However, by speaking one word alone to assure me, the Lord left me feeling as I usually did: quiet, favored, and without any fear." Like the Magdalene, Teresa fails at first to comprehend the identity of her companion and her bewildered distress is expressed in copious weeping. The single word spoken, however, like the Magdalene's name addressed to her by Christ in the garden, at once recalls her to the blessed intimacy she had been seeking. Indeed, Teresa's yearning for the Magdalene's closeness to Christ is so palpable that she even "complains that Jesus loves Mary Magdalene more than herself." This yearning is resolved in a vision that assures Teresa that she does, in fact, have the same union with Christ that the Magdalene had known: "One day in Toledo, Teresa was envying St. Mary Magdalene for the love our Lord had for her. The Lord then appeared to Teresa and said: 'While I was on earth, I took her for my friend; but now that I am in heaven, I have chosen you.'"[19]

The promise of a relation to the divine like that of the Magdalene encouraged Teresa's own imitation of the saint, a piety she recommended to others. Again, she begins with her own experience. Writing of her early life in the convent, she describes her desire to be like her model. "I was very devoted to the glorious Magdalene and frequently thought about her conversion, especially when I received Communion. For since I knew the Lord was certainly present there within me, I, thinking that He would not despise my tears, placed myself at His feet . . . (He did a great deal who allowed me to shed them for Him, since I so quickly forgot that sentiment); and I commended myself to this glorious saint that she might obtain pardon for me." The reliance on the good desire of the soul as a guide shows the influence of the *Spiritual*

Exercises of Ignatius. God is portrayed as encouraging the believer with such impulses, with the Magdalene again used as the exemplar for the proper response to God's direction: "Since the soul receives permission to remain at the feet of Christ, it should endeavor not to leave that place. Let it remain there as it desires; let it imitate the Magdalene, for if it is strong, God will lead it into the desert." The inverse of holy desire, the temptation of the desert, is also an experience through which one must follow Mary Magdalene. Teresa's reading of God as testing strong Christians with a dark night of the soul is an example of the popular Counter-Reformation spiritual practice of self-examination. Her self-conscious imitation of Mary Magdalene produces resolutions and reflections specifically associated with the observance of the saint's festival, as Teresa recounts in the *Spiritual Testimonies*: "The desires and impulses for death, which were so strong, have left me, especially since the feast day of St. Mary Magdalene; for I resolved to live very willingly in order to render much service to God." And in another year, on the same date, she writes, "On the feast of St. Mary Magdalene while I was reflecting on the friendship with our Lord I'm obliged to maintain and also on the words He spoke to me about this saint, and having insistent desires to imitate her, the Lord granted me a great favor and told me that from now on I should try hard."[20]

The strength of this bond, and of the desire for it, is what prompts Teresa's own writing, and she gives it as her justification for public testimony. On the irrepressible nature of the spiritual experience, producing a speech that cannot be denied, she writes, "I receive a very intense, consuming impulse for God that I cannot resist . . . this impulse makes me cry out and call to God." This impulse led at times to frustration at not being able to pursue a more active vocation. The perception that she was teaching publicly, in contravention of the biblical prohibition, was another of the charges for which Teresa was investigated by the Inquisition.[21]

In such circumstances, Teresa writes, "A woman in this stage of prayer is distressed by the natural hindrance there is to her entering the world, and she has great envy of those who have the freedom to cry out and spread the news abroad about who this great God of hosts is."[22] This apparent tension ought to be resolved, Teresa counsels her sisters, by a return to the understanding of the dual roles of Mary and Martha. In discussing the need to combine active service with contemplation, Teresa has attempted to address her reader's

objections to this project. In addition to the fact that Mary's role has traditionally been interpreted as

> the better part. . . . The other objection you will make is that you are
> unable to bring souls to God, that you do not have the means; that you
> would do it willingly but that not being teachers or preachers, as were
> the apostles, you do not know how. . . . Sometimes the devil gives us
> great desires so that we will avoid setting ourselves to the task at hand,
> serving our Lord in possible things, and instead be content with having
> desired the impossible. Apart from the fact that by prayer you will be
> helping greatly, you need not be desiring to benefit the whole world
> but must concentrate on those who are in your company.[23]

The humble work of Martha, among those nearest to her, is the religious
woman's best means of extending the fruits of contemplation beyond herself,
and so joining in the church's larger mission.

Exploring the relationship between Martha and Mary allowed Teresa to
theorize about some of her chief concerns in ordering the spirituality of her
fellow nuns as well as in discerning her own vocation, but she also engaged
some of the other images from the Magdalene tradition. The saint's identity
as penitent sinner provided Teresa with language for confessions of her sinfulness. Her characterization of her debt to divine mercy makes reference to
the absolution given in Luke 7: "What I owe God is much more since He has
pardoned me more." She resolves the question of divine justice by observing
the unreasonable grace of God's forgiveness of notorious sinners such as the
Magdalene, or Paul, the persecutor of the early church: "[God] doesn't grant
[favors] because the sanctity of the recipients is greater than that of those who
don't receive them but so that His glory may be known, as we see in St. Paul
and the Magdalene."[24]

Assuring believers of her experience of God's pardon, Teresa emphasizes
the penitent's inherent unworthiness, an awareness that creates ongoing misery. "No relief is afforded for this suffering by the thought that our Lord has
already pardoned and forgotten the sins. Rather, it adds to the suffering to
see so much goodness and realize that favors are granted to one who deserves
nothing but hell. I think such a realization was a great martyrdom for St. Peter
and the Magdalene."[25] This attitude of continuous torment over her sin places

Teresa in accord with orthodox Catholic doctrine that insisted on the penitent's perpetual uncertainty about salvation, a medieval teaching reasserted in opposition to Lutheran proclamations of the joyful comfort of the Gospel.[26]

Also demonstrating her Counter-Reformation theological orientation is Teresa's reading of Mary Magdalene's conversion. Luther and his followers had noted the instantaneous nature of the Magdalene's redemption as a model for all believers, and Teresa agrees that her change from sin to grace is swift, as it had been with Paul: "Look at St. Paul or the Magdalene. Within three days the one began to realize he was sick with love; that was St. Paul. The Magdalene knew from the first day; and how well she knew!" Though she celebrates the Magdalene's insight, however, she is careful to warn others to pursue a more measured course, just as François de Sales had advised Jeanne de Chantal. Teresa calls such a swift conversion anomalous and does not wish it to discourage her contemporaries from a lifetime's labor of cooperating with their salvation: "What He did in a short time for the Magdalene His Majesty does for other persons in conformity with what they themselves do in order to allow Him to work." The saint is held up as an example of God's defense of those whom he favors, and particularly vulnerable women: "Observe how the Lord answered for the Magdalene both in the house of the Pharisee and when her sister accused her." Teresa's sisters are left with the assurance that though they may face opposition in the reform of their order, God will protect them as he did the Magdalene who fled to his feet, both in contrition and in contemplation: "He defends these souls in all things; when they are persecuted and criticized He answers for them as He did for the Magdalene."[27]

Teresa's reading of the saint influenced the piety of her followers, strengthening them to face attacks on the reforms she had begun. Faced with the challenge of increasingly strict enclosure regulations and the end of an autonomous reform movement, Teresa's protégée María de San José Salazar (1548–1603) appealed to the Magdalene to defend her order. Salazar became prioress of the Discalced Carmelite convent in Seville after Teresa was ordered to leave by local ecclesial authorities. In 1590, Salazar led "the nuns' revolt," appealing to Pope Sixtus V to have Teresa's reforms safeguarded from interference by the local clergy.[28]

Salazar's *Book of the Hour of Recreation* was written in 1585 as a protest against a new provincial supervisor's attempt to end the Discalced Carmelites' daily practice of theological discussion. The text is an imagined conversation between nuns during such an hour of recreation. The work was never published, surviving only in a fragmentary manuscript copy, and must therefore be considered as evidence for a dissenting view on the Counter-Reformation Magdalene, not as a popular interpretation.[29] Salazar offers a complex reading of scriptural examples of women speaking, centered on the post-resurrection appearance to the Magdalene:

> Our sweet Master acted in favor of women with that kindness He showed them when He did not disdain to hold a long and lofty conversation with the Samaritan woman . . . teaching her and making her the one to divulge His holy word. We also know that He first revealed the most high mystery of His Resurrection to Mary Magdalene and the other Marys and commanded them to announce it to their brothers. So there is no reason for us to be excluded from speaking and communicating with God, nor should we be kept from telling of His greatness or from wanting to know of the teachings; and in this lies what should serve as a bridle to curb bold women. I say we should speak and know of the teachings, not that we should teach. I believe the Lord Himself showed Mary Magdalene this point when, after having revealed to her a mystery so high and so necessary to our faith, and having commanded her to be the messenger of this good news to the grieving apostles, He did not allow her to come to Him, saying, "Touch me not." For in this we can see that, although we may be allowed to tell of God's greatness and to help our brothers, it is not ours to pry into mysteries.[30]

Women may announce teaching given to them, after the model of the Magdalene's passing on the news of the resurrection, but they cannot engage in speculative theology; this is the exclusive province of men and any aspiration to that kind of intellectual work is the "touching" prohibited by Christ's *noli me tangere*.[31] Even such a circumscribed vision of women's public ministry, however, proved unacceptable to the church officials in authority over the Spanish Carmelites, as can be seen from the suppression of Salazar's work.

While her convent did not participate in the Teresian reform, the Italian Carmelite mystic Maria Maddalena de' Pazzi (1566–1607) also reflects the influence of Counter-Reformation spirituality—particularly Ignatius of Loyola's *Spiritual Exercises*—in her very visual and impassioned piety. Maria

Maddalena was shaped by the penitential emphasis of the era, but without the challenges to the exercise of her vocation that would face those who attempted a more radical response to reform.[32]

Born into a noble Florentine family, she entered the Convent of Little St. John's of the Knights at fourteen, and then joined the Carmelite Convent of Santa Maria degli Angeli at sixteen. Entering the order of which the Magdalene was patron, Maria Maddalena described the fruits of ascetic withdrawal using Magdalene imagery. Despite her early vocation, her self-understanding was that of an abject sinner, as mired in crimes of the soul and body as the youthful Magdalene. She experienced union with Christ in several visions, often during imagined reenactments of scriptural events, in which she accompanied Christ in his Passion. She constantly used the title of lover or spouse for Christ, adopting the language of the Song of Songs with which the Magdalene had been associated in medieval theology. In parallel with Mary Magdalene's legendary later life in the grotto at Sainte-Baume, Maria Maddalena refused most food and otherwise followed a life of extreme discipline in her pursuit of a spiritual union with God.[33]

The depth of her mystical connection with the divine was such that it could not help but seek expression—the typical justification for women's religious speech or writing in the Catholic Reformation. The ecstatic vision in which she embraced a crucifix implicitly alluded to both the artistic convention of the Magdalene's embrace of the cross at the Crucifixion and the saint's role in carrying the message of the Good News after the resurrection. Her audible cries about the love of God during this vision—the love that we saw emphasized in the writing of Charles Vialart—voiced an irrepressible call to mission. In her recorded conversation, she described a wish to have been a man and so to have been able to evangelize like Francis Xavier, the Jesuit missionary to India and Japan. Her mysticism displayed a decidedly worldly savvy, with a concern for the ecclesiastical issues of her day. Even from the sickbed where she spent most of her life, she actively confronted the threat of Protestantism. She had visions in 1584 and in 1603 of Elizabeth I of England being punished by God for leading souls to hell in continuing that country's apostasy from papal control.[34]

Although Maria Maddalena's spirituality incorporated many of the traditional characteristics of the Magdalene, her self-professed ideal was not her namesake, but the Virgin Mary. The description of the Virgin that she offers, however, also makes reference to both the Magdalene and her sister: "In heaven Mary fills the offices of both Mary and Martha. Like Mary Magdalene she enjoys God; like Martha she intercedes for us."[35] The Virgin Mary exceeds Mary and Martha because she combines both of their virtues, being both contemplative and active, a blessed witness of Christ's suffering, and offering her testimony on behalf of supplicant sinners. Maria Maddalena here voices a desire to reconcile active and contemplative vocations, a desire that was to characterize the piety of nuns in the Catholic Reformation. She achieves a balance by substituting the Virgin Mary as the model of a flexible integration of the two paths.

The Carmelite reform movement spread to France at the beginning of the seventeenth century, bringing with it the Magdalene spirituality developed by Teresa. Pierre de Bérulle, the cardinal who oversaw the introduction of the Discalced Carmelite Order in France, saw the Magdalene as the pattern for prayerful withdrawal from the world that characterized Carmelite life. This apparent emphasis on the cloister is somewhat misleading. The spirituality that flourished among French Carmelites in fact incorporated much of the reconciliation of active and contemplative vocations that Teresa and her followers had pursued with varying success in Spain. Still, the Carmelite ideal of flight from worldly temptation into the cloister remained a compelling image for many women through the end of the seventeenth century. Indeed, it was so attractive that at least one renowned courtesan, from the cohort who had their likenesses painted as sensual, preconversion Magdalenes, was moved to leave behind royal dalliances and settle in a convent. Louise de la Vallière had been Louis XIV's first mistress; she later regretted her position and entered a Carmelite convent for the rest of her life.[36] Given her history, an identification with Mary Magdalene was natural. In her *Réflexions sur la miséricorde de Dieu* (1680), she wrote extensively about the saint. She addressed Christ, begging that he "above all look at me without ceasing as you looked at Mary Magdalene and allow me, like this holy penitent, to wash your feet with my tears, and in attempting to love you much, try to erase the multitude of my crimes." Her personal connection to the Magdalene sprang from her self-understanding as a sexual sinner in parallel with the beautiful and promiscuous young woman who became the beloved saint.[37]

Dramatic conversions and amendments of life could follow from such identifications, producing zealous devotions to Christ that shared the unbridled passion of both the Magdalene's sensuality and her asceticism. These very public conversions then themselves became the models for subsequent imitators, through autobiography or the records made by male confessors. The *Refléxions* includes a section clearly intended to shape the piety of Vallière's readers after the pattern of scriptural examples and, by implication, after her own pattern as well. Reflection 3 is titled, "On the virtues necessary to approach Christ, according to the example of the Canaanite woman, the Samaritan woman, and Mary Magdalene."[38] She prays to Christ, with the three women as mediators: "In the name of these three holy women who, one might say, are still living witnesses of your mercy towards us, and who teach us what must be, in return, our hope in your goodness."[39] For Vallière, what the Magdalene and the other women give witness to is that which they have received: Christ's merciful forgiveness of their sins. They teach other sinful women to hope chiefly by their example; if they can be pardoned and redeemed, so might other prostitutes or mistresses. They teach not by words spoken aloud, but through the mutely eloquent testimony of their changed circumstances. The character of witness displayed in Vallière's writing is one that informed the Carmelite appropriations of the Magdalene that we have explored in Teresa and her followers: it is the witness of a transformed life, in which uniting the individual will to the will of God reconciles the divided nature—divided between sin and virtue, secular and sacred, action and contemplation—of the human person.

Despite the persistence of the penitential, ascetic Magdalene as an attractive model, the central theme that emerges from a survey of Magdalene piety among early modern Catholic nuns is that of reconciliation of Mary and Martha. Women felt the need to maintain their identity as contemplatives even in the midst of everyday tasks, to see mundane or public work as an expression of the passions and guiding of the interior life. Early modern nuns' effort to discern a spirituality of daily work that connected it to contemplation places them closer to Protestant women—and men—than has previously been understood. The concern to find sacred worth in secular vocations, so commonly ascribed to the Protestant reformers, was a direction in which Catholic religious women also sought to reform their own rules of life. They maintained that charitable and teaching work, by their nature often done outside the cloister, were the purest expressions of the contemplative's union with God's will.[40]

Among the most prominent examples of active female vocations are those of the Ursulines, founded by Angela Merici in the early sixteenth century. The new foundations called themselves congregations or societies rather than religious orders because they favored active, public ministries such as teaching, nursing, and charitable work rather than a cloistered vocation. The Ursuline Order in France was started in 1592, with a teaching mandate. Even after the French Ursulines became a formal, enclosed order, the attempt to unite the vocations of Mary and Martha remained. The Ursulines' guidelines for the integration of teaching into convent life assert that they must remain contemplatives on the model of Mary of Bethany: "The sisters . . . will not take charge of more boarders than their regular institute will permit, lest the continual occupation occasioned by these girls . . . should cause them to lose the spirit of Mary, without which they cannot fulfill their vocations with dignity." Laurence Lux-Sterritt has argued that the enclosure of the Ursulines represented the order's understanding that the cloistered, contemplative life was fundamental to the exercise of a public vocation. The Ursulines interpreted an active apostolate as the most demanding, and therefore the highest form of penance. Less self-indulgent than pure contemplation, the "mixed life" of Mary and Martha was seen as a worthy sacrifice to offer to God, a conception not opposed to the Counter-Reformation's emphasis on penitential withdrawal, but situated deep within it, seeking the most rigorous possible retreat, a retreat from God into the world, for God's sake.[41]

An active vocation could offer options for women who could not, for various reasons, join a convent. Marguerite Bourgeoys (1620–1700) was denied entry into an enclosed order—in this case, the Carmelites—and instead pursued the mixed life as a missionary member of a lay confraternity dedicated to education in New France. Because of the very active nature of her work, Bourgeoys found that she was unable to integrate the images of Mary and Martha. In an autobiographical reminiscence, she wrote about how her confessor formed her understanding of possible vocations for women: "Monsieur Gendret once said to me that our Lord had left three states in which women could follow and serve the Church; that of Saint Mary Magdalen was observed by the Carmelites and other recluses, and that of Saint Martha by the cloistered religious who serve their neighbour; but that the outgoing life of the Blessed Virgin was not honoured as it should be, and that even without veil and wimple one could be truly religious." According to Gendret,

Mary Magdalene was clearly and exclusively associated with the cloistered contemplative life, as opposed to the kind of work in the world that Bourgeoys sought for herself and the women she led in Québec as missionaries. In describing the very different vocation of one of her colleagues, Jeanne Le Ber, Bourgeoys associates Le Ber's entry into silent seclusion with the Magdalene's desert retreat: "M. Dollier, vicar general of the diocese and superior of the seminary, conducted her to the room built for this purpose, in the chapel but outside the main part of the house. He spoke to her exhorting her to perseverance. Like St. Magdalene in her grotto, she never went out and she spoke to no one."[42] Like Teresa of Avila and Maria Maddalena de' Pazzi, Bourgeoys herself seemed to be searching for a means of combining the supposedly disparate vocations of activity and contemplation, to be "truly religious" after the manner of a devout contemplative while venturing outside of the constraints of that life in order to perform works of service. There was, for Bourgeoys, a desirable humility in turning away from the rewards and status of a cloistered retreat, to embrace the hard work of mission. Bourgeoys also wrote, in distinguishing the two kinds of life, that "the contemplative life was 'austere,' 'in the deserts.' [This was a clear allusion to the image of Mary Magdalen living as a hermit in her later years, and hence to the Carmelites, whose patron she was.] But it was also the portion of the rich. The 'little life' of hard work and simplicity was 'fitted to the condition of a poor woman.'" The new asceticism proposed here is one that welcomes not only a vow of material poverty, such as had always accompanied the religious life, but the spiritual poverty of the Beatitudes: "Blessed are the poor in spirit, for theirs is the kingdom of Heaven."[43]

Whether this impulse arose out of dissatisfaction with existing religious options in the cloister or emerged to meet a perceived need in the world is difficult to distinguish. Women such as Bourgeoys witnessed the role many convents played in society, as respectable retreats for aristocratic daughters and widows. While formal religious vows and a focus on contemplation offered precisely the challenging, rigorous vocation for which some women longed, Bourgeoys typifies the stories of many women who felt called to work beyond convent walls in education and mission.[44]

Jeanne de Chantal's Visitandines, a religious foundation of the late sixteenth century for laywomen who wished to engage in charitable work, initially identified themselves simply with Martha. They wanted to take the name Filles de Sainte-Marthe, expressing their active vocation. While the Visitandines were envisioned as being free to come and go as their work demanded, they became an enclosed order with formal religious vows in 1618.[45] One means by which their charitable work could continue was through a form of cloistered mission work, through the supervision of a convent for reformed prostitutes, the Filles de la Madeleine. So Martha was finally to get the better of her wayward sister! Though the opposition of identities is suggested by the names associated with the orders, a more nuanced interpretation of roles for the Visitandines eventually emerged. In a letter advising Jeanne, her mentor François de Sales offers counsel similar to Teresa's, pleading that both kinds of life should be possible for every person; to segregate women between actives and contemplatives is inhumane, and contrary to the divine will: "Do you know how I would have wanted to resolve those differences? . . . I would have wanted Saint Martha, our dear patron, to come to the feet of our Lord in the place of her sister, and her sister to have gone off to finish preparing supper; in this way they would have shared the work and the repose like good sisters."[46] Male clergy, too, participated in establishing appropriate models for Counter-Reformation women's orders by renegotiating the dialogue between Mary and Martha.

Women engaged images of a new partnership between Mary and Martha to articulate their sense of call to serve the Counter-Reformation church's mission drives, both at home and abroad. The integration of new vocations in church institutions was a complex process in which women encountered unintended consequences and faced opposition. Their work gave them relative independence and the chance to live the lives to which they felt called, though it also involved them in the exploitative enterprise of colonialism, or perpetuated economic inequality for women. In gaining their own freedom, female missionaries became part of the subjugation of other women, whether indigenous women in the mission fields of the Americas or prostitutes and poor women in European cities. For the most part, women like Marguerite Bourgeoys were arguing for their speech and activity as part of their vocation as Christians rather than making political or social equality their goal. The inequalities of power that female missionaries helped to create supports the conclusion that most early modern women were invested in public evangelism as part of a Christian vocation, not as a modern, feminist project of achieving agency for all women as such. Despite the fact that women's ministries generally supported the church's mission programs, however, new kinds of activity could still be seen as suspect.[47]

Again, the Magdalene provided a ready explanation when women's missionary work seemed to threaten cultural norms. The biographers of female missionaries in the New World often struggled to describe these women in terms that would meet the expectations of their readers. Many of these nuns' lives echoed the active aspects of the Magdalene tradition, as a precedent for female evangelism. Women managed to accomplish impressive feats simply in order to reach the field of their work in the Americas. Both Marie de St-Joseph and Catherine de St-Augustin, for example, had contemporary biographies that described their dangerous sea crossings on the way to mission work— surely evoking, for many in the seventeenth century, Mary Magdalene's legendary sea journey to pagan France.[48]

In Europe, parishioners could see and assess for themselves new models of women's mission activity in aid of the Counter-Reformation. Accounts of Ursuline teachers resemble the medieval legends of Mary Magdalene converting pagans in Marseilles, to the point of including conflicts with local officials, though those are now not pagan priests but Catholic aristocrats: "Anne de Vesvres went like a missionary from village to village. . . . 'She even reproved the local nobility for their injustices and frankly told them that they were offending God.' The crowds that gathered around her, 'both men and women,' were so great that she sometimes simply sat down on the ground, and taught them as the Spirit dictated." The overwhelming crowds and her directness of approach to them recall not only the medieval Magdalene legend but the descriptions of Christ himself preaching in the Gospels. Similar is the story of Geneviève Fayet, a laywoman who catechized French villagers and recorded an instance of her own public speaking "in the presence of their priest and at least one hundred people." Like Marguerite Bourgeoys, Fayet was a member of a confraternity, in this case the Dames de la Charité; their examples indicate that some lay Catholic women did take up a public teaching ministry. Fayet's teaching produced such devotion that it inspired one priest to express his wish "to be able to end his days near me . . . just to listen to the words that would come from my lips," again alluding to the posture of the Magdalene listening at Christ's feet, but this time with a female speaker in the place of Christ, and a male listener. Fayet and the biographer of Anne de Vesvres used these allusions to assert the popularity of their messages, arguing for legitimacy through appeals to scripture and to early church models. Contemporary comparisons were even made between Ursulines and male preachers, including John the Baptist and Paul.[49]

Such direct endorsements of female preaching could prove problematic, and they existed alongside more cautious statements about women's roles. The rule of life developed for the Ursuline congregations in Paris warned that "Ursulines should instruct visitors without seeming to preach." Claude Martin, son and biographer of Marie de l'Incarnation, a missionary in Canada, defended her ministry by arguing that she was not an apostle herself, but rather a euphemistically termed, "apostolic woman" who supported male apostles through her prayer.[50] These efforts were part of a public demonstration of placing constraints on women's ministry, a feature of Catholic rhetoric noted earlier. Though this rhetorical posture may not always have been tied to the actual disruption of women's church work, it was, nevertheless, a factor with which women had to contend. In Paris, Barbe Acarie, a prominent laywoman who had founded the Discalced Carmelite order in France, "was reproved from the pulpit for neglecting her responsibilities as a wife and mother,"[51] a public counterargument to Teresa's claim that a woman could perform the duties of Martha while pursuing the contemplation of Mary. Teresa herself had faced opposition to her work; other women were likewise vulnerable to rebuke for seeking an improperly public and active role. Mère Perrette de Bermond, an Ursuline who preached and taught in Moulins, was celebrated by her male biographer for her "unusual activity," but he also praised the male superiors who eventually stopped her.[52]

Women themselves recognized the apostolic nature of the work of teaching, and took different positions on how and when that mission could be accomplished by female voices. Some demonstrated ambivalence about their right to engage in it, an ambivalence born perhaps out of their own sense of themselves as women, but just as much arising from a conviction of humility. Marie Barbier, a schoolmistress in Montréal, was to write about teaching, "It is a sublime employment, worthy of the apostles; it is the continuation of the work of the Saviour; I have never performed it without fear and confusion."[53]

Women's public ministry was viewed ambiguously in the Catholic Reformation, feared as threatening and unorthodox, yet also recognized as valuable work that helped individuals, communities, and institutions. The mixed life of Mary and Martha contributed to the vitality of early modern

Catholicism, becoming an indispensable part of the network of social care and education in Catholic regions. Language that mitigated the appearance of radical change—couching the women's work carefully in terms of teaching, rather than preaching, and emphasizing female humility—helped make new vocations for women acceptable to their society.

The posture of humility is common to both Catholic and Protestant women in defending their ministry. The same strategy is evident in the art produced by early modern Catholic women. Following the Council of Trent, which had established a strongly directive program of pedagogical goals for religious art, artistic decisions were made based on a complex calculus of aesthetic and doctrinal considerations.[54] An examination of women's connection to Mary Magdalene as artists and as patrons will therefore provide important insights into how early modern Catholic women navigated institutional circumstances, coming to understand themselves as religious subjects.

Artists and Scholars: "He Whom My Soul Seeks"

Identifications with Mary Magdalene are abundant in the work of female spiritual writers and monastic reformers of the Counter-Reformation; such self-comparisons went a step further in the artistic production of women who authored poetry, plays, and music, and created visual art in which they could become new incarnations of the Magdalene—not just as a contemplative exercise, but before an audience. In the case of dramatic productions and musical compositions, women actually performed as the saint herself, taking on her persona but, more than that, speaking their own words with her authority. Plays about the saint's life, written by nuns, were a common feature in celebrations of the feast of Mary Magdalene at convents such as San Guglielmo in Bologna, for example. In the context of the cloister, women could shape an environment of Magdalene piety in which they encouraged each other's vocations by regularly enacting her story in their communities.[55]

This kind of dramatic self-identification was actively cultivated by Federico Borromeo, one of the most important patrons of convent music and of female composers in the Counter-Reformation era. The Milanese cardinal encouraged Magdalene piety in his correspondence with nuns.[56] Borromeo's letter 30 tells the reader that the intimacy of her relationship with Christ makes the Magdalene, and therefore the contemporary nun, a true disciple: "So then, you should do the office of the sweetest disciple Magdalene, who was a disciple of Christ. . . . Oh true disciple at what hour would you think to go? [This is a reference to the Magdalene's visit to the tomb at dawn.] I will pray that you be the most devoted to the Magdalene, because in love she can be the mistress of all souls. . . . Yet take for your advocate this Magdalene, because she is the sweetest and greatest, resting in peace with the contemplatives."[57] The title of disciple was again applied to the Magdalene and her imitators in letter 83: "The thought has come to me of calling you by the . . . name of disciple . . . of this great disciple, Magdalene, who so loved the Savior."[58] In letter 15, written for her feast day, the reason for her discipleship is made clear, using language drawn from the Gospel text for the feast, Luke 7:47; she is the same woman who was forgiven at the house of Simon the Pharisee: "This is the feast of the Magdalene, who was a disciple of love, and was so because she loved much." (Quel giorno è proprio della Madalena, che fu discepola dell'amore, et fu quella, che dilexit multum.) Borromeo also draws on the medieval legend for his Magdalene imagery. In letter 10, he writes about the saint being lifted up by the angels in the daily ravishing she was said to have experienced during her desert sojourn.[59]

His encouragement worked. Borromeo's female monastic correspondents frequently referred to themselves in their letters as the bride from the Song of Songs, adopting the imagery from the motet repertory of the convent choirs on his explicit recommendation.[60] Borromeo's spiritual direction inspired one of his female correspondents, Suor Aurelia Maria at the Convent of Santa Caterina, Brera, to write,

> Bitterly I prayed my Lord, with humility, that He would reveal to me what He wanted of me . . . and I seemed to hear an inner voice which said, "Why are you crying, my daughter?" and this made me break out in greater tears than before; and I saw St. Mary Magdalene, when she mourned at the Tomb, and the Lord asked her, "Woman, why are you mourning?" and she responded, "They have taken away my Lord and I don't know where they put him; if you took Him, tell me and I will take Him." And that is how my soul could respond, and it did; namely, I find myself without, deprived of my Lord's presence, and I don't know why.[61]

Aurelia Maria compares her own sorrowful weeping to that of the mourning Magdalene at the tomb. The shared grief makes possible a parallel dialogue with Christ, even as it arises from a sense of despairing absence. The language she uses was likely suggested by Federico's own application of the Magdalene as a model, but it also draws on the nuns' musical environment. Contemporary motets featuring Mary Magdalene included *Dic nobis, Maria,* published by Agostino Soderini in 1598, in which the disciples ask the Magdalene what she has seen of the risen Christ.[62] Published in the same year, Giuseppe Gallo's *Sacer opus musici . . . liber primus,* contained a "Dialogue of the Angels with the Women [at the tomb]."[63]

Milanese nuns were not only surrounded by music and guided by clergy describing the life of the Magdalene; they also hymned her in their own words. In 1650 Chiara Margarita Cozzolani composed a motet dialogue on the Magdalene at the empty tomb. Cozzolani (1602–c. 1676) was part of the second generation of nuns under the leadership of Federico Borromeo. She was from a wealthy family, served as abbess and prioress of her convent, and composed and published choral music between 1640 and 1650. Her Easter motet, *Maria Magdalene Stabat,* gives the Magdalene a detailed role, embellishing on the material from the scriptures. The added material combines the Gospel dialogue with the angels and quotations from the Song of Songs as Cozzolani's Magdalene speaks of and to "her beloved,"[64] Christ:

> Mary Magdalene stood at the tomb, mourning; as she wept, she turned to the tomb, and saw two angels in white sitting there, and said to them:
> "Have you seen him whom my soul seeks? . . . My beloved is white and ruddy, chosen among thousands. . . . My beloved, my love is beautiful among the sons of men. He is the crucified Jesus. O my light, where are you? O my love, where are you? O my life, where are you? Come, my beloved, come, for I languish for your love, come, for I am dying for your love."[65]

Dramatic and vocal performance was one way in which Catholic women were permitted to engage with biblical texts directly, and to do a certain amount of interpretive work: linking different passages and characters to each other, and developing prosopopoeia that fostered their audience's experience of these ancient stories as their own.

Just as it is possible to find examples of a vigorous Magdalene piety among nuns reflecting artistically on their own spiritual lives, there is also evidence of secular female artists applying Magdalene imagery to help create images and worship spaces that would express the concerns of women's lives to the broader community. In Italy, the painter Artemisia Gentileschi may well have identified the Magdalene's tragic sexual history with her own experience as a rape victim.[66] Her *Penitent Mary Magdalene* (1615–1620), commissioned by the Grand Duchess Maria Maddalena of Florence, vividly portrays the psychological torment of the saint's suffering. The English noblewoman Helena Wintour embroidered vestments for Catholic priests in the mid-seventeenth century, linking the activity of the Magdalene to the liturgical roles of the male clergy. Her work uses garden imagery suggestive of both the garden in which Christ appeared to Mary Magdalene and the lovers' bower in the Song of Songs.[67] The man celebrating the Eucharist, clothed in visual references to Eden and Gethsemane and to the Magdalene's gardens, enacted within himself the Fall and redemption of humanity, which would have reminded the assembled congregation of themselves as the sinful, yet forgiven, woman in the garden, the Magdalene as everywoman. Through drama, music, and material objects, women surrounded themselves with Magdalene imagery that inspired and supported their vocations. While the environment of secular women was oriented toward different goals, they, too, produced work that reflected on the various aspects of the Magdalene legacy through two centuries of Catholic reform.

The Italian poet and humanist scholar Vittoria Colonna (1490–1547) represents a transitional figure, a noblewoman who lived a privileged life at the opening of the early modern period. Not bound by religious vows, and widowed early, she was able to experiment with theological innovation relatively free of institutional constraints. An almost exact contemporary of Luther's, her life coincided with the very beginning of the church's reaction to his reform, though she died just as the official response was being developed at the opening sessions of the Council of Trent. Her interpretation of the Magdalene can inform us about how the saint was being discussed in the evangelical-leaning circles that existed in early modern Catholicism before Trent. Alongside her interest in reform, Colonna was active in traditional practices of the Magdalene cult: she was involved with the reform of prostitutes through the Convent of the Convertite in Rome, and planned a trip, even applying for and receiving papal permission, to visit the saint's pilgrimage site in Provence. As a woman of means, Colonna also patronized the arts with the saint in mind, collecting Magdalene images through the 1530s, perhaps with the intention of decorating a chapel.[68]

So unusually renowned was Colonna for her learning and creative ability that her correspondence was published in 1544, the first collection of letters by a woman to be published during her own lifetime.[69] In a letter to her aunt, Constanza D'Avalos Piccolomini, Duchess of Amalfi, Colonna offers the Magdalene as a model in giving spiritual counsel, indicating that the saint is, in her estimation, to be ranked with Paul and Augustine as among the great religious guides: "When you already feel that earthly weights drag you back . . . pause a while with my most observant father Paul, or with my great luminary Augustine, or with my most ardent servant Mary Magdalene."[70] Another letter published in the same collection discusses Mary Magdalene and St. Catherine of Alexandria, comparing their public, prophetic roles: "Both of them through their passionate, wise, and sweet words I see converting queens with their kingdoms and a huge number of people." Here Colonna uses an evangelical interpretation of preaching as speech that leads to conversion, a definition that could embrace women's work for the church even without trespassing on the office of the clergy. Colonna's interpretation of the saint combined a focus on her eloquent preaching with an emphasis on her great love for Christ and intimacy with him, which led to her selection as the first witness of the resurrection.[71]

This ability to hold multiple images of the Magdalene together, to join an evangelical interest in the Magdalene as a preacher to a more Catholic attention to her character as Christ's beloved, may be traced to Colonna's location as a Protestant sympathizer who remained loyal to the Catholic tradition; she was one of the leaders of the Nicodemite group in Renaissance Italy that included Michelangelo. Colonna's spiritual director was Bernardino Ochino, a famous convert to Protestantism, whose preaching on Mary Magdalene inspired Colonna's sonnet "Donna acessa animosa, e da l'errante." In a letter from 1544, Colonna compares both herself and her male correspondent, Cardinal Giovanni Morone, himself imprisoned for three years on suspicion of Lutheranism, to Mary Magdalene. She excuses herself for writing so boldly by asking Christ's forgiveness for her words, as he forgave the Magdalene. Colonna then observes that the cardinal "would probably have preferred a life of

FIG 5.1 Artemisia Gentileschi, *Penitent Mary Magdalene*, c. 1616. Oil on canvas. Photo: Galleria Palatina, Palazzo Pitti, Florence / Scala / Art Resource, NY.

contemplation and retreat, but that he was compelled by Christ to actively serve his brothers, as the Magdalene did."[72]

Colonna's contemporaries also associated her with the saint. She was described in a 1543 publication as a disciple of Ochino, just as Mary Magdalene was a disciple of Christ. Colonna commissioned a noli me tangere painting from Michelangelo, with herself as the model for the Magdalene.[73] In her "Spiritual Poem No. 8," Colonna described the scene:

> Seized in her sadness by that great desire
> which banishes all fear, this beautiful woman,
> all alone, by night, helpless, humble, pure,
> and armed only with a living, burning hope.
> Entered the sepulcher and wept and lamented;
> Ignoring the angels, caring nothing for herself,
> She fell at the feet of the Lord, secure,
> For her heart, aflame with love, feared nothing.
> And the men, chosen to share so many graces,
> Though strong, were shut up together in fear;
> The true Light seemed to them only a shadow.
> If, then, the true is not a friend to the false,
> We must give to women all due recognition
> For having a more loving and more constant heart.[74]

She draws on the traditional comparison between the loyal woman and the fearful male disciples but extends the Magdalene's womanly devotion to all her sex, pleading for recognition of the faith of women, particularly in the strength of its affection.[75] Here Colonna prefigures the arguments of seventeenth-century Quakers such as Margaret Fox, who would claim women's right to preach publicly because of the Magdalene's female compassion and courage. Neither Colonna nor Fox made such claims out of a belief purely in their own inherent value as persons, but as sinners redeemed by divine grace, the model for which they found in Mary Magdalene. The "recognition" due to women was not an end in itself, but a move in the reform of Christianity that replaced doctrine with loving and constant hearts—that is, with the faith of the ordinary believer. These examples testify that appreciation of the worth of women did not arise only out of the secular philosophical traditions of modernity, but owes a debt to the earlier devotional discourse of the era of Catholic and Protestant reform, which was often expressed in self-identifications with the woman whom Christ had chosen as both friend and messenger.

Some female authors did adapt the Magdalene to provide arguments for explicitly feminist goals. The French philosopher and author Marie le Jars de Gournay (who had produced editions of Michel de Montaigne and Latin classics) celebrated the Magdalene as a hopeful precedent for women's public speech. She deployed the saint in her treatise "Egalité des hommes et des femmes" (1622), arguing against the exclusion of women from the priesthood. Gournay appealed specifically to the saint's medieval title of *apostola apostolorum*, identifying a surviving reference to her as such in the Eastern Orthodox liturgy. In a passage addressing Paul's prohibition on women's speech from 1 Corinthians 14, Gournay notes exceptional women, from the scriptural Phoebe to the legendary daughter of St. Peter, who had held public roles in the church. In her catalog she includes Mary Magdalene as perhaps the greatest of such exceptions: "And so also the Magdalene is called in the Church 'Equal to the Apostles'—*par apostolis*. [Marginal note: "Among others, in the Greek liturgical calendar, published by Génebrard."] See how they themselves and the Church permitted an exception to this rule of silence for her who preached for thirty years in La-Baume-de-Marseilles, according to all of Provence."[76] Gournay takes up the Magdalene's legendary preaching career, which had moved to the background in many seventeenth-century iterations of the saint's life. She locates Mary Magdalene within the tradition of female prophets, beginning with the Sibyls, and explicitly defines their speech as preaching. She links two of the Magdalene's scriptural identities, as Mary of Bethany who anointed Jesus and as first witness of the resurrection: "Let us add that Mary Magdalene was the only one to whom the Redeemer said the following words and promised this most magnificent favour: 'They will talk about you in every place where the Gospel is preached.' Besides, Jesus Christ declared his most joyful and glorious resurrection in the first instance to ladies, so as to make them apostles of the original apostles . . . and, as we know, with a definite mission." Making her argument for an active ministry for women from outside the confines of the church hierarchy, Gournay clearly had greater freedom to explore images of female activity without wrestling with the requirements of silence and humility, than did avowed religious women.[77]

Though Gournay may have achieved such freedom, other female writers still often faced opposition to their public testimony of faith. Descriptions of an experience of union with Christ could create official suspicion, as hap-· pened to Jeanne Guyon (1648–1717). Guyon, who was born into a wealthy family, had wanted to become a nun but was married off by her parents at a young age. A celebrated beauty in court society, she wrote that following her marriage she had been "tempted by the worldly life of Paris." Influenced by François de Sales's *Introduction to the Devout Life,* she wrote her own devotional manual, *A Short and Easy Method of Prayer.* As with Teresa of Avila and Maria Maddalena de' Pazzi, part of Guyon's religious enthusiasm was directly inspired by the confrontation with Protestantism.[78]

The two primary spiritual turning points in her life both occurred on the Feast of the Magdalene, and her interpretations of those events feature language connecting herself with the saint and the bride in the Song of Songs. In the vision from July 22, 1676, she experienced a spiritual marriage to Christ in which she saw herself as his spouse, united to him in suffering.[79] The dowry of this marriage was "crosses, scorn, confusion, opposition, ignominy. . . . These words were first placed in my mind, that he would be 'a bridegroom of blood.' Since then he has taken me so strongly as his own, that he has perfectly consecrated my body and my mind unto himself by the cross."[80] On July 22, 1680, she experienced another feeling of unity with God, but this time in joy, with a profound sense of the forgiveness of sins and newness of life. After the death of her husband, Guyon entered the Ursuline convent at Thonon in 1682, then began to practice automatic writing, feeling that in this state she was communicating as God's "instrument." The church was critical of her writing, particularly of the claims about mystical experience, which was perceived as dangerously idiosyncratic by contrast with participation in the church's sacramental program. The medieval conflict between the orthodoxy of Peter and the prophecy of Mary Magdalene persisted into the early modern period as a suspicion of women's intimate, personal encounters with the divine in mystical visions. Guyon was tried for heresy and imprisoned for the final years of her life. As such, her work has had little influence in the Catholic tradition, but she was celebrated among Pietists, both during her lifetime and since, for an interior spirituality that they found sympathetic to their theology. Only her commentary on the Song of Songs was published while she lived, though her poetry was published posthumously and cherished by

Protestants—especially those of the Radical Reformation traditions. Like the work of María de San José Salazar, then, Guyon's interpretation of the Magdalene must remain a record of possibility that she strove to sustain for the future of the tradition rather than a representation of popular Catholic piety or a vocation that was recognized and praised by her contemporaries.[81]

Other women's vocations could not help but be recognized when they were expressed in service to a worldly call in a prominent and public role, as in the case of noblewomen whose education and responsibilities meant that they read and wrote with greater freedom than the majority of women. Still, these unusual instances of female leadership had to be justified, typically by connecting these women's authority to that of revered figures from scripture or the classical tradition. Many women in the context of court life—especially those who ruled their territories as regents—took Mary Magdalene as their personal patroness.

Women in Power: "Her Name and Her Virtue"

Abstracted spirit, rapt in ecstasy,
Who while you haunt the skies, your origin,
Have left your servant host as you roam free,
Your well-matched body—quick to discipline,
Heeding you, for this pilgrim's life we're in—
Sans sentiment, and to emotion slow;
Wouldn't you care for just a while to go
Out of the heavenly manor where you dwell?[82]

A sixteenth-century reader could have been forgiven for thinking this a prayer to Mary Magdalene in her legendary, austere exile in Southern France, when she was taken up into the clouds each day by angels for the Eucharistic nourishment that was her only food. It was, however, François Rabelais's dedication of the third book of his *Gargantua and Pantagruel* (1546) to Marguerite de Navarre. Known as a supporter of Protestants within her sphere of influence in France, Marguerite had been the subject of a similar literary comparison before, though less favorably. A play produced by students at the Collège de Navarre in 1533 mocked Marguerite as abandoning proper female pursuits for the anarchy of Luther's new teaching. She was, in their eyes, "a Queen who, in womanly fashion, was taken up with spinning, and wholly occupied with the rock (distaff) and the needle; then the fury Maegera appeared, bringing lighted torches near to her that she might throw away the rock and the needle. For a little while she opposed and struggled; but when she had yielded, she received the Gospel into her hand, and straightway forgets all she had formerly got into the habit of, and almost even herself."[83] In both texts, Marguerite is a woman so involved in her study of theology and scripture that she has left behind her duties as woman and as queen. The student agitators had found this contemptible, while Rabelais implored her to return from her musings and continue her public championing of humanism and religious toleration by reading his book.

However divisive Marguerite's actions may have been, the Christian tradition's model for such behavior in a woman, whose story Rabelais alludes to, was Mary Magdalene. How had the sister of the King of France come to be linked with such a controversial figure? Like the Magdalene, Marguerite had indeed sat at the feet of her religious and intellectual mentors, having received a humanist education at the direction of her mother, Louise of Savoy. The saint and her controversial roles played a part in shaping that education. The works of Christine de Pizan, the fifteenth-century author who had argued for the preaching and teaching of women using the example of Mary Magdalene, were included in Marguerite's childhood library. In 1515–1516, Marguerite, her mother, and Queen Claude (wife of Marguerite's brother, Francis I) went on a pilgrimage to the center of the Magdalene's cult, Saint-Maximin-la-Sainte-Baume in Marseilles, making gifts to support the shrine. The visit inspired Louise to commission her son's tutor, François de Moulins, to write a life of the saint, the *Vie de la Magdaleine,* on which he consulted with the eminent humanist scholar Jacques Lefèvre d'Étaples. It was this consultation that led Lefèvre d'Étaples to his own inquiry about the identity of the Magdalene, resulting in his 1519 tract rejecting her medieval legend as false and unscriptural, a characterization that would be taken up by Reformation polemicists. Through the war of words that followed, including the placing of Lefèvre d'Étaples's works on the Inquisition's list of forbidden books and his denunciation by the theology faculty of the University of Paris, he found protection and employment with Marguerite and her family. She secured him the position of tutor to her brother's children, then housed him at her court in Nérac during his retirement and until his death.[84]

Lefèvre d'Étaples was not the only reformer to benefit from Marguerite's interest and influence. She maintained a correspondence with the leader of Lefèvre's circle of reform-minded humanist scholars, Guillaume Briçonnet, the bishop of Meaux, who served as her spiritual adviser from 1521 to 1524. As a result of her relationship with this group and its ideas, Marguerite sent evangelical preachers to Berry, the territory she ruled following her appointment as duke-peer in 1517. Her creation as Duchess of Berry in her own right, by her brother Francis I, gave her the political status of an "honorary man," a parallel to the Magdalene's public activity, which had been so unusual for a woman in late antiquity. As a public advocate for religious causes, Marguerite followed the Magdalene's model of testimony to the Gospel in her role as first witness and preacher of the resurrection, as well as her material support of the ministry of Christ and his disciples. She sheltered John Calvin on his flight from France in 1534. Calvin's fellow evangelical exile in Geneva, Marie Dentière, solicited Marguerite's patronage for further reform in her 1539 treatise, proclaiming women's right to preach and teach in public and appealing to the Magdalene as an exemplar.[85]

Despite her manifest commitment to many of the ideas of the Reformation, Marguerite herself never converted from Catholicism, determined instead to reform the church from within. Her ambitious program included vernacular biblical translation and charitable works, as well as correcting the abuses of monasticism. Her efforts did not escape censure, however, as we have seen. In addition to the student protests, she was condemned by the theology faculty of the University of Paris in 1533 for the ideas espoused in her devotional work, *Mirror of a Sinful Soul*.[86]

Marguerite de Navarre's biography and career suggested the comparison with Mary Magdalene to her contemporaries, to François Rabelais and Marie Dentière, who both invoked the saint in connection to discussions of female religious leadership. Other aspects of the likeness were explored as well. Another derisive theatrical portrayal, this time by Parisian students, had mocked her as possessed by demons, one of the descriptions of the Magdalene's condition, from which she was said to have been released by Christ. The group of humanist reformers at Meaux with which Marguerite was associated referred to the Gospel as "le seul necessaire," the one thing necessary, alluding to Christ's praise in Luke 10:42 for Mary's devotion to him. As a humanist scholar herself and the author of devotional poetry and prose, Marguerite displayed the intimacy with Christ as the incarnate word of God that had characterized the Magdalene of medieval legend.[87]

Given these parallels, some of them displaying a self-conscious orientation toward Magdalene piety on the part of Marguerite and her associates, it is interesting to examine the references to the saint that Marguerite makes in her own writing. The Magdalene appears in the moral at the end of story 19 in Marguerite's *Heptaméron,* a collection of moral fables on the pattern of Giovanni Boccaccio's *Decameron.* Concluding the saga of a pair of star-crossed lovers who both enter the religious life, Marguerite writes, "Thenceforward Pauline and her lover lived such holy and devout lives, observing all the rules of their order, that we cannot doubt that He whose law is love told them when their lives were ended, as He had told Mary Magdalene, 'Your sins are forgiven, for ye have loved much'; and doubtless He removed them in peace to that place where the recompense surpasses all the merits of man." The celibate, monastic life is praised as providing the solution to the lovers' unhappy circumstances and their faithfulness in pursuing it guarantees them a place in heaven as reward for their labors. If Marguerite may be said to have had a foot in both evangelical and Catholic camps, this Magdalene reference displays her loyalty to elements of Catholic tradition, with reform meaning simply a purification of that tradition.[88]

Elsewhere in the *Heptaméron,* glimpses of a more evangelical adaptation of the Magdalene tradition can be seen. Marguerite gives an account of an unfaithful wife who is made to do penance by being locked in a room with her lover's skeleton, forced to drink from his skull. A painting that is made of her likeness then moves viewers with the image of her beauty and penitence. An intimate and penitential interaction with human remains, like the saints' relics venerated in medieval piety, is presented here to harrowing and perhaps critical effect, though the woman and her penitence still emerge as inspiring and exemplary. The allusions to Mary Magdalene in the female protagonist serve as a positive image of penitence, while distancing the saint from cult practice that the author viewed as harmful. The story is told within the framing narrative of the *Heptaméron* by Oisille, a devout widow commonly thought to represent Louise de Savoy, whose special devotion to the Magdalene had led to the humanist investigation of her identity.[89]

A more overtly evangelical message is found in the discussion of the Magdalene herself that follows between the characters in the framing narrative that links the morality fables. Ennasuite compares the unfaithful wife to Mary Magdalene, and receives the following response:

"How could you make up for such loss of honor?" said Longarine. "Don't you know that nothing a woman can do after such a crime can ever restore her honor?" To which Ennasuite replied, "Tell me, I beg you, whether the Magdalene does or does not have more honor amongst men than her sister, who was a virgin?" "I admit," said Longarine, "that she is praised for her great love for Jesus Christ and for her great penitence, but even so she is still given the name of *Sinner*." "I don't care," said Ennasuite, "what names men call me, only that God pardons me."[90]

The emphasis here is on God's gracious forgiveness, which overcomes the saint's dubious reputation. The idea of an insurmountable stain of sexual sin for women is rejected, as is the medieval hierarchy of virtue that values virginity as the highest ideal of Christian life.[91]

The Magdalene's role in the New Testament resurrection narrative is the sole subject of a poem Marguerite dedicated to her brother the king. Titled "The Faith of the Magdalene," the poem responds to Francis's own, "Do Not Blame Love That Errs Through Ignorance." Expressing a strongly evangelical position, Marguerite disputes the traditional value of the Magdalene's renowned love, noting the impotence of a love that lacks faith:

Love without faith makes the Magdalene weep.
For faith, seeking something in our God
More sovereign than humanity
Scarce permits such great sorrow to hold sway
Because of the loss of a body, when it is certain
That he has risen for us from death.
The ignorance of this truth
Makes her feel an unbelievable pang.
It is love that drives her to such blindness
That we see her forgetting the divinity
To go no farther than the human nature [of Christ].
O beggar love, and vain hope,

It is you who treat her with such great miserliness
Faith gives her the source and the spring,
And you make [her] go out ceaselessly
Looking for water, in her faithlessness,
Amid a torrent. But this love
Which blinds faith is neither praiseworthy nor sound.
For, possessing all things, it still stands in need.[92]

The Magdalene of the poem is a pathetic figure, disabled by human love and grief when she should trust in the abundant revelation of God's nature and purpose. We will see Calvin interpret the saint in very similar terms, rejecting a religion of sentiment in favor of an intellectual assent of faith.

For Marguerite, Mary Magdalene was a figure that allowed her to explore the questions that activated her, from the reform of monasticism to the nature of redemption, with a special focus on female religious experience. The multiple identities of the saint made her a flexible model for several different kinds of investigation, not limited to one particular theological orientation or spiritual goal. Like Vittoria Colonna, Marguerite incorporated elements of both Catholic and Protestant theology in her life and writing. In the first years of the era of reform, this kind of religious inquiry, seemingly not limited by an exclusive loyalty to one confession or the other, was possible especially for women at elite levels of society. Women's faith commitments could be less politically fraught than those of their male counterparts, especially as rulers' religious affiliations were tied to the religious identity of their territories, following the Peace of Augsburg. Thus, wealthy and aristocratic women could pursue a certain amount of theological experimentation with fewer risks than men would have run—the exception being those women who held positions of great power, such as Mary I and Elizabeth I of England, whose faith had to be less equivocal and more guarded. As the age of reform went on, other noblewomen negotiated their own positions of authority amid polemical debates over confessional boundaries and more personal reflections on the life and practice of faith; for them the Magdalene would also provide a compelling and malleable image. Though these women faced public duties, it was not always the vocal, preaching Magdalene who inspired them.[93]

Women in positions of power, paradoxically, often found the penitential, contemplative image of the Magdalene most appealing. The medieval tradition's connection between the Magdalene and sacred retreat endured throughout the early modern period; it was allegorized in a seventeenth-century French devotional work, Antoine de Nervèze's *L'Hermitage de l'Isle saincte* (1612), in which the Magdalene's body itself, which had shared in Christ's physical suffering, became the hermitage into which the reader could retreat. So prevalent did the Magdalene's association with ascetic withdrawal become for the laity that a fashion arose for aristocratic retreats located in lonely and wild places, known as Magdalene cells, a phenomenon which persisted in southern Germany as late as the early eighteenth century, at Rastatt and Nymphenburg. The same saint who led world-weary rulers into the wilderness, however, could also accompany them on the journey back. The legendary Magdalene of the desert continued to be adapted by women in positions of political leadership as a provider of spiritual solace for a woman forced into society at need.[94]

Following the examples of Louise of Savoy and Marguerite de Navarre, the precedent of a special relationship between the Magdalene and French female leaders influenced regent queens through the seventeenth century. French ruling houses were especially likely to associate themselves with the Magdalene because of her legendary conversion of the pagan king in Provence, drawing on the traditional connection between the Magdalene and the House of Burgundy for both political and personal reasons, but the association persisted even after the transition from the Valois to the Bourbon dynasties. Marie de' Medici donated a chapel with a decorative scheme depicting the penitent Magdalene to the Carmelite Order in Paris in 1611. And in the mid-seventeenth century, Anne of Austria commissioned decoration from Philippe de Champaigne for her suite at the Abbey of Val-de-Grâce when she retired there following the end of her own responsibilities as French regent. The dominant elements of the interior are a painting of Mary Magdalene paired with a depiction of the assumption of the Virgin Mary. Both portray images of female escape from the world into the life of the spirit, symbolizing Anne's desired retreat from the demands of court life.[95]

Mary Magdalene's retreat from the world, from the sorrowful city into the joyful garden where she found an ecstatic intimacy with Christ, served as a model for contemplation in the secular context across Europe, demonstrating the ubiquity of the saint in the life and work of the laity as well as in religious life, and in the creativity with which her multiple identities were used to meet the needs of women's particular circumstances. Among the Italian nobility, one early example of this practice is found in the life of Ludovica Torelli, Countess of Guastalla. Widowed in 1527 and ruling for over forty years in her own right (she had no children), she felt called to deepen her spiritual life and took the Magdalene as her pattern of perfect conversion, engaging in contemplative prayer at her court and working with a confessor to shape a life of holy hermitage. She founded a secular school for girls, the Collegio della Guastalla, in Milan.[96]

Mary Magdalene's contemplative, penitential image was also used in support of the regency of Archduchess Maria Maddalena in Florence at the turn of the seventeenth century. The association suggested by her name may well have played a part in fostering the archduchess's devotion to the Magdalene, who was the saint most featured in art of her patronage. In addition to Artemisia Gentileschi's *Penitent Magdalene,* the archduchess commissioned a painting cycle of the saint's life for her private chapel at Poggio Imperiale, and her villa contained more than twenty-five other paintings of the subject. Joining in the trend of aristocratic portraiture in the guise of the Magdalene, Maria Maddalena had herself painted as the saint by Justus Sustermans around 1625–1630. In the painting she appears with all of the typical Baroque iconography: her hair down, hands clasped and gaze directed soulfully upward, the ointment jar at her feet, a cross in the background, and a memento mori skull next to her, though the tone of the painting suggests not so much sensuality as a spiritual longing. The duchess and her family celebrated the Feast of the Magdalene each year with a Mass followed by a ceremonial dinner and the performance of a play about the saint.[97] Riccardo Riccardi's *Conversione di Santa Maria Maddalena* had been written to form part of the festivities for the marriage between Maria Maddalena and Cosimo de' Medici in 1608. A surviving manuscript version of the play contains the following stanza:

> And here, to the new goddess of Florence,
> Whence she is happy and serene,
> O gracious Astraea of Austria and Graz [the birthplace of Maria Maddalena],
> I want to reenact, on this humble stage,
> The lofty conversion of the Magdalen;
> Of your Magdalen, whom you so honor,
> For her name and her virtue adorn you.[98]

The action of the play focuses on the penitent, weeping Magdalene in her grotto. The identity of Mary Magdalene that was valued by the archduchess, it seems, was not the public preacher boldly carrying the Gospel around the Mediterranean world, but the impassioned soul yearning for Christ.[99]

In none of these royal examples does the Magdalene's identity as a prostitute receive emphasis, and her preaching career is also not of apparent interest. In all cases, her heavenly intimacy with Christ promises relief from the rigors of a political career. That intimacy also lent a holiness that gave authority to women who would not ordinarily have held positions of such responsibility. Women in power adopted the Magdalene as their patron with a pragmatic understanding of the safest and most useful aspect of her identity: a devout soul who would never seek power on her own initiative, whose very reluctance for public life made her a trustworthy ruler.

THE MAGDALENES that emerged from women's writing, artistic production, and patronage in early modern Catholicism testify to both the possibilities and the challenges for women's vocations during a creative and turbulent era. A rich variety of Magdalene images were adapted to meet the needs perceived by women in their spiritual lives. As women negotiated their place within the Counter-Reformation's religious culture, they most often turned to the relationship between Mary and Martha to assert the necessity of an active expression for a contemplative vocation. This was a negotiation difficult but rewarding, between the demands and expectations of institutional life and the ineffable call of the spirit. Women such as Teresa of Avila insisted, when they praised the contemplative Magdalene, that she must represent one part of a whole life, reconciled with her more pragmatic sister to achieve the will of God in the self and for the world.

Alongside this innovation, with its effect on the institutions of religious life, charity, and education, evidence exists for the continued presence of the preaching Magdalene from the resurrection narrative. She was celebrated among early feminist authors and Protestant sympathizers but was also a model for religious women discerning their identity as bearers of the incarnate Word, through long-standing expressions of the contemplative life such as prayer and music.[100]

The penitent Magdalene also remained a central focus of devotion, from spiritual writers contemplating human sinfulness to secular leaders seeking an escape from the press of worldly responsibility—and who may have found their positions strengthened by a posture of preferring her humility. There is less evidence, though, of women voluntarily assigning themselves the role of degraded sexual sinner. The promotion of an eroticized, debased Magdalene may explain some women's desire to explore alternate models for self-identification, such as an industrious Martha or the Virgin Mary.

The question of patronage leads us to a larger truth behind the different identities of the Catholic Magdalene: women's identification with the Magdalene held dangers, and they pursued that identification often at their peril. Women who claimed her as their patroness, whether for a religious vocation or in their art and writing, could be perceived as threatening; they often suffered the consequences of their temerity, having their work suppressed. The Magdalene occupied a precarious position, between presumption and humility—and as such she could, if carefully deployed, be a strategic model for royal women justifying their authority as rulers or regents. Those women who were portrayed as the sexualized, sinful Magdalene, prostitutes and mistresses, were the most vulnerable. Women in these circumstances were made to be objects of both censure and consumption, their images made to serve the moralizing agenda of the Counter-Reformation, the aspirations of artists anxious to create a successful genre piece, or the power of wealthy male patrons. For the aristocratic mistresses who were the subjects of many of these paintings, any religious impulse behind the connection seems doubtful. The association with a notoriously beautiful prostitute added sensual mystique to their court personas and prestige to their royal lovers; the Magdalene's ultimate redemption merely suggested a respectable chastity that was surely, in Augustine's words, "not yet." It is when the commission came from its female subject, such as in the portrait of Archduchess Maria Maddalena of Florence as the Magdalene, that we find devotional and political goals expressed in the depiction of a less sexualized, more contemplative figure.

In viewing the paintings of the eroticized Magdalene, or reading the rhetoric of the Counter-Reformation, it can appear as though the male clerics of that movement were determined to force the Magdalene, and all religious women with her, to vanish behind convent walls in order to preserve a ladylike sainthood—or to retrieve a damaged womanhood, in the case of the image presented to former prostitutes. The dangers of the world were simply too great, from sexual sin to unsupervised reading of the scriptures. The cloistered life that the Magdalene represented in that rhetoric did indeed hold great power for early modern Catholic women; many sought its disciplines in grateful retreat while others were forced into involuntary confinement. Women did not simply receive those images and institutions, however; they themselves shaped and transformed them, influencing the church in their turn. Counter-Reformation culture presents a diverse picture of Magdalene imagery as it was preached and then adopted for a variety of projects by Catholic women. The rhetorical posture of the church, in which the Magdalene was rejected as a precedent for lay and female preaching, contrasts with the profusion of Magdalenes that women used in the service of contemplative and active vocations. Through their persistence and resourcefulness, the Magdalene remained their own: a flexible, potent model of female sanctity in a variety of expressions.

In Chapter 6 we will turn to an examination of the Protestantism that took shape in tandem with the Counter-Reformation, looking at how the communities and authors of the Reformed traditions defined their own Magdalenes in opposition and response to Catholic models.

CHAPTER SIX

These Magdalens

Diversity in the Reformed Tradition

A DISCREPANCY between doctrine and popular practice is evident in the Magdalene interpretations of the Reformed tradition, just as it was in Counter-Reformation religious culture. Although Martin Luther and his colleagues embraced her emotional piety and adopted her as a model of evangelism, this approach was not shared across the Protestant world. Other reformers argued against women's public preaching, claiming that Mary Magdalene was a special exception, criticizing her character, and taking up Jacques Lefèvre d'Étaples's deconstruction of her entwined identities.

This school of Magdalene interpretation characterized the Reformed tradition at its beginning, in John Calvin's teaching on the New Testament texts involving Mary Magdalene. His interpretation, much different from Luther's, exerted a profound influence over the image of the Magdalene in Reformed preaching and discourse. Far from praising her as exemplary, Calvin contended that her preaching, like that of other women in the Bible, served principally to shame educated men who ought themselves to be preaching and teaching correct doctrine. And where Lutheran pastors commended the Magdalene's emotional expressions of devotion to Christ, Calvin dismissed her weeping at Christ's tomb as a feminine display of "idle and useless" emotion.[1]

Calvin's legacy to the tradition he founded includes a rejection of emotional piety, documented by Susan Karant-Nunn, who argues that "the establishment of greater distance between the individual soul and its divine Progenitor is a feature of Reformed preaching in general." This meant that one of the most important themes of the Magdalene tradition, the intimacy of her relationship with Christ, would be absent from Calvin's theology. His aim in preaching was not to console his audience with the promise of an almost

167

familial connection to the divine (arguably one of the chief elements of Lutheran sermons), but rather to convey the seriousness of humanity's predicament as "sinners in the hand of an angry God," as a later Calvinist would famously put it. Calvin also avoided preaching about Christ's suffering almost entirely, leaving it unlikely that he would have dwelt on another strand of the Magdalene tradition, her great compassion. Instead he hoped to impress his audience with an appalled sense of the total depravity of human nature: "Everything that humankind is able to contrive in his spirit is nothing but unseemliness and vanity. From our infancy we show that we are steeped in all the infection of sin."[2]

David Whitford and Larissa Taylor have both argued that Calvin's dismissive interpretation of the Magdalene was "typical" of her treatment by Reformed preachers. Whitford concludes that Calvin's reduction of her composite identity to the scriptural figure alone amounted to a "denunciation of the Medieval Magdalene" that stripped away the tradition of her conversion of France, her title of apostle to the apostles, and her position as a prominent disciple, leaving her only "a redeemed hooker." Taylor similarly laments Calvin's Reformation as the "turning point" for the Magdalene, simplifying and diminishing her role: "Gone is the beautiful woman, the playful siren, the dancer, but gone too is the preacher and apostle to the apostles."[3]

Further study reveals, however, that Calvin's stern disapproval of Mary Magdalene as an exemplar for believers did not prove definitive for the Reformed tradition, even among his closest followers. The dichotomy between theology and practice in the Reformed tradition was complicated by a diversity across Reformed communities in different regions, resulting in patterns of devotion that sometimes renewed and adapted her identity in ways that Calvin himself had been unwilling to consider.[4]

A variety of Magdalenes were available in the religious cultures of communities that claimed their origins in Calvin's theology. England especially provided a remarkable diversity and depth of Reformed interpretations of the saint. The Magdalene was adopted in English drama and poetry to express aspects of Reformed teaching, including the ideal of penitence, the nature of salvation, and the understanding of the sacraments. The Magdalene's role in the cultural transmission of Calvin's theology is not, however, the sole focus of a poetic tradition that also features intricate biographical narratives, incorporating aspects of her legendary history and celebrating her emotional attachment to Christ. Such literary portraits, appearing alongside moralizing Puritan homilies, can reveal a surprising range to the Reformed devotional repertoire. Perhaps the common element that can be identified among Reformed Magdalenes is the earnestness of the attempt to reconcile her image with theology faithful to Calvin's teaching, even though this resulted in very different readings across the Reformed world.[5]

Calvin's Exegesis on Mary Magdalene

Calvin's attention to the Magdalene was limited to her role in the resurrection narrative, and his interpretation restricted her still more by belittling her agency and character. He published his *Commentary on the Gospel of John* in 1553, two years before his work on the remaining Gospels, indicating the importance that John's text held for his theology. The exalted view of Christ conveyed in John comes for Calvin at the expense of Mary Magdalene, who acts as an all too human counterpoint to divine Providence, and even to the righteousness of the other disciples. The male disciples had often been compared unfavorably to Mary Magdalene in the tradition, a practice Luther upheld, but Calvin takes the opposite approach. In his reading of the Easter morning narrative, Calvin sees Peter and John sympathetically, excusing them both for leaving the tomb and for not yet having faith in the resurrection. Indeed, expecting faith at that point would have been nonsensical, he argues, until it had been confirmed by experience and reason: "Their faith was not strong, but was only some confused remembrance of the miracle and resembled a trace, until it was more fully confirmed; and indeed, a strong faith could not be produced merely by the sight which they had beheld."[6]

If Peter and John are not at fault for a lack of faith since belief was not yet justifiable, then those who did remain at the tomb—the women—must have done so for no good reason. Why did they stay? Calvin notes, "As to the women remaining at the sepulcher, while the disciples return to the city, they are not entitled to great accommodation on this account; for the disciples carry with them consolation and joy, but the women torment themselves by idle and useless weeping. In short, it is superstition alone, accompanied by carnal feelings, that keeps them near the sepulcher." Calvin deliberately scorns previous interpretations that praised the women's loyalty and instead denigrates their reasons for remaining when the men had fled. The male disciples had apparently already seen enough to give them hope until the resurrection would be confirmed by an appearance from Christ. The women stayed only to indulge in excessive grief, fueled by their natural tendency to look for some occult explanation, or else because they were simply in thrall to primitive emotions. Grouping the women and their reactions together, as they are in the other three Gospels, Calvin purposefully rejects the unique focus on Mary Magdalene in John's Gospel. Calvin surmises that Mary was most likely not alone in returning to the tomb after Peter and John had left, but that she was probably accompanied by the other women.[7]

Calvin pauses in his narrative to marvel over the unworthiness of any women as witnesses to the resurrection: "What an amazing forbearance displayed by our Lord, in bearing with so many faults in Mary and her companions! . . . One purpose, surely, which Christ had in view in selecting the women, to make the first manifestation of himself to them, was to fill the apostles with shame." Even though Peter and John have already been excused for having left the scene, Calvin contradicts himself by explaining that Christ has only chosen such miserable vessels for the good news in order to blame the men for not being there.[8]

Mary herself is shown to be the worst of a bad lot. The women as a group had already been condemned for their inappropriate tears, but Calvin interprets the angel's question in John 20:13, "Woman, why are you weeping?," as a special rebuke to her. He notes that "the angel reproves Mary for her excessive weeping, [for which there is] no reason," implicitly contrasting Mary with Peter and John, who were praiseworthy for their reasonable behavior because they had refused to believe in a resurrection with no sensible proof. He then ponders why the Magdalene does not recognize Jesus as soon as he appears, deciding that the fault lies with her eyes. Calvin acknowledges that both she and the male disciples were kept in ignorance by God, but more than that, he claims that her eyes were "bewitched by the world and by Satan, that they may have no perception of the truth." Among the witnesses present on Easter Sunday, Mary is the most pointed example of a person so bound by sin that her intellect and perceptions are clouded: "In Mary we have an example of the mistakes into which the human mind frequently falls." Calvin then addresses an inconsistency between the different Gospel resurrection narratives, again using the occasion to heap particular opprobrium on Mary Magdalene. The other women are portrayed in Matthew 28:9 as being allowed to touch Christ's feet to assure themselves of his resurrection, but Mary takes this impulse too far in John 20, according to Calvin. In her attempt to reach out and embrace the risen Christ she has gone "to excess . . . perceiving that their attention was too much occupied with embracing his feet, he restrained and corrected that immoderate zeal." Luther had taken pains to contradict medieval readings of the noli me tangere text, arguing that Mary Magdalene simply did not yet understand the nature of Christ's resurrected relationship to humanity, but Calvin returns to the older interpretations of the text, which condemn her vulgar longing for physical contact. She and the other women are irredeemably carnal: "Christ saw that, by their foolish and unreasonable desire, they wished to keep him in the world."[9]

The misogynistic rhetoric in which Calvin engages, identifying women as more subject to emotion than men are, their natures more animal, was a literary convention of the sixteenth century, one of the sides of the *querelle des femmes* debate over the status of women. John Lee Thompson has explored Calvin's engagement with the *querelle* literature and concludes that Calvin was influenced by the negative assessments of women inherited from the classical tradition, and he deployed them when it served his polemical goals, while maintaining the evangelical principal of spiritual liberty for all, men and women alike.[10]

When he wishes to speak about the condition of all Christians, Calvin's study of John 20 does make some positive use of the Magdalene. In a sermon preached on the same text, the fact of the women's having gone to the sepulcher is used as a model of seeking God in faith, though the insistence on their ignorance is still made. "We will have no profit from the resurrection of our Lord Jesus Christ unless we seek him by faith, to be united to him. . . . And the example for that is offered to us here, when it is said that Mary Magdalene and her companions came to the sepulcher. It is true that there is some fault and roughness, . . . in that they wanted to anoint our Lord Jesus Christ and they never thought of what he had foretold and testified so many times, that he must be resurrected." And again in the John commentary, he explores Jesus's calling of Mary by name as an example of how God calls all persons. The praiseworthy action is, however, all Christ's; Mary's passive receipt of grace is the only good thing that can be said of her. In dealing with an unambiguous example of the Magdalene's own action, discussing the mission Christ gives her to the disciples, Calvin grudgingly concedes, "It must also be admitted that Mary Magdalene fully obeyed the injunctions of

Christ." He goes on to reiterate his interpretation that Mary Magdalene and the other women were used in order to shame the male disciples into taking up the office of evangelism. The disciples were so much at fault, indeed, that they ought to have had not just women deliver Christ's Word to them, but animals: "I consider that this was done by way of reproach, because they had been so tardy and sluggish to believe. And, indeed, they deserve not only to have women for their teachers, but also oxen and asses, since the Son of God had been so long and laboriously employed in teaching, and yet they had made so little, or hardly any progress. Yet this is a mild and gentle chastisement, when Christ sends his disciples to the school of the women."[11]

Calvin's mocking tone diminishes the importance of the choice of women as messengers, making its only purpose a negative one, goading the true preachers into doing their work. In this way he moves to an assertion that the action of Mary and the other women must therefore not be taken as a precedent or rule for the practice of the church, forestalling the claims of those, such as Marie Dentière, who used the Magdalene to argue for women's right to preach. Calvin also rejects the Lutherans' argument that women can baptize in case of need, and the related claim that they might also preach in a similar necessity:

> It ought likewise to be observed, however, that this occurrence was extraordinary, and—we might almost say—accidental. They are commanded to make known to the Apostles what they afterwards, in the exercise of the office commanded to them, proclaimed to the whole world. But, in executing this injunction, they do not act as if they had been Apostles; and therefore it is wrong to frame a law out of this injunction of Christ, and to allow women to perform the office of baptizing. Let us be satisfied with knowing that Christ displayed in them the boundless treasures of his grace, when he once appointed them to be the teachers of the Apostles, and yet did not intend that what was done by a singular privilege should be viewed as an example.[12]

Here Mary's reputation as a notorious sinner serves his point particularly well. Calvin points out the unworthiness of Mary Magdalene even among women, capping his discussion of women's preaching as neither endorsed nor even permitted by scripture.

Mary Magdalene is fundamentally, for Calvin, an example of the sinful human person at her most depraved. His only reference to her in his *Institutes of the Christian Religion* offers the Magdalene as proof of the overwhelming complexity of the devil's assaults and the need for surrender to God rather than reliance on works: "That we may feel the more strongly urged to do so, the Scripture declares that the enemies who war against us are not one or two, or few in number, but a great host. Mary Magdalene is said to have been delivered from seven devils by which she was possessed." As in the John commentary, her example is most positive when her individuality is lost in the magnitude of her existential predicament and the intervention of divine grace.[13]

The character that Luther and his colleagues had found worthy of praise and imitation in her profound affection for Christ, especially as expressed in her copious weeping, is for Calvin merely self-indulgence. Calvin's attitude toward tears is a theological stance. Weeping is a vain show of emotion, in women as in men; but worse, tears could be an appeal for mercy from one's fellows and from God. To stop and give way to tears before the abyss of hellfire might come dangerously close to a suspicion that one was deserving of divine pity or could earn it through pathetic displays. In Calvin's theology it is not compassion that ensures the salvation of the elect, but the necessary fulfillment of the glory of God. Emotional outbursts simply got in the way of Calvin's clear-eyed contemplation of the soul's peril before God's just wrath.[14]

The Reformed Community

The piety Calvin sought to instill in his followers included unflinching submission to an arbitrary Providence. There was no room in this conception of the world and humanity's place in it for sentimental pleading with God on behalf of sinners. Calvin's particular brand of reform demanded the complete renunciation of medieval popular religion, with its colorful pantheon of supernatural intercessors. Iconoclasm, removing images of the saints from places of worship, was a central impulse of the Calvinist Reformation. That program is typified by the polemical work of Pierre Viret (1511–1571), a Reformed pastor in Lausanne but also a friend and supporter of Calvin in the reform of Geneva, and an influential figure for the English Reformation as well.[15] Viret's 1560 *De le vraie et fausse religion* presents a catalog of pagan practices and Christian heresies—including the cult of the saints—from the classical period through Viret's own time. Among them is the traditional identification of the Magdalene with the sinful woman and with Mary of Bethany. While Viret takes pains to correct the misidentifications, it is clearly the association with prostitution that disturbs him most, and which he connects to the Cathars: "This Mary Magdalene was not the sister of Martha and Lazarus. . . . On this, we have the testimony of Chrysostom, who says clearly, that this Mary was not a whore [*putain*], but honest and virtuous, the one who cared for Jesus Christ, and loved him strongly with her sister: and who was not at all a whore, the one whom St. Luke mentions. Thus it is a great impudence of the Cathars, having dared to create these fables, and preach them publicly to people."[16] Viret is dismayed that in Rome the Magdalene was being portrayed as a new incarnation of Venus, an equation that was being made in Counter-Reformation art, as we have seen. This connection has made the saint into "a patroness of lechers and prostitutes [*des paillars et des paillardes*]," with her festival having devolved into a drunken orgy in Rome and at her shrine in southern France. No longer the simple adulteress of the Luke 7 account, she has become a "public whore, the most notorious, debauched, and infamous that ever was in the world [*elle auoit esté vne putain publique, voire la plus diuulguée & la plus desbauchée et infame, que iamais fust au monde*]," and her story gives misguided hope to those in that profession: "I do not know if the priests and monks wrote these things of Mary Magdalene . . . in order to give greater courage to women to prostitute themselves, seeing that such great prostitutes were received in paradise in such honor." (Ie ne say si les Prestres et les Moynes ont escrit ces choses de Marie Magdaleine et de saincte Thaïs à celle fin qu'ils donassent meilleur courage à femmes de paillarder, veu que si grandes paillardes ont esté receues en paradis en tel honneur.) In discussing the Magdalene houses, he shares the concern of Counter-Reformation clerics that old and unattractive prostitutes may be pretending to convert so that they can seek a comfortable retirement when they can no longer ply their trade profitably. Similarly derogatory is his logical proof that the woman named Mary Magdalene in the New Testament could not have been this sinful woman, for Mary Magdalene was known as the one from whom Christ had exorcised seven demons, and what man, he asks, would desire a demon-possessed prostitute?[17]

FIG 6.1 Jan Gossaert, *Mary Magdalen*, c. 1525–1530. Oil on panel. 49.53 × 39.37 cm (19 1/2 x 15 1/2 in.). Gift of William A. Coolidge, 1991.585. Photograph: © 2018 Museum of Fine Arts, Boston.

Viret's description of Mary of Bethany is scarcely more flattering. He mocks the idea that Martha's preaching had converted her, and mentions a variation on the story in which Martha had told her promiscuous sister that Jesus was the most beautiful man she had ever known, and this is what had convinced Mary to go and see for herself. Ridiculing the identification of the wedding at

Cana as that of the Magdalene and John the Evangelist, he points out causti-
cally that it was hardly honorable of Christ to ruin a marriage contracted in
accordance with divine law, making a prostitute out of a respectable woman
in order to gain a disciple. Finally, having dispensed with most of the legend,
he even dismisses her preaching role: "I leave aside also what they have written, that she performed the office of Apostle and minister, preaching the
Gospel, and that she had this authority from St. Peter, the pope of Rome.
For these are such weighty lies."(Ie laisse aussi, ce qu'ils ont escrit, qu'elle a
fait office d'Apostre & de ministre preschat l'Evangile, et qu'elle a eu ceste
authorité par S. Pierre Pape de Rome. Car ce sont mensonges si lourd.) His
tone throughout echoes Calvin's in belittling Catholic tradition by linking it
to a culture promoting women's speech and sinfulness.[18]

    Both Calvin and Viret endorsed the scholarship of Lefèvre d'Étaples that
attacked the traditions of the Magdalene, and Calvin criticized the cult of the
saints as it existed in the France of his youth. One of the centers of the Magdalene cult in France, Vézelay, had been touched by this fever of iconoclasm,
when it became home to a Protestant community in 1557. The town was one of
the few designated sites for Protestant worship when it was permitted under
Charles IX. In the late 1560s members of that community engaged in vandal-
ism at the abbey church that had housed the saint's relics in the Middle Ages.
The town faced attack and ultimate capture by Catholic royal forces in the
fall and winter of 1569–1570. With its reputation for Protestant loyalty, it was
there that surviving Protestants fled from Paris after the St. Bartholomew's
Day Massacre. Vézelay's brief tenure as a Protestant refuge came to a final end,
however, with the reconquest of the town and the murder of the refugees in
1572, on what became known as the Champ des Huguenots.[19]

    Not all of Calvin's closest partners in reform shared in the destruction of
the Magdalene's image, however. Vézelay had been the birthplace of Theodore Beza (1519–1605), Calvin's successor as the religious leader of Geneva.
Beza's origins in a stronghold of Mary Magdalene's cult perhaps informed his
divergence from the dismissive tone with which his mentor and his colleague
Viret rejected the Magdalene tradition. Beza adopted the Magdalene as a
metaphor for the church, a positive image developed by theologians in the
early church and in the Middle Ages. And although certainly aware of Lefèvre
d'Étaples's work on the saint's scriptural identity and of Calvin's scorn for
her as a model, Beza invokes her connection to the sinful woman of Luke 7,

identifying the beginning of the church with Mary Magdalene's anointing of Christ. In his *Sermons on the Song of Songs* (1586), also a text traditionally associated with the Magdalene, Beza writes, "The Christian Church began with a small flock: when Mary Magdalene poured oil over Christ's head (Luke 7:37ff.) the Church consisted only of Christ's disciples and her."[20]

The connection between the Magdalene and the church is also made in a series of sermons published by Beza in 1593, *Sermons sur l'histoire de la resurrection de nostre Seigneur Jesus Christ*. The first several sermons in the series constitute a fascinating attempt to reengage many of the medieval Magdalene traditions in teaching Calvinist doctrine on salvation and the soul. The first sermon establishes the Magdalene's great and ardent devotion in coming so early to the tomb. While Calvin had explained the women's presence at the sepulcher as superstition and "useless emotion," for Beza, Mary Magdalene and the other women are "courageous," and her perseverance is rewarded by Christ with the first resurrection appearance.[21]

The third sermon maintains that the resurrection was announced first to women in order to spur the male disciples to action, but with a very different emphasis than Calvin had chosen. Beza takes up the traditional contrast between the women and the men, noting the women's greater constancy:

> This is the reason we must also place before those who could find it strange that He was manifested sooner to these women than to His Apostles or to some other disciples. Because in all things the will of God is true and forever rules all that can and should be said and properly done. But in spite of this, the story clearly shows us again that there were many faults in these women, as we will see later, and that the Apostles showed less faith and constancy than these poor women, who had accompanied Him to death and to burial, and now visited Him again at the sepulcher, in place of the disciples, who were so lost that it was as if they had forgotten their Master.[22]

Rather than dwelling on the degradation the men faced in being schooled by women, Beza instead compares this reversal of expectation to the reform and rebuke of human authority that must always purify the church.[23]

Here and elsewhere in the series, Beza seems conflicted between a desire to recognize the women's great love for Christ and faulting them for their lack of faith in the resurrection. He condemns ignorance as no excuse for neglecting our duty of faith and obedience, a position that recalls Marguerite de Navarre's poem on the Magdalene's tragic ignorance. Searching for Christ among the dead, as the angels reprimand the women for doing, is here equated with Catholic "superstitions," expressing the Reformed theology that Christ is now to be encountered only spiritually, not as a physical presence in the sacraments.²⁴

Fundamentally, however, Christ's forgiveness of the women, and their response, is presented as a message of hope to everyone: "Notwithstanding this great fault [of not believing in the resurrection], the Lord had regard for this sincere love, that these women showed him in life and death, . . . [and] passed over all this imperfection, making himself better known to them than ever before." (Mais nonobstant ce grand defaut, le Seigneur ayant esgard à cette sincere dilectio, que ces femmes lui auoyent monstree en la vie & en la mort . . . qui a passé par dessus toute cette imperfection, se faisant mieux cognoistre à elles que iamais au parauant.) The great fault Beza laments in the women is not associated with them uniquely, nor even with women in general, but with all sinners. He then praises the women for obeying the angels, exhorting his audience to follow their good example. He concludes by claiming that Christ's commission to the women to tell the news to the disciples should show us two things: first, the importance of preaching the mercy of God, and second, that not all are prophets and apostles, as these women were not, and that everything must be done according to order in the church, referring to the prohibition on women's public speech in 1 Corinthians 14:40. He thus includes an affirmation of Calvin's position on women's religious leadership, but his tone is markedly more positive, seeing the women more as praiseworthy, universal examples rather than as notably flawed and unworthy.²⁵

Beza's fourth sermon, also on Christ's command to the women, elaborates on the same interpretations. The women's search for a dead Christ is inexcusable, showing all the more Christ's goodness in tolerating human frailty. This misconception is again connected with Catholic theology and practice. Like Calvin, Beza believes that the commission to the women of public evangelism is not a precedent, but "another singular favor from the Savior [vne autre faveur singulaire]." Immediately after this, though, he introduces the Magdalene's medieval title, observing that the women "indeed, were like apostles to the apostles in this message, with an infallible consolation [de forte, qu'elles furent

comme Apostres des Apostres en ce message, auec vne consolation inerrable]." The
time for such a direct encounter with Christ is over, Beza cautions, and now
things must be conducted in the church with proper order. As in the previous sermon, the women's actions in response to Christ are commended as
exemplary. In an imagined dialogue, they confess that they had come seeking to anoint a dead body, testifying joyfully that they had instead found the
Savior seeking them with the balm of consolation. The Savior is seeking all
sinners in the same way, and all should respond in the same way.[26]

The fifth sermon, on the disciples' not believing the women's testimony,
begins with a remarkable discussion on the sinful woman of Luke 7. Though
Beza introduces the section by noting the falseness of the identification of
this figure (and of Mary of Bethany) with Mary Magdalene, he nonetheless
launches into a three-page exploration of the value of this woman's story for
believers. Again, he uses the text to teach a Reformed theology of justification. Pardon and repentance cannot be separated, for amendment of life is
the fruit and goal of pardon; true repentance comes not from us but from God.
Again, she is held up as a model: all should ask God for the same grace she
received. Her image of loving service to God gives Beza an opportunity to
criticize others in the history of the church and in his own day: "We have in
this woman a beautiful witness. . . . For is it not true of all time, that rarest
among men is a true and constant love?" (Nous auons vn beau temoignage
en ceste femme. . . . Car n'est-il pas trop vraye de tous temps, qu'il n'y a rien
plus rare entre les homes qu'vne vraie et constante amitié?) He gives many
examples of conflict in the church, contrasting them with the example of the
woman who followed Jesus out of ardent affection and gratitude, courageously
exposing herself to danger in doing so. He then returns to Mary Magdalene
at the tomb without distinguishing her from the penitent woman, lauding her
"perseverance," a formula for holiness from Calvin's *Institutes*.[27] Calvin had
compared the Magdalene unfavorably to Peter and John after the Crucifixion,
maintaining that their reasonable consideration of events led them to an
appropriate measure of belief, while she was simply emotional and unproduc-
tively distraught. Beza describes her instead as wrestling with the competing
claims of faith and reason within herself, an example of the self-inflicted
torments of any who engage in such a futile effort. Dismissing the loyalty
to sense and reason that confused her, Beza points to faith as the "one thing
necessary [*qui est seul necessaire*]," referring to Luke 10:42, Christ's praise of

Mary of Bethany. Even when she is presented as a cautionary lesson, though, her character has inherent value for Beza, as when he explains her temerity in speaking to the angels at the tomb as if they were ordinary people, asking "how could she have thought that they were simply men [*comment eust elle peu penser que ce fust simplement des hommes*]?" Yet "nevertheless, she speaks to them as one would to a few men … nothing less than the extreme desire to know what became of the body of Jesus Christ … consumed all her spirit such that she could think of nothing else [*toutefois elle parle à eux comme on feroit à quelques hommes … ce neantmoins ceste extreme désir de sauoir qu'estoit devenu le corps du Iesus Christ … a tenu tous ses esprits tellement occupés, qu'elle n'a pensé à autre chose*]." He notes that her ardent devotion to Christ should be a rebuke us in our coldness to grace. This sermon thus includes praise for all three of the figures and characteristics traditionally associated with the Magdalene, in interpretations that advance a Reformed theological program.[28]

Beza generally achieves a reconciliation between Calvin's theology and a more positive view of the Magdalene than his mentor had taken, though there are passages where the tension between the two positions becomes evident. He departs most pointedly from Calvin's readings of the Magdalene texts in his sixth sermon, on the noli me tangere scene. Beza begins with his most emphatic statement yet in celebration of Mary Magdalene and her role in the resurrection narrative. Christ gives her a "special, double grace" in choosing her to be the first witness of his rising from the dead, and "he made her as an apostle to the apostles: they were taught by her, where they must go, and we after them [*qu'il l'a faicte comme Apostre des Apostres, leur enseignant par elle, où les deuoit amener, et nous après eux*]." He considers her famous weeping not derisively, as Calvin had, but as a mark of her fidelity, approved by God: "But to whom does the Savior manifest himself here? To the one who wept, not to those who enjoyed themselves in Jerusalem." (Mais à qui se manifeste ici le Seigneur? À celle qui pleuroit, non pas à ceux qui se gaudissoyent en Ierusalem.) Tears coming before joy will often be the lot of God's children, as other biblical texts are used to confirm, though Beza admits that much of her sorrow came from her own lack of faith. He alternates between finding fault with her imperfect faith and acknowledging that her grief came from a real affection for Christ, rewarded by him with this consolation and yet reprimanded as well. This oscillation illustrates the predicament of all sinners before the gift of grace, at once condemned and saved. Beza uses the ambiguity of Mary's role to advantage here, directing his audience to accept blame for their own faults and lack of faith, responding to Christ with joyful humility. She becomes a symbol for the church again in a discussion of Christ's calling her by name. Beza uses this example to urge pastors to know their congregations, unlike absentee bishops in Catholic territories. Strikingly, the example given for the ideal response of the church to pastoral direction is that of Lydia, in Acts 16:15, a woman who was converted by Paul's preaching, afterward hosting him for his ministry in Thyatira and converting her household.[29]

Beza acknowledges that the discussion that follows, an explanation of Jesus's command to the Magdalene not to touch him, is his own "opinion [à mon advis]," which he has decided on as the simplest reading of a much-misunderstood passage. Where medieval interpreters and Calvin had seen this as proof of the Magdalene's—and all women's—carnality being condemned by God, and even Luther had found her uncomprehending of the nature of the risen Christ, Beza simply sees Christ hurrying her on to her evangelical mission. He argues that Christ knew that her great love would have made her wish to stay with him, to embrace him and talk about everything that had happened to him since the Crucifixion. There was not time for this at the moment, though there would be, later. "The Lord simply did not want to reprimand her touching, but wanted Mary to delay it for another time." (Le Seigneur donc n'aura pas voulu simplement reprendre ceste attouchement, mais a voulu que Marie delayast cela à vne autre fois.)[30] Not only is there nothing wrong with her desire to touch Jesus, but she is again offered as a universal example, in this case of those who tarry in doing God's work for reasons of their own. Concluding the sermon, Beza affirms the importance of her role in the strongest terms, while being careful to note that it still does not permit other women to preach. The Magdalene held "the greatest and most honorable commission that was ever given by our Lord to any prophet or apostle whatsoever, and containing a teaching exceeding the capacity even of angels. But it must not be held, however, as a consequence of the person to whom, in this case, this charge was given; it is not the ordinary administration of the house of God, that women teach in the assembly, but on the contrary they are commanded to listen in silence, 1 Cor. 14:34."[31] Despite the caution, Beza's emphasis remains on the affirmation of God's call. He maintains that God can open the mouth of the least, making even stones speak (Luke 19:40), not observing distinctions of sex or age. Finally, Beza expresses incredulity that the disciples did not believe Mary Magdalene, when she bore witness with such vivid expression and from the direct evidence of her own eyes and ears.[32]

Taken altogether, Beza's narrative offers an unusually positive interpretation of the Magdalene's character and role. Where she is criticized for her lack of faith in the resurrection, the connection is immediately drawn to the faithlessness of all sinners, and her response to Christ's and the angels' correction is commended to all believers as exemplary. Her personal history and character are therefore not faulted uniquely, but only as typical of human imperfection. Beza includes elements from the medieval tradition to emphasize Reformed ideals and to expand them. He advances the sinful woman of Luke 7 to describe the theology of justification, and uses Mary of Bethany's example to value faith above all else. The "apostle to the apostles" title serves to emphasize the importance of evangelical testimony and perseverance in adhering to the Word of God in the face of opposition. The Magdalene's weeping and intimate attachment to Christ foster an emotive piety not present in Calvin's own preaching (except where it is criticized). Beza's interpretation of the resurrection narrative represents a contribution to Reformed religious culture from someone whose faith was surely formed by a youth immersed in Magdalene piety, who sought to preserve the value of that tradition and to ally its strengths with Reformed theology.

Thus, while Calvin himself did not embrace Mary Magdalene in the same way as Luther and his followers had, she did not pass from sight even in the culture of his most immediate influence. Another Reformed pastor whose interpretation of the Magdalene was markedly more positive than Calvin's, Georg Spindler (1525–1605), also came from an environment in which the Magdalene was celebrated. Spindler had been educated in the Lutheran culture of Wittenberg University, but eventually converted to Calvinism. In his 1596 devotional work *The Passion and Resurrection of Christ* Spindler offered praise for the Magdalene's role at the sepulcher: "Even though Mary [Magdalene] errs and is betrayed by her emotions when she thinks that the Lord has been stolen, nonetheless she is correct in seeking Christ and in wanting to have him again." Spindler's willingness to draw on the Magdalene tradition in Calvinist piety may have been influenced by his Lutheran origins, but he was not alone in his attempt to retain and adapt this figure of the medieval religious culture to serve the needs of a Reformed audience.[33]

Reformed pastors such as Beza and Spindler evidently maintained significant attachments to the Magdalene even as they demonstrated allegiance
to their Reformed faith. Such attachments existed among the laity as well, and
are better interpreted as a combination of enduring cultural ties and authentic
faith commitments rather than as religious confusion. French Huguenots continued to participate in local and regional Catholic festivals such as those held
for Mary Magdalene. The practice of naming women after the saint persisted
even in Huguenot exile communities, as can be seen from probate records in
North America.[34] The other major site where Calvinist theology came to
dominate the religious landscape, outside of France and Switzerland, was
in England and its colonies. There, too, the Magdalene found an enduring
home. Where we might have expected to find only a scarred and empty niche
left behind after iconoclastic purges, instead we see a space carved out for a
reinterpreted figure, one who illustrates Reformed ideas about penitence and
faithfulness.

Puritanical Magdalenes

To be sure, many relics of the Catholic tradition had been consciously removed
from England's state church, beginning with the dissolution of the monaster-
ies under Henry VIII in the late 1530s, through the reform of worship under
Edward VII and Elizabeth I. All aspects of religious life were affected, from
images to institutions, though the result was not as complete as some advocates of English reform desired. While some elements of Catholic tradition
endured, such as bishops, other areas of religious culture, such as monasticism,
were almost erased. Few options remained for single, Anglican women to live
in community in the cloistered, contemplative model that the Magdalene had
represented. As part of the general Protestant rejection of the religious life
for women, the saint's role as a patron for houses of redeemed prostitutes
was emphatically scorned. Documented exceptions to the ban on religious
foundations, such as the house endowed by Mary Wandesforde in York, were
strictly policed. The York community, under the control of the cathedral,
refused entrants below the age of fifty and with any history of scandal or even
low birth, so as not to be thought a Magdalene house.[35]

Though Mary Magdalene's identity as an exemplar for avowed contemplatives had ended, she continued to be a popular saint for English Protestants.

She was the only female saint whose feast was observed in the 1549 Book of Common Prayer, though the collect for the feast was altered to emphasize her exemplary penitence and proclaim the theology of justification by faith. Her penitence was the focus of Lewis Wager's 1567 Protestant morality play, *The Life and Repentaunce of Marie Magdalene*. Patricia Badir has argued that the saint's conversion parallels the conversion of England underway at the time of the play's production. Over the course of the drama the Magdalene is transformed from an attractive image for viewers' consumption into an example of Calvinist morality, right down to her new, plain dress. This shift in identity is clearly meant to guide viewers' own process of embracing and internalizing the nation's reform.[36]

The use of the Magdalene to stand for the religious experience of believers in general renews the medieval interpretation of Mary Magdalene as an allegorical figure of the church, linking it with Protestant polemics that described the Catholic Church as a whore. The Magdalene, the reformed whore, is thus a perfect symbol of the new Reformed church. The play's language exploits both sides of the comparison. In her sinful state, she is a "house" that the seven deadly sins enter. Like Calvin's interpretation of the Magdalene, Wager's imagery is dependent on the misogyny of early modern discourse for its power: the Catholic Church is effeminate when compared to a sexually sinful woman, and makes those who belong to it effeminate as well. England's manhood is better served, in the rhetoric of the play, by the courageous, masculine theology of the Reformation than by a Catholicism that encouraged a slavish and feminine devotion to precious idols.[37]

The play's language of conversion reinterprets an ancient theme, first developed by Gregory the Great, of cataloging the Magdalene's senses and comparing their uses in her sinful and saved states:

As thus, like as the eyes have been vainly spent,
Upon worldly and carnal delectations,
So henceforth to weeping and tears must be spent,
And wholly given to godly contemplations.

Likewise as the ears have been open alway,
To here the blaspheming of Gods holy name,

And filthy talking evermore night and day,
Now they must be turned away from the same.

. . . .

The tongue which blasphemy hath spoken,
Yea and filthily, to the hurt of soul and body,
Whereby the precepts of God have been broken,
Must henceforth praise God for his mercy daily.[38]

The Magdalene's conversion, like the church's, is accomplished as a purification of feminine attributes once given over to sinful temptation but now rightly directed to spiritual ends.

A generation after Wager's polemical drama, Gervase Markham wrote a long poem in praise of Mary Magdalene, *Marie Magdalens Lamentations for the Losse of Her Master Iesus* (1601). The poem's emphasis differs from that of Wager's more didactic play; Markham meditates on the Magdalene's experience. Rather than being a symbol of Protestant conversion, she has become a fully drawn character whose emotions contribute to the reader's understanding of faith. Although this work was clearly influenced by the poetry of the Jesuit Robert Southwell, Markham's religious identity is a subject of debate. His work lacks an explicitly Catholic sacramental theology and any expression of mourning over the loss of that tradition, elements that dominate Southwell's verse. It is possible that that perhaps Markham was trying to redeem the saint for Protestantism in the wake of the popularity, even among confessed Anglicans, of Southwell's work.[39]

The poem can be read as a Protestant theological statement about the power of the divine Word to bring the sinner to salvation. Mary Magdalene is grieving in the garden at the injustice of Christ's death; he speaks her name, and she is instantly filled with confidence and joy: "His words authority which all obey, / this foggy darkness clean away doth chase, / and brings a calm and bright well-tempered day." Unlike in Southwell's version, where her distress is so overwhelming that she loses her judgment and almost her senses, Markham's Magdalene has enough self-awareness to rebuke herself for having mistaken the risen Christ for the gardener.[40] Markham suggests in his preface that this quality of self-awareness, particularly as it informs her penitence, is what ordinary believers should emulate, to the point of weeping:

> Ah could they see what sin from sense hath shut,
> How sweet it were to summon deeds misdone,
> To have their lives in equal balance put,
> To weigh each work ere that the judge do come:
> Ah then their tears would trickle like the rain.
>
> .   .   .   .
>
> They would with Mary send forth bitter cries,
> To get the joys of their soul-saving love,
> They would gush forth fresh fountains from their eyes,
> To win his favour, and his mercy prove:
> Eyes, heart, and tongue, should pour, breathe out, and send,
> Tears, sighs, and plaints, until their love they find.[41]

This passage seems to call readers to evaluate their deeds and condemn them, and then to perform works of contrition and penance, in order to "win [God's] favour," which would place the poem within a Catholic framework. Elsewhere in the poem, however, Markham seems to reject Catholic ritual and the theology of works:

> But being too precise to keep the Law;
> The laws sweet maker I have thereby lost
> And bearing to his ceremonies too much awe,
> I miss his sweet self, of far more cost,
> Since rather with the Truth I should have been,
> Than working that, which by a Type was seen.[42]

Despite its arguably Protestant theology, Markham's poem has been included in lists of English Catholic devotional poetry about the Magdalene. Such lists often also include Thomas Robinson's *The Life and Death of Marie Magdalen* (1620).[43]

Scholars have been divided on Robinson's identity and confessional allegiance. One school of thought identifies him as Protestant, reworking the story of the Magdalene to counter the well-known interpretation of Southwell and to offer a Magdalene suitable for Reformed piety. Heinrich Oskar Sommer's introduction to his 1887 edition of the poem indicates that the work testifies to a Protestant context of authorship, comparing the allegory of the poem to the work of Edmund Spenser and John Bunyan. In discussing Robinson's possible sources, including medieval legends and Passion plays, Sommer concludes that Robinson's main source was the Bible, evidence of Protestant authorship. Götz Schmitz also identifies Robinson as Protestant, claiming that "The legend was probably devised to counteract the elegiac Magdalen literature of the Counter-Reformation." The existence of a contemporary author of the same name, the explicitly Protestant Thomas Robinson who wrote a polemical, antimonastic pamphlet, *The Anatomy of the English Nunnery at Lisbon* (1622), suggests an interesting possible identification for the obscure creator of the Magdalene poem. Other scholars have concluded that Robinson was Catholic. Margaret Hannay lists Thomas Robinson among the Catholic authors of seventeenth-century Magdalene literature, though she includes no explanation for so locating him and his work. Likewise, Lily Campbell thought that Robinson was Catholic, proposing the possibility that he was the Dean of Durham under Queen Mary.[44]

The first section of Robinson's poem chronicles the pleasures of her sinful past, while the second describes her conversion. The youthful devotion to pleasure is an expression of her character at the time: she is vain, fickle, and spoiled. Robinson dwells at length on the sensual delights of these years in a literary parallel to erotic Baroque portraits of the Magdalene. The second section is shorter and focuses on the radical nature of her penitence, both in the instantaneous joy it produces and in the continuing need for such an attitude for the believer.

The binary structure of the poem, encouraging the reader to compare her life before and after her conversion, is assisted by literary devices and inverted parallelisms. Like Markham, Robinson engages the tradition of contrasting the sinful uses of the Magdalene's features or senses to the way they would be rightly used in faithfulness to Christ.[45] In this early passage, he compares the Magdalene herself to a sepulcher, prefiguring the resurrection scene:

A breast so white, and yet so black a heart;
Her worst the best, her best the worser part.
Can such fair hues enclose such idle Drones?

So white a wall immure such worthless stones?
So beauteous a sepulcher, such rotten bones?
A 'sepulchre' that cave I rightly call,
Wherein her soul so long immured hath been,
Bound with the fetters of a willing thrall:
And yet that sepulcher must bury sin.[46]

When she comes to the tomb on Easter morning, her faithful heart, consumed by grief, will finally be a proper sepulcher for Christ, as fitting then as it is now unfit, a body caught in the living death of a wasted existence. Later in the poem, the catalog of transgressions is presented alongside the list of the true uses to which she will put her body after her conversion, the same trope of a purified body that Lewis Wager had used:

These cheeks should blush at sin with crimson dye,
But they to lewdness chiefly do invite,
With smiles deceiving the beholder's eye:
These lips were made to praise, and pray aright,
Not to delude the soon-deluded sight:
This tongue should sing out Hallelujahs,
Not accent vain lascivious essays:
Hands, feet, heart, all were made, to speak their maker's praise.[47]

In her purified state she will be able, and indeed obliged, to speak with the testimony of a converted life, an interpretation of her role as witness that many female authors embraced.

The contradictions between wrong and right uses of her body suggest the need for change and resolution, and the crucial turning point of self-awareness. The carefree Magdalene is suddenly gripped by a burning pain, a physical realization of her predicament. The bitter truth is put off for a while, however, "But sorrow soon in streams of pleasure's drowned, / And conscience away doth vanish quite; / So little truth in women's tears are found." As Mary Magdalene is sinful and inconstant, so are all women. The echo of Calvin's contempt for the saint's traditional weeping, and of the carnal emotionalism of women in general, can be heard in Robinson's dismissal of the Magdalene's first experience of contrition. She cannot return to the ease of her former pleasure garden, however, as her moral landscape has already been irrevocably altered. There follows a long description of haunting by demons and snakes, with a wasteland replacing the lovers' bower. The ravaged form of melancholy takes the place of the beautiful young body of Mary. The confrontation with a blighted nature, reflecting the barren reality of her soul, produces self-knowledge: "A guilty conscience she within her breast can find."[48]

A Calvinist emphasis on conscience is evident in the description of how Mary is brought to her senses. The traditional seven demons are set upon her by Nemesis and the young Magdalene goes mad and roves through the devastated land.[49] Her journey is a parable of conscience, in which she is all but destroyed by its stark revelations:

> Witness distressed Mary's sad estate,
> Who erst with worldly happinness was blest,
> And lived in Pleasure's affluence of late:
> But gnawing Conscience, devoid of rest,
> Her short-lived pleasure quickly disposed,
> Her former jollity, tormenting thought,
> Terror of conscience, melancholy wrought
> That misery, and misery to Mercy brought.[50]

The theme of the terror of conscience bringing the sinner to recognition of her peril was central to Calvin's theology;[51] Calvin himself had used the metaphor of a dangerous natural environment to evoke the soul's vulnerability, even to the point of insanity, in the grip of conscience:

> The metaphor of the sea is elegant and very well fitted to describe the uneasiness of the wicked, for in itself the sea is troubled. Though it is not driven by the wind or agitated by frightful tempests, its billows carry on mutual war and dash against each other with terrible violence. In the same manner wicked men are disturbed by inner distress which originates in their spirits. They are terrified and confused by conscience, which is the most agonizing of all torments and the most cruel of all executioners. The furies agitate and pursue the wicked, not with burning torches, as in fables, but with anguish of

conscience and torment of deceit. For everyone is distressed by his own deceit, and his own terror grows; everyone is driven to madness by his own wickedness; he is terrified by his own evil thoughts and by conscience.[52]

Robinson constructs his fable of the Magdalene's early life and conversion precisely on such terms, and peoples it with demonic personifications of the terrible powers of Calvin's conscience. Though Robinson's own theological formation is unknown, this imagery for the terrors of conscience was in common use in early seventeenth-century Reformed sermons. Wildernesses, storms, and pirates figured heavily in sermons as metaphors for the dangers facing the soul in Puritan preaching from England and North America.[53]

Once the soul is stricken with the awareness of her peril, salvation is not long in coming. The transition to the second part, "Mary Magdalene's Death to Sin, or Her Life in Righteousness," is instantaneous. In this the Magdalene's experience is not exceptional, as Catholic devotional writers such as Teresa of Avila and François de Sales had cautioned, warning that the ordinary believer's path toward righteousness is a prolonged labor through good works and increasing fluency in prayer. For Protestants, the night-and-day opposition between sin and salvation in the Magdalene's story represents the existential position of all Christians, resembling the simultaneity of the *Law and Gospel* paintings of Lucas Cranach, Luther's artistic interpreter.[54] Robinson relates how quickly the peril is overcome by the presence of Christ:

> So night with sable weeds 'gan disapear,
> So melancholy vanished quite away;
> So joy her cheerful countenance did rear,
> So did the orient day-spring bring the day,
> And all the trees were clad with blooming May.[55]

In contrast to the destroyed garden of her illicit pleasure, now Mary Magdalene meets Christ in a verdant springtime. Robinson describes him with the language of the bridegroom from the Song of Songs. Christ casts out the demons that had been tormenting her, and Mary's release is so complete that she does not even need to weep:

Soon as they took their leave, that caused her thrall,
Down sunk the Damsel in amazement deep,
(After an earth-quake, so the ground doth fall,)
And sounding, yielded to a senseless sleep,
Nor could she speak a word, nor could she weep:
But he yet conquered all the powers beneath,
The Hell of sin, and sin of Hell, and Death.[56]

Robinson's Magdalene is thus more Calvinist than the one Calvin had balked at in the Gospel of John: not preaching and not weeping, but silently awestruck, she is the perfect Protestant penitent, utterly submissive to grace.

After her conversion, the need for an attitude of perpetual penitence remains. The saved soul must be constantly vigilant, in continual fear of sin. As Christ orders her,

Go to the courts of Wisdom, gentle guest;
There seek Repentance, and with her, find rest:
Repentance hath a flood, doth ever flow,
A flood of brinish tears and bitter woe,
That, be thou n'er so black, will make thee white as snow.[57]

The Magdalene goes toward the tower of Wisdom, facing the challenges of another allegorical landscape, guided by the figure of Humility. She meets the beautiful Wisdom and then the miserable Repentance, who sits weeping, guarded by angels. There follows an ode on tears of repentance and their salutary effect, in which Robinson reclaims the value of tears for Reformed piety. Now tears are again appropriate, not in the moment of evangelical confidence, when they are only wasted sentiment, but in a lifetime's anxious vigilance against the soul's depravity.[58]

Having portrayed her story as the model of a perfect Calvinist conversion, Robinson offers the Magdalene's response as an example to the believer. She hears of Christ in the house of the Pharisee, brings her costly ointment, and enters to perform her deed of love. The poet advises the reader to imitate her, and this imitative piety begins with the author himself. He writes of her love and its captivating effect on him:

Fain would I leave of Mary's love to write,
But still her love yet will not let me leave:
In love she lived, and now with love's delight,
Her former love, yet did her eyes deceive,
Instead of love, of life she doth bereave:
Fair maid, redeemed from the jaws of Hell,
How hardly can I bid thy love farewell!
That which thou lovst to do, so do I love to tell.[59]

This love is framed in strictly Reformed terms as the awareness of the sinner's need for grace, not as the impressive quality that earns her absolution. Robinson reads the forgiveness she receives with the evangelical interpretation we observed in Lutheran preaching, making her love the response of gratitude: "Great is her love, because her Sin is great."[60]

Her future after this episode is suggested, but not chronicled in detail. Robinson tells very briefly how she then followed Jesus with the other Marys. He closes with a short section on her witness of the Crucifixion and her visit to the tomb, comparing her favorably with Peter and John, a departure from Calvin's interpretation of this text. In Southwell's poem, the saint's grief over the absent Christ is inescapable and perhaps even worsened by his temporary reappearance. By contrast, Robinson's Magdalene is made joyful by the news of the resurrection and gladly goes to spread it to the disciples. "Joy closes all, (such ioy no style hath penned) / So end I with their ioy; n'er may that joy have end!"[61]

The theology behind Robinson's reading of the Magdalene may be assessed by contrasting it with Southwell's overtly Catholic poem, but also by comparing it with other Protestant poetry on the saint. Daniel Cudmore (1637?–1701) was the Anglican rector of Holsworthy, in Devon. He is recorded as having studied at Oxford University, though his life is otherwise undocumented. His collection of poems published in 1657, *Euchodia. Or, A prayer-song; being sacred poems on the history of the birth and passion of our blessed Saviour, and several other choice texts of scripture,* contains a section, "On Mary Magdalene," which takes as its text the Matthew 26:6–7 account of the anointing at Bethany. Cudmore begins by describing the surpassing sweetness of her copious tears. Attempting to find a place for tears in Calvinist piety, like Beza and Markham, he uses her example to condemn contemporary people who are hard of heart and dry-eyed. In describing her, he makes a statement against cosmetics and elaborate hairdressing, taking up a theme seen in both Catholic and Protestant authors, from Juan Luis de Vives to the Anabaptist Menno Simons. The passage commends genuine sorrow over sin, with weeping as its proper manifestation: "Good-woman! Who esteem'd no paint / Like to a face blubber'd with tears; / All other tinctures are but faint, / But these outwear all age and years. / No Venus-mole bespeaks a Saint, / No beauty-spot like these appears."[62] As in Robinson's poem, the author enters into a relationship with the Magdalene as his spiritual muse. Cudmore describes himself as Lazarus because of his sinful mortality, with Mary Magdalene (in her character as Mary of Bethany) mourning him. He concludes with praise for her great love and faithfulness, stronger than that of men:

> For Lazarus my outward man,
> Is sick, my Mary, Lord, can mourn;
> Groan like a dove, throb like a swan,
> Til thou hast rais'd him from his urn:
> But for her self she now and than [sic]
> Can weep, but doth her grief adjourn.
> And yet we see, when thou dost move
> Womens devotion unto love,
> Men ever doth the weaker vessel prove.[63]

In Cudmore's seventeenth-century English context, Catholic and Protestant literary traditions mingled productively, allowing Reformed authors to employ conventions from the Catholic Magdalene heritage that Calvin himself had scorned, such as celebrations of her weeping or the positive comparison between her and the male disciples. These images expanded the language of Reformed piety while still expressing fundamental elements of Calvinist theology: the mortal peril of the sinful soul and its dependence on divine grace.

Radical Puritans

The development of the Reformed tradition in England also included radical elements, particularly during the English Civil War (1642–1651) and the Commonwealth (1649–1660); this strand of the tradition persisted as

nonconformism following the restoration of the monarchy. The application
of ancient Magdalene images to radical Reformed polemics and pastoral counsel presents a striking contrast to Calvin's own dismissal of Mary
Magdalene. Even in strictly iconoclastic communities, the utility of this
time-honored story for teaching lessons old and new proved impossible
to resist.[64]

The Presbyterian minister John Rogers wrote a five-hundred-page pamphlet, *Ohel or Beth-shemesh* (1653), addressed to Oliver Cromwell, leader of
the Puritan government. Among his prophetic and apocalyptic concerns,
Rogers included the spiritual equality of women. In a list of scriptural figures
including Abigail, Priscilla, the Canaanite woman, Deborah, Lydia, and the
Samaritan woman, Rogers's pamphlet gives evidence of women "surpassing
men for piety and judgment; and therefore [they] ought to have equal liberty
with them in church-affairs." The resurrection narrative takes pride of place
in this enumeration of biblical examples, featuring Mary's comparison to
the male disciples and celebrating her role as apostle to the apostles: "And
Mary Magdalene, for piety and spirit, outran, and outreached all the twelve
disciples in her diligence to seek out Christ: to whom Christ first discovered
himself after his resurrection, and bid her declare it to his disciples; she was
the first preacher of Christ's resurrection." In the same passage, Rogers also
notes the metaphor linking the kingdom of heaven to the woman in the Song
of Songs. He goes on to address the thorny problem of the injunctions to
women's silence in church from 1 Corinthians 14 and 1 Timothy 2. He concedes
that Paul meant that women are not to preach and minister as public officers
of the church, as men do, but claims that they ought to be allowed to testify
to the Gospel and vote on the business of the church as equal members.[65]

Richard Baxter, a more widely influential but still nonconformist Puritan theologian, addressed his *A Christian Directory: Or, A Summ of Practical
Theologie, and Cases of Conscience* (1673) to both men and women. His text
is engaged with questions that might preoccupy any believer, as well as those
more specifically applicable to women, such as the hardships women bear
in marriage and childbirth. His advice on how to manage the distractions
of a family and household invoke the conflict between Mary and Martha.
While noting the superiority of a pure devotion to the divine, he does not
simply relegate women to one sphere or another exclusively, but notes with
the realism of the married person—as Baxter was at the time he wrote

A Christian Directory—that life does not always permit such undivided attention: "The business, care, and trouble of a married life, is a great temptation to call down our thoughts from God, and to divert them from the 'one thing necessary' (Luke 10:42). . . . How hard it is to pray, or meditate with any serious fervency, when you come out of a crowd of cares and businesses. . . . You think yourselves (as Martha) under a greater necessity of dispatching your business, than of sitting at Christ's feet to hear his Word. O that single persons knew . . . the preciousness of their leisure!" The wistfulness of his closing implies an acquaintance with the frustrations of everyday demands, on the part of husbands as well as wives. He seems to be recommending faithfulness within the challenging vocation of family life rather than either a postponement of spiritual pursuits or an abandonment of daily responsibilities.[66]

Magdalene language was being used to describe the exemplary faith of contemporary Reformed women, both ideal and real. The author of a 1675 epitaph for a noted female patron of the Anglican church, Lady Mary Armine, engaged the Magdalene tradition, including the saint's multiple identities, in order to praise his subject as a defender of the Reformed faith. Though a loyal Anglican, Armine gave money in support of dissenting clergy in 1662, and apparently took an interest in the case of Richard Baxter, who faced persecution as a dissenter. Armine lived in Lincolnshire, but used her means to support church missions in Massachusetts—particularly John Eliot's schools in Grafton and Natick. This patronage led to her biography's preservation in a nineteenth-century study of Massachusetts's history whose focus was the Reformed heritage of the region, including accounts of the Huguenot community that immigrated to Massachusetts.[67] Armine's epitaph was held up by the study's authors, Chrystia and Mary DeWitt Freeland, as part of that collective legacy:

An Epitaph for Lady Mary Armine (1675)
Hail Mary, full of grace, 'bove women blest;
A Name more rich in Saints than all the rest;
An army of them fam'd in sacred Story:
All good, none bad, an unparallel'd Glory!

. . . .

Next follows Mary the Bethanien;

. . . .

How much is spoke of Mary Magdalen?

. . . .

A Mary was the Mother of our Lord.
A Mary 'twas laid up in heart his word.
A Mary 'twas that chose the better part.
A Mary 'twas that wept with broken heart.
A Mary 'twas that did anoint Christ's feet.
A Mary pour'd on's Head the Spikenard sweet.
At Christ's Cross standing Maries three I find.
When others fled, they were not so unkind.
Christ dead, interr'd, at the Sepulchre door
Two Maries stand, I find no Women more.

So that from the Cradle to the Passion;
From Passion to the Resurrection;
From Resurrection to the Ascension;
Observe you may a Mary still was one,
The Army of such Ladies so divine,
This Lady said, I'le follow they all Ar-mine,

Lady Elect! In whom there did combine
So many Maries, might'st say all Ar-mine.
Thou Mother Sister, Spouse wa'st of the Lord,
In that in Heart and Life thou kept'st his Word,
With th'other Mary chose the better part;
With Mary Magdalen had'st a most tender heart.

On Christ a Mary spent all that she could;
Tho' others grudg'd, more if she had she would,
To th'Head above could'st not, on the Feet below
Thou did'st not spare much cost for to bestow.
Thy name a precious Ointment, and the Armies
Of Saints, and Angels are the Lady Armines.

Now God and Christ are thine, and what's Divine
In Heaven's enjoyment, Blest Soul! Now All are thine.[68]

Here we see another Reformed author apparently comfortable exploring aspects of the Magdalene tradition that Calvin had attempted to purge from popular piety. And, again, we observe the theme of incorporating a variety of roles, active and contemplative, within the life of the individual, as part of fulfilling the vocation of the priesthood of all believers. The saint's position as a scriptural figure would certainly have given her some legitimacy for Protestants considering suitable role models for their communities. It is evident, too, that the English context—in which both Catholic and Protestant texts were widely read and published, and in which confessional identity continued to be a matter of some fluidity in the lives of families and individuals—permitted or even encouraged more diversity in devotional options.

One prominent example of a Protestant author whose own religious identity had been Catholic in his youth is John Donne, the metaphysical poet and Anglican clergyman. His poem celebrating the piety of Lady Magdalen Herbert, the mother of Donne's fellow poet and cleric George Herbert, was offered as a gift to its subject on the Feast of the Magdalene in 1607.[69] Like Mary Armine's epitaph, it uses the many Marys of scripture as a literary device. Though he had renounced Catholicism, Donne was apparently unwilling, at least within the poem, to abandon the Magdalene of tradition, and his poem even gently mocks the attempt to sort out her multiple identities:

> Her of your name, whose fair inheritance
>   Bethina was, and jointure Magdalo,
> An active faith so highly did advance,
>   That she once knew, more than the Church did know,
> The Resurrection; so much good there is
>   Deliver'd of her, that some Fathers be
> Loth to believe one woman could do this;
>   But think these Magdalens were two or three.
> Increase their number, Lady, and their fame;
>   To their devotion add your innocence;
> Take so much of th' example as of the name,
>   The latter half; and in some recompense,
> That they did harbour Christ Himself, a guest,
>   Harbour these hymns, to His dear Name address'd.[70]

Though he includes all of her potential identities in the poem, listing both Bethany and Magdala as places associated with her, it is her "active faith," marked by her special, early knowledge of the resurrection, that Donne selects for his chief praise.

Such celebrations of aristocratic women's faith activity stood within a context of debate over the proper role for women in religious life in England. Women had been forbidden to read the scriptures aloud in male hearing in 1543, an offense for which some had been arrested, including one "Mrs. Castle of St. Andrews, Holborn known as 'a reader of the scripture in church,' or for 'disturbing the service of the church with brabbling of the New Testament.'" The law against reading was reversed by Edward VI, acknowledging the validity of the evangelical argument in favor of women's public ministry in time of need. The question of the Magdalene, of her active ministry as an expression of her personal relationship to Christ, was therefore central to the working out of the English Reformation's religious culture, to its interpretation of how individuals, including women, were called to be members of the community of the elect.[71]

ALTHOUGH THE Reformed Magdalene was primarily a figure of penitence, of divine accommodation to human frailty and of the radical nature of conversion, there is evidence for a surprising diversity of interpretation at the level of popular devotion and literature. Even the continued attachment of these themes to the Magdalene, whom Calvin had separated from the Luke 7 text, demonstrates the latitude of theology and devotional practice that existed in the larger Reformed community. Loyalty to the figure of the Magdalene that included Mary of Bethany and the sinful woman persisted among Calvinists, from French exiles in Geneva and the Americas to English clergymen serving an increasingly Puritan church.

That diversity is apparent in Reformed preaching on the Gospel texts involving the saint; our case study of the English church can provide numerous examples of this, as well. Nicholas Breton's 1595 sermon on John 20, *Marie Magdalen's Love, upon the Twentieth Chapter of John*, invokes Mary to discuss "divine love, proper humility, and repentance." Lancelot Andrewes's 1620 Easter sermon offers the Magdalene as a model of faith, remaining at the tomb in evangelical hope and rewarded with the commission to serve as Christ's chosen preacher. Like Beza, Andrewes uses her medieval title, "to be an Apostle, and that to the Apostles themselves, to bring them the first good newes of Christs rising again." John Bunyan's *Good News for the Vilest of Men* mentions Mary Magdalene in defending a Reformed theology of repentance and forgiveness. Reformed preaching both conveyed the Magdalene of Calvin's own interpretation and adapted elements from Catholic culture to present Protestant theology in a familiar and beloved form.[72]

While the positive role of the Reformed Magdalene as a figure of exemplary penitence and faith is attested to by these sermons and texts, the mocking misogyny of Calvin's exegesis is also visible in Reformed English culture. A late seventeenth-century play, *The Damoiselle,* by Richard Brome, features a comical, drunken Mrs. Magdalen, who is always in tears: "She's in her maudlin fit; all her wine showers out in tears." Brome's figure of fun signifies the confidence of his society's iconoclasm, recalling the strident derision of Calvin and Viret. Images that had been venerated for centuries, sanctifying various elements of religious experience, were often displaced by the rigor of reform movements. In a religious context deeply distrustful of emotive, mystical experience, the Magdalene could be used to tell cautionary tales about sin or doubt, with the more extravagant manifestations of Magdalene spirituality explained away as the ravings of female hysteria.[73]

There were those, however, who chose to pause with the weeping Magdalene at the empty tomb. Authors from Theodore Beza to Richard Baxter and John Donne found valuable lessons in the story of a sinner's profound devotion to Christ, lessons they applied to the lives of congregations and fellow Christians. The Calvinist clerics and poets who took up her story as a tool for encouraging Protestant piety saw something still of use in the long tradition of the Magdalene legend. With her as their inspiration, they dared to sketch captivating dramas of conversion, pity, and passion on the whitewashed walls of the Reformed imagination.

CHAPTER SEVEN

Mark This, Ye Despisers of the Weakness of Women

The Magdalene of the Radical Reformation

FROM ITS FIRST DAYS, the Protestant movement gave rise to more radical theologies and practices of reform than Martin Luther had espoused. His immediate colleagues and contemporaries, such as Andreas Bodenstein von Karlstadt, Caspar Schwenckfeld, and Ulrich Zwingli, broke with Luther's teaching on the Eucharist and infant baptism.[1] Anabaptism was named for the fourth-century groups that had been condemned for promoting rebaptism of those who had received the sacrament from morally tainted clergy.[2] Sixteenth-century Anabaptists espoused a believer's baptism, which could not be undertaken for those beneath the age of consent and religious education; its promises could not be pledged for another, such as a godchild, but must be made as expressions of an individual's conversion and self-dedication to God. Those whom Luther labeled "Spiritualists" and "Enthusiasts" sought a direct, personal encounter with the spirit through an unorthodox reading of the scriptures or through the channels of mystical experience.[3] Some, such as the militant revolutionary Thomas Münzer, attempted to create new communities limited to those who had themselves experienced authentic conversions, purging the so-called ungodly through violence.[4] Following the failure of experiments in politicizing the vision of a purified community, Anabaptists resolved to live in the surrounding world but distinct from it, setting themselves apart by their confessions of faith. Those who insisted on nonconformity to the established religion of a territory often faced persecution and even death for their beliefs.

In this chapter we will examine interpretations of Mary Magdalene to be found among the adherents of two communities that emerged from the Radical Reformation, from its beginnings through the close of the seventeenth century, when wider toleration for these groups changed the nature of their identity. We will look first at continental Anabaptists from the sixteenth century, as a group that documented considerable activity among women through its martyrological literature, and then at Quakers in seventeenth-century England, a movement whose founders embraced the Magdalene as an example of women's public leadership.[5]

Just as we have seen in the other denominations that emerged from the age of reform, the churches of the Radical Reformation had their own theological programs to advance and would take up aspects of the Magdalene tradition that served those goals. References to Mary Magdalene and to Mary of Bethany are infrequent in the documents preserved from the Anabaptist martyrs, despite the martyrs' overwhelming reliance on scriptural citation as the means of confession, exhortation, and spiritual counsel. There are some instances of her use, however, which indicate the parts of the saint's identity that were most relevant to Anabaptist theology. The relative absence of Magdalene references, even as other scriptural figures did become common rallying points, leads to questions about her appeal in different church contexts. Mary Magdalene's identification with prostitution may have been an undesirable connection for Anabaptists, who emphasized the moral life as an expression of conversion and who sought to distance themselves from Lutheran clergy and communities whom they criticized for immorality. Though the woman whom Jesus commanded to speak his message may have inspired evangelical churches, churches that needed to grow through the work of their members, she may have been less useful in a context of severe persecution, when open proselytizing was dangerous for illegal sects, and because the Magdalene's story did not feature a martyrdom with which the reader could identify.

In seventeenth-century England, members of new sects faced persecution, but execution was more rare than it was for continental Anabaptists. In the English context, we do find more confident adaptations of the Magdalene tradition. The founders of the English Quaker movement, Margaret Fell and her husband George Fox, held up the Magdalene of the resurrection narrative as the center of their argument for female preaching; their work would come to form the theology and practice of that denomination. The Quakers' embrace of Mary Magdalene alongside other prominent female scriptural prophets established a foundation for women's leadership in the Society of Friends.[6]

Both Anabaptists and Quakers engaged the Magdalene in different ways appropriate to their contexts and theology, even though these Free Church traditions did not emphasize sainthood apart from the lives of ordinary believers. As they saw other reformers around them doing, members of the Radical Reformation reinterpreted the Magdalene's legacy and derived authority from her story.[7]

Anabaptists

Anabaptists confronted persecution from their beginnings in the sixteenth century, as documented in the martyrs' testimonies that shaped the piety of the members of the movement. This literature participated in larger impulses of the era of Reformation, including attempts to establish legitimacy by connecting reform movements to the early church and its martyrs, and expressions of an apocalyptic worldview. After more than a century of persecution, Thieleman van Braght's The bloody theater: or, Martyrs mirror (1660) collected narratives of torture and execution, legal sentences, interrogation records, and letters from those imprisoned and condemned, written to their communities and loved ones. Van Braght presents these accounts of Anabaptist persecutions with a long introductory section on the Christian martyrs of the early church and medieval era, clearly proclaiming that the Anabaptists represent the true heirs of such faithful perseverance unto death.[8]

Explicit references to Mary Magdalene are few in the Martyrs mirror, despite a rhetorical culture that seems almost exclusively composed of biblical citations in both the original letters and the editorial material. In a movement strongly oriented toward iconoclasm, one might expect to find an absence of medieval saints used as examples. The lack of references even to the biblical figure of Mary Magdalene, and the subtlety of those that can be uncovered, require some interpretation of the sources and the theological goals of the communities they present. Anabaptists' relative silence on the Magdalene is unusual across the different faith communities that emerged from the age of reform. While there is insufficient evidence to explain her absence on the basis of contemporary sources—there are no explicit rejections of the Magdalene as a model for identification—there are some possible inferences we can draw from the context of early modern Anabaptism.[9]

Early Anabaptists often adopted a strategy of silence and equivocation. In many cases, silence was the safest course, and a self-comparison to an active preacher of the Gospel would simply have been too dangerous. Silence in the face of persecution went beyond a pragmatic caution for Anabaptists, however. Passive resistance to suffering, including silent endurance, was held by Anabaptists to be a mark of the true church, following Christ's counsel to turn the other cheek and his silence during his own trial and torture. Anabaptist communities established their authority, paradoxically, by *not* claiming it with eloquent arguments.[10]

In the third-person narratives of executions—particularly those of female martyrs—there are many descriptions of Anabaptists facing death eagerly, going joyfully to meet Christ, their promised bridegroom. This image for the relationship between the believer and Christ begs the question of a woman's proper allegiance, to her heavenly bridegroom or to her earthly home and duties, the dilemma in the story of Mary and Martha. This conflict underlies one such use of the marriage metaphor, in the account of the deaths of martyrs David and Levina, in 1554. Van Braght writes of Levina that she "rather forsook, not only her six dear children, but also her temporal life, than her dear Lord and Bridegroom Jesus Christ."[11] The Anabaptist martyrs' loyalty to Christ above all else makes the leave-taking of children a frequent subject of the condemned believers' letters to family members.[12] The assertion that Christ is one's true spouse, taking priority over an earthly husband and children, therefore implicitly invokes two of the themes of the Magdalene tradition: Mary of Bethany's intimacy with Christ and the marriage imagery of the Song of Songs. References to particular passages from the Song of Songs in the martyrs' documents establish the profound nature of the bond between believers and Christ, as in the narrative for Maria and Ursula van Beckum, executed in 1544. The two women accompany one another to death, and van Braght notes, "Here love was stronger than death, and firmer than the grave. Cant. 8:6." The same text figures in a contemporary Anabaptist hymn that praised the two women. The use of marital language to describe faith as making an absolute claim is especially significant in light of the permission and even encouragement granted to an Anabaptist woman to divorce a spouse who did not share her religious affiliation. The obligation to Christ took priority over the human wedding vows, as an early Swiss Anabaptist tract affirmed. "The spiritual marriage and obligation to Christ, yea, faith, love, and obedience to God . . . takes precedence over the earthly marriage, and one ought rather forsake such earthly companion than the spiritual companion. And by not removing the designated one from the bond of marriage we [mistakenly] care more for earthly than for spiritual obligations and debts." If the spiritual life is akin to a marital relationship, martyrdom then becomes the act of consummation, or the public wedding ceremony of the spiritual marriage.[13]

While the reference to bridal imagery from the Song of Songs is present, however, it remains largely general, with the identification of Christ as the believer's spouse often made abstractly. There are no explicit references at all in the *Martyrs mirror* to Mary Magdalene's traditional association with the female figure of the Song of Songs. Marriage language is also used in connection with the parable of the wise and foolish virgins, whose preparation for the coming of the bridegroom made the difference between those who would go into the wedding feast and those who would be cast into the outer darkness.[14] And by contrast with the absence of the Magdalene, the figures of Susannah and Judith are openly recommended as examples of suffering and sacrifice; perhaps the violence attached to their stories made them more appealing models for those facing immediate persecution.[15]

The only places where unambiguous references to Mary Magdalene—in her various identities—are to be found is in the letters Anabaptists wrote to their families as they awaited execution. Two of the features of the Magdalene's character—her intimacy with Christ, including the implicit echo in references to the bride from the Song of Songs, and the primacy that Mary of Bethany gave to her devotion to Christ, before her role in the family—persist as strong theological currents in the martyrs' letters. The special importance Anabaptists placed on the scriptures as the sole means of salvation suggested a suitable theological role for Mary of Bethany, with her particular dedication to the Word incarnate, listening attentively to the person of Christ.[16] A letter from Jerome Segers to his wife, Lijksen Dircks, in 1551, while both were imprisoned, makes use of Mary's example at a crucial time of testing. He encourages his wife to persevere in reading the Bible for herself, even though she may be urged otherwise by those anxious to turn her from the faith: "And though they may tell you to attend to your sewing, this does not prevent us; for Christ has called us all, and commanded us to search the Scriptures, since they testify of Him; and Christ also said that Magdalene had chosen the better part, because she searched the Scriptures. Matt. 11.28, John 5:39, Luke 10:42."[17] Segers here continues the identification of the Magdalene as Mary of Bethany and uses her example to argue for the supreme importance of the spiritual life for both men and women, even at the expense of domestic responsibilities. The "sewing" Dircks was advised to concentrate on may have had a more pointed meaning than simply a standard female task. It likely meant the preparation of clothing for the child she was expecting; she was executed by drowning shortly after giving birth. One can conclude from Segers's entreaty that reminders to consider one's traditional duties and family loyalties were one part of the approach that was taken to reconvert Anabaptist women. Segers and his wife were imprisoned and killed in Antwerp, a Catholic community, where arguments against female scripture reading might be expected as part of the standard arsenal against Protestantism, more than they might be in a Lutheran or Reformed context.

Similar language was used by Jan Wouters, who was imprisoned and burned at the stake in Dordrecht in March 1572, just before the Dutch rebellion against Hapsburg rule achieved a coup in the city, establishing Protestant rule.[18] Though Dordrecht had, by that time, developed as a staunch outpost of Reformed theology, it was confessionally divided and officially loyal to Catholic Spain at the time of Wouters's death. Indeed, some of Wouters's own family remained Catholic, and so, as for Segers, the very reading of the scriptures was in jeopardy for his female correspondents.[19] In a letter to the family of his sister and brother-in-law, written in 1572, Wouters offered parting counsel to his nieces and nephews, encouraging them all to follow Christ's teaching. The particular advice he gives to one niece includes a reference to Mary of Bethany: "Hence I beseech you, my dear, beloved niece, to shun evil, diligently to seek the kingdom of God and His righteousness, and to work to satisfy [your soul's] hunger with bread, and quench her thirst with drink. If you do this, my dear niece, you will be one who with Mary has chosen the good part; and I will then await you there with Christ Jesus."[20]

Anabaptist men can thus be seen applying the identity of the Magdalene— especially as Mary of Bethany—to their correspondents, mostly intimate members of their families. The identification is an interesting one in the context of the early modern family, in which men held authority over their households and women were generally understood to be relegated to domestic roles. In the case of religious persecution, however, that hierarchy of value appears to have been disrupted, with the spiritual equality of the priesthood of all believers and the evangelical imperative of a public confession of faith taking precedence over social conventions and duties. Though many of the letters include discussions of a couple's children, they never counsel abandonment of the faith in order to protect them or maintain a home for them. Under the conditions of imprisonment and martyrdom, Anabaptist husbands and fathers felt compelled to call their wives away from home and hearth, to a devotion to the Word of God that might cost them their families and lives. The women who followed that call were celebrated in the community, in stories such as that of Anneken Jansz, who went to her martyrdom after handing her small child to a stranger in the crowd. This act reversed cultural expectations of women's maternal attachment and devotion to duty. Yet women had been doing what they were not supposed to do in the Christian tradition from its beginnings, from Mary of Bethany abandoning the housework to sit at Christ's feet, to the Magdalene preaching publicly about the resurrection.[21]

The Magdalene's traditional identities were used to fortify Anabaptist martyrs for a radical commitment to God, though other figures were more common. For those who were not in contexts of immediate persecution, the question of women's preaching and public testimony in Anabaptist communities also demonstrated subtle but enduring echoes of the Magdalene's roles as preacher and as one possessed by an emphatically undomesticated spirituality. These echoes can be detected by looking carefully at how women's activity developed among Anabaptists, and how it was characterized by contemporaries. That Anabaptist women did speak and teach in public is attested to by the mockery of the movement for its departure from conventional gender roles. In Antwerp, the home of many Anabaptist martyrs, the Catholic poet Anna Bijns derided a situation in which, as she saw it, "doctors, clergymen, licentiates, / are now taught by women." Anabaptist women engaged in a range of practices such as teaching and proselytizing, Bible reading and interpretation, hymn writing, hosting religious gatherings in their homes, and prophetic speech, as well as authoring farewell letters and public testimonies at the time of their martyrdom. These activities combine two commonly acknowledged characteristics of preaching: communication that produces conversion and teaching that claims a degree of authority.[22]

Contemporary observers recorded various kinds of public testimony by women. Some of the first descriptions of Anabaptist meetings feature demonstrations of charisms by both women and men who testified by confessing the faith and speaking in tongues, as happened in Germany and Switzerland in the mid-1520s. The spiritual authority thus established was translated into the terms of Anabaptist polity. The Schleitheim Confession gave congregations, including women, the power to evaluate and discipline pastors. Anabaptist women as a whole contributed to the mutual governance of the community.[23]

In addition to participating in public, mixed gatherings, they also proclaimed the Gospel among themselves, and to convert other women. Women evangelized through networks of female occupations, such as the teaching of children and servants in the home, and in work as itinerant seamstresses. Women's meeting together was sometimes regarded by local authorities as merely domestic, social, or simply not as ominous as a male gathering, and so women's proselytizing proved crucial—through evading some persecution—for the survival of the movement. Despite the relative invisibility of these kinds of networks, such efforts did not pass entirely unnoticed. In Switzerland, for example, Margaret Hellwart was punished for her successful evangelism of women.[24]

The recorded testimonies of those women tried and punished for their Anabaptist faith constitute one of the most visible kinds of female religious leadership. Women used the forum of public persecution to give voice to their theological commitments. Not only the women's words, but the ways in which they were interpreted by contemporary biographers conveyed their character through preached messages to the faithful. These courtroom and scaffold sermons feature standard elements of the preaching genre: they outline the speaker's theological position, distinguishing it from opposing positions, and they use evidence from scripture. Margret Hottinger, when questioned in Zurich in 1525–1526, denied the validity of infant baptism. One of her companions, Winbrat Fanwiler, supported this claim by noting the absence of infant baptism in scripture, showing that she was confident in interpreting scripture in public. Agnes Linck, interrogated in 1528 in Solothurn, Switzerland, openly questioned both Catholic and Lutheran sacramental theology and proclaimed her own baptism "in spirit and in truth," directly from God. She affirmed this understanding of baptism, as well as the importance of living a biblical life and of condemning the cult of the saints, in another public interrogation two years later in Basel. Her confession includes an admission that she had been teaching children in her household. She criticized the preaching of local clergy, with the implication that her own publicly voiced theological opinions were, by contrast, true. Because she was also accused of having purchased a New Testament, all of this activity can be said to have a scriptural origin; like the pronouncements and programs of male clergy, the "preaching" of Linck and other Anabaptist women was the expression of their own interpretation of the Bible. This intimate experience of the Word of God, which transformed the believer's life and commanded her to speak, parallels the Magdalene's relationship to Christ, her devotion to the Word incarnate as "the one thing necessary." While members of other confessional traditions made this parallel openly in describing their impulse to speak or write, for Anabaptist women the comparison was more implicit.[25]

Implicit, subtle, or coded messages were a common feature of Anabaptist discourse. Sometimes the speech made by Anabaptist women was not a straightforward confession of faith but demonstrated the strategy of silence or carefully manipulated speech in order to safeguard the movement. One tactic was a pretense of mental defect or "simplemindedness." Adelheit Schwartz and her companions, interrogated in Zurich in 1529, gave answers that stymied the questioners through mumbling, self-contradiction, and the offering of statements too generic to contest. Margaret Hellwart's demeanor, smiling and laughing through her interrogations in Beutelsbach in the early seventeenth century, conveyed courage and disdain for other religious authorities. Women staged public religious actions, such as mocking ecclesiastical visitors and preachers, desecrating holy water, and proclaiming visions of violence against prominent members of the clergy. Women evangelized through such subversive actions and speech acts as well as through the wordless but powerful testimony of their lives. Margret Hottinger was renowned and respected for her disciplined manner of life; this authority gave credibility to her claims about a direct connection to God, which she justified with scriptural references.[26]

Thus, although they were not permitted to serve as preachers and pastors of congregations, women in early modern Anabaptism effectively "preached" in a variety of ways, including conversation, hospitality, teaching, civil disobedience, religious protest, singing and ecstatic utterance, and testimony in the face of persecution. While their work was not described as preaching by either the women or their audiences, it was clearly understood and feared for its power to convert and for its claims of authoritative teaching. Women's public speech was crucial to the spread of the Anabaptist movement through informal networks of evangelism and the more formal statements made by martyred women, whose words were treasured and recorded by their local communities and in the wider Anabaptist tradition. The very importance of women's evangelism links their work to the role of the Magdalene, the first preacher of the Christian church. Other features of women's activity in early modern Anabaptism recall other aspects of the Magdalene legacy: persistent devotion to Christ in the face of physical suffering and at the expense of one's family duties; prophetic testimony that is viewed as insubordinate or at least inappropriate; and support of the church's growth (and of a charismatic preacher) from within a community of women.

Anabaptist Preachers

Just as laypersons can be found invoking the scriptural images and cultural resonances of Mary Magdalene at need, the professional theologians of the Anabaptist movement also adapted the Magdalene legacy to address pastoral and theoretical questions. The leader of the Anabaptist movement in the Netherlands, Menno Simons, explored the story of the sinful woman from Luke 7 in his essay *The True Christian Faith* (1541). Simons assumed the leadership of the Dutch movement after the violent defeat of the Anabaptist revolution in Münster, where activists had attempted to convert the city by force.

Simons's concern to direct the community away from the dangers of social activism and instead toward personal holiness is evident in the use he makes of the Magdalene. Following the traditional association—Simons had been a Catholic priest before becoming an Anabaptist—he connects the woman in Luke 7 with Mary Magdalene, though he does allude to the controversy over her identity: "She had been possessed of seven devils (if indeed she was that woman, or Mary, of whom the evangelists make mention)." Simons describes her conversion, which produced in her the virtuous response of humility. He uses her example to embark on a long tirade, reproving the proud in his community and congregation. In particular, he attacks those who wear fine clothes, depicting the Magdalene as a worldly sensualist, a wealthy heiress tempted to sin by her beauty, which she had exploited with cosmetics, elaborate hair arrangements, and fashionable dress. Christian women, he writes, should not do so, and even if they are inclined to, their husbands should curb such inclinations. This last counsel indicates that Anabaptist culture in this period affirmed a traditional hierarchy of marital authority, only encouraging departure from it under conditions of persecution. As the Dutch Anabaptist community retreated from the political experiments of their earlier history, the assertion of an ethical emphasis that would support social order promoted the long-term survival of the movement.[27]

Distancing themselves from the anarchic freedom of revolution, Anabaptists focused on adherence to a strict moral code. In a text that engaged the community on the fraught question of the role of good works in Christian life, the penitent woman provided Simons with an important example of amendment of life. According to his reading, her story should shame those who profess to be Christians and yet continue in sin, especially sexual sin. In this, Simons applies the caution equally to men and women. Indeed, he goes on mostly to criticize those men who seduce and use women for selfish pleasure, without any commitment to honorable marriage. Simons lists the admirable characteristics of the woman after her conversion: she "adorned her soul inwardly and not her appearance outwardly"; she "sighed and wept and feared the wrath and judgment of the Lord"; she "was compassionate and merciful"; she "sought the company of the righteous"; she "sat at the feet of Jesus and heard his holy Word." The character he sketches includes all of the elements of the composite, medieval Magdalene: asceticism, penitence, compassion, weeping, discipleship, and Mary of Bethany's complete devotion to the incarnate Word. He then portrays sinful men and women doing the opposite in each case, adorning themselves with fancy clothes, wasting themselves in frivolity, being proud and cruel, keeping bad company, and turning away from the study of God's word.[28]

In the conclusion of his essay, Simons returns to the story's special application to women, using the Magdalene as an instructive image of ideal female spirituality: "I, therefore, entreat and desire all women through the mercy of the Lord to take this sorrowful, sorrowing woman as a pattern and follow her faith." Simons, though, draws the opposite conclusion to the one that Anabaptist martyr Jerome Segers found in this text. Where Segers urged his wife to remain true by reading the scriptures for herself, even if others remind her to attend to her sewing, Simons advises women to display their faithfulness *through* domestic labor. The imitation of Mary that Simons recommends means being humble and obedient and staying quietly and dutifully at home: "Remain within your houses and gates . . . attend faithfully to your charge, to your children, house, and family . . . and walk in all things as the sinful woman did after her conversion." The lesson drawn here is unusual, given that amid the Magdalene's numerous identities, that of mother is nowhere to be found. The figure of Mary of Bethany was a traditional symbol of the neglect of household duties in favor of spiritual pursuits, and the Magdalene herself was known to have wandered stubbornly out of doors on the morning of the resurrection, when the male disciples remained prudently at home. Again, Simons's interpretation confirms that outside of the context of persecution, in more pastoral situations, Anabaptists emphasized moral duties, reshaping the Magdalene tradition to convey ethical positions on marriage and the family that conflicted with what they taught when salvation was at stake.[29]

In another pastoral context, that of teaching about the sacraments, Mary Magdalene's example was also used to support and advance Anabaptist theology as distinct from that of other reform movements. Mary Magdalene's daring actions following the resurrection are the subject of a letter written on Easter Sunday 1561 by the Silesian pastor Caspar Schwenckfeld. Schwenckfeld was influenced by Luther, but went on to formulate his own doctrine on the sacraments, resulting in his eventual exile and the condemnation of his teaching by Lutheran authorities. In Schwenckfeld's letter to Sibilla Eisler, he uses the resurrection narrative to describe the Lord's Supper as a memorial of Christ rather than as the real presence of Christ's body and blood that Lutherans maintained. He begins conventionally, by repeating the traditional comparison between the faith of the women who remained at the tomb and that of the male disciples: "Dear sister in Christ: There is not time today to write much, except to meditate upon the joyful resurrection of our dear Lord Christ and how he consoled and cheered his disconsolate disciples and the beloved women. The latter remained more faithful to the Lord Christ than the men, leaving him neither at the Cross nor at his burial. . . . Oh how heart-warming to reflect on Mary Magdalene who loved the Lord so fervently and to whom he also appeared first." In his praise of the saint's loyalty, Schwenckfeld notes that her devotion was rewarded with the first appearance of the risen Christ, therefore distinguishing her among his followers. He then goes on to say that Mary Magdalene loved Christ so much that she reached out to touch him, but he refused. She could not touch the risen Lord except spiritually, and that becomes the pattern for all believers' contact with the post-resurrection Jesus; hence, the faithful do not consume Christ bodily in the Eucharist. Where medieval theologians—and John Calvin—engaged the noli me tangere pericope to disparage women's carnality, Schwenckfeld insists that this text is a teaching about sacramental theology, without attributing frailty of character to all women thereby. As we saw her in the late medieval and early Lutheran preaching on the forgiveness of sins, Mary Magdalene is again functioning in the place of the prototypical believer, revealing the touchstone of the particular theological formula on offer.[30]

The diversity of interpretations within early Anabaptism illustrates the flexibility of the Magdalene tradition, supplying models for what were, at times, conflicting theological goals. Absolute commitment to a radically personal experience of the scriptures, concern for moral conduct among the faithful, and a Reformed sacramental theology were all part of the Anabaptist movement from its beginnings. Mary Magdalene stands at the Reformation nexus of Gospel and Law, sacred revelation and secular order, able to speak to both worlds. She demonstrates a selfless, absolute commitment to the Word of God and helps reformers argue for the kind of self, and society, that should follow from that allegiance.

Quakers

Anabaptists' engagement with the Magdalene tradition presents a contradictory and ambiguous picture, resonating with the themes of her various roles yet demonstrating a hesitance, on the part of early modern Anabaptist women, to identify themselves directly with the famous sinner-saint or to claim the title of preacher. Many traditions emerged from the Radical Reformation, including large Free Church bodies, small sects, and individual teachings. From among this diverse movement, one well-known and influential Free Church community, the Quakers, makes a useful comparison to Anabaptists' coded interpretation of the Magdalene because of the very explicit use of some of the same texts and images. Quakers adopted the Magdalene to argue boldly and openly for women's religious leadership, though even there we can find evidence of tensions between different Magdalene interpretations.

The messages carried by the Magdalene tradition were enthusiastically taken up and expanded by the Quakers from the first years of their founding in the mid-seventeenth century. The Quakers shared many of the core concerns of radical reform with the Anabaptists, though they were not parallel movements and, indeed, they came into conflict with each other in the English context. Both groups had broken away from other reform communities—the Anabaptists from the early evangelical reform on the

Continent, the Quakers from the Church of England—because they thought that those efforts did not take conversion to a biblical life seriously enough. Like the Anabaptists, the Quakers emphasized the direct experience of the spirit, permitting individual biblical interpretation and charismatic, unprogrammed liturgy. Also like the Anabaptists, for the Quakers the formation of a community of those who gave testimony of a profound conversion led to concern with the shape of moral life. The gathered faithful should reflect the depth of their transformation through purity of conduct. Both Anabaptists and Quakers were persecuted for this attempt to proclaim a visible community of the elect, and for departing from orthodox interpretations of baptism and the Eucharist. But while the Anabaptists had sought after the trauma of Münster to remove themselves from the wider society, Quakers worked within that society as activists. Anabaptist women had found ways of preaching indirectly or covertly, through a series of evangelical ministries and testimonies; Quaker women openly claimed the mantle of preacher in the name of the Magdalene.[31]

Quakerism's founder, George Fox, promoted a more equal role for women in the new church he envisioned with his treatise *The Woman Learning in Silence* (1656), in which he addressed the prohibition on women's speech from 1 Timothy 2 with the examples of Priscilla and Phoebe in the early church and Mary Magdalene in the Gospels. This was not an abstract hope for the future; Fox used the Magdalene to advocate for the public ministry of his contemporaries. In 1684, for example, he wrote to the Duke of Holstein, defending the preaching of Elizabeth Hendricks to the Quakers in that territory: "Was it not Mary Magdalene and other women that first preached Christ's resurrection to the apostles? . . . Christ sent these women to preach his resurrection; so it is no shame for such women to preach Christ Jesus; neither are they to be silent when Christ sends them."[32]

Another of the founders of the movement, and also Fox's wife, Margaret Askew Fell (tradition held that she was the great granddaughter of the English Reformation martyr, Anne Askew), discussed the saint in her own treatise arguing for women's right to preach and teach publicly.[33] *Women's Speaking Justified, Proved and Allowed of by the Scriptures* (1666) rejects the prohibitions from 1 Corinthians 14 and 1 Timothy 2, opposing them with counterexamples taken from the life of Christ, an approach we saw in the *querelle des femmes* tradition. The worthiness of women is attested by the love Christ showed for them and received from them, as Fell writes: "Thus

FIG 7.1 *A Quaker Assembly in London,* 1735. Engraving. Photo: Bibliothèque des Arts Décoratifs, Paris / © DeA Picture Library / Art Resource, New York.

we see that Jesus owned the love and grace that appeared in women, and did not despise it, and by what is recorded in the Scriptures, he received as much love, kindness, compassion, and tender dealing towards him from women, as he did from any others, both in his life time, and also after they had exercised their cruelty upon him, for Mary Magdalene, and Mary the mother of Joses, beheld where he was laid."[34]

The Magdalene's compassion for Christ and intimate relationship with him represent the character of all women. Her spirituality is a pattern for imitation for all believers, as it had been throughout the medieval church. At the dawning of the Pietist era, however, this kind of meditation on the Magdalene took on a new rigor. Fell's argument is less a delicate hymn to the feminine qualities of all gentle and compassionate followers of Christ and more clearly a legitimation of female, affective spirituality in which the actions and experiences of women speak in bold opposition to academic—and traditionally male—theology. This exploration of women's religious experience is remarkably similar in tone, albeit with very different practical implications, to the devotional writing of the Lutheran mystic Catharina Regina von Greiffenberg, Fell's contemporary.[35]

Fell goes on to discuss the crucial role played by the female witnesses of the resurrection in the spread of the Gospel and the life of the early church, but with a more openly confrontational stance than we have witnessed so far: "It was Mary Magdalene, and Joanna, and Mary the mother of James, and the other women that were with them, which told these things to the Apostles, 'And their words seemed unto them as idle tales, and they believed them not.' Mark this, ye despisers of the weakness of women, and look upon yourselves to be so wise: but Christ Jesus doth not so, for he makes use of the weak. . . . Mark this, you that despise and oppose the message of the Lord God that he sends by women, what had become of the redemption of the whole body of mankind if they had not believed the message that the Lord Jesus sent by these women, of and concerning his resurrection?"[36] The message of Mary and the other women coming from the tomb was almost discounted because of their gender. Fell blames the male disciples for this—not because they failed to preach themselves, but because they failed to listen. Her interpretation draws on the same theological framework as Calvin's: God has decided to make special use of the weakness of women in delivering the news of salvation to humanity. Her aim is different, however. She is not trying to shock men into taking their rightful place as the true preachers of the Gospel, but simply to make them ashamed at their reluctance to believe God's chosen messenger, and to warn them against ignoring or silencing women's speech in the future.

Two parts of the Magdalene's identity, her compassion and her preaching, are joined together by Fell as being paradigmatic for women; both the tenderness and the testimony of women, when combined, are the necessary foundation of the church. The giving and receiving of love in intimate exchange has ultimately forged a stronger bond between Christ and his female followers than has the intellectual teaching and ecclesiastical debate conducted among the male disciples. Fell's Radical Reformation emphasis on the inner stirrings of heart and spirit is evident in this movement of women to the foreground of the church's mission. The Gospel is not carried *despite* the weakness of its first vessel, but *because* of it; the Magdalene's feminine character offers a paradoxical source of strength and insight to the church, from which men are called to learn: "And if these women had not thus, out of their tenderness and bowels of love, who had received mercy, and grace, and forgiveness of sins, and virtue, and healing from him, which many men also had received the like, if their hearts had not been so united, and knit unto him in love, that they could not depart as the men did, but sat watching, and waiting, and weeping about the sepulcher until the time of his resurrection, and so were ready to carry his message, as is manifested, else how should his Disciples have known, who were not there?" This is the school of women in earnest. Fell urges her readers to reflect on the vital necessity of the women's presence, attitude, and response, and then to take up the task of securing equal participation in the church's life.[37]

One important forum for female church activity was in the women's meetings favored by Quakers. While Anabaptist women's preaching has to be excavated from a study of evangelical activities and interrogation records, Quaker women can be seen self-consciously coming together and training each other to preach and teach; they left a published history of instructions for doing so. George Fox's letter from 1679, "To the Men and Women's Meetings," sent to Bedfordshire, Leicestershire, and Northamptonshire, continues Fell's embrace of the positive contributions of women's nurturing character, working for the good of the church, especially as Quakerism matured and became a "family religion." He hoped that women "would become like Sarah, Deborah, Miriam, Dorcas, Priscilla, and the repentant Mary Magdalene, 'to give suck to nurse up the seed and heir of the promise.'" Another pamphlet encouraging the formation of women's meetings in particular was published between 1675 and 1680, and sent from the Lancashire Meeting of Women Friends to other women's meetings in Britain and North America. The text was likely written under the guidance of Sarah Fell, Margaret Fell's daughter. The letter was widely circulated and had significant influence on the development of Quakerism.[38]

The Lancashire Meeting's letter explores several scriptural figures as examples of Christ's relationships with women. The Canaanite woman and the Samaritan woman are discussed as objects of Christ's mercy. Mary Magdalene is mentioned among the women Christ had healed, and who had "ministered to him of their substance." The woman who anointed him with oil and washed his feet with her hair is included next, but seems to be understood as a separate woman from Mary Magdalene, though also an important one. Her proximate position to the figure named as the Magdalene represents a strong echo of the traditional conflation of identities. Caring for Christ's body and nurturing his spiritual body, the church, are shown to be parallel activities, even if they are not necessarily supposed to have been performed by a single individual.[39]

The letter's central exegetical study celebrates the church's debt to the women who went to the tomb on Easter Sunday; the treatment takes its pattern from Margaret Fell's *Women's Speaking Justified:*

> And they remembered his words, and returned from the Sepulchre, and told all these things unto the eleven, and to all the rest, It was Mary Magdalen, and Joanna, and Mary the Mother of James, and other women that were with them, which told these things unto the Apostles, and their words seemed to them as Idle tales, and they believed them not, as you may see in Luke 24. and Mark 15.40.41. Math: 28.5. So these women were the first preachers of the Resurrection of Jesus . . . and Jesus himself spake with Mary . . . and Mary Magdalen came and told the disciples. . . . Soe here the lord Jesus Christ sent his first message of his resurrection by women unto his own disciples: And they were faithful unto him, and did his message, and yet they could hardly be believed.[40]

After establishing the crucial role of women in the early Christian community, the pamphlet then exhorts the women to meet monthly, just as the men do, to discern and follow God's will for them and to live upright lives. The Radical Reformation's embrace of early church practices is here manifested as a desire to return to the conditions thought to have existed for women before the institutionalization of the church, the vision of communal life found in Acts. Quaker anticlericalism thus goes hand in hand with an egalitarian vision of religious community. The text's vision of the early church is not idealized, however. The caution about the disciples' initial unwillingness to listen to Mary Magdalene and her companions is intended to brace women against potential conflicts over their role in the present-day church. The pamphlet spurs women's meetings to go forward with a determination made resolute by a realistic understanding of the challenges faced by all female proclaimers of the Gospel in order to claim the legacy of Christ's own commissioning of the Magdalene and her companions: "And so here in the power and spirit, of the Lord God, women come to be co-heirs, and fellow labourers, in the Gospel, as it was in the Apostles' days."[41]

That legacy was celebrated in the poetry of the Scottish Quaker Lilias Skene. Raised as a radical Presbyterian in Aberdeen, Skene converted to Quakerism in 1666 and pursued a public ministry, publishing letters and sermons defending her fellow Quakers from persecution. Her untitled poem from 1695 acknowledges women's central role in the salvation history of humanity, from Eve to Mary Magdalene, whose first preaching of the Gospel was the founding example that authorized Skene's own work: "A women was the instroment / Of mankinds los and fall / A woman brought the ferst report / Christ had restored all." Women here are the chosen agents of God's action throughout human history, supporting Quaker teaching that contemporary women must continue to allow the spirit to work through them.[42]

The Quaker theologian Elizabeth Bathurst's large pamphlet *The Sayings of Women* (1683) argued for women's ministry and leadership by presenting a survey of prominent scriptural women, including several of the Magdalene's traditional identities. Though she does not conflate them, she discusses the woman who anointed Christ—Mary choosing the better part and sitting at the feet of Christ "that all people might chiefly prefer the better part and esteem the Word of Truth as the one thing needful," and Mary Magdalene and the other women in the synoptic Gospels "giving Testimony of his resurrection." The Johannine resurrection narrative is given its own extended section, noting that "Christ conferred with Mary, and she with him; unto whom he first shewed himself after his resurrection." At the end of the list of examples, Bathurst concludes, "so Women receive an Office in the Truth as well as Men, and they have a Stewardship, and must give an account of their Stewardship to their Lord, as well as the Men."[43]

The Quakers are well known for their early feminist rhetoric, for which they found support in the Magdalene's scriptural preaching role. A different element of the Magdalene tradition can be found in some less prominent seventeenth-century Quaker documents, in identifications of the ideal Quaker life with the contemplation of Mary of Bethany. Elizabeth Stirredge (1634–1706) wrote in 1692, describing the persecution she and her husband had faced over the course of a long lifetime of Quaker witness in Bristol, England. Stirredge evokes the experience of reading the Bible with a frustrating sense of the distance between herself and the original events, seeking comfort from the standard Christian source of the scriptures yet unable to achieve the personal contact for which she longs: "Many hours have I been alone, reading and mourning, when no eye saw me, nor ear heard me, neither could I find comfort in reading, because it was a book sealed unto me. Then did I mourn, and say, 'Oh! That I had been born in the days when our blessed saviour Jesus Christ was upon the earth; how would I have followed him, and sat at his feet, as Mary did."[44] The author voices the urgency that characterized radical reform: mere acquaintance with sacred texts and traditions is not enough to produce the desired spiritual connection with Christ as it had been felt by those who had surrounded him intimately. Only a direct experience of Christ's presence, such as Mary Magdalene had, could satisfy those whom Luther had labeled the "Enthusiasts." Though Stirredge expresses a Quaker sentiment, desiring an encounter with the divine more personal than that available through sacred texts, her language recalls the spiritual envy described by many female authors, from Margery Kempe to Teresa of Avila, in their own longing for intimacy with Christ. The Magdalene's model of friendship with Christ evidently held enduring power for women across confessional boundaries through the early modern period.

Alongside this self-identification among Quakers, we also find descriptions of a profound, unmediated relationship to Christ in comparisons of Quaker mothers to Mary of Bethany, as preserved in remembrances by their daughters. This phenomenon is part of the innovative adaptation of the Magdalene legacy in Protestant religious culture, transforming the medieval use of the Mary and Martha story in defense of the cloistered, celibate life into a spirituality of the family. As we had observed in the case of the Reformed scholar Anna Maria van Schurman, Mary's devotion could be reinterpreted as part of a faithful pursuit of vocation that includes new elements: a woman's life incorporating secular scholarship or, in this case, the demands of motherhood. In the spiritual counsel that Anabaptist martyrs offered to one another, the moral ambiguities of so deep a devotion were revealed, as parents encouraged each other in a faithfulness that would ultimately remove them from their children. The Quaker daughters' spiritual biographies are not so conflicted. Quaker daughters who pay tribute to their mothers using the model of Mary of Bethany do not cast doubt on the purity of their parents' dedication to either God or family, but rather affirm that such powerful examples shaped the faith of their children, forming the vital core of their motherhood. Joan Wintrow recorded the dying words of her daughter, Susannah, as she praised her mother, in "These are the Dying Words of the

Maid." Susannah assures Joan that she has been the best sort of mother, precisely in showing her children how fiercely she sought communion with Christ: "Thou art *Mary*, thou art *Mary*; My Mother, thou hast chosen the good part." Elizabeth Bols also makes the comparison in a remembrance of her mother, Mary Watson, and the reference to female weakness, common in different Magdalene narratives, underscores the ardor of her piety: "My dear Mother, tho' but weak of Body, yet formerly was much given to fasting on Religious Accounts, and spending much of her time in private Retirements, fervent prayers, and praising the Lord, delighting much in Meditations and like *Mary*, that Christ said, *had chosen that better part*."[45] These published accounts described the orientation of individual and family piety and helped to shape Christian family life for their readers, creating an image of Quaker motherhood as being first and foremost a testimony of faith to one's children.

The encouragement of praise for a wholesome example was not the only way in which Mary of Bethany could be used, however. Toward the close of the seventeenth century, as Quakerism became a tolerated denomination, the radical ideology of its first decades gave way to an acceptance of conventional social patterns. In 1700 Susanna Blandford, a dissenting Quaker, in *A Small Treatise Writ by One of the True Christian Faith, Who Believes in God and in His Son Jesus Christ*, argued against women's public preaching by saying that Mary "sat silently at Christ's feet" and therefore so should her opponent in a debate on the question![46]

The Magdalene's complex identity remained supple enough, even within a single tradition, to contain multiple meanings and to support conflicting or shifting theological positions. More than simply offering a diversity of options, though, Quaker theology and practice engaged the Magdalene tradition in order to argue for a greater degree of public participation and leadership than women had in any other community that emerged from the age of reform. In a polity where the priesthood of all believers was in contention with no ordained priesthood, where there existed no theological separation between laity and clergy, the potential of the *apostola apostolorum* legacy could be realized as nowhere else.

THE PASTORS AND COMMUNITIES of the Radical Reformation, who were even more preoccupied with iconoclasm and the rejection of medieval saints' legends than were the Lutheran and Calvinist reformers, can nevertheless be seen adapting the Magdalene tradition to advance their own goals. As a scriptural figure, the Magdalene could not be ignored entirely; moreover, aspects of her traditional identity proved extremely useful in addressing the concerns of radical reform, particularly in establishing models of lay and female preaching and in considerations of how to achieve intimacy with Christ. Although Anabaptists and Quakers avoided the legendary elements of her cult, such as her preaching career in Marseilles or accounts of her death, the connections among Mary Magdalene, Mary of Bethany, and the sinful woman of Luke 7 remained common in these movements through the seventeenth century, ensuring that her historical character would remain a part of the spirituality of the Free Church traditions.

Different elements of Mary Magdalene's character were put to use according to the various programs of the churches that emerged from the Radical Reformation. Where the encouragement of lay and female preaching was seen as both important and relatively safe, as it was for the Quakers, the focus was on the Magdalene's role in the resurrection narrative and her delivery of the good news to the apostles. In communities facing violent persecution, where public religious testimony was dangerous and possibly fatal, another face of the Magdalene comes to the fore. Mary of Bethany's quiet yet absolute dedication to Jesus, standing in opposition to societal pressures, offered an image of comfort and strength for imprisoned Anabaptists under threat of torture and death.[47]

Despite the restraint of the Anabaptists in publicly embracing the Magdalene's female model of evangelism, the emerging pattern among Protestant interpretations of Mary Magdalene is clear, and was so to contemporaries on both sides of the confessional divide in the age of reform. Whether her intimacy with Christ is emphasized, or the focus is on her preaching of the first news of the resurrection, Protestants found in her an accessible pattern for the spiritual life and activity of every Christian. Her sinfulness was that of every man and woman, and so, therefore, was her response: a profound union with Christ, expressed in the common vocation of all believers, a priesthood of the heart and mind and a ministry of the Word.

CONCLUSION

An Army of Such Ladies

COULD IT be possible to explain the persistence of the Magdalene tradition in early modern Protestant circles as simply a lingering remnant of medieval piety, which eventually grew less and less compelling as Protestant religious culture became established? Perhaps the iconoclasm of the age of reform simply took several generations to be internalized, but the common assumptions about the Magdalene's disappearance for Protestants would ultimately prove accurate. Was Protestant culture as unkind to this saint as scholars of religion and even of the Magdalene herself have claimed? Did she really vanish—either all at once, or gradually—from Protestant spiritual life?

The Reformation era was defined by new encounters with the Word of God in scripture as printed texts, vernacular translations, and increasing literacy combined to make the Bible more accessible than ever before. The Magdalene is a central figure in the Gospel stories, and especially in the narrative of Christ's death and resurrection. As such, she became an inherent part of reformers' wrestling with these texts, as they interpreted them in innovative ways and in conversation with each other's arguments. Far from confirming her disappearance, our survey of early modern Magdalenes has discovered her at the heart of Protestant theological formation, where the Magdalene's flexible image helped mold new vocations for the clergy and the laity. And our exploration has revealed Catholic Magdalenes that shifted dramatically from medieval models, in response to Protestantism and to changing internal needs within Catholic communities, as part of institutional reform, devotional movements, and the church's involvement with colonialism.

These Magdalene interpretations emerged partly through the work of male preachers and authors, but they are especially conspicuous in the work of early modern women. One way to characterize much of the scholarship on women in the Reformation era is as a chronicle of loss, of things that reform of theology and culture took away from women: the autonomy of convent life, the diverse cast of female saints, the freedoms of the early years of most reform efforts. My work differs in presenting a story of things that were added, and often added by women themselves. Women supplied images and arguments using the Magdalene to advance their own theological commitments and expressions of vocation. Recent scholarship has noted ways in which women have subverted the narrative of increased restriction on their activity, but it has tended to expose exceptionalism, instances when women somehow worked around an oppressive system. Mary Magdalene presents an unusual case in which women aligned themselves with influential reformers— Martin Luther, John Foxe, Teresa of Avila, Theodore Beza, Federico Borromeo, Margaret Fell, and George Fox—who offered a positive assessment of this important female figure. Reinterpreting Mary Magdalene was central to several key elements of sixteenth-century religious reform, and the debates in which she figured so prominently—justification by faith, the priesthood of all believers, lay and female preaching, education, the reorganization of convents, morality and sex, vocation and the individual—allowed women to claim their own right to confess the faith with their words and with their lives.

The Magdalenes that emerged from that era have shaped understandings of women's religious identity and authority. In the words of the epitaph for Mary Armine, the age of reform saw "an army of such ladies" come forward to preach, encourage, challenge, and direct the church by following the example of Mary Magdalene. Like her, these women supported the church with their means and testified to its truth. They endowed the churches of the modern world with a legacy of leadership tested by conflict and proved by endurance. In response to Natalie Zemon Davis's influential contention that the Reformation ultimately did not have a positive effect for women, I would argue that these early modern Magdalenes laid important groundwork for discussions of women's rights in the modern world as they established God's valuing of women and command to them to speak and teach publicly. Again and again through the generations, women took courage from the Magdalene's example and from the authority she derived from Christ, who forgave her, loved her, and called her into ministry. By way of epilogue for this inquiry, we might consider the discussions of the Magdalene that appear in the work of two women who argued for women's right to preach and teach, more than three centuries after the beginning of the Reformation, in a very different political and cultural context from Europe at the close of the Middle Ages.

Maria Stewart was an African American activist and lecturer working in Massachusetts and New York in the first half of the nineteenth century, mentored by the radical abolitionist David Walker. She was the first American woman to speak in public in front of an audience of women and men of different races. Though she would go on to a long career as a schoolteacher and hospital matron in Washington, DC, her final speech as an activist was delivered when she was only thirty, at the Belknap Street Church in Boston in 1833. At that point she withdrew from public speaking, having faced violent opposition and after suffering the deaths of both her mentor and her husband.[1]

Her "Farewell Address" to the Boston community adopts a tactic familiar from the female writers of the Reformation: in asserting her right to speak, she offers a list of scriptural women, including Mary Magdalene, who demonstrate God's endorsement of women's leadership:

> What if I am a woman; is not the God of ancient times the God of these modern days? Did he not raise up Deborah, to be a mother, and a judge in Israel? Did not Queen Esther save the lives of the Jews? And Mary Magdalene first declare the resurrection of Christ from the dead? . . . Did Saint Paul but know of our wrongs and deprivations, I presume he would make no objection to our pleading in public for our rights. . . . What if such women as are here described should rise among our sable race?[2]

Like Marie Dentière and Margaret Fell before her, Stewart uses biblical prophecy to rebuke the injustices of modern society. Far from accepting the chasm between divine truth and human reality, Stewart invokes the record of the biblical era as proof and promise of God's will to transform the sinful world.

Despite the shared strategy, her argument differs from the work of early modern women like Dentière and Fell, both in her aim and in the authorities to which she appeals. Although she uses religious language and evidence in her speech, Stewart seeks a public voice for women beyond religious leadership, in political participation. She affirms openly that her goal is "our rights," drawing on the rhetoric of the Enlightenment revolutions as well as the (as yet unrealized) legal terms of the U.S. Constitution. Stewart uses the sacred past to speak prophetically to the present, as had the women of the Reformation, but her conception of justice also corrects the faults of the past. In her own grappling with the proscriptions on women's speech in 1 Corinthians and 2 Timothy, Stewart insists that the sufferings of modern women and slaves must broaden St. Paul's limited vision. Human experience is thus used to inform the interpretation of sacred texts in a way that would not have been possible before the influence of John Locke and the First Great Awakening.[3]

Near the close of the nineteenth century, the African American Baptist scholar Mary V. Cook chronicled the experiences and contributions of women to the church as she argued for greater credit for their accomplishments and scope for their leadership. Born in Kentucky just months before the Emancipation Proclamation was issued, Cook was able to attend school and university, becoming a professor of Latin in the Normal School of the State University of Kentucky. Cook opens her 1890 essay "The Work for Baptist Women" with a discussion of Luke 8:1–3, in which Mary Magdalene is described as one among Jesus's female followers, who supported him and his ministry from their means, and with the sinful woman of Luke 7. "When Christ came into the world to redeem man from the curse of the Law, he found among his followers faithful women ready to do him service. . . . He did not spurn their devotion, as his disciples often suggested, but acknowledged their love and good deeds, and commanded that wherever the gospel should be preached throughout the world that mention should be made of the woman who anointed his head, as a memorial of her." The actions of these women, and Christ's acknowledgment of them, are to serve as the pattern for the modern church as it begins, finally, to give women's work its true value.[4]

Cook spends the remainder of her essay listing the women's groups, missionary societies, teaching ministries, fund-raising programs, and activism that demonstrate how contemporary women are continuing to answer Christ's call faithfully, albeit without adequate recognition from the church. By this point in the century, Cook would have been influenced not only by democratic and abolitionist rhetoric but also by the arguments of the emerging feminist movement. She brings those tools to her aid, using the vocabulary of modernity as well as biblical language, just as Maria Stewart had. The memorial that Christ had commanded—of celebrating women's devoted service following the Magdalene's example—was being neglected, and the activist women of the nineteenth-century African American Baptist church were stepping forward to right that wrong in her name.

Intimacy with the Word

The work of Maria Stewart and Mary V. Cook can be said to display continuity with the Magdalene tradition as it had developed through the Middle Ages in the sense that, for both of them, her authority came from her intimacy with Christ. The medieval Magdalene, as lover of Christ, had given mystical experience the vocabulary of romantic desire. We have observed the intimate character of that relationship being explored, praised, envied, and imitated across the religious boundaries of the early modern period. Early modern women claimed that same intimacy and the same authority to speak, even as they gained strength for their arguments by experiencing that intimacy in a new way, reading the Bible for themselves, and in their own languages. Through this direct experience of the incarnate Word of God, women were able to see themselves as sitting at Christ's feet, listening with rapt attention, even in the midst of family life and its responsibilities. Devotion to "the one thing necessary" was no longer the exclusive province of cloistered nuns; it became accessible to wives and mothers, who could discover their own vocations as sacred, authorizing their testimony. Perhaps the clearest example is the funeral oration delivered by Katharina Schütz Zell, in which she justified eulogizing her husband, and his passage to eternal life, by citing the Magdalene's joyful proclamation of her beloved Christ, risen from the dead.

The ways in which Protestants described the intimacy between Christ and the Magdalene reflect their theological commitments and social contexts. Luther lingered over the Magdalene's grief at Christ's death, calling her profound attachment to and desire for him a model for all Christians, and especially for preachers who must cultivate the same familiarity with the Word. The Calvinist preacher Theodore Beza, though he condemned her lack of confidence in the promised resurrection, could not help but praise her closeness to Christ, claiming that Christ appeared to her in his risen form and named her as the first messenger of the Gospel because of it. Even John Calvin, who scorned the emotional piety represented by the Magdalene, had to address so obvious a fact as her dedication, visiting the tomb of an executed outlaw, seeking to anoint the body within. That he deals with this feature of the biblical narrative by deriding her, seeing her popular appeal as something to be corrected, indicates the enduring power and attraction of this intimate relationship for Christians.

Protestant women—from Argula von Grumbach at the very beginning of the Reformation, through Catharina Regina von Greiffenberg, a seventeenth-century Lutheran in Catholic Bohemia—found in the friendship between the Magdalene and Christ a model for their own encounter with the Word and the public testimony it engendered in them. Grumbach pointed to Christ's conversation with the Magdalene and other women as permitting women's entry into theological debates over reform. After those debates had hardened into persecution, Greiffenberg noted the potential cost of such devotion, which women might have to place above their family duties, at least for a time. That was also the chief theme of Anabaptist references to the Magdalene, who encouraged each other to take up Mary of Bethany's "better part" of direct experience of the Word, no matter what punishments or temptations they might face.

The affection between the Magdalene and Christ was an equally compelling subject for early modern Catholics, both male and female, though they faced a more restricted context of scripture reading and interpretation. Charles Vialart, like the Reformed Beza, identified her love for Christ as the reason for Christ's appearing first to her after the resurrection. Vialart's devotional work was aimed at an audience of cloistered women. As it had been during the Middle Ages, nuns' spirituality continued to be dominated by the metaphor of the bride of Christ. The Carmelite nun and reformer Teresa of Avila was so jealous of Christ's favor that she openly expressed her longing for a relationship with him that would be as close as, or closer than, his intimacy with Mary Magdalene. And yet she, like Katharina Schütz Zell, found that intimate relationship calling her out into the world, to engage in projects of reform and mission, despite institutional constraints.

For both Catholics and Protestants, the intimacy shared by Christ and Mary Magdalene was an important source of her spiritual authority. Sixteenth-century Christians believed that devout reading and correct interpretation of scripture allowed them to experience that intimacy and gain that authority, though the assessment of what a correct interpretation was, and who might do it, varied according to the different traditions that developed in the Reformation era. The extent to which that authority would or could find expression in public

ministry varied widely between institutions and according to local circumstances. An intimate friendship with Christ, the Word incarnate, remained
a goal of piety across theological boundaries, however, as the promise of the
character of Christian life for all believers.

The medieval church had gone beyond the relationship recorded between
Christ and the Magdalene in the New Testament. Unable to resist elaborating
on the story of this prominent yet enigmatic woman, medieval authors had
developed a complex system of associations and images to explain her place
in the narrative of salvation. Each of the three scriptural roles that had come to
be associated with the Magdalene in the medieval Magdalene tradition—the
ideal penitent of Luke 7, the contemplative Mary who irked her sister Martha,
and the first witness of the Gospel—would be adapted to advance the theological programs of the age of reform. Her story addressed the fundamental
questions of the Reformation: how are individuals saved, and how are they
to live in the world, in right relation to God and the neighbor? What better
story to reframe for evangelical theology, as it touches on the nature and
work of justification, on the validity of the clergy / lay hierarchy, understandings of vocation, and the priesthood of all believers? And what better story
for Catholics to revisit in their turn, to promote a vigorous piety of absolute
commitment to the church?

The Perfect Penitent

Catholic and Protestant reformers interpreted Mary Magdalene's role as the
ideal penitent in a dialogue that helped construct their theological divergence.
The story of the sinful woman of Luke 7 had been crucial to the establishment
and teaching of medieval doctrines for the Sacrament of Penance. Preachers
of this doctrine had focused on her contrition and her acts of humble service
as that which merited Christ's pronunciation of absolution. Penitents were
encouraged to see themselves entering into that same narrative with their own
confessors and in performing works of satisfaction. Rather than discarding
this key text as antithetical to evangelical theology (as did happen to other
texts, such as the Epistle of James), Luther and his colleagues appropriated
it for their movement, reinterpreting it as a confirmation of justification by
grace alone. They emphasized Christ's mercy in granting forgiveness, an action
that should offer hope to all sinners. The Magdalene's faith lay not in the work

of washing Christ's feet but in her trust that she would be forgiven. Her works are the fruit that naturally follows faith, the proper expression of gratitude for what she has received.

In response, Catholic readings continued to affirm the Magdalene's contrition and works as exemplary, if potentially daunting in their perfection. Catholic preachers, particularly in areas where the Reformation was making significant gains, took up this text as a means of rebutting the new teaching on justification. Meanwhile, devotional writers sought to prevent the attacks of conscience that might tempt Catholics to turn toward the evangelical promise of grace for everyone who seeks forgiveness. Teresa of Avila and François de Sales both describe the saint's conversion as miraculously quick and complete, cautioning their readers to attempt something more gradual in their own lives. Indeed, François de Sales finds Mary Magdalene's penitence so perfect that what Christ pronounces for her is less an absolution than an acknowledgment of the state of grace she has already achieved. Through such opposing interpretations, the Luke 7 text became a central locus of debate over the different programs of salvation proposed by different confessions.

The Ideal of Contemplation

The Magdalene's penitence had been directly linked in her medieval legend with her future as an ascetic contemplative. Following her conversion, she demonstrated the absolute devotion to the Word that was praised by Christ in his comparison of Mary and Martha, leading to her role as a patroness of the contemplative life. Both Catholics and Protestants in the age of reform offer interpretations of this role as well. For Catholics, her association with the cloistered religious life continued and developed according to new circumstances and needs. In response to Protestant attacks on Catholic immorality, the Catholic Church expanded its program of Magdalene houses for reformed prostitutes. Such was the strength of the Magdalene's identification with the cloister that those who sought more active vocations sometimes looked for other models, such as the Virgin Mary, or reinterpreted the relation between Mary and Martha as one of complementarity rather than opposition, following the reading of Teresa of Avila.

Protestants also gave attention to Christ's praise of Mary's contemplation, adapting it to support the priesthood of all believers. All the faithful, men and women, married and single, were encouraged in devotion to the Word as the constituent of true faith, the one thing necessary. Martha was not neglected, however, but was given her due as a reliable and hard worker, serving the community in her divinely appointed secular vocation. Like Teresa, Protestant interpreters advised a combined pursuit of the paths of both Mary and Martha in the life of each individual, rejecting the hierarchical separation of work and prayer that this text had long been used to enforce. Teresa reconciled the two vocations as a means of bringing humility and pragmatism into the contemplative life, making each nun into a housekeeper for the good of her soul and of the convent's floors! Protestants, meanwhile, elevated each layperson to the status of priest, claiming that the prosaic duties of mothers and fathers held the sacred poetry of pastoral offices and insisting that all Christians needed the fortification of spiritual practices—scripture reading and worship—in order to exercise their priesthood.

In Memory of Her

Just as theologically fraught as the nature of penitence and of contemplation was the fact of the Magdalene's identity as a woman, and one with a potentially sinful sexual history. Another enduring theme from the medieval tradition was the Magdalene as a symbol of the church, an image in which her gender could be used to signify the divine-human union but also corruption in need of purification. Both Catholics and Protestants engaged this image in the course of advancing their theological and ecclesiastical reform programs. The collective nature of the image made it appealing to both groups, as they worked to uphold different forms of religious community, from the household to the convent. The sexualized nature of the image would, however, prove problematic for women as they sought to become full members of churches and colleagues in ministry.

The spousal language for the relationship between Christ and the church remained a feature of Protestant piety despite the medieval connection between that imagery and the cloister. Protestant discussions of the marital bond between Christ and his church tended to assert the authority of new churches by declaring them to be Christ's true bride. This constituted a communal version of the way in which self-identifications with the Magdalene allowed female Protestant authors to justify their public speech. Katharina

Schütz Zell had comforted the widows of an evangelical uprising by comparing them to the bride in the Song of Songs. Women of the English Reformation often invoked the vocabulary of mystical marriage to testify to the strength of their connection to God and to propose a spiritual equality that they longed for in their contemporary church. The Anabaptist martyrs of the sixteenth and seventeenth centuries—concerned to separate themselves from the wider society and to establish a sanctified, apostolic community—in turn used the language of the Song of Songs to identify themselves as the true church.

Other aspects of the Magdalene's femininity were adopted to proclaim authority for the churches emerging from the Reformation. The Reformed churchman Theodore Beza used the surprising choice of the Magdalene and the other women, those unlikely witnesses of the resurrection, as an example of the ideal character of the church, always reforming itself by overturning expectations, allowing the weak to expose the corruption in powerful human institutions. Beza departed from the purely scriptural identity approved for the Magdalene by Calvin, discussing her anointing (as Mary of Bethany) of Christ before his death as the founding act of the church—a comparison Beza made in his sermons on the Song of Songs. The Magdalene's role as an image of female patronage provided a model for Elizabeth I's defense and maintenance of a reformed church in George Ashe's late seventeenth-century sermon commemorating her support for the founding of Trinity College Dublin. Like Beza, Ashe also praised her nurture of the church by comparing it to Mary of Bethany's anointing of Christ. Less positively, but more typically, the Magdalene as reformed prostitute enacts the role of a purified church, purged of sinful theologies and practices, as in Lewis Wager's Reformed morality play *The Life and Repentance of Marie Magdalene*.

Perhaps not surprisingly given the popularity of that comparison in Protestant polemics, Counter-Reformation portrayals of the Magdalene tend not to compare the Magdalene, in her identity as a prostitute, to a church in need of reform and purification. But her gender and sexual history remained a troubling question. In an age of religious strife, the Magdalene's identification with the Catholic Church was reinterpreted to convey more ambivalent or problematic experiences of religious commitment. Catholics could adopt the grieving Magdalene at the empty tomb, a lonely and sorrowful woman, as an image of the church in a persecuted context, as Robert Southwell's *Marie*

Magdalens Funeral Teares did for English Catholicism under the Elizabethan settlement. The Magdalene's preconversion appearance formed a template for scores of visual representations, lending a titillating aura of sanctity to portraits of royal mistresses. When women themselves faced the prospect of ruling, they often modeled themselves on the Magdalene, to excuse the unusual situation of female leadership. Or the marriage metaphor of the Song of Songs could express the challenges and sacrifices faced by an author accused of unorthodox beliefs, as in the case of the mystic Jeanne Guyon in France, for whom Christ was "a bridegroom of blood."

More broadly across the Catholic context there was a new recognition, derived from engagement with Protestant reforms, that both celibate and married persons could understand their ways of life as sacred. In this project the sexuality of the Magdalene could be redeemed as a valued part of human experience. The Jesuit poet Friedrich Spee interpreted the Song of Songs' imagery of the Magdalene as the bride of Christ, the church, to foster the spirituality of married women in the home. This imagery remained popular in the spiritual direction offered to women in Catholic religious orders as well, as can be seen in the letters of Federico Borromeo, cardinal of Milan, to the nuns of his city. In both cases, the language of desire was used to express the character of women's spirituality—not in a way that brought different vocations into competition with each other, but as a means of encouraging an embodied devotion to God, involving the fullness of the self.

In assessing the influence of Mary Magdalene's sexuality in early modern religious culture, we can observe a continuity with the gendered treatment that Katherine Jansen has demonstrated in medieval preaching about her. When the Magdalene is described as the other, she is pointed to as something the male author is not: she is presented as an object for the viewer's evaluation, either for his moral education or his desire. In these kinds of interpretations her own possibility is not explored; she is merely offered up for condemnation or consumption. But when the Magdalene is discovered as an image of the self, she becomes the subject of a liberating identification, lending her voice to subjects, both male and female, speaking of their own religious commitment and claiming their own spiritual authority. Mary Magdalene's gender and sexuality offered believers a model for honesty and authenticity in the life of faith. Rather than needing to escape or transcend this fundamental part of humanity, the problem that preoccupied humanist scholars and religious institutions, these self-professed Magdalenes claimed their entire selves, the whole range of their identity and experience, for the service of Christ. For those who found their own voice because of her story, perhaps the question of her sexual history ultimately did not matter, at least not as a cause for judgment and condemnation. As Catharina Regina von Greiffenberg wrote, "poor womenfolk, on account of being completely despised and defamed by most men, seek and find their honor in the apologia of the Holy Spirit. And why ask in the end about the disgrace of people who have God himself eulogizing them? If it is God who takes care of our honor, we are thus free from care."[5]

Witness of the Resurrection

Whether later interpreters would regret or celebrate the fact, the Gospels are unequivocal in their testimony that the Magdalene and her female companions had been the first witnesses to Christ's resurrection. This role had fascinated medieval theologians to such an extent that they had created the Magdalene's complex legend, identifying her with two other New Testament figures in order to explain her presence at that crucial moment in humanity's salvation history. The centrality of that role was not lost on the theologians of Catholic and Protestant reform, though they adapted its character in order to express different understandings of the vocation of Christian life.

What was the character of being a "witness" to the resurrection for Protestants and for Catholics? The difference is a somewhat paradoxical one given the importance ordinarily given to passive reception of grace in Protestant theology and to activity in cooperation with divine grace for Catholics. Though Luther emphasized the believer's passive role in justification, his interpretation of the Magdalene at the resurrection celebrates her activity as a model for Christians, preachers and laity alike. After the work of salvation is accomplished by Christ, the Christian is called to labor in the vineyard, offering service to the neighbor. Perhaps the most important kind of service any Christian could give to another was to deliver the good news of her forgiveness in Christ. That role was given equally to men and women at the individual level—as opposed to the level of community leadership—as Luther affirms in his discussions of the Magdalene as preacher and disciple. The conditions of religious persecution intensified this vocation of bearing witness, turning it into an existential commitment. A commonality across Protestant communities is the encouragement of their members to bear witness to Christ in public confessions of faith, persisting in their faithful testimony even to the point of death, with the Magdalene serving as exemplar, not only in her identity as preacher of the resurrection but also in her other guises. The English martyr Anne Askew's courage was praised by John Bale and John Foxe in terms that recalled the devotion of Mary of Bethany. Anabaptist martyrs encouraged their wives to remain as loyal to the Word as Mary of Bethany had, resisting attempts to urge them to their family duty.

In contrast to this model of witness as active testimony, Catholic interpretations of the appropriate response to the resurrection describe a more internal sense of awe and a need to overcome Christ's absence through the spiritual and sacramental program of the church. For some this necessitated a negotiation over the imperative of participation in the Counter-Reformation. Teresa of Avila explicitly addressed the frustration she felt at not being able to give public testimony to her faith as part of confronting the Protestant threat and evangelizing in the mission field. She called her fellow nuns to turn away from what she counseled was a misdirected sense of vocation and instead to devote themselves to prayer and service within their communities, among their nearest neighbors. This inward turn fulfilled the vocation to which many women felt called. Former royal mistress Louise de la Vallière embraced the model of silent witness offered by the Magdalene as a penitent, demonstrating in her own complicated past the mercy of God toward sinners.

The contrast between Catholic and Protestant interpretations of the resurrection narrative is exemplified by their focus on two different parts of the story. Protestant interpreters, such as Nicolaus Herman in his hymns for Mary Magdalene, typically explored the dialogue the Magdalene has with Christ in the road, in which he instructs her to give his message to the apostles. Catholic interest, especially in poetry and the visual arts, was often preoccupied with the noli me tangere scene, which forecasts the believer's need to approach Christ in a new way through the mediation of the church. Catholic nun María de San José Salazar, in advocating that she and her fellow Carmelites be allowed to continue a practice of communal discussion, was careful to maintain that they would be refraining from speculative theology, the direct spiritual and intellectual "touching" prohibited by Christ's refusal of the Magdalene's gesture.

The dichotomy is one of emphasis between two different experiences of the human encounter with the divine: permission and encouragement or refusal and frustration. Of course, theoretical permission and encouragement can prove confusing and infuriating when real opportunities for women in public ministry are closed. And an open acknowledgment of refusal and frustration as an inherent part of the spiritual life can foster creativity in crafting a vocation amid the world's challenges. The contrast is not a simple one between being commanded to preach or being warned against touching God's majesty, but it does inform the orientations of the two strands of reform, from which different promises and solutions would develop, affecting the shape of life in the churches of the modern world.

On the question of the Magdalene's role as preacher of the Gospel as a precedent for how preaching will be done in the church, there are both overt debates and telling silences. Luther and his followers who published sermons on the resurrection narrative opened the possibility of women's preaching after the Magdalene's example. Although they rejected women's institutional leadership as incompatible with the order of the church, they did maintain that women might—and, indeed, ought to—preach in case of need.

The influence of these discussions was far-reaching, as can be seen from the trial records of the English Protestant martyr John Lambert (d. 1538), as published in John Foxe's *Acts and Monuments of the Church.* Lambert had been part of the evangelical community in Antwerp, and also of the reform-minded group that met at the White Horse Tavern in Cambridge, associating with Robert Barnes and William Tyndale.[6] Questioned as to the right of laypersons to preach and administer the sacraments, Lambert affirms the position outlined by Luther and elaborated by his colleagues. Lambert invokes the same scriptural examples Luther had used, as well as introducing the Virgin Mary as a model of preaching:

> In time of great necessity lay people may preach, & that of both kinds both men & women, as you may see in the Epistle to the Corinthians, wheras he saith: but it is a shame for a woman to speak in a multitude or congregation, yet in an other place he saith: that every woman praying or prophesying, having any thing upon her head, doth dishonor her head. To this accordeth the prophecy of Joel recited Acts. ii. wherein the parson of god is thus said, I shall pour out of my sprite

upon all flesh, & both your sons & your daughters shall prophecy. Thus did Anna the prophet's daughter of Phanuel give praise unto Christ in the temple, & spake of him to all men of Jerusalem that looked after the redemption of Israel. This also doth yet speak unto us in scripture our Lady by the song which she made that is daily recited in the church called Magnificat.[7]

This opening was seized by early modern evangelical women, such as Marie Dentière, Argula von Grumbach, and Katharina Schütz Zell, who argued for their own right to engage in public religious debate and in preaching, supporting their claims with the Magdalene's divinely granted preaching role. Their arguments were perceived as dangerous presumption, as is evident from the careful qualifications by evangelical pastors, as well as from the polemics raised on the Catholic side in response. The renowned Catholic preacher François Le Picart openly scorned "Lutherans" who were claiming women's right to preach based on scriptural examples.

The preaching Magdalene was clearly problematic for Counter-Reformation religious culture. The medieval *apostola apostolorum*, so inspiring to Dominican preachers in the late Middle Ages, was not taken up as the model for Jesuit preachers and teachers as they confronted and checked the spread of evangelical theology. With the Reformation's introduction of the concept of the priesthood of all believers, including preaching, teaching, and even the administration of the sacraments at need by the laity, the Magdalene too closely suggested divine approval for such subversions of the clerical hierarchy.

Generally speaking, the Magdalene's preaching was most minimized or qualified in those traditions with the highest clerical authority, and it was most embraced in emerging reform traditions with less regard for the distinction between clergy and laity. The implications of the Magdalene's biblical preaching, carefully considered and tentatively advanced by evangelicals beginning with the Lutheran Reformation, were much more fully exploited by the Quaker activists of the seventeenth century. The founders of Quakerism, Margaret Fell and George Fox, both cited the Magdalene of the resurrection narrative among their justifications for women's public preaching. The Society of Friends established women's leadership with this theoretical basis, but also through a structure of women's meetings for worship, Bible study, and organized charitable ministry and political activism. The example of Mary

Magdalene and the other women at the tomb was used to inspire and guide women as they formed Quaker communities of faith and action.

The Anabaptist tradition represents an interestingly isolated case within the narrative of Protestant preaching Magdalenes. Though Anabaptist martyrs certainly made use of her identities as Mary of Bethany and as the Song of Songs' bride of Christ, there are no comparisons of Anabaptist women to the Magdalene as preacher. This may be explained in part by their strategies of silence and prevarication under interrogation, designed to protect other members of the community and the movement as a whole. There may also have been wariness, among a group so concerned with identifying the true church by purity of conduct, about connecting themselves with the image of the notorious sinner-saint. Nevertheless, Anabaptism survived and grew, thanks in large part to the unofficial "preaching" of women, through proselytizing, prophetic utterance, biblical interpretation, and the eloquent testimony of female martyrs. They were encouraged in these activities by their male companions in the faith, and praised for them after death, using images drawn from the composite, medieval Magdalene tradition.

Discontinuities

The principal elements of the Magdalene tradition established in the early church and the Middle Ages endured into the early modern period through their adaptation by reform movements looking to serve both internal and polemical goals. There are, however, important discontinuities to observe in our survey of the Magdalene in the age of reform. Chief among them is the beginning of the separation of the three figures long associated with the saint, identifying Mary Magdalene only as the woman mentioned by name in the Bible who supported Jesus's ministry and witnessed his death and resurrection.

The motivations of the humanist scholars who debunked her composite identity included, according to Jacques Lefèvre d'Étaples's account, a concern for the purity of the woman to whom the risen Christ first appeared. Moral questions were among those that fomented the Reformation, and many of the communities that emerged from it gave morality a special prominence in their theological orientation. Humanists and Reformed Protestants, as well as Anabaptists, were especially interested in the ethical life as an aim of their reform efforts or as a proof of the individual's state of grace. That God would have given so central a role to a woman who had been sexually promiscuous, the idea on which the medieval legend had embroidered to such an extent, was ridiculed as a distortion of the true pattern; it contradicted God's glory for such an incongruous choice to have been made—therefore, it had not happened.

There are both positive and negative implications of the shift away from a composite Magdalene. On the one hand, the association with prostitution had tainted the reputation of one of Christ's most trusted followers, perhaps preventing a full acknowledgment of her leadership in the early church and, as such, of the religious leadership of all women. On the other hand, the redemption of so notorious a sinner had offered comfort, throughout Christian history, to sinners desperate for the hope of redemption. Luther and his followers pointed to this as one of the greatest benefits of the story of the Magdalene, and it is precisely this possibility of universal hope that made her such a compelling example for evangelical theology.

In weighing the influence of a composite or a purely scriptural Magdalene on the different traditions' attitudes toward women, it is difficult to identify one interpretation as having resulted in clear advances for women and the other as tending to be uniquely oppressive. The presence of a disciple with a complex sexual history may allow more of the story of women's lives to be told than is included in a tradition determined to keep such unsavory characters off the list of true disciples. If given too much attention, though, the Magdalene's exciting past becomes the focus of prurient fascination, distracting from her conversion and apostolic vocation and precluding her use as a model for other Christians.

The Magdalene's composite identity addressed women's sexuality as part of discipleship for better or worse, while the limitation of the Magdalene to her scriptural role of supporter and witness effectively separated female sexuality from discipleship in those strands of the Christian tradition that adopted Lefèvre's reform, in theory creating a more neutral ground for spiritual life and leadership. Yet generalizations about which organizational structures and ideologies might best foster women's spirituality in its fullness can be misleading. Celibate nuns such as Maria Maddalena de' Pazzi and Teresa of Avila were fluent in a vocabulary of desire for Christ as the beloved spouse; the silences of the cloister were enlivened by practical discussions of how that spouse needed good meals and a well-run household just as much as adoration. A tradition known for radical activism and profound spirituality, Quakerism, used the Magdalene to express a vision of motherhood as courageous mentoring in the faith, demonstrating the importance of familial bonds and models in a supposedly individualistic piety. And the preaching of Reformed Geneva could echo, contrary to all expectations, with the praise of a woman's devoted tears, which Christ was said to honor with his divine approval for the apostle to the apostles.

The discontinuities between early modern Magdalenes and the medieval tradition go beyond treatments of her sexuality. This study began as an investigation into changes in how her preaching role was interpreted among the different confessions that emerged from the Reformation era. Magdalene scholarship has demonstrated the importance of the *apostola apostolorum* title as an inspiration for medieval preachers. With the Reformation's emphasis on the responsibilities of the laity in confessing the faith came a new focus on the Magdalene's role in the resurrection narrative. Early modern theologians either seized on this example of a layperson and woman being commanded to preach, or worked to explain why this scene did not establish such a precedent. Our survey of Protestant Magdalene interpretation has clearly shown that the preaching Magdalene was a live issue in the debates of the early years of the Reformation—about the priesthood of all believers and especially about how the duties of that vocation applied to women. In those early years and well beyond, Protestant women identified themselves with Mary Magdalene as being empowered to preach and teach the Gospel. This kind of direct self-identification with the preaching Magdalene did not take place in the same way in early modern Catholicism; allegations of women's preaching and inappropriate study of scripture were among the polemical attacks launched at Protestants as the culture of the Counter-Reformation was defined in opposition to perceived threats and heresies.

The early modern period thus saw the Magdalene tradition lose some of the flexibility it had in medieval piety. Though Protestants embraced her as a universal image of a redeemed sinner who could still be useful to God, some—although not all—of the particularity of her female experience of the encounter with the divine was neglected or rejected. Catholic piety, by contrast, continued to draw on the Magdalene tradition as a model for female spirituality, even expanding on her compassion with Christ's suffering through her intimate connection with him. The essentially female nature of her early modern Catholic character, especially as it was proposed by male authors—fundamental carnality replaced with radical asceticism, her devotion arising from the same source as romantic and sexual attachments—reduced the likelihood that she would be a model for public preaching by male clergy.

The separation between clergy and laity was not what it had been in the medieval period, however; this marks one of the signal shifts of the age of reform as a social and cultural transition. The medieval church had developed a hierarchy of social roles, in which different orders prayed, fought, and worked. Each order was dependent on the others and was rewarded for performing functions that were understood to bring tangible, necessary benefits to those in the other groups. Beginning in the twelfth century, with the gradual commercialization and urbanization of European society, this structure was complicated and undermined in various ways until it ultimately succumbed to the tensions of an emerging modernity. As the medieval separation between those who work and those who pray became obsolete, reform-minded Christians began to explore new understandings of the shape of Christian life. The contemplation of Mary and the worldly work of Martha could no longer be divided among different groups, but had to be integrated by each believer in a life devoted to God. Authors male and female, Catholic and Protestant, discussed the terms of this reconciliation, attempting to understand secular work as a vocation, the fruit and expression of contemplation. What have often been taken to be the distinct preoccupations of the different confessions are revealed to have shared a common dialogue. Early modern nuns reflected on the meaning of ascetic withdrawal in an age of mission, Protestant pastors and their wives strove to find the sacredness of diaper changes and household budgets, and both groups resorted to the relationship between Mary and Martha to make sense of what they were doing.

The figure of the Magdalene, in the multiplicity of her composite tradition, was at the center of both the practical and the theoretical debates of the Reformation era. As reformers wrestled with the problem of the nature of Christian life, and the character of the priesthood of all believers and the vocation of religious orders was worked out in the terms of reconciling the roles of Mary and Martha, so were Catholic and Protestant conceptions of salvation developed using the narrative of the sinful woman in Luke 7. The interpretation of the story allowed theologians on both sides of the confessional divide to identity the definitive action: either the woman's work of penance or the gracious absolution offered by Christ. So crucial was this text to establishing Protestant theology as distinct from Catholic teaching that Theodore Beza could not resist including it in a sermon on the Magdalene of the resurrection, even as he admitted that it was a false custom that had associated the two women. And, finally, the role of the Magdalene on Easter morning was one through which all Christians understood their relation to their church's mission. If the modern world may be said to have evolved in large measure through encounters with differences both confessional and cultural, in religious upheaval and the beginning of colonialism, then the Magdalene's example as the first evangelist was surely formative for early modern individuals and churches as they sought to proclaim their faith and inspire conversion.

Looking together at the Magdalene's three identities and their interpretations in the traditions that emerged from the age of reform, we find a common concern, one that is only underscored by the diversity of its expressions. Early modern Christians were grappling with the question of vocation: the call to testify to salvation and to live a sanctified life in the world. The Magdalenes of the age gave shape to new understandings of the self before God and before others. Through the image of the Magdalene, previous conceptions of the obligations of Christian life were variously rejected or refined, argued with and adapted. The innovation of that project can be seen in the gradual transition it helped to accomplish, from a compartmentalized understanding of society, in which some stand before God or serve others on behalf of the whole community, toward a model in which each person discerns her own obligations to God and her participation in communities of her own choice.

MARY MAGDALENE, the disciple of Christ and patron of his movement, has been central to the church's teaching about witness and vocation, religious commitment and reform, throughout the history of Christianity. In the age of reform, during the sixteenth and seventeenth centuries, the scriptural woman and the figure of legend provided new generations of church leaders with images and stories to challenge, correct, sustain, and renew the communities of faith that emerged from that turbulent era. Invoking her example to justify themselves, prophetic voices within the church came forward to call its teaching, liturgy, and institutions into greater faithfulness to its Gospel mission. Although she was often adopted by women to argue for their own authority, men also found in her story the solace of the forgiven sinner and an inspiring model of love for Christ and the proclamation of his message. The early modern Magdalene tradition witnesses the rich legacy of testimony, dissent, negotiation, and vision that has shaped the different confessions of the Christian tradition, sometimes speaking from its margins and sometimes, surprisingly, from its very heart. It is the duty of the historian—and, I might add, of the preacher—not to allow these faithful voices to be forgotten. One might well ask, with Margaret Fell, "If these women had not thus [been] ready to carry his message . . . how should his Disciples have known, who were not there?"[8] An army of eloquent Magdalenes has carried the message of the Gospel through the centuries, despite facing violence, oppression, insult, and mockery. The church owes them its life.

Notes

Abbreviations

CWT Teresa of Avila. *The Collected Works of Teresa of Avila*. Translated by Kieran Kavanaugh and Otilio Rodriguez. 2nd ed. 3 vols. Washington, DC: ICS Publications, 1989.

LW   Luther, Martin. *Luther's Works: American Edition*. Vols. 1–30, ed. Jaroslav Pelikan. St. Louis: Concordia, 1955–76. Vols. 31–55, ed. Helmut Lehmann. Philadelphia: Muhlenberg / Minneapolis: Fortress, 1957–86. Vols. 56–, ed. Christopher Boyd Brown, 2008–. St. Louis: Concordia.

PL   Migne, J.-P., ed. *Patrologiae cursus completus: Series Latina*. 221 vols. in 223. Paris: Garnier, 1844–64.

WA Luther, Martin. *D. Martin Luthers Werke: Kritische Gesamtausgabe [Weimarer Ausgabe]*. 73 vols. in 85. Weimar: Böhlau, 1883–.

Introduction: A Woman for All Seasons

Unless otherwise noted, all translations are the author's own.

1. Katherine Ludwig Jansen, *The Making of the Magdalen: Preaching and Popular Devotion in the Later Middle Ages* (Princeton, NJ: Princeton University Press, 2000), 334.

2. Susan Haskins, *Mary Magdalen: Myth and Metaphor* (New York: HarperCollins, 1993), 249.

3. Jansen, *The Making of the Magdalen*, 335; Larissa Juliet Taylor, *Heresy and Orthodoxy in Sixteenth-Century Paris: François le Picart and the Beginnings of the Catholic Reformation*, Studies in Medieval and Reformation Thought 77 (Leiden: Brill, 1999), 179.

4. Haskins, *Mary Magdalen*, 249.

5. David M. Whitford, "The Moste Folyshe Fable of the Worlde: Preaching the Maudlin," in *Calvinus Pastor Ecclesiae: Papers of the Eleventh International Congress on Calvin Research*, ed. Herman J. Selderhuis and Arnold Huijgen (Göttingen: Vandenhoeck und Ruprecht, 2016), 450.

6. Patricia Badir, *The Maudlin Impression: English Literary Images of Mary Magdalen, 1550–1700* (Notre Dame, IN: University of Notre Dame Press, 2009).

7. Joan Kelly, "Did Women Have a Renaissance?," in *Women, History, and Theory: The Essays of Joan Kelly* (Chicago: University of Chicago Press, 1984), 19–50; Haskins, *Mary Magdalen*, 248.

8. On confessionalization, see John M. Headley, Hans J. Hillerbrand, and Anthony J. Papalas, eds., *Confessionalization in Europe, 1555–1700: Essays in Honor and Memory of Bodo Nischan* (Aldershot, England: Ashgate, 2004); Jeffrey R. Watt, ed., *The Long Reformation,* Problems in European Civilization 93 (Boston: Houghton Mifflin, 2006); Robert Kolb, ed., *Lutheran Ecclesiastical Culture, 1550–1675,* Brill's Companions to the Christian Tradition 11 (Leiden: Brill, 2008); and Susan C. Karant-Nunn, *The Reformation of Feeling: Shaping the Religious Emotions in Early Modern Germany* (New York: Oxford University Press, 2010). On preaching's role in confessionalization, see Phyllis Mack Crew, *Calvinist Preaching and Iconoclasm in the Netherlands, 1544–1569,* Cambridge Studies in Early Modern History (Cambridge: Cambridge University Press, 1978); Patrick T. Ferry, "Confessionalization and Popular Preaching: Sermons against Synergism in Reformation Saxony," *Sixteenth Century Journal* 28, no. 4 (1997): 1143–66; Amy Nelson Burnett, *Teaching the Reformation: Ministers and Their Message in Basel, 1529–1629,* Oxford Studies in Historical Theology (Oxford: Oxford University Press, 2006); John M. Frymire, *The Primacy of the Postils: Catholics, Protestants, and the Dissemination of Ideas in Early Modern Germany,* Studies in Medieval and Reformation Traditions 147 (Leiden: Brill, 2010); Howard Louthan, *Converting Bohemia: Force and Persuasion in the Catholic Reformation* (Cambridge: Cambridge University Press, 2009); and Philip M. Soergel, *Wondrous in His Saints: Counter-Reformation Propaganda in Bavaria,* Studies on the History of Society and Culture 17 (Berkeley: University of California Press, 1993).

9. Carol Piper Heming, *Protestants and the Cult of the Saints in German-Speaking Europe, 1517–1531,* Sixteenth Century Essays and Studies 65 (Kirksville, MO: Truman State University Press, 2003), 8, 65, 66; Robert Kolb, *For All the Saints: Changing Perceptions of Martyrdom and Sainthood in the Lutheran Reformation* (Macon, GA: Mercer University Press, 1987). See also Thomas Fuchs, "Protestantische Heiligen-memoria im 16. Jahrhundert," *Historische Zeitschrift* 267 (1998): 587–614.

10. David J. Collins, *Reforming Saints: Saints' Lives and Their Authors in Germany, 1470–1530,* Oxford Studies in Historical Theology (New York: Oxford University Press, 2008), 8, 9–10, 16; Alison Knowles Frazier, *Possible Lives: Authors and Saints in Renaissance Italy* (New York: Columbia University Press, 2005), 61–63.

11. Jodi Bilinkoff, *Related Lives: Confessors and Their Female Penitents, 1450–1750* (Ithaca, NY: Cornell University Press, 2005), 3–7.

12. Roland Bainton, *Women of the Reformation: From Spain to Scandinavia* (Minneapolis: Augsburg, 1977), 9, 10.

13. Natalie Zemon Davis, "City Women and Religious Change," in *Society and Culture in Early Modern France: Eight Essays* (Stanford, CA: Stanford University Press, 1975), 66, 79, 81, 83.

14. Ibid., 86.

15. Kirsi Irmeli Stjerna, *Women and the Reformation* (Malden, MA: Blackwell Pub., 2009), 14. See also Sherrin Marshall, ed., *Women in Reformation and Counter-Reformation Europe: Public and Private Worlds* (Bloomington: Indiana University Press, 1989).

16. Lyndal Roper, *The Holy Household: Women and Morals in Reformation Augsburg* (Oxford: Oxford University Press, 1989), 1, 2, 5.

17. Merry E. Wiesner[-Hanks], *Women and Gender in Early Modern Europe*, 2nd ed., New Approaches to European History 20 (Cambridge: Cambridge University Press, 2000), 214, 222–24, 232–34, 239.

18. Susan C. Karant-Nunn, "Reformation Society, Women and the Family," in *The Reformation World*, ed. Andrew Pettegree (London: Routledge, 2000), 435, 438–39, 443–44.

19. Susan C. Karant-Nunn and Merry E. Wiesner-Hanks, "Introduction," in *Luther on Women: A Sourcebook* (Cambridge: Cambridge University Press, 2003), 9, 10, 12.

20. Margaret L. King and Albert Rabil Jr., eds., *Teaching Other Voices: Women and Religion in Early Modern Europe*, The Other Voice in Early Modern Europe (Chicago: University of Chicago Press, 2007), 14, 17.

21. Sylvia Brown, "Introduction," in *Women, Gender, and Radical Religion in Early Modern Europe*, ed. Sylvia Brown, Studies in Medieval and Reformation Traditions 129 (Leiden: Brill, 2007), 2.

22. Stjerna, *Women and the Reformation*, 2, 4; Marshall, *Women in Reformation and Counter-Reformation Europe*, 2.

23. Stjerna, *Women and the Reformation*, 11–13, 214, 218; King and Rabil, *Teaching Other Voices*, 20.

24. Karant-Nunn, *The Reformation of Feeling*, 6. See also Karant-Nunn, "Reformation Society, Women and the Family," 440, 458; and Karant-Nunn and Wiesner-Hanks, *Luther on Women*, 13.

25. Badir, *The Maudlin Impression*, 2.

1. The Medieval Magdalene: Establishing a Cult of Personality

1. Nicolaus Herman, *Die Sontags Evangelia, und von den fürnemsten Festen uber das gantze Jar, In Gesenge gefasset fur Christliche Haussveter und ire Kinder, Mit vleis corrigiert, gebessert und gemehret* (Wittenberg: Georg Rhau Erben, 1560; 2nd ed. 1561), fol. 61r. On medieval Passion drama, see Charles Edmond Henri de Coussemaker, *Les drames liturgiques du Moyen Âge (texte et musique)* (Paris: V. Didron, 1861), 48–48.

2. See Christa Grössinger, *Picturing Women in Late Medieval and Renaissance Art*, Manchester Medieval Studies (Manchester, England: Manchester University Press, 1997), 34; Jacques Dalarun, "The Clerical Gaze," in *A History of Women in the West*, vol. 2, *Silences of the Middle Ages*, ed. Christine Klapisch-Zuber (Cambridge, MA: Belknap Press, 1992), 37.

3. Theresa Coletti, *Mary Magdalene and the Drama of Saints: Theater, Gender, and Religion in Late Medieval England* (Philadelphia: University of Pennsylvania Press, 2004), 129.

4. Helen Meredith Garth, *Saint Mary Magdalene in Mediaeval Literature* (Baltimore: Johns Hopkins Press, 1950), 60–63, 106.

5. For an investigation of the scriptural record, see Helen Schüngel-Straumann, "Maria von Magdala—Apostolin und erste Verkünderin der Osterbotschaft," in *Maria Magdalena: Zu*

einem Bild der Frau in der christlichen Verkündigung, ed. Dietmar Bader, Schriftenreihe der Katholischen Akademie der Erzdiözese Freiburg (Munich: Schnell und Steiner, 1990). On Gnosticism, see Luci Halliwell, *Mary of Magdala: The Evolution of an Image* (Saarbrücken, Germany: VDM Verlag Dr. Müller, 2008), 27; Karen King, *The Gospel of Mary of Magdala: Jesus and the First Woman Apostle* (Santa Rosa, CA: Polebridge Press, 2003); and Elaine Pagels, *The Gnostic Gospels* (New York: Random House, 1979).

6. Gregory the Great, *Homilia* 33, in *Homiliarum in evangelia,* in PL, 76:1239; see also Katherine Ludwig Jansen, *The Making of the Magdalen: Preaching and Popular Devotion in the Later Middle Ages* (Princeton, NJ: Princeton University Press, 2000), 32–35. The other women with whom the Magdalene was associated were those taken in adultery in John 7:53–8:11; the bride in the Song of Songs; the eremite Mary of Egypt; and also, less frequently, the Virgin Mary.

7. John Rees Smith, ed., *The Lives of St Mary Magdalene and St Martha (MS Esc. h-I-13),* Exeter Hispanic Texts 48 (Exeter: University of Exeter Press, 1989), xi; Jane Cartwright, *Mary Magdalene and Her Sister Martha: An Edition and Translation of the Medieval Welsh Lives* (Washington, DC: The Catholic University of America Press, 2013), 18; Jansen, *The Making of the Magdalen,* 6, 18, 36, 38, 41–46. The legendary ministry in Marseilles first appears in a tenth-century life, the *Vita apostolica Mariae Magdalenae;* see *The Life of Saint Mary Magdalene and of Her Sister Saint Martha: A Medieval Biography,* trans. David Mycoff, Cistercian Studies Series 108 (Kalamazoo, MI: Cistercian Publications, 1989), 5

8. Rabanus Maurus, in PL, 112:1495–96, translated in Garth, *Saint Mary Magdalene in Mediaeval Literature,* 53.

9. *The Life of Saint Mary Magdalene and of Her Sister Saint Martha,* 41. Cf. Song of Solomon 2:3.

10. *The Life of Saint Mary Magdalene and of Her Sister Saint Martha,* 14–16, 60. On Cistercian spirituality, see Caroline Walker Bynum, *Jesus as Mother: Studies in the Spirituality of the High Middle Ages* (Berkeley: University of California Press, 1982), 59–81.

11. *The Life of Saint Mary Magdalene and of Her Sister Saint Martha,* 27.

12. M. Amelia [Klenke], *Three Saints' Lives by Nicholas Bozon,* Franciscan Institute Publications History Series 1 (St. Bonaventure, NY: Franciscan Institute, 1947), 3, 4.

13. *The Life of Saint Mary Magdalen. Translated from the Italian of an Unknown Fourteenth Century Writer,* trans. Valentina Hawtrey (London: John Lane, The Bodley Head, 1904), vii, 2–4, 9, 47–48, 94. This work was originally printed with some editions of Domenico Cavalca's translations of Jerome's *Lives of the Saints.*

14. Ibid., 171–72, 176, 197–98. See also Jansen, *The Making of the Magdalen,* 91–96.

15. Anne T. Thayer, *Penitence, Preaching, and the Coming of the Reformation,* St. Andrews Studies in Reformation History (Aldershot, England: Ashgate, 2002), 83, 10.

16. Bonaventure, *Rooted in Faith: Homilies to a Contemporary World,* trans. Marigwen Schumacher (Chicago: Franciscan Herald Press, 1973), 53, 54.

17. Thayer, *Penitence, Preaching, and the Coming of the Reformation,* 55, 62. The saint's tears were also praised by Michael of Hungary in his collection, *Sermones praedicabiles per totum*

annum, licet breves, s. Sermones tredecim (Strasbourg, France: Georgius Husner, 1494); see Sermon 7, 113.

18. Thayer, *Penitence, Preaching, and the Coming of the Reformation,* 85.

19. Ibid., 87.

20. Jane Lahr, ed., *Searching for Mary Magdalene: A Journey Through Art and Literature* (New York: Welcome, 2006), 61.

21. Hans H. Hofstätter, "Darstellungen der Maria Magdalena in der bildenden Kunst," in Bader, ed., *Maria Magdalena,* 82, and plate 14; Andreas Tacke, ed., *"Ich armer sundiger mensch" Heiligen- und Reliquienkult am Übergang zum konfessionellen Zeitalter,* Schriftenreihe der Stiften Moritzburg 2 (Göttingen, Germany: Wallstein, 2004), 255 and frontispiece.

22. Jansen, *The Making of the Magdalen,* 54–99; see esp. 58–59.

23. Rebecca Lea McCarthy, *Origins of the Magdalene Laundries: An Analytical History* (Jefferson, NC: McFarland and Company, Inc., Publishers, 2010), 1, 76–80.

24. Caroline Walker Bynum, *Holy Feast and Holy Fast: The Religious Significance of Food to Medieval Women,* The New Historicism: Studies in Cultural Poetics (Berkeley: University of California Press, 1987), 166; Nancy Bradley Warren, *Women of God and Arms: Female Spirituality and Political Conflict, 1380–1600* (Philadelphia: University of Pennsylvania Press, 2005), 25–26, 29; Pierre de Vaux, *Vie de Soeur Colette,* trans. Elisabeth Lopez, CERCOR Travaux et Recherches / C. E. R. C. O. R. 6 (Saint-Etienne, France: Publications de l'Université de Saint-Etienne, 1994), 112, 152, 157; Jansen, *The Making of the Magdalen,* 19.

25. See Elisabeth Gössmann, "Maria Magdalena als Typus der Kirche," in Bader, ed. *Maria Magdalena,* 52, 60–61, 63.

26. Jansen, *The Making of the Magdalen,* 84–89.

27. Beverly Mayne Kienzle, "Penitents and Preachers: The Figure of Saint Peter and His Relationship to Saint Mary Magdalene," in *La figura di san Pietro nelle fonti del medioevo: atti del convegno tenutosi in occasione dello Studiorum universitatum docentium congressus: Viterbo e Roma 5–8 settembre 2000,* ed. Loredana Lazzari and Anna Maria Valente Bacci, Textes et etudes du moyen âge 17 (Louvain-la-Neuve: FIDEM, 2001), 272. Halliwell, *Mary of Magdala,* 27, traces this conflict to the early church and the era of composition of the Gnostic Gospels, such as the Gospels of Thomas and of Phillip, which portray men resenting Mary for speaking and seeking prominence among the disciples.

28. Kienzle, "Penitents and Preachers," 272; Garth, *Saint Mary Magdalene in Mediaeval Literature,* 66–7.

29. Garth, *Saint Mary Magdalene in Mediaeval Literature,* 36, 64; Jacob Bennett, "The 'Mary Magdalene' of Bishop's Lynn," *Studies in Philology* 75, no. 1 (1978): 5, 6; Elisabeth Pinto-Mathieu, *Marie-Madeleine dans la littérature du Moyen Âge* (Paris: Beauchesne, 1997), 209. On the Magdalene and anti-Semitism in medieval Passion plays, see Pinto-Mathieu, *Marie-Madeleine dans la littérature du Moyen Âge,* 236–37; Elizabeth Monroe, "'Fair and Friendly, Sweet and Beautiful': Hopes for Jewish Conversion in Synagoga's Song of Songs Imagery," in *Beyond the Yellow Badge: Anti-Judaism and Antisemitism in Medieval and Early*

Modern Visual Culture, ed. Mitchell B. Merback, Brill's Series in Jewish Studies 37 (Leiden: Brill, 2007), 41–42; and Brett Edward Whalen, *Dominion of God: Christendom and Apocalypse in the Middle Ages* (Cambridge, MA: Harvard University Press, 2009), 135–36. See also Maria Norberta Hoffmann, *Die Magdalenenszenen im geistlichen Spiel des deutschen Mittelalters* (Würzburg, Germany: K. Triltsch, 1933), 64.

30. Joanne Findon, *Lady, Hero, Saint: The Digby Play's Mary Magdalene,* Studies and Texts 173 (Toronto: Pontifical Institute of Medieval Studies, 2011), 6, 42, 155, 182, 192; Bennett, "The 'Mary Magdalene' of Bishop's Lynn," 9. See also Evans Lansing Smith, *The Hero Journey in Literature: Parables of Poesis* (Lanham, MD: University Press of America, 1997), 81–166.

31. Jane Lahr, ed., *Searching for Mary Magdalene,* 24, 28. As Isabelle Chamska, *Marie-Madeleine en tous ses états: typologie d'une figure dans les arts et les littérature, IVᵉ–XXIᵉ siècle,* Histoire (Paris: Cerf, 2008), 131, notes, the Magdalene is "beaucoup plus humaine, tendre et passionnée" than the Virgin.

32. Kienzle, "Penitents and Preachers," 270; Battista da Varano, *The Mental Sorrows of Christ in His Passion,* trans. Joseph Berrigan, Peregrina Translation Series. Matrologia Latina 6 (Saskatoon, Saskatchewan: Peregrina, 1986), 18, quoted in Jeryldene M. Wood, *Women, Art, and Spirituality: The Poor Clares of Early Modern Italy* (Cambridge: Cambridge University Press, 1996), 118–19.

33. Catherine Sanok, *Her Life Historical: Exemplarity and Female Saints' Lives in Late Medieval England.* The Middle Ages Series (Philadelphia: University of Pennsylvania Press, 2007), 126–32; Suzanne L. Craymer, "Margery Kempe's Imitation of Mary Magdalene and the 'Digby Plays,'" *Mystics Quarterly* 19, no. 4 (1993): 173, 174.

34. Craymer, "Margery Kempe's Imitation," 176–78. See also Katharine Goodland, *Female Mourning and Tragedy in Medieval and Renaissance English Drama: From the Raising of Lazarus to King Lear,* Studies in Performance and Early Modern Drama (Aldershot, England: Ashgate, 2005), 50–53.

35. Craymer, "Margery Kempe's Imitation," 178. On the Magdalene's preaching, especially to convert pagans or debunk heresy, see Victor I. Scherb, "Blasphemy and the Grotesque in the Digby Mary Magdalene," *Studies in Philology* 96, no. 3 (1999): 231, 237–38; Gyorgy Galamb, "Sainthood in the Propaganda of Mendicant Orders: The Case of the *Dialogus contra fraticellos* of James of the Marches," in *Promoting the Saints: Cults and Their Contexts from Late Antiquity until the Early Modern Period: Essays in Honor of Gábor Klaniczay for His 60th Birthday,* ed. Ottó Gecser, CEU Medievalia 12 (Budapest: Central European University Press, 2011), 255.

36. *The Life of Saint Mary Magdalene and of Her Sister Saint Martha,* 73, 82, 84. See also Herbert L. Kessler, *Spiritual Seeing: Picturing God's Invisibility in Medieval Art,* The Middle Ages Series (Philadelphia: University of Pennsylvania Press, 2000), 37.

37. *The Life of Saint Mary Magdalene and of Her Sister Saint Martha,* 86.

38. Second Council of Lyons, 1274, cited in Jansen, *The Making of the Magdalen,* 49; Madeleine Boxler, *"Ich bin ein predigerin und appostlorin": die deutschen Maria Magdalena-Legenden*

des Mittelalters (1300–1550): Untersuchungen und Text, Deutsche Literatur von den Anfängen bis 1700 22 (Bern: Lang, 1996), 190; see also 52, 76.

39. Klenke, *Three Saints' Lives*, 8, 9–10.

40. Jansen, *The Making of the Magdalen*, 41; Jacobus de Voragine, *The Golden Legend: Readings on the Saints*, vol. 1, trans. William Granger Ryan (Princeton, NJ: Princeton University Press, 1993), 376, 377.

41. Smith, ed., *The Lives of St Mary Magdalene and St Martha (MS Esc. h-I-13)*, 14: "Il vindrent au port de Marseille, et issirent hors de la nef e trouverent la Magdaleine a touz ses desciples que preschoit a grant multitude de gent. E il se lessierent cheoir a ses piez e si distrent, 'O benoite Magdaleine, ton Dieu que tu as aoree e qui tu presches.'"

42. *The Life of Saint Mary Magdalen*, trans. Valentina Hawtrey, 51, 71, 159.

43. Ibid., 101–2, 131. Cf. John 21:25.

44. Christine de Pizan, *The Book of the City of Ladies*, trans. Earl Jeffrey Richards (New York: Persea, 1982), 27–28.

45. Kienzle, "Penitents and Preachers," 272; Jansen, *The Making of the Magdalen*, 27, 49.

46. John 20:17; Hofstätter, "Darstellungen der Maria Magdalena in der Bildenden Kunst," 79, 80; *The Life of Saint Mary Magdalene and of Her Sister Saint Martha*, 73; Jansen, *The Making of the Magdalen*, 54–55, 79. On the origins of the trope comparing the Magdalene to Eve, see Jansen, *The Making of the Magdalen*, 31.

47. Chamska, *Marie-Madeleine en tous ses états*, 33, 159; Coletti, *Mary Magdalene and the Drama of Saints*, 139; Gerhard Piccard, *Der Magdalenenaltar des Lukas Moser in Tiefenbronn, Ein Beitrag zur europäischen Kunstgeschichte mit einer Untersuchung die Tiefenbronner Patrozinien und ihre (Hirsauer) Herkunft* (Wiesbaden, Germany: O. Harrassowitz, 1969).

48. Faber Stapulensis [Jacques Lefèvre d'Étaples], *De Maria Magdalena, et Triduo Christi Disceptatio, ad Clarissimum virum D. Franciscum Molineum, Christianissimi Francorum Regis Francisci Primi Magistrum* (Paris: Stephani, 1517); John Fisher, *Reuerendi patris Joannis Fisscher Rossensis in Anglia episcopi, necnon Cantibrigieñ. academię cãcellarii dignissimi, de vnica Magdalena, libri tres* (Paris: Iodoci Badii Ascēsii, 1519). On Fisher's motivation for taking up this controversy, see Richard Rex, *The Theology of John Fisher* (Cambridge: Cambridge University Press, 1991), 65–77, esp. 69. For English translations of the documents involved in the controversy, see Jacques Lefèvre d'Étaples, *Jacques Lefèvre d'Étaples and the Three Maries Debates*, trans. and ed. Sheila M. Porrer, Travaux d'humanisme et Renaissance 451 (Geneva: Librairie Droz, 2009).

49. Yves Giraud, ed., *L'image de la Madeleine: du XVᵉ au XIXᵉ siècle: actes du colloque de Fribourg, 31 mai–2 juin 1990* (Fribourg, Switzerland: Editions universitaires, 1996), 73, 75–76.

50. Ibid., 37–50, 73.

51. Porrer, *Jacques Lefèvre d'Étaples and the Three Maries Debates*, 165; Coletti, *Mary Magdalene and the Drama of Saints*, 226–27.

2. Teacher of the Dear Apostles:
Lutheran Preaching on Mary Magdalene

1. Martin Luther, *Sermons on John 18–20* (1528–1529), in WA, 28:448–57, translated in LW, 69:298–305; John A. Maxfield, *Luther's Lectures on Genesis and the Formation of Evangelical Identity,* Sixteenth Century Essays and Studies 80 (Kirksville, MO: Truman State University Press, 2008), 155.

2. Amy Nelson Burnett, *Teaching the Reformation: Ministers and Their Message in Basel, 1529–1629,* Oxford Studies in Historical Theology (Oxford: Oxford University Press, 2006), 222.

3. Giles Constable, *Three Studies in Medieval Religious and Social Thought* (Cambridge: Cambridge University Press, 1995), 8; Gregory the Great, *Sermon 33,* in PL, 76:1239; Martin Luther, *Auslegung und Deutung des heiligen Vaterunsers* (1518), in WA, 9:150.

4. Martin Luther, *Sermon on Marriage* (1525), in WA, 17.1:17; in this he followed the *Golden Legend.* See also Martin Luther, *Sermon for the Second Sunday after Epiphany* (1525), WA, 17.2:60–61, translated in *The Sermons of Martin Luther: The Church Postils,* vol. 2, ed. John Nicholas Lenker (Grand Rapids, MI: Baker, 1983), 55–57.

5. On the popularity and good reputation of Spangenberg's and Corvinus's postil collections among their evangelical contemporaries, see Ronald K. Rittgers, *The Reformation of Suffering: Pastoral Theology and Lay Piety in Late Medieval and Early Modern Germany,* Oxford Studies in Historical Theology (New York: Oxford University Press, 2012), 5.

6. "Saint Mary Magdalene," in *Exemplary Lives: Selected Sermons on the Saints, from Rheinau,* ed. and trans. James C. Wilkinson, Reformation Texts with Translation (1350–1650), Theology and Piety 3 (Milwaukee, WI: Marquette University Press, 2006), 135, 137, 139.

7. See Jaroslav Pelikan, *Divine Rhetoric: The Sermon on the Mount as Message and as Model in Augustine, Chrysostom, and Luther* (Crestwood, NY: St. Vladimir's Seminary Press, 2001), 86; Bernhard Lohse, *Martin Luther: An Introduction to His Life and Work,* trans. Robert C. Schultz (Philadelphia: Fortress, 1986), 58; and Rittgers, *The Reformation of Suffering,* 111. On the pastoral Luther, see Arthur H. Becker, "Luther as *Seelsorger,*" in *Interpreting Luther's Legacy: Essays in Honor of Edward C. Fendt,* ed. Fred W. Meuser and Stanley D. Schneider (Minneapolis: Augsburg Pub. House, 1969); and Timothy J. Wengert, ed., *The Pastoral Luther: Essays on Luther's Practical Theology,* Lutheran Quarterly Books (Grand Rapids, MI: Eerdmans, 2009). Luther was much grieved, for example, by the suicide of Johann Krause, an adviser to the archbishop of Mainz who had condemned himself for wavering between an evangelical conversion and loyalty to Catholic teaching; see the description in Luther's letter to Justus Jonas (1527), in LW, 49:181–82. See also Randall C. Zachman, *The Assurance of Faith: Conscience in the Theology of Martin Luther and John Calvin* (Louisville, KY: Westminster John Knox, 2005).

8. Jared Wicks, "Fides sacramenti—fides specialis: Luther's Development in 1518," *Gregorianum* 65, no. 1 (1984): 73; see also Martin Brecht, *Martin Luther,* vol. 1, *His Road to Reformation, 1483–1521,* trans. James L. Schaaf (Philadelphia: Fortress, 1985), 255.

9. "Sic b. Augustinus super Ioannem: accedit verbum ad elementum, et fit sacramentum, non quia fit, sed quia creditur. Ecce baptismus abluit, non quia fit, sed quia creditur abluere.

Inde et Mariam absolvens [Luc. 7, 50.] dicit: Fides tua te salvam fecit, vade in pace. Inde illud dictum commune: 'non sacramentum fidei, sed fides sacramenti iustificat', sine qua impossibile [Röm. 5, 1.] est, ut sit pax in conscientia, ut Ro: v. Iustificati ergo ex fide, pacem habemus ad deum." Martin Luther, *Acta Augustana* (1518), in *WA*, 2:15. See also Martin Luther, *Die sieben Bußpsalmen* (1517), in *WA*, 1:170; Martin Luther, *Ein Sermon von Ablaß und Gnade* (1517), in *WA*, 1:244; Martin Luther, *Assertio omnium articulorum M. Lutheri per bullam Leonis X. novissimam damnatorum* (1520), in *WA*, 7:119; Martin Luther, *Resolutiones disputationum de indulgentiarum virtute* (1518), in *WA*, 1:537, 541; and Martin Luther, *Auslegung deutsch des Vaterunsers für die einfältigen Laien* (1519), in *WA*, 2:117.

10. Martin Luther, *Sermon on Two Kinds of Righteousness* (1519), *WA* 2:149, translated in *LW*, 31:303.

11. See Martin Luther, *[Sermon] an S. Jacobs Tag*, in *Hauspostille* (1544), *WA*, 52:679.

12. "Die heuchler und werckheiligen schreiben solchen zeychen oder wercken die gerechtigkait zů, Aber Christus spricht: Dein glaube hat dir geholffen." Martin Luther, *[Sermon] am Tag Magdalene* (1527), in *WA*, 17.2:464.

13. Martin Luther, *Sermon for the Day of St. Mary Magdalene* (1536), in *Hauspostille* (1544), *WA*, 52:664–73; cf. the translation in *The Sermons of Martin Luther: The House Postils*, vol. 3, ed. Eugene F. A. Klug (Grand Rapids, MI: Baker, 1996), 367–70.

14. "Denn also spricht Paulus: 'Wir halten, das der mensch durch den glauben und nicht durch des Gesetzes werck gerecht werde'. Unnd der Prophet Abacuck spricht: 'Der gerechte wirdt seines glaubens leben'. Unnd Christus spricht zu Maria, der jre sünd vergeben wurden: 'Gehe hin, dein glaub hat dir geholffen'." Martin Luther, *Sermon for Trinity 21*, in *Hauspostille* (1544), *WA*, 52:516.

15. Johann Bugenhagen, *Postillatio in evangelia usui temporum et Sanctoru(m) totius anni servientia, ad preces Georgij Spalatini scripta* (Wittenberg, 1524), A7v, B1v, C2r; Urbanus Rhegius, *Preaching the Reformation: The Homiletical Handbook of Urbanus Rhegius*, ed. and trans. Scott Hendrix, Reformation Texts with Translation (1350–1650), Theology and Piety 2 (Milwaukee, WI: Marquette University Press, 2003), 7, 77. Lüneburg's reformation had begun in the mid-1520s and was still in progress in the 1530s; see Hendrix, *Preaching the Reformation*, 8–9.

16. Robert Kolb, *Bound Choice, Election, and Wittenberg Theological Method: From Martin Luther to the Formula of Concord*, Lutheran Quarterly Books (Grand Rapids, MI: Eerdmans, 2005), 198–99; Robin A. Leaver, *Luther's Liturgical Music: Principles and Implications*, Lutheran Quarterly Books (Grand Rapids, MI: Eerdmans, 2007), 212.

17. Johann Spangenberg, *Postilla Deütsch. Fur die jungen Christen / Knaben vnd Meidlein / jnn fragstücke verfasst / Von den fürnemesten Festen / durche gantze Jar* (Wittenberg, 1544), 128r, 128v. Spangenberg refuses to take a position on whether or not the Magdalene is this sinful woman; he claims that her specific identity is unimportant, but the message that Christ comes for sinners is all that Christians need to know.

18. Spangenberg, *Postilla Deütsch*, 127v, 128v, 129r, 129v, 130v, 133r, 130r, 132v–133r. On evangelical repentance, see also Martin Luther, *Against the Antinomians* (1539), *WA*, 50:461–77,

translated in *LW*, 47:99–120; and Bernhard Lohse, *Martin Luther's Theology: Its Historical and Systematic Development*, trans. and ed. Roy A. Harrisville (Minneapolis: Fortress, 1999), 178–84.

19. Christopher Boyd Brown, *Singing the Gospel: Lutheran Hymns and the Spread of the Reformation*, Harvard Historical Studies 148 (Cambridge, MA: Harvard University Press, 2005), 27.

20. "Dir Sünder vnd Sünderin / Lernet von dieser Büsserin / Wie Gott auffnimpt so gnediglich / Die Bus thun / gleubn vnd bessern / sich." Nicolaus Herman, "Am tage Marie Magdalene / Luc. 7," in *Die Sontags-evangelia von Nicolaus Herman (1561)*, ed. Rudolf Wolkan, Bibliothek deutscher Schriftsteller aus Böhmen 2 (Prague: F. Tempsky / Leipzig: Freytag, 1895), 207.

21. "Denn jr Lieb gegen mir ist gros, / Drumb wird sie vieler Sünden los. / Wem man aber nicht viel vergibt, / Derselb auch dester weniger liebt." Nicolaus Herman, "Das vorige Euangelium von Maria Magdalena, zum andernmal gemacht," in *Die Sontags-evangelia*, 210. My thanks to Christopher Boyd Brown for assistance with the translation.

22. Brown, *Singing the Gospel*, 91–92. Johannes Mathesius, *Postilla / Das ist / Außlegung der Sontags vnd fürnemesten Fest Euangelien / über das gantze Jar. Jetzund von neuem gedruckt / vnd gemehret mit etlichen zugethanen Predigten.* (Nuremberg: Katharina Gerlach [Erben], 1593).

23. Mathesius, *Postilla*, 54v, 55r, 55v, 56r; Johannes Mathesius, *De Profundis*, in *Ausgewählte Werke*, vol. 4, ed. Georg Loesche, Bibliothek deutscher Schriftsteller aus Böhmen 14 (Prague: Calve, 1908), 463.

24. Mathesius, *Postilla*, 55v, 56r, 56v.

25. David C. Steinmetz, *Reformers in the Wings: From Geiler von Kaysersberg to Theodore Beza*, 2nd ed. (Oxford: Oxford University Press, 2001), 71, 72; Johann Paul Christian Philipp, *Geschichte des Stiftes Naumburg und Zeitz oder allgemeine Nachrichten* (Zeitz, Germany: Webel, 1800), 268. Habermann's sermon collections were published fifteen times in the years 1575–1600; see Patrick T. Ferry, "Confessionalization and Popular Preaching: Sermons against Synergism in Reformation Saxony," in *The Reformation: Critical Concepts in Historical Studies*, vol. 1, ed. Andrew Pettegree (New York: Routledge, 2004), 214.

26. Of the legendary preaching in France, he writes, "das kan gar wol sein." Johannes Habermann, *Postilla / Das ist: Auslegung der Sontags Euangelien / wie sie durchs Jar vber in der Kirchen gelesen vnd gepredigt werden / Mit sondern fleis vnd treuen beschriben* (Jena, Germany: Donat Richtzenhan, 1575), 154r.

27. Habermann, *Postilla*, 149v, 150r, 150v, 154v–155r, 155v, 156r.

28. Edward Muir, *Ritual in Early Modern Europe*, 2nd ed., New Approaches to European History 33 (Cambridge: Cambridge University Press, 2005), 204–5; Constable, *Three Studies*, 15–16, 18.

29. Martin Luther, *Sermon on the Assumption of Mary* (1523), in *WA*, 12:651; translated in Susan C. Karant-Nunn and Merry E. Wiesner-Hanks, *Luther on Women: A Sourcebook* (Cambridge: Cambridge University Press, 2003), 78, 79; Martin Luther, *Sermon on the Assumption of Mary* (1522), in *WA*, 10.3:272.

30. "Jch habe meyne lere auß keynen buchern und nerrischen religionibus kunnen erlangen. Den do ich mich doher gab, quid Christus doceret, und seczt die andern lerer unter die bang, et cum Maria ad pedes audirem, tunc discebam. Nam nos Christiani habemus difficilem fidem." Martin Luther, *Sermon for Trinity 12* (1531), in *WA*, 34.2:148.

31. Cf. Anselm of Canterbury's "faith seeking understanding"; see Giles E. M. Gasper, *Anselm of Canterbury and His Theological Inheritance* (Aldershot, England: Ashgate, 2004), 107–9. Luther's opposition to this conception of faith is demonstrated in his contempt for the "theologians of glory"; see Martin Luther, *Heidelberg Disputation* (1518), *WA*, 1:354, translated in *LW*, 31:40. His praise for the faith of children and young women can be found in his frequent celebration of the early Christian virgin martyrs; see Margaret Arnold, "To Sweeten the Bitter Dance: The Virgin Martyrs in the Lutheran Reformation," *Archiv für Reformationsgeschichte* 104 (2013): 110–33.

32. Johann Spangenberg, *Postilla Teütsch für die jungen Christen, Knaben vnd Meydlin, in fragstücke verfassetn . . . Von den fürnemsten festen* (Augsburg, 1544), 76r, 77v. On Luther's approach to scriptural interpretation according to the rule of the Gospel, see Martin Luther, *On Translating: An Open Letter* (1530), *WA* 30.2:633, 636–37, 640–41, translated in *LW*, 35:182, 187–89, 195; and Robert Kolb, *Martin Luther: Confessor of the Faith*, Christian Theology in Context (Oxford: Oxford University Press, 2009), 48–49. On Luther's two kingdoms theology, see Lohse, *Martin Luther's Theology*, 314–24.

33. "So müsten alle weltliche handlung / handtwercken / burger vnd bauren / verlorn sein / Wz wolt daraus werden?" Spangenberg, *Postilla Teütsch . . . Von den fürnemsten festen*, 77v.

34. "Dein werck seind zwarnutz vnd güt / aber Marie werck ist allein dz nötigst / Deine werck seind vergängcklich / Marien werck / (nämlich / Gottes wort hören) ist ewig / vnd bringt den zühörer endlich dahin / da das wort wesentlich sitzet / zü der rechten des Vatters / im ewigen leben." Spangenberg, *Postilla Teütsch . . . Von den fürnemsten festen*, 78v. The parenthetical clarification that Mary's work is hearing God's word is Spangenberg's own.

35. "Das die wercke nicht rechtfertigen vor Got / Sondern sitzen zü den füssen Christi / vnd hören sein wort / das rechtfertiget vnd macht selig." Spangenberg, *Postilla Teütsch . . . Von den fürnemsten festen*, 79v.

36. Martin Luther, *Sermon for Easter Thursday* (1530), in *WA*, 32:85 (see also 90); Martin Luther, *Against the Heavenly Prophets* (1525), in *WA*, 18:107, translated in *LW*, 40:124f; Martin Luther, *Lectures on Genesis* (1535–45), in *WA*, 44:46, translated in *LW*, 6:371; Martin Luther, *Sermon for Easter Sunday* (1530), in *WA*, 32:46; Martin Luther, *Sermon for Trinity 24*, in *Sommerpostil* (1526), in *WA*, 10.1.2:432f, translated in Lenker, *The Sermons of Martin Luther: The Church Postils*, vol. 5, 332–333. For other examples of the same comparison, see Martin Luther, *Second Sermon on the First Sunday after Epiphany* (1524), in *WA*, 15:416; Martin Luther, *Magnificat* (1521), in *WA*, 7:569, translated in *LW* 21:323; Martin Luther, *Lectures on 1 Timothy* (1528), in *WA*, 26:24, translated in *LW* 28:246; Martin Luther, *Sermon for Trinity 11* (1537), in *WA*, 45:128. The very unequal comparison of Peter (and Paul) with Mary Magdalene as penitents was an element of the medieval tradition of the two saints; see Beverly Mayne Kienzle, "Penitents and Preachers: The Figure of Saint Peter and His Relationship to Saint

Mary Magdalene," in *La figura di san Pietro nelle fonti del medioevo: atti del convegno tenutosi in occasione dello Studiorum universitatum docentium congressus: Viterbo e Roma 5–8 settembre 2000*, ed. Loredana Lazzari and Anna Maria Valente Bacci, Textes et etudes du moyen âge 17 (Louvain-la-Neuve: FIDEM, 2001), 258–59.

37. See, e.g., Martin Luther, *Wochenpredigten über Joh. 16–20* (1528–1529), in WA, 28:450; and Martin Luther, *Reihenpredigten über 2. Mose* (1524), in WA, 16:38. On Luther's relationship to the papacy, see Scott H. Hendrix, *Luther and the Papacy: Stages in a Reformation Conflict* (Philadelphia: Fortress, 1981); Mark U. Edwards Jr., *Luther's Last Battles: Politics and Polemics, 1531–46* (Philadelphia: Fortress, 2004); James M. Kittelson, *Luther the Reformer: The Story of the Man and His Career* (Minneapolis: Augsburg, 1986), 290; and David M. Whitford, "The Papal Antichrist: Luther and the Underappreciated Influence of Lorenzo Valla," *Renaissance Quarterly* 61, no. 1 (2008): 26–52.

38. "Maria habebat 7 demonia. Si diceret Petrus: non potest mihi equari Maria, deus responderet: si tantum vel plus darem Magdalenae, quam tibi. Hic totum diem laboravit nihil consecutus." Martin Luther, *Sermon for Septuagesima* (1524), in WA, 15:425.

39. Martin Luther, *Sermon for Epiphany 3*, in *Winterpostille* (1528), in WA, 21:82–83; Martin Luther, *Sermon for Easter Monday*, in *Sommerpostille* (1544), in WA, 21:231.

40. "Vides in illis mulieribus ein gros trefflich unuberwindlich sterck quam habent ex verbo quod stat contra omnes insultus diaboli." Martin Luther, *Sermon on Easter Monday* (1529), in WA, 29:277.

41. This runs contra Karant-Nunn and Wiesner-Hanks, who offer this text as an example of Luther's references to the particular weakness of women; see Karant-Nunn and Wiesner-Hanks, *Luther on Women*, 60–61, 84.

42. See Martin Marty, *Martin Luther* (London: Penguin, 2004), 22; and Katherine Ludwig Jansen, *The Making of the Magdalen: Preaching and Popular Devotion in the Later Middle Ages* (Princeton, NJ: Princeton University Press, 2000), 54–55.

43. Luther, *Sermons on John 18–20*, in LW, 69:304–5.

44. Ibid., LW, 69:289–91.

45. Martin Luther, *Sermon for Easter Thursday* (1530), in WA, 32:78; Luther, *Sermons on John 18–20*, 69:299, 303.

46. Luther, *Sermon for Easter Thursday*, WA, 32:80; Martin Luther, *Eine Schoene Oster Predigt, fur dem Churfursten zu Sachssen gethan.* (1538), in WA, 46:331.

47. Martin Luther, *Disputatio inter Ioannem Eccium et Martinum Lutherum* (1519), in WA, 59:577.

48. "Invenies discipulos esse non solum apostolos, sed quotquot cred iderunt in Christum. Luc. 'Erat discipula Lyddae' &c . . . Cap. 9. Act. In hoc verbo omnes sumus comprehensi, ut indocta capita erubescant, quod mulier expresso nomine &c . . . et proculdubio in caena fuerunt mulieres Maria Magdalena, Martha, Iohanna und haben freilich mit yhm gessen, quae coxerunt, pascha und osterlamb. Non dixit apostolis, sacerdotibus, sed discipulis, darauff sihe du. Euangelistae cum maximo discrimine loquuntur de discipulis. Discipuli sunt etiam

illi qui adheserunt in Christo, non Apostoli. Antiochiae coeptum est discipulos vocari Christianos. Hierosolymis non, sed dicebatur: sunt discipuli, schuler, Junger Iesu Christi, donec usque in hunc diem. Sicut nomen Christiani et discipuli est commune omnibus hominibus viris et mulieribus, so bleibt der text uns auch gemein." Martin Luther, *Sermon for Palm Sunday* (1529), in WA, 29:158–59.

49. Brecht concurs; see Martin Brecht, *Martin Luther,* vol. 3, *The Preservation of the Church, 1532–1546,* trans. James L. Schaaf (Minneapolis: Fortress, 1999), 76. Cf. Carl R. Trueman, "Reformers, Puritans and Evangelicals: The Lay Connection," in *The Rise of the Laity in Evangelical Protestantism,* ed. Deryck W. Lovegrove (London: Routledge, 2002), 23.

50. Martin Luther, in WA, 6:370; Martin Luther, in LW, 35:101–2.

51. Timothy J. Wengert, *Priesthood, Pastors, Bishops: Public Ministry for the Reformation and Today* (Minneapolis: Fortress, 2008), 52, emphasis added.

52. Martin Luther, *The Misuse of the Mass* (1521), WA 8:487, 495, translated in LW, 36:138–39, 149; Robert C. Croken, *Luther's First Front: The Eucharist as Sacrifice* (Ottawa: University of Ottawa Press, 1990), 30, 31–32; Martin Brecht, *Martin Luther,* vol. 2, *Shaping and Defining the Reformation, 1521–1532,* trans. James L. Schaaf (Minneapolis: Fortress, 1990), 27–29; Kittelson, *Luther the Reformer,* 170; Lee Palmer Wandel, *The Eucharist in the Reformation: Incarnation and Liturgy* (Cambridge: Cambridge University Press, 2006), 98. There is an excellent survey of the events of 1521, and the theological development that led up to them, in Amy Nelson Burnett, *Karlstadt and the Origins of the Eucharistic Controversy: A Study in the Circulation of Ideas,* Oxford Studies in Historical Theology (New York: Oxford University Press, 2011), 10–35.

53. Luther, *The Misuse of the Mass,* WA 8:498, translated in LW, 36:151–52.

54. For interpretations of Luther as increasingly conservative through the 1520s in relation to the question of clerical authority, see Brad C. Pardue, *Printing, Power, and Piety: Appeals to the Public During the Early Years of the English Reformation,* Studies in Medieval and Reformation Traditions 162 (Leiden: Brill, 2012), 40; and Mark U. Edwards Jr., *Printing, Propaganda, and Martin Luther* (Minneapolis: Fortress, 1994), 167–68.

55. Martin Luther, *To the Christian Nobility of the German Nation* (1521), WA 6:407–8, translated in LW, 44:128.

56. Martin Luther, *Lectures on 1 Timothy* (1527–1528), WA 26:46–47, translated in LW, 28:277. On the *Lectures on 1 Timothy* and Luther's ecclesiastical goals there, see Brecht, *Martin Luther,* 2:248–49.

57. Johann Spangenberg, *Postilla Teütsch Für die jungen Christen, Knaben vnd Meidlein, in Fragstück verfasset . . . Von Ostern bis auff das Aduendt* (Augsburg, 1543), 6v, 8v–9r.

58. "Sanct Paulus mainung ist nicht / das die weiber Christum nicht sollen leren vnd bekennen / sonder er will das es in Christlicher gemain soll ordenlich zügeen / Wonun Männer seind / die das Leerampt künden ausrichten / da schweigen billich die weiber / Wa aber kain man ist geschickt zü Predigen / warumb solt ainem weibe da nicht gestattet werden zü leren? Mügen die weiber / als Christen / in der not Teüffen / so mügen sy auch wol inir der not Predigen / nicht durch jr aigen verdienst / sonder durch den Tod

vnd Auffersteheeung Christi." Spangenberg, *Postilla Teütsch . . . Von Ostern bis auff das Aduendt,* 9r.

59. Spangenberg's dedication to the sermon collection for Advent to Easter notes his attempt to formulate the work of Corvinus, as well as Luther and Johannes Brenz, for a young audience. Spangenberg, *Postilla Deütsch,* 3r–3v. Corvinus and Spangenberg apparently met in 1544, when Corvinus, in his role as confessor to Elisabeth Braunschweig-Lüneburg, accompanied her and her son on a trip to Saxony, which included a visit to Spangenberg in Nordhausen. See Carl Lorenz Collmann, "Anton Corvinus Leben," in *Das Leben der Altväter der lutherischen Kirche,* ed. Moritz Meurer (Leipzig: Justus Naumann, 1864), 43; and Paul Tschackert, *Antonius Corvinus Leben und Schriften,* Quellen und Darstellungen zur Geschichte Niedersachsens 3 (Hanover: Hahn'sche, 1900), 151.

60. Rittgers, *The Reformation of Suffering,* 180. Such removal was the case for the Marian antiphons, which were taken out of the worship practice in Calenberg-Göttingen. See Mary E. Frandsen, "'Salve Regina / Salve rex Christi': Lutheran Engagement with the Marian Antiphons in the Age of Orthodoxy and Piety," *Musica Disciplina* 55 (2010): 153.

61. Anton Corvinus, quoted in Frandsen, "'Salve Regina / Salve rex Christi,'" 153.

62. "Mercke / das die weiber hie ein Priesterlich ampt thun sollen / Wer hat sie dennzu Priestern geweihet? Der Bapst? Nein / sondern Gott durch seinen Son vnd vnsern Hohen priester Christum / Wer an den Christum gleubt / vnd durch sein wort den Heiligen geist empfangen hat / der gehört je vnter den hauffen / von welchem S. Peter gesagt hat / Gott geb ersey man oder weib." Anton Corvinus, *Kurtze und einfeltige Auslegung der Episteln vnd Euangelien so aufff die Sontage vnd furnemisten Feste durchs gantze jar jnn der Kirchen gelesen werden* (Wittenberg, 1539), 4r.

63. "Wirr alle sampt weiber vnd menner / müssen bekennen / das wir wider geboren sein / zu einer lebendigen hoffnung / durch die aufferstehung Jhesu Christi von den todten." Corvinus, *Kurtze und einfeltige Auslegung der Episteln vnd Euangelien,* 4r.

64. Spangenberg, *Postilla Deütsch,* 3r–3v; Elisabeth von Braunschweig-Lüneburg, *Ein Christlicher Sendebrieff* (Hanover, 1545); Irene Dingel, "The Culture of Conflict in the Controversies Leading to the Formula of Concord, 1548–1580," in *Lutheran Ecclesiastical Culture, 1550–1675,* ed. Robert Kolb, Brill's Companions to the Christian Tradition 11 (Leiden: Brill, 2008), 29. See also Ulrike Zitzlsperger, "Mother, Martyr and Mary Magdalene: German Female Pamphleteers and their Self-Images," *History* 88, no. 291 (2003): 383; and "Elisabeth, Duchess of Brunswick-Calenberg," in *Late-Medieval German Women's Poetry: Secular and Religious Songs,* ed. and trans. Albrecht Classen, Library of Medieval Women (Cambridge: D. S. Brewer, 2004), 86.

3. Publish the Coming of the Lord: Evangelical Magdalenes

1. Katherine Ludwig Jansen, *The Making of the Magdalen: Preaching and Popular Devotion in the Later Middle Ages* (Princeton, NJ: Princeton University Press, 2000), 334; Susan Haskins, *Mary Magdalen: Myth and Metaphor* (New York: HarperCollins, 1993), 249.

2. This was what Luther argued; see Martin Luther, *The Keys* (1530), in LW, 40:321, 323, 364–73.

3. Katharina Schütz Zell, "Lamentation and Exhortation at the Burial of Matthew Zell" in *Katharina Schütz Zell,* vol. 2, *The Writings: A Critical Edition,* ed. Elsie Anne McKee (Leiden: Brill, 1999), 71, 83f. See also Katharina Schütz Zell, *Church Mother: The Writings of a Protestant Reformer in Sixteenth-Century Germany,* ed. and trans. Elsie McKee, The Other Voice in Early Modern Europe (Chicago: University of Chicago Press, 2006), 104, 115.

4. Margaret Patterson Hannay, *Silent but for the Word: Tudor Women as Patrons, Translators, and Writers of Religious Works* (Kent, OH: Kent State University Press, 1985), 85; Kimberly Ann Coles, *Religion, Reform, and Women's Writing in Early Modern England* (Cambridge: Cambridge University Press, 2008), 18–45; Patricia Badir, *The Maudlin Impression: English Literary Images of Mary Magdalen, 1550–1700* (Notre Dame, IN: University of Notre Dame Press, 2009), 197.

5. M. Marsin, *Good News to the Good Women* (London, 1700), cited in Sarah Apetrei, "A 'Remarkable Female of Womankind': Gender, Scripture, and Knowledge in the Writings of M. Marsin," in *Women, Gender, and Radical Religion in Early Modern Europe,* ed. Sylvia Brown, Studies in Medieval and Reformation Traditions 129 (Leiden: Brill, 2007), 150; Susan C. Karant-Nunn, *The Reformation of Feeling: Shaping the Religious Emotions in Early Modern Germany* (New York: Oxford University Press, 2010), 229.

6. Ulrike Zitzlsperger, "Mother, Martyr and Mary Magdalene: German Female Pamphleteers and their Self-images," *History* 88, no. 291 (2003): 381.

7. Argula von Grumbach, "To the University of Ingolstadt," in *Argula von Grumbach: A Woman's Voice in the Reformation,* ed. Peter Matheson (Edinburgh: T & T Clark, 1995), 88–89.

8. Ibid., 83.

9. Zitzlsperger, "Mother, Martyr and Mary Magdalene," 380, 382; Jansen, *The Making of the Magdalen,* 64. On sexual slander in Renaissance rhetoric, see Rachel Heard, "Caught *in medias res:* Female Intercession, 'Regulation,' and 'Exchange,'" in *Rhetoric, Women, and Politics in Early Modern England,* eds. Jennifer Richards and Alison Thorne (Abingdon, England: Routledge, 2006), 53–54.

10. For example, Luther and his colleagues were depicted as the disciples in Lucas Cranach's *Wittenberg Altarpiece* (1547); see John Dillenberger, *Images and Relics: Theological Perceptions and Visual Images in Sixteenth-Century Europe,* Oxford Studies in Historical Theology (Oxford: Oxford University Press, 1999), 102–5.

11. Zitzlsperger, "Mother, Martyr and Mary Magdalene," 381. See also *Johannes Kesslers Sabbata, mit kleinerin Schriften und Briefen,* ed. Emil Egli and Rudolf Schoch (St. Gallen, Switzerland: Fehr, 1902), 132; Zitzlsperger gives an incorrect reference to p. 102.

12. Zitzlsperger, "Mother, Martyr and Mary Magdalene," 384; Zell, *Church Mother,* 219; Ulrike Wiethaus, "Female Authority and Religiosity in the Letters of Katharina Zell and Caritas Pirckheimer," in *Mystics Quarterly* 19, no. 3 (1993): 127–28. On the duty of the congregation to

monitor the character of preaching, see Martin Luther, *Infiltrating and Clandestine Preachers* (1532), in *LW*, 40:384–85.

13. Christ also called to Anna, Hannah, Martha, Sarah, Rebecca, and the Virgin Mary; see Kirsi Stjerna, *Women and the Reformation* (Hoboken, NJ: Wiley-Blackwell, 2009), 127.

14. Zell, *Church Mother*, 104.

15. Zitzlsperger, "Mother, Martyr and Mary Magdalene," 390; Katharina Schütz Zell, "Meditations on Psalms and Lord's Prayer," in *Katharina Schütz Zell*, 2:361; Katharina Schütz Zell, "Letter to the Suffering Women of the Community of Kentzigen Who Believe in Christ, Sisters with Me in Jesus Christ," in *Early Protestant Spirituality*, ed. and trans. Scott H. Hendrix (New York: Paulist, 2009), 110; Elsie Anne McKee, *Katharina Schütz Zell*, vol. 1, *The Life and Thought of a Sixteenth-Century Reformer*, (Leiden: Brill, 1999), 470–71.

16. Stjerna, *Women and the Reformation*, 141; Mary B. McKinley, "The Early Modern Teacher—Marie Dentière: An Outspoken Reformer Enters the French Literary Canon," in *Sixteenth Century Journal* 37, no. 2 (2006): 408.

17. Marie Dentière, *Epistle to Marguerite de Navarre*, in *Epistle to Marguerite de Navarre and Preface to a Sermon by John Calvin*, ed. and trans. Mary B. McKinley, The Other Voice in Early Modern Europe (Chicago: University of Chicago Press, 2004), 53.

18. Ibid., 55.

19. Dentière, *Epistle to Marguerite de Navarre*, 54–55, 55–56; McKinley, "The Early Modern Teacher," 406, 410; Beverly Mayne Kienzle, "The Prostitute-Preacher: Patterns of Polemic against Medieval Waldensian Women Preachers," in *Women Preachers and Prophets through Two Millennia of Christianity*, ed. Beverly Mayne Kienzle and Pamela J. Walker (Berkeley: University of California Press, 1998), 105. On the Waldensians joining the Reformation, see George Huntston Williams, *The Radical Reformation*, 3rd ed., Sixteenth Century Essays and Studies 15 (Kirksville, MO: Truman State University Press, 1992), 808–9.

20. Larissa Taylor, *Soldiers of Christ: Preaching in Late Medieval and Reformation France* (Toronto: University of Toronto Press, 2002), 174–75.

21. Dentière, *Epistle to Marguerite de Navarre*, 19. See also Calvin to Farel, 1 September 1546, in *Ioannis Calvini Opera quae supersunt omnia*, vol. 12, ed. G. Baum, E. Cunitz, and E. Reus (New York: Johnson Reprints, 1964), no. 824, cols. 377–78.

22. Hannay, *Silent but for the Word*, 85; John Foxe, *Foxe's Book of Martyrs: Select Narratives*, ed. John N. King (Oxford: Oxford University Press, 2009), 23; Anne Askew, "The first examination of Ann Askew," in *Renaissance Woman: A Sourcebook: Constructions of Femininity in England*, ed. Kate Aughterson (New York: Routledge, 1995), 20. See also *The first examinacyon of Anne Askewe, lately martyred in Smythfelde, by the Romysh popes upholders, with the Elucydacyon of John Bale* (Wesel, Germany, 1546).

23. Patrick Collinson, "English Reformations," in Michael Hattaway, ed., *A New Companion to English Renaissance Literature and Culture* (Chichester, England: Wiley-Blackwell, 2010), 404; Elaine V. Beilin, "Introduction," in Anne Askew, *The Examinations of Anne Askew*, ed. Elaine V. Beilin, Women Writers in English 1350–1850 (New York: Oxford

University Press, 1996); xix; Edith Wilks Dolnikowski, "Feminine Exemplars for Reform: Women's Voices in John Foxe's *Acts and Monuments,*" in Kienzle and Walker, eds., *Women Preachers and Prophets,* 200.

24. John Foxe, *Acts and Monuments of the Church,* 1563 ed., book 5, 1104, The Acts and Monuments Online, http://www.johnfoxe.org/index.php?realm=text&gototype=modern&edition =1563&pageid=1104 (on David, Peter, and the Magdalene as sinners); Foxe, *Acts and Monuments,* 1563 ed., book 5, 1383, The Acts and Monuments Online, https://www.johnfoxe.org /index.php?realm=text&gototype=&edition=1563&pageid=1383 ("Magdalene did not know Christ to be God, before his resurrection"); and M. Philpot to John Careless, n.d., in Foxe, *Acts and Monuments,* 1563 ed., book 5, 1604, The Acts and Monuments Online, https://www .johnfoxe.org/index.php?realm=text&gototype=&edition=1563&pageid=1604 (on Mary's "sevenfold sins"); John Foxe, *Fox's Book of Martyrs: The Acts and Monuments of the Church,* vol 3, ed. John Cumming (London: George Virtue, 1844), 704. On the question of whether Mary Magdalene had understood Jesus to be the Son of God before the resurrection, as it was explored in the medieval hagiography, see Sister M. Amelia [Klenke], *Three Saints' Lives by Nicholas of Bozon,* Franciscan Institute Publications Historical Series 1 (St. Bonaventure, NY: Franciscan Institute, 1947), 8; and *The Life of St. Mary Magdalen. Translated from the Italian of an Unknown Fourteenth Century Writer,* trans. Valentina Hawtrey (London: John Lane, The Bodley Head, 1904), 51, 71.

25. Jane Eade, "Reflections on a Glass *Madeleine Pénitente,*" in *Mary Magdalene: Iconographic Studies from the Middle Ages to the Baroque,* ed. Michelle A. Erhardt and Amy M. Morris, Studies in Religion and the Arts 7 (Leiden: Brill, 2012), 320; Elizabeth I, "A Godly Meditation of the Christian Soul," in *Queen Elizabeth I: Selected Works,* ed. Steven W. May (New York: Washington Square Press, 2004), 65; David Loades, *Elizabeth I* (London: Hambledon Continuum, 2006), 61; Patrick Collinson, *Elizabethans* (Cambridge: Cambridge University Press, 2003), 95; Patrick Collinson, "What Are the Women Doing in Foxe's 'Book of Martyrs'?," in *Women and Religion in the Atlantic Age: 1550–1900,* ed. Emily Clark and Mary Laven (Aldershot, England: Ashgate, 2013), 30.

26. George Ashe, quoted in Badir, *Maudlin Impression,* 197, emphasis in the original.

27. Catharina Regina von Greiffenberg, *Meditations on the Incarnation, Passion, and Death of Jesus Christ,* ed. and trans. Lynne Tatlock, The Other Voice in Early Modern Europe (Chicago: University of Chicago Press, 2009), 6–7, 28, 31.

28. Ibid., 30, 69.

29. Christine de Pizan, *The Book of the City of Ladies,* trans. Earl Jeffrey Richards (New York: Persea Books, 1982), 28; Greiffenberg, *Meditations on the Incarnation,* 69, 70 (cf. Matthew 16:23). On Greiffenberg's desired imitation of the anointing in her speech and writing, see Karant-Nunn, *The Reformation of Feeling,* 229. On Luther's discussion of Mary Magdalene being enflamed by the love of Christ, see Martin Luther, *Sermons on the Gospel of St. John, Chapters 18–20:18* (1528–1529), in LW, 69:299, 303.

30. Greiffenberg, *Meditations on the Incarnation,* 70. See also Martin Luther, *Lectures on Galatians* (1535), in LW, 26:232.

31. Greiffenberg, *Meditations on the Incarnation,* 85, 99. See also Karant-Nunn, *The Reformation of Feeling,* chapter 3, "The Reformed Churches."

32. Greiffenberg, *Meditations on the Incarnation,* 111; Silke R. Falkner, "Rhetorical Tropes and Realities—A Double Strategy Confronts a Double Standard: Catharina Regina von Greiffenberg Negotiates a Solution in the Seventeenth Century," in *Women in German Yearbook: Feminist Studies in German Literature and Culture* 17 (2001): 31–56.

33. Greiffenberg, *Meditations on the Incarnation,* 113. See also Anne T. Thayer, *Penitence, Preaching, and the Coming of the Reformation,* St. Andrews Studies in Reformation History (Aldershot, England: Ashgate, 2002), 87.

34. Greiffenberg, *Meditations on the Incarnation,* 129–30.

35. See Martin Luther, *Freedom of a Christian* (1520), in *LW,* 31:352.

36. Apetrei, "A 'Remarkable Female of Womankind,'" 142–43.

37. Sarah Apetrei, *Women, Feminism, and Religion in Early Enlightenment England,* Cambridge Studies in Early Modern British History (Cambridge: Cambridge University Press, 2010), 185; M. Marsin, quoted in Apetrei, "A 'Remarkable Female of Womankind,'" 145, 149, 150. See also William E. Burns, "'By Him the Women will be delivered from that Bondage, which some has found Intolerable': M. Marsin, English Millenarian Feminist," in *Eighteenth Century Women: Studies in Their Lives, Work and Culture,* vol. 1, ed. Linda V. Troost (New York: AMS, 2001), 19–38

38. Karen Lee, "'I Wish to Be Nothing': The Role of Self-Denial in the Mystical Theology of Anna Maria van Schurman," in Brown, ed., *Women, Gender, and Radical Religion,* 189, 190, 192; see also Joyce Irwin, "Anna Maria van Schurman: From Feminism to Pietism," in *Church History: Studies in Christianity and Culture* 46, no. 1 (1977): 49; Mirjam de Baar, Machteld Löwensteyn, Marit Monteiro, and A. Agnes Sneller, eds., *Choosing the Better Part: Anna Maria van Schurman (1607–1678),* International Archives of the History of Ideas 146 (Dordrecht: Kluwer Academic, 1996).

39. Anna Maria van Schurman, quoted in Lee, "'I Wish to Be Nothing',"189, 197; Anna Maria van Schurman, *Whether a Christian Woman Should Be Educated and Other Writings from Her Intellectual Circle,* trans. and ed. Joyce L. Irwin, The Other Voice in Early Modern Europe (Chicago: University of Chicago Press, 1998), 9.

40. Teresa Feroli, *Political Speaking Justified: Women Prophets and the English Revolution* (Newark: University of Delaware Press, 2006), 97, 100.

41. Anna Trapnel, *The Cry of a Stone,* quoted in Erica Longfellow, *Women and Religious Writing in Early Modern England* (Cambridge: Cambridge University Press, 2004), 168.

42. Longfellow, *Women and Religious Writing,* 210–11.

43. Ibid., 3–4, 12–13.

44. This was the case of Ursula of Munsterberg leaving the Freiberg Convent of the Order of Mary Magdalene the Penitent, for example; see Stjerna, *Women and the Reformation,* 29; and Sonja Domröse, *Frauen der Reformationszeit: Gelehrt, mutig und glaubensfest* (Göttingen, Germany: Vandenhoeck und Ruprecht, 2013), 73.

45. Jansen, *The Making of the Magdalen,* 251–56, 264.

4. A Most Holy Penitent: Preaching and
Teaching the Magdalene in the Catholic Reformation

1. Susan Haskins, *Mary Magdalen: Myth and Metaphor* (New York: Harcourt, Brace & Co., 1993), 235, 245, 261; Sara F. Matthews-Grieco, "Models of Female Sanctity in Renaissance and Counter-Reformation Italy," in *Women and Faith: Catholic Religious Life in Italy from Late Antiquity to the Present,* ed. Lucetta Scaraffia and Gabrielle Zarri (Cambridge, MA: Harvard University Press, 1999), 165.

2. On the pattern of female fidelity to early modern Catholic congregations, see Kathryn Norberg, *Rich and Poor in Grenoble, 1600–1814* (Berkeley: University of California Press, 1985), 251.

3. See Ian MacLean, *The Renaissance Notion of Woman: A Study in the Fortunes of Scholasticism and Medieval Science in European Intellectual Life,* Cambridge Monographs on the History of Medicine (Cambridge: Cambridge University Press, 1980).

4. Robert L. Kendrick, *Celestial Sirens: Nuns and Their Music in Early Modern Milan,* Oxford Monographs on Music (Oxford: Clarendon, 1996), 77.

5. See Jean Delumeau, *Le Catholicisme entre Luther et Voltaire,* 4th ed., Nouvelle Clio 30 (Paris: Presses universitaires de France, 1992), 241–42, 256–58. For an evaluation of the success of this program, see Robert Bireley, *The Refashioning of Catholicism, 1450–1700: A Reassessment of the Counter-Reformation,* European History in Perspective (Basingstoke: Macmillan, 1999), 96–120. The First and Second Decrees (1546) of the Council of Trent established the canonical books of the Bible, mandated the use of the Latin Vulgate, and banned individual scripture interpretation, even in private; see Dean P. Béchard, trans. and ed., *The Scripture Documents: An Anthology of Official Catholic Teachings* (Collegeville, MN: Liturgical Press, 2002), 3–5. See also Hughes Oliphant Old, *The Reading and Preaching of the Scriptures in the Worship of the Christian Church,* vol. 4, *The Age of the Reformation* (Grand Rapids, MI: Eerdmans, 2002), 165.

6. See, e.g., the study of the reform of prostitutes in the Spanish context in Mary Elizabeth Perry, "Magdalens and Jezebels in Counter-Reformation Spain," in *Culture and Control in Counter-Reformation Spain,* ed. Anne J. Cruz and Mary Elizabeth Perry, Hispanic Issues 7 (Minneapolis: University of Minnesota Press, 1992), 124–44, especially 132–41.

7. Tommaso de Vio Cajetan, *De fide et operibus contra Lutheranos* (Rome: Antonius Bladus Asulanus, 1532), fols. B1v–B2r, translated in Tommaso de Vio Cajetan, *Cajetan Responds: A Reader in Reformation Controversy,* ed. and trans. Jared Wicks (Washington, DC: Catholic University of America Press, 1978), 224–25; Lewis W. Spitz, *The Renaissance and Reformation Movements,* vol. 2, *The Reformation* (St. Louis: Concordia Pub. House, 1980), 563; Allyson F. Creasman, *Censorship and Civic Order in Reformation Germany, 1517–1648: "Printed Poison and Evil Talk"* (New York: Routledge, 2016), 125–26; Peter Canisius, *Notae In Evangelicas Lectiones, Qvae Per Totvm Annvm Festis Sanctorvm Diebvs In Ecclesia Catholica Recitantvr: Opvs Ad Pie Meditandvm* (Fribourg, Switzerland: Gemperlin, 1593), 385, 386.

8. Johann Hoffmeister, *Homiliae In Evangelia, Qvae In Dominicis, Et Aliis Festis Diebvs Legvntvr Per Totvm Annum : cu[m] duabus vnaquaque hebdomade quadragesimae, Tertia videlicet & Quinta Feriis, depraedicatae* (Paris: Sonnius, 1567), 241v.

9. Peter G. Wallace, *Communities and Conflict in Early Modern Colmar, 1575–1730* (Atlantic Highlands, NJ: Humanities Press, 1995), 19; Nikolaus Paulus, *Der Augustinermönch, Johannes Hoffmeister: Ein Lebensbild aus der Reformationszeit* (Freiburg im Breisgau, Germany: Herder'sche Verlagshandlung, 1891), 40–41, 197–220; Hoffmeister, *Homiliae In Evangelia,* 242r.

10. "Hic duae sententiae in magna sunt controuersia inter patres dum alii iustificationem fidei per dilectionem, alii sursum vtrique, hoc est, fidei per dilectionem operanti adseribunt. . . . Certem praestaret fide & dilectione praeditum esse, quam de his inaniter disputare." Hoffmeister, *Homiliae In Evangelia,* 243r.

11. John M Frymire, *The Primacy of the Postils: Catholics, Protestants, and the Dissemination of Ideas in Early Modern Germany,* Studies in Medieval and Reformation Traditions 147 (Leiden: Brill, 2010), 52.

12. "Ante omnia mutuam charitatem in vobis continuam habentes, quoniam charitas operit multitudienm peccatorum, quandoquidem feruor dilectionis sit spiritualis ignis, peccata simul cum poena consumens." Friedrich Nausea, *Catholicarum postillarum et homiliarum in totius anni tam de Tempore quàm de sanctis Euangelia, epitome* (Cologne, 1576), 527.

13. Frymire, *The Primacy of the Postils,* 304–5.

14. "(Darumb ists nit wahr das die neuwen Christen Narrieren: allein der Glaube seye von nöten vnd gnüg verzeihung der Sünden vnd die Seligkeit zu erlangen, die Liebe thüt solchs, dann Marie Magdalene seynd vil Sünd vergeben, darumb, das sie vil geliebt hat.)" Jakob Feucht, *Postilla catholica Euangeliorum de sanctis totius Anni : das ist Catholische Außlegung aller Fest un[d] Feyertäglichen Euangelien durch das gantze Jar . . . Getheilt in drey theil* (Cologne: Quentel, 1597), 136.

15. Johann Hoffmeister, *Predig Vber die Suntäglichen Euangelien des gantzen Jars* (Ingolstadt, Germany: Weissenhorn, 1548), 78r; Hoffmeister, *Homiliae In Evangelia,* 146r, 148r.

16. Hoffmeister, *Homiliae In Evangelia,* 148r; Nausea, *Catholicarum postillarum epitome,* 526; Craig S. Farmer, *The Gospel of John in the Sixteenth Century: The Johannine Exegesis of Wolfgang Musculus,* Oxford Studies in Historical Theology (New York: Oxford University Press, 1997), 111; Antonius Broickwy von Königstein, *Postillae seu enarrationes, in lectiones epistolarum & evangeliorum : quas tam in dominicis diebus, [at]q[ue] in divorum memoria orthodoxa ecclesia hactenus lege re co[n]suevit* (Cologne: Quentell, 1530), 125v.

17. Irena Backus, *Historical Method and Confessional Identity in the Era of the Reformation (1378–1615),* Studies in Medieval and Reformation Thought 94 (Leiden: Brill, 2003), 46, 47–48; Robert J. Christman, *Doctrinal Controversy and Lay Religiosity in Late Reformation Germany: The Case of Mansfeld,* Studies in Medieval and Reformation Traditions 157 (Leiden: Brill, 2012), 29; Georg Witzel, *Dn. Georgii Wicelii Postilla, Hoc Est, Enarratio Epistolarvm Et Evangeliorvm De Tempore Et De Sanctis Per totum annum* (Cologne: Quentel, 1553), 329, 332, 849, 851–52.

18. R. Po-chia Hsia, *The World of Catholic Renewal, 1540–1770,* 2nd ed. (New York: Cambridge University Press, 2005), 33, 39. Elizabeth Lehfehldt's study of Spanish convents confirms a trend toward increasingly upper-class composition of convent populations through

the early modern period; see Elizabeth A. Lehfehldt, *Religious Women in Golden-Age Spain: The Permeable Cloister,* Women and Gender in the Early Modern World (Aldershot, England: Ashgate, 2005), 75–76. The percentage of patrician women who were nuns ranged between 53 percent and 81 percent in sixteenth- and seventeenth-century Venice; for an extensive exploration of the complex web of social, economic, and religious causes, see Jutta Gisela Sperling, *Convents and the Body Politic in Late Renaissance Venice,* Women in Culture and Society (Chicago: University of Chicago Press, 1999), 18–71.

19. Barbara B. Diefendorf, "Rethinking the Catholic Reformation: The Role of Women," in *Women, Religion, and the Atlantic World (1600–1800),* ed. Daniella Kostroun and Lisa Vollendorf, UCLA Center / Clark Series (Toronto: University of Toronto Press, 2009), 31–34, 36–37, 38, 50–51; Barbara B. Diefendorf, *From Penitence to Charity: Pious Women and the Catholic Reformation in Paris* (New York: Oxford University Press, 2004), 248; Susan E. Dinan, *Women and Poor Relief in Seventeenth-Century France: The Early History of the Daughters of Charity,* Women and Gender in the Early Modern World (Aldershot, England: Ashgate, 2006), 3–5, 26, 31. On the difference between practice and official dogma as a trope of the historiography of early modern Catholicism, see Jill Fehleison, *Boundaries of Faith: Catholics and Protestants in the Diocese of Geneva,* Early Modern Studies 5 (Kirksville, MO: Truman State University Press, 2010), 4. On women as mediators between popular and elite culture, see Peter Burke, *Popular Culture in Early Modern Europe,* 3rd ed. (Farnham, England: Ashgate, 2009), 84. For the opposition characterized as between church and local religion, see William A. Christian, Jr., *Local Religion in Sixteenth-Century Spain* (Princeton, NJ: Princeton University Press, 1981), 3.

20. Ruth P. Liebowitz, "Virgins in the Service of Christ: The Dispute over an Active Apostolate for Women during the Counter-Reformation," in *Women of Spirit: Female Leadership in the Jewish and Christian Traditions,* ed. Rosemary Ruether and Eleanor McLaughlin (New York: Simon and Schuster, 1979), 143, 145.

21. Elizabeth Rapley, *The Dévotes: Women and Church in Seventeenth-Century France,* McGill-Queen's Studies in the History of Religion 4 (Montreal and Kingston: McGill-Queen's University Press, 1990), 42–43; *Reglement de la confrerie de la charité qui se pratique dans plusieurs paroisses de Paris et ailleurs. Avec un formulaire de l'instruction que l'on peut faire en visitant les Malades. Dressé à l'instance des Dames employés en ce pieux exercice* (Paris: Pierre de Bresche, 1655), 30. On confraternities' involvement with religious education in Counter-Reformation Italy, see Christopher F. Black, *Italian Confraternities in the Sixteenth Century* (Cambridge: Cambridge University Press, 1989), 224–28. This represented a continuity of late medieval efforts; see the discussion of fifteenth- sixteenth-century Milan in Bireley, *The Refashioning of Catholicism,* 122–24.

22. John Bossy formulates this dilemma elegantly, noting that "[the Counter-Reformation] was obliged to promote education, and in promoting education tended to abolish itself." John Bossy, "The Counter-Reformation and the People of Catholic Europe," in *The Counter-Reformation: The Essential Readings,* ed. David M. Luebke (Malden, MA: Blackwell, 1999), 102.

23. Rapley, *Dévotes,* 117; S. Hosias is cited in Keith Thomas, "Women and the Civil War Sects," *Past and Present* 13 (1958): 60. Michael Mullett points to the situation in the Netherlands,

where there was a shortage of priests, nothing that "the result . . . was to hand the every-day direction of the Church to the laity and especially to women"; Michael A. Mullett, *The Catholic Reformation* (London: Routledge, 1999), 171. See also Virginia Cox, *The Prodigious Muse: Women's Writing in Counter-Reformation Italy* (Baltimore: Johns Hopkins University Press, 2011), 21.

24. Kirstin Noreen, "Ecclesiae militantis triumphi: Jesuit Iconography and the Counter-Reformation," *Sixteenth Century Journal* 29, no. 3 (1998): 697; Zoran Velagić, "Reading Aloud: Between Oral and Literate Communication," in *Friars, Nobles and Burghers—Sermons, Images and Prints: Studies of Culture and Society in Early-Modern Europe, In Memoriam István György Tóth*, ed. Jaroslav Miller and László Kontler (Budapest: Central European University Press, 2010), 384. For a study of Germany's educational literary production for girls, see Cornelia Niekus Moore, *The Maiden's Mirror: Reading Material for German Girls in the Sixteenth and Seventeenth Centuries*, Wolfenbütteler Forschungen 36 (Wiesbaden, Germany: In Kommission bei O. Harrassowitz, 1987).

25. Desiderius Erasmus, "The Abbot and the Learned Woman," in *Erasmus on Women*, ed. Erika Rummel (Toronto: University of Toronto Press, 1996), 174–79; cf. Rummel's discussion of the dialogue p. 10. Charles Fantazzi, "Vives and the Emarginati," in *A Companion to Juan Luis Vives*, ed. Charles Fantazzi, Brill's Companions to the Christian Tradition 12 (Leiden: Brill, 2008), 65–86; Christine Christ-von Wedel, *Erasmus of Rotterdam: Advocate of a New Christianity* (Toronto: University of Toronto Press, 2013), 241. See also John Lee Thompson, *John Calvin and the Daughters of Sarah: Women in Regular and Exceptional Roles in the Exegesis of Calvin, His Predecessors, and His Contemporaries*, Travaux d'humanisme et Renaissance 259 (Geneva: Librairie Droz, 1992), 4; and J. K. Sowards, "Erasmus and the Education of Women," *Sixteenth Century Journal* 13, no. 4 (1982): 77–89.

26. Erasmus, "The Abbot and the Learned Woman," 176.

27. Susan Haskins, "Foreword," in *Mary Magdalene: Iconographic Studies from the Middle Ages to the Baroque*, ed. Michelle A. Erhardt and Amy M. Morris, Studies in Religion and the Arts 7 (Leiden: Brill, 2012), xxxiv; Desiderius Erasmus, "The Christian Widow," in Rummel, ed., *Erasmus on Women*, 189, 212–13.

28. Juan Luis Vives, *The Education of a Christian Woman: A Sixteenth-Century Manual*, ed. and trans. Charles Fantazzi, The Other Voice in Early Modern Europe (Chicago: University of Chicago Press, 2000), 72, 78, 113.

29. Ibid., 132, 133.

30. Erasmus himself stepped back from the controversy, supportive of Fisher's defense of popular piety but satirizing the Magdalene's composite identity; see Haskins, *Mary Magdalen*, 250. See also Jonathan Arnold, *The Great Humanists: An Introduction* (London: Tauris, 2011), 219. On the reform of the cult of the saints, see Alison Knowles Frazier, *Possible Lives: Authors and Saints in Renaissance Italy* (New York: Columbia University Press, 2005); Simon Ditchfield, "Thinking with the Saints: Sanctity and Society in Early Modern Europe," *Critical Theory* 35, no. 3 (2009): 552–84; Simon Ditchfield, "Tridentine Worship and the Cult of the Saints," in *The Cambridge History of Christianity*, vol. 6, *Reform and Expansion*,

1500–1660, ed. R. Po-chia Hsia (Cambridge: Cambridge University Press, 2007), 201–24; and Peter Burke, "How to Be a Counter-Reformation Saint," in *The Reformation,* ed. Andrew Pettegree, Critical Concepts in Historical Studies 4 (London: Routledge, 2004), esp. 154–55.

31. Vives, *Education of a Christian Woman,* 100, 207.

32. Ibid., 319. Vives's reading of Martha's duties as those of a wife, while Mary represents the single life, is a variation, though not a unique one, of the traditional separation between the active and the contemplative life. Jo Ann MacNamara has noted the early church fathers' use of Martha as a model for married women; see Jo Ann MacNamara, "Sexual Equality and the Cult of Virginity in Early Christian Thought," in *Women in Early Christianity,* ed. David M. Scholer, Studies in Early Christianity 14 (New York: Garland, 1993), 148–49. Meister Eckhart's homilies on Luke 10, for example, described Martha as a "wife," though also a virgin, modeling the medieval ideal of a celibate marriage; see Edward P. Hahnenberg, *Awakening Vocation: A Theology of Christian Call* (Collegeville, MN: Liturgical Press, 2010), 10; and Amy Hollywood, "Preaching as Social Practice in Meister Eckhart," in *Mysticism and Social Transformation,* ed. Janet K. Ruffing (Syracuse, NY: Syracuse University Press, 2001), 80.

33. See the section on appropriate reading material, "Which Writers Are to Be Read and Which Not to Be Read," in Vives, *Education of a Christian Woman,* 73–79.

34. Frederick J. McGinness, *Right Thinking and Sacred Oratory in Counter-Reformation Rome* (Princeton, NJ: Princeton University Press, 1995), 83; Rachel Geschwind, "The Printed Penitent: Magdalene Imagery and Prostitution Reform in Early Modern Italian Chapbooks and Broadsheets," in Erhardt and Morris, eds., *Mary Magdalene,* 107–9. For Luther's scathing judgment of Roman morals, following his visit there in 1510 or 1511, see Martin Luther, *Table Talk* no. 3478 (1536–1537), in LW, 54:207–8; and no. 3582a (1537), in LW, 54:237. On the oral transmission of printed material, including sermons, in early modern societies with mixed degrees of literacy, so that literacy rate does not equate directly to the level of dissemination, see Velagić, "Reading Aloud," 379–83, 387. See also Robert Scribner, "Oral Culture and the Diffusion of Reformation Ideas," in *Literacy and Historical Development: A Reader,* ed. Harvey J. Graff (Carbondale: Southern Illinois University Press, 2007), 161–82; cf. Bernd Moeller, "Stadt und Buch: Bemerkungen zur Struktur der reformatorischen Bewegung in Deutschland," in *The Urban Classes, the Nobility, and the Reformation: Studies on the Social History of the Reformation in England and Germany,* ed. Wolfgang J. Mommsen, Publications of the German Historical Institute, London, 5 (Stuttgart: Klett-Cotta, 1979), 25–39.

35. Geschwind, "The Printed Penitent," 116, 120–21, 125.

36. François de Sales, *Introduction to the Devout Life* (London: Longmans, Green, 1891), 173, 35. *Introduction to the Devout Life* was the most printed book in seventeenth-century France, after the Bible; see Barbara R. Woshinsky, *Imagining Women's Conventual Spaces in France, 1600–1800: The Cloister Disclosed,* Women and Gender in the Early Modern World (Farnham, England: Ashgate, 2010), 80. Cf. François de Sales to Madame Brûlart, *Letter 277,* March 1605, in Francis de Sales and Jeanne de Chantal, *Letters of Spiritual Direction,* trans.

Péronne Marie Thibert, ed. Wendy M. Wright and Joseph F. Power, Classics of Western Spirituality (New York: Paulist Press, 1988), 108.

37. Sales, *Introduction to the Devout Life*, 15, 11; François de Sales to Mademoiselle de Soulfour, *Letter 190*, July 22, 1603, in Sales and Chantal, *Letters of Spiritual Direction*, 98. On Sales's theology of the freedom of the will, which included cooperation with God's saving grace, see Eunan McDonnell, *The Concept of Freedom in the Writings of Saint Francis de Sales* (New York: Peter Lang, 2009), especially p. 89.

38. Zur Shalev, *Sacred Words and Worlds: Geography, Religion, and Scholarship, 1550–1700*, Scientific and Learned Cultures and Their Institutions 2 (Leiden: Brill, 2012), 239; Charles Vialart, *Tableau de la Magdelaine en l'état de parfaite amante de Jésus: 1628*, ed. Jean-Luc Boucherat, Petite collection atopia 11 (Grenoble, France: Millon, 1997), 9, 34.

39. "L'Amour de la Madeleine a été plus parfait que celui des Apotres," in Vialart, *Tableau de la Magdelaine*, 36, 37–38.

40. "C'est à elle, que vous avez preièrement parlé, après que vous futes sorti du tombeau, son nom est le premier que votre sacrée bouche a prononcé, vous lui avez donné le première commission que vous délivrates, que fut d'annoncer à vos Apotres votre gloire et votre résurrection." Vialart, *Tableau de la Magdelaine*, 39.

41. *Chroniques de l'ordre des Carmélites de la réforme de Sainte-Thérèse depuis leur introduction en France*, vol. 3 (Troyes, France: Imprimerie d'Anner-André, 1856), 284–85.

42. "Les révérends pères de la Compagnie de Jésus le regardait aussi comme leur bienfaiteur: il fit ériger dans leur église une chapelle en l'honneur de sainte Madeleine, que lui, et toute sa famille, vénéraient d'un culte particulier. Il obtint pour cette chapelle un autel privilegié en faveur des ames du Purgatoire." *Chroniques de l'ordre des Carmélites*, 3:53.

43. Ignatius of Loyola, *Spiritual Exercises*, in *Ignatius of Loyola: The Spiritual Exercises and Selected Works*, ed. George E. Ganss, Classics of Western Spirituality (New York: Paulist Press, 1991), 197, 198; Jerome Nadal, *Adnotationes et Meditationes in Evangelia: Quae in sacrosancto missae sacrificio toto anno leguntur, cum evangeliorum concordantia, historiae integritati sufficienti*, 2nd ed. (Antwerp: Nutius, 1595). See also "Illustrations of Gospel Stories from Jerome Nadal, S.J.," Catholic Resources, http://www.catholic-resources.org/Art/Nadal.htm, and the illustrations presented at http://www.catholic-resources.org/Nadal/139.jpg and http://www.catholic-resources.org/Nadal/141.jpg.

44. Michael Mullett uses her portrait as the representation of the Sacrament of Penance as his example of the importance of the visual arts for conveying theological instruction to the illiterate; see Mullet, *The Catholic Reformation*, 163. See also Anne Hollander, *Feeding the Eye: Essays* (Berkeley: University of California Press, 2000), 249.

45. Michelle Erhardt and Amy Morris, "Introduction," in Erhardt and Morris, eds., *Mary Magdalene*, 1; Ingrid Maisch, *Mary Magdalene: The Image of a Woman through the Centuries*, trans. Linda M. Maloney (Collegeville, MN: Liturgical Press, 1998), 65, 66; Ignatius of Loyola, *Spiritual Exercises*, in Ganss, ed., *Ignatius of Loyola*, 113–214.

46. See, e.g., Perry, "Magdalens and Jezebels," 132–41.

47. Bernardino Ochino, "Nove Prediche," in *Predicazione dei Cappucchini nel Cinquecento in Italia* (Loreto, Italy: Libreria "S. Francesco d'Assisi," 1956), 556, 558, 561; Alonso Franco y Ortega, quoted in Karen Melvin, *Building Colonial Cities of God: Mendicant Orders and Urban Culture in New Spain* (Stanford, CA: Stanford University Press, 2012), 122; Matthews-Grieco, "Models of Female Sanctity," 168; Elizabeth Carroll Consavari, "Tintoretto's Holy Hermits at the Scuola Grande di San Rocco," in Erhardt and Morris, eds., *Mary Magdalene,* 160. The connection between Mary Magdalene's beauty and prostitution in early modern Catholicism is also made in Laura J. McGough, "Quarantining Beauty: The French Disease in Early Modern Venice," in *Sins of the Flesh: Responding to Sexual Disease in Early Modern Europe,* ed. Kevin Siena, Essays and Studies 7 (Toronto: Centre for Reformation and Renaissance Studies, 2005), 224.

48. H. Colin Slim, *Painting Music in the Sixteenth Century: Essays in Iconography,* Variorum Collected Studies Series 727 (Aldershot, England: Ashgate, 2002), fig. 1, 465–66.

49. These are attributed to either Jan van Hemessen or Jan van Amstel; Slim, *Painting Music in the Sixteenth Century,* 818.

50. The dating is approximately 1524–1546, making it unclear whether this painting would have belonged to a Catholic or Protestant context, though the inclusion of "before" and "after" states of a soul in a single visual space is similar to Lucas Cranach's *Law and Gospel* compositions, in which a sinner is shown in a single garden divided by the tree of life, mired in sin and condemned by the law on the left and simultaneously saved by the death and resurrection of Christ on the right. See Carl C. Christensen, *Art and the Reformation in Germany* (Athens, OH: Ohio State University Press / Detroit: Wayne State University Press, 1979), 112–14.

51. Consavari, "Tintoretto's Holy Hermits," 152. On the theology of the Magdalene presented in Titian's influential work, see Diane Apostolos-Cappadona, "'Pray with Your Tears and Your Request Will Find a Hearing': On the Iconology of the Magdalene's Tears," in *Holy Tears: Weeping in the Religious Imagination,* ed. Kimberly Christine Patton and John Stratton Hawley (Princeton, NJ: Princeton University Press, 2005), 216–18.

52. Patrick Hunt, "Irony and Realism in the Iconography of Caravaggio's *Penitent Magdalene,*" in Erhardt and Morris, eds., *Mary Magdalene,* 164. Cf. Haskins, *Mary Magdalene,* 252, 296.

53. Hunt, "Irony and Realism," 166, discussing the views of Sergio Benedetti.

54. Ibid., 162–64, 171–72, 173.

55. Francesco Panigarola, quoted in Hunt, "Irony and Realism," 175.

56. Badir, *Maudlin Impression,* 171, 189. For another typical source image, see Michael Jaffé, "'The Penitent Magdalene in a Landscape' by Annibale Carracci. For Peter Murray," *Burlington Magazine* 123, no. 935 (1981): 90. See also John Hale, *England and the Italian Renaissance: The Growth of Interest in Its History and Art,* 4th ed., Blackwell Classic Histories of Europe (Malden, MA: Blackwell, 2005).

57. Maisch, *Mary Magdalene,* 64–65.

58. Badir, *Maudlin Impression,* figs. 33–35, 193.

59. Slim, *Painting Music in the Sixteenth Century,* fig. 2, 461, 463.

60. Ibid., 462. This composition may have influenced Lucas Cranach's later *Law and Gospel* works; see Christensen, *Art and the Reformation in Germany*, 112–14.

61. Slim, *Painting Music in the Sixteenth Century*, 462.

62. Ibid., 465.

63. Ibid., 467.

64. Ibid., 463.

65. Lorenzo Pericolo, "Love in the Mirror: A Comparative Reading of Titian's *Woman at Her Toilet* and Caravaggio's *Conversion of Mary Magdalene*," *I Tatti Studies: Essays in the Renaissance* 12 (2009): 173; Badir, *Maudlin Impression*, 81, 82.

66. Badir, *Maudlin Impression*, 82.

67. Ibid., 136.

68. Robert Southwell, *Marie Magdalens Funeral Teares* (1591), quoted in Badir, *Maudlin Impression*, 71.

69. Badir, *Maudlin Impression*, 73.

70. Southwell, *Marie Magdalens Funeral Teares*, quoted in Badir, *Maudlin Impression*, 76. Subsequent editions of Southwell's work were published in 1594, 1594, 1602, and 1608; see Badir, *Maudlin Impression*, 65, 83.

71. Paul Cefalu, *The Johannine Renaissance in Early Modern English Literature and Theology* (Oxford: Oxford University Press, 2017), 97–130; Badir, *Maudlin Impression*, 76.

72. Thomas M. Carr, "Remi de Beauvais' *La Magdeleine* (1617)," in *Le Savoir au XVIIᵉ siècle: Actes du 34ᵉ congrès annuel de la North American Society for Seventeenth-Century French Literature, University of Virginia, Charlottesville, 14–16 mars 2002*, ed. John D. Lyons and Cara Welch, Biblio 17, 147 (Tübingen, Germany: Narr, 2003), 140–41, 144–47.

73. "Fourby ta langue évangélique! / Annonce! réjouy la troupe apostolique! / Presche! esleve ta voix! enseigne le Salut!" Carr, "Remi de Beauvais' *La Magdeleine*," 142–44.

74. Carr, "Remi de Beauvais' *La Magdeleine*," 146.

75. Maisch, *Mary Magdalene*, 86.

76. Ibid., 83–85.

77. Agustin de la Madre de Dios, quoted in Melvin, *Building Colonial Cities of God*, 102.

78. On Mary of Bethany's contemplation in Carmelite theology, see Mary Jo Weaver, *Cloister and Community: Life within a Carmelite Monastery* (Bloomington: Indiana University Press, 2002), 26.

5. Love Made Her Dare: The Magdalene among Catholic Women

1. Belinda Jack, *The Woman Reader* (New Haven, CT: Yale University Press, 2012), 115.

2. Barbara B. Diefendorf, "Rethinking the Catholic Reformation: The Role of Women," in *Women, Religion, and the Atlantic World (1600–1800)*, ed. Daniella Kostroun and

Lisa Vollendorf, UCLA Center / Clark Series (Toronto: University of Toronto Press, 2009), 40.

3. Indeed, the appeal was so successful that it spread to secular philosophers; see, e.g., the work of Gabrielle Suchon, esp. *On the Celibate Life*, in *A Woman Who Defends All the Persons of Her Sex: Selected Philosophical and Moral Writings*, ed. and trans. Donna C. Stanton and Rebecca M. Wilton, The Other Voice in Early Modern Europe (Chicago: University of Chicago Press, 2010), 229–94.

4. For the relationship between holy women and their confessors and biographers, see Jodi Bilinkoff, *The Avila of Teresa: Religious Reform in a Sixteenth-Century City* (Ithaca, NY: Cornell University Press, 1992).

5. This follows Merry E. Wiesner, *Women and Gender in Early Modern Europe*, 2nd ed., New Approaches to European History (Cambridge: Cambridge University Press, 2000), 231.

6. On Teresa and her context, see Alison Weber, *Teresa of Avila and the Rhetoric of Femininity* (Princeton, NJ: Princeton University Press, 1990); Bilinkoff, *The Avila of Teresa*; Gillian T. W. Ahlgren, *Teresa of Avila and the Politics of Sanctity* (Ithaca, NY: Cornell University Press, 1996); and Erin Kathleen Rowe, *Saint and Nation: Santiago, Teresa of Avila, and Plural Identities in Early Modern Spain* (University Park: Pennsylvania State University Press, 2011).

7. Teresa of Avila, *The Way of Perfection*, in CWT, 2:102.

8. On the reality of such tensions between sisters explicitly identified with the Magdalene or with Martha, see Barbara B. Diefendorf, *From Penitence to Charity: Pious Women and the Catholic Reformation in Paris* (New York: Oxford University Press, 2004), 186.

9. Teresa of Avila, *The Interior Castle*, in CWT, 2:431–32, 448; Teresa of Avila, *The Book of Her Life*, in CWT, 1:188.

10. The other two faculties are the intellect and the soul. Teresa of Avila, *Spiritual Testimonies*, no. 59 (1576), in CWT, 1:426.

11. Teresa of Avila, *The Way of Perfection*, in CWT, 2:155; Teresa of Avila, *Meditations on the Song of Songs*, in CWT, 2:257; Teresa of Avila, *The Interior Castle*, in CWT, 2:448.

12. Teresa of Avila, *Soliloquies*, no. 5, in CWT, 1:448.

13. Teresa of Avila, *The Interior Castle* 7.4.2, in CWT, 2:448, cited in Tessa Bielecki, *Teresa of Avila: Mystical Writings*, The Crossroad Spiritual Legacy Series (New York: Crossroad, 1994), 194.

14. Teresa of Avila, *The Way of Perfection*, in CWT, 2:100; see also Teresa of Avila, *The Interior Castle*, in CWT, 2:448.

15. Teresa of Avila, *The Book of Her Life*, in CWT, 1:195.

16. See Giles Constable, *Three Studies in Medieval Religious and Social Thought* (Cambridge; New York: Cambridge University Press, 1995), 18; and Antonio Pérez-Romero, *Subversion and Liberation in the Writings of St. Teresa of Avila*, Portada Hispánica 2 (Amsterdam: Rodopi, 1996), 200, citing the criticism of the Dominican Alonso de la Fuente during the period

1589–1591. On the threat posed by the Protestant license to interpret scripture, which caused Teresa's *Meditations* to be ordered burned, her confessor Jerónimo Gracián wrote, "She was ordered to burn this book, since it seemed . . . very unorthodox and dangerous for a woman to write about the *Song of Songs*. . . . And since at the time Luther's heresy was doing much harm, for it had opened the doors for ignorant women and men to read and explicate divine works, . . . it seemed to him that the book should be burned." Jerónimo Gracián, quoted in Weber, *Teresa of Avila and the Rhetoric of Femininity*, 117.

17. This is from a series of comments made on a theological discussion held at the Abbey of St. Joseph in Avila in 1576, including comments on John of the Cross; see Teresa of Avila, "A Satirical Critique," in *CWT*, 3:360–61.

18. Teresa of Avila, quoted in Bielecki, *Teresa of Avila*, 186; Teresa of Avila, *The Book of Her Life*, in *CWT*, 1:153–54; Teresa of Avila, *The Way of Perfection*, in *CWT*, 2:171–72. On Teresa's identification with the Magdalene as a source for her own authority, see Elena Carrera, *Teresa of Avila's Autobiography: Authority, Power and the Self in Mid-Sixteenth-Century Spain* (London: Modern Humanities Research Association / Maney, 2005), 53–54, 173–74, 176.

19. Teresa of Avila, quoted in Bielecki, *Teresa of Avila*, 151, 176, 177; Teresa of Avila, *The Way of Perfection*, in *CWT*, 2:135–36; Teresa of Avila, *Spiritual Testimonies*, no. 28 (July 22, 1572), in *CWT*, 1:400; see note p. 494.

20. Teresa of Avila, *The Book of Her Life*, in *CWT*, 1:101; Teresa of Avila, *Spiritual Testimonies*, no. 37 (dated July 22 of uncertain year), in *CWT*, 1:408; Teresa of Avila, *The Book of Her Life*, in *CWT*, 1:197; Keith P. Luria, *Territories of Grace: Cultural Change in the Seventeenth-Century Diocese of Grenoble*, Studies on the History of Society and Culture 11 (Berkeley: University of California Press, 1991), 130; Teresa of Avila, *Spiritual Testimonies*, no. 17 (1571), in *CWT*, 1:394; Teresa of Avila, *Spiritual Testimonies*, no. 37 (July 22, no year), in *CWT*, 1:408.

21. Teresa of Avila, quoted in Bielecki, *Teresa of Avila*, 185; Weber, *Teresa of Avila and the Rhetoric of Femininity*, 4, 18.

22. Teresa of Avila, quoted in Bielecki, *Teresa of Avila*, 79.

23. Teresa of Avila, *The Interior Castle*, in *CWT*, 2:449–50.

24. Teresa of Avila, *The Book of Her Life*, in *CWT*, 1:139; Teresa of Avila, *The Interior Castle*, in *CWT*, 2:285.

25. Teresa of Avila, *The Interior Castle*, in *CWT*, 2:398.

26. For Cajetan's pronouncement on the uncertainty of grace, see Tommaso de Vio Cajetan, *Augsburg Treatises*, translated in *Cajetan Responds: A Reader in Reformation Controversy*, ed. and trans. Jared Wicks (Washington, DC: Catholic University of America Press, 1978), 52; cf. Martin Luther, *Proceedings at Augsburg* (1518), in *LW*, 31:270–74.

27. Teresa of Avila, *The Way of Perfection*, in *CWT*, 2:193; Teresa of Avila, *The Book of Her Life*, in *CWT*, 1:199; Teresa of Avila, *The Way of Perfection*, in *CWT*, 2:93; Teresa of Avila, *The Interior Castle*, in *CWT*, 2:426.

28. María de San José Salazar, *Book for the Hour of Recreation*, ed. Alison Weber, trans. Amanda Powell, The Other Voice in Early Modern Europe (Chicago: University of Chicago Press,

2002), 4, 8–9. Salazar was imprisoned by the Inquisition several times over the course of her career for alleged sexual offenses, including an inappropriate relationship with the Carmelites' first provincial, Jerónimo Gracián, and was finally exiled to a remote convent in Cuerva, where she died shortly after making the arduous journey. On Teresa's mentoring of Carmelite nuns, see Elizabeth Teresa Howe, *Education and Women in the Early Modern Hispanic World*, Women and Gender in the Early Modern World (Aldershot, England: Ashgate, 2008), chapter 3, "The New Judith: Teresa de Jesús as Conventual Example."

29. Salazar, *Book for the Hour of Recreation*, 16, 22–23.

30. Ibid., 101–2.

31. Ibid., 26.

32. Clare Copeland, *Maria Maddalena de' Pazzi: The Making of a Counter-Reformation Saint*, Oxford Theology and Religion Monographs (Oxford: Oxford University Press, 2016), 15.

33. Mary Minima, *Seraph among Angels: The Life of St. Mary Magdalene de' Pazzi, Carmelite and Mystic*, trans. and ed. Gabriel N. Pausback (Chicago: Carmelite Press, 1958), 24, 51–52. The convent would not have participated in Teresa's Carmelite reform at this point; the Discalced Carmelite order came to Italy in 1584, first at Genoa, then at Rome two years later, at which point an Italian edition of Teresa's spiritual autobiography became available. See Rowe, *Saint and Nation*, 201.

34. Minima, *Seraph among Angels*, 50–51, 212–13.

35. Maria Maddalena, quoted in Minima, *Seraph among Angels*, 248.

36. Elizabeth Rapley, *The Dévotes: Women and Church in Seventeenth Century France*, McGill–Queen's Studies in the History of Religion 4 (Montreal: McGill-Queen's University Press, 1990), 5, 170; Barbara Diefendorf, "Barbe Acarie and Her Spiritual Daughters: Women's Spiritual Authority in Seventeenth-Century France," in *Female Monasticism in Early Modern Europe: An Interdisciplinary View*, ed. Cordula van Whye, Catholic Christendom, 1300–1700 (Aldershot, England: Ashgate, 2008); Jane Eade, "Reflections on a Glass *Madeleine Pénitente*," in *Mary Magdalene: Iconographic Studies from the Middle Ages to the Baroque*, ed. Michelle A. Erhardt and Amy M. Morris, Studies in Religion and the Arts 7 (Leiden: Brill, 2012), 326. See also Philip F. Riley, *A Lust for Virtue: Louis XIV's Attack on Sin in Seventeenth-Century France*, Contributions to the Study of World History 88 (Westport, CT: Greenwood Press, 2001), 85–86.

37. Louise de la Vallière, *Réflexions sur la miséricorde de Dieu par une dame pénitente*, 2nd ed. (Paris: Antione Dézallier, 1680), 12; partly translated in Eade, "Reflections," 327. Alison Weber has noted that Teresa of Avila may have felt guilt over a flirtation in her adolescence and thereby felt a connection to the Magdalene's sinful sexual history; see Weber, *Teresa of Avila and the Rhetoric of Femininity*, 53–54.

38. De la Vallière, *Réflexions*, 9; translated in John J. Conley, *The Suspicion of Virtue: Women Philosophers in Neoclassical France* (Ithaca: Cornell University Press, 2002), 106.

39. De la Vallière, *Réflexions*, 12–13.

40. Ruth P. Liebowitz, "Virgins in the Service of Christ: The Dispute over an Active Apostolate for Women during the Counter-Reformation," in *Women of Spirit: Female Leadership in the Jewish and Christian Traditions,* ed. Rosemary Ruether and Eleanor McLaughlin (New York: Simon and Schuster, 1979), 133.

41. Liebowitz, "Virgins in the Service of Christ," 135; Linda Lierheimer, "Preaching or Teaching? Defining the Ursuline Mission in Seventeenth-Century France," in *Women Preachers and Prophets through Two Millennia of Christianity,* ed. Beverly Mayne Kienzle and Pamela J. Walker (Berkeley: University of California Press, 1998), 214; Laurence Lux-Sterritt, *Redefining Female Religious Life: French Ursulines and English Ladies in Seventeenth-Century Catholicism,* Catholic Christendom, 1300–1700 (Aldershot, England: Ashgate, 2005), 140, 189. See also Diefendorf, *From Penitence to Charity,* 90, 243; and Querciolo Mazzonis, *Spirituality, Gender, and the Self in Renaissance Italy: Angela Merici and the Company of St. Ursula (1474–1540)* (Washington, DC: Catholic University of America Press, 2007).

42. Marguerite Bourgeoys, quoted in Rapley, *The Dévotes,* 101; Marguerite Bourgeoys, quoted in Patricia Simpson, *Marguerite Bourgeoys and the Congregation of Notre-Dame, 1665–1700,* McGill–Queen's Studies in the History of Religion 42 (Montreal: McGill-Queens University Press, 2005), 188.

43. Marguerite Bourgeoys, quoted in Rapley, *The Dévotes,* 191; Matthew 5:3, NIV.

44. Diefendorf, *From Penitence to Charity,* 173. See also Helen Hills, *The Architecture of Devotion in Seventeenth-Century Neapolitan Convents* (Oxford: Oxford University Press, 2004).

45. Diefendorf, *From Penitence to Charity,* 176; Silvia Evangelisti, *Nuns: A History of Convent Life, 1450–1700* (Oxford: Oxford University Press, 2007), 222.

46. François de Sales to Jeanne de Chantal, 16 August 1607, quoted in Diefendorf, *From Penitence to Charity,* 176–77.

47. See James Axtell, *The Invasion Within: The Contest of Cultures in Colonial North America,* The Cultural Origins of North America 1 (Oxford: Oxford University Press, 1985), 40, 48, 54; Mark A. Noll, *A History of Christianity in the United States and Canada* (Grand Rapids, MI: Eerdmans, 1992), 20–21; Marie-Florine Bruneau, *Women Mystics Confront the Modern World: Marie de l'Incarnation (1599–1672) and Madame Guyon (1648–1717)* (Albany: State University of New York Press, 1999), 24–25; Dorothy A. Mays, *Women in Early America: Struggle, Survival, and Freedom in a New World* (Santa Barbara, CA: ABC-CLIO, 2004), 64–65; Rosemary Skinner Keller and Rosemary Radford Ruether, eds., *Encyclopedia of Women and Religion in North America* (Bloomington: Indiana University Press, 2006), 143–46.

48. Allan Greer, "Colonial Saints: Gender, Race, and Hagiography in New France," *William and Mary Quarterly,* 3rd ser., 57, no. 2 (2000): 338. The biography of Marie de St-Joseph (1652) was by Marie de l'Incarnation; the biography of Catherine de St-Augustin (1671) was by Paul Ragueneau. See Greer, "Colonial Saints," 339.

49. Rapley, *The Dévotes,* 51–52; Diefendorf, *From Penitence to Charity,* 227; Lierheimer, "Preaching or Teaching?," 216–17.

50. Lierheimer, "Preaching or Teaching?," 219, 220. Teresa of Avila's biographer found it desirable to make claims for his subject's lack of presumption, reporting that she once rebuked

a novice with a Bible, "Bible, daughter? Don't come around here, we don't need you or your Bible, for we are ignorant women and we only know how to spin and do what we are ordered." Father Yepes, quoted in Weber, *Teresa of Avila and the Rhetoric of Femininity*, 106. Weber herself argues that Teresa's informal diction constituted a similar tactic to avoid competition with male homiletic discourse (78).

51. Rapley, *The Dévotes*, 17; see also Diefendorf, *From Penitence to Charity*, 21.

52. Lierheimer, "Preaching or Teaching?," 212–13.

53. Ibid., 154, 213, 221–22. Lierheimer describes the self-conscious development of a "female apostolate" involved in charity, teaching, nursing, and mission during the Counter-Reformation, and the tensions this caused. She notes that Ursulines (and their male supporters) defended their activity by making a distinction between acceptable teaching and inappropriate preaching, claiming that teaching was private, domestic work.

54. John O'Malley, "Trent, Sacred Images, and Catholics' Senses of the Sensuous," in *The Sensuous in the Counter-Reformation Church*, ed. Marcia B. Hall and Tracy E. Cooper (New York: Cambridge University Press, 2013), 28–29.

55. Elissa Weaver, *Convent Theatre in Early Modern Italy: Spiritual Fun and Learning for Women*, Cambridge Studies in Italian History and Culture (Cambridge: Cambridge University Press, 2002), 61.

56. Robert L. Kendrick, *Celestial Sirens: Nuns and Their Music in Early Modern Milan*, Oxford Monographs on Music (Oxford: Clarendon, 1996), 168.

57. "Allora voi fate l'officio di quella dolcissima Discepola Madalena che fu discepola di Christo e dell'amore Tulerunt Dominum meum etc. O vera discepola dove hora pensi di andare? . . . Io vi priego ad essere divotissima della Madalena, perchè ella nell'amare può essere a tutte l'anime la maestra. . . . Però pigliatela per vostra avvocata questa Madalena perchè ella è dolcissima et massimamente con I contemplative restate in pace." Federico Borromeo, Letter 30, quoted in Carlo Marcora, "Lettere del cardinale Federico alle claustrali," *Memorie storiche della diocesi di Milano* 11 (1964): 327.

58. "Mi è venuto pensiero di chiamarvi alle volte nelle mie letter ecol nome di discepola, essendo racordevole di quella gran discepola Madalena, tanto amata dal Signore, et di quell Discepolo, quem diligebat Jesus." Federico Borromeo, Letter 83, quoted in Marcora, "Lettere del cardinale Federico alle claustrali," 303.

59. Federico Borromeo, Letter 15, quoted in Marcora, "Lettere del cardinale Federico alle claustrali," 247; Federico Borromeo, Letter 10, cited in Marcora, "Lettere del cardinale Federico alle claustrali," 241.

60. Kendrick, *Celestial Sirens*, 169.

61. Ibid. 168.

62. Ibid., 223.

63. Ibid., 222.

64. Ibid., 83, 334, 335.

65. "Maria Magdalene stabat ad monumentum foris, plorans; dum ergo fleret, inclinavit se in monumentum, et vidit duos angelos in albis sedentes, et dixit eis: 'Num quem diligit anima mea vidistis? . . . Dilectus meus candidus et rubicundus, electus, electus, ex milibus. . . . Dilectus meus, amor meus speciosus forma prae filiis hominum. Crucifixus Jesus est. O mea lux, ubi es? O amor meus, ubi es? O vita mea, ubi es? Veni, dilecte mi, veni, amor tuo langueo, veni, amor tuo morior.'" Chiara Margarita Cozzolani, *Maria Magdalene Stabat,* in *Motets,* ed. and trans. Robert L. Kendrick, Recent Researches in the Music of the Baroque Era 87 (Madison, WI: AR, 1998), xxix–xxx.

66. Heidi J. Hornik, "The Invention and Development of the 'Secular' Mary Magdalene in Late Renaissance Florentine Painting," in *Mary Magdalene in Medieval Culture: Conflicted Roles,* ed. Peter V. Loewen and Robin Waugh, Routledge Studies in Medieval Literature and Culture 4 (New York: Routledge, 2014), 87.

67. Sophie Holroyd, "'Rich Embrodered Churchstuffe': The Vestments of Helena Wintour," in *Catholic Culture in Early Modern England,* ed. Ronald Corthell, Frances E. Dolan, Christopher Highley, and Arthur F. Marotti (Notre Dame, IN: University of Notre Dame Press, 2007), 90.

68. Lisa M. Rafanelli, "Michelangelo's *Noli me tangere* for Vittoria Colonna, and the Changing Status of Women in Renaissance Italy," in Erhardt and Morris, eds., *Mary Magdalene,* 241. On Colonna and her circle, see Diana Robin, *Publishing Women: Salons, the Presses, and the Counter-Reformation in Sixteenth-Century Italy,* Women in Culture and Society (Chicago: University of Chicago Press, 2007), 14–15, 28–32.

69. Abigail Brundin, *Vittoria Colonna and the Spiritual Poetics of the Italian Reformation,* Catholic Christendom, 1300–1700 (Aldershot, England: Ashgate, 2008), 147, 148.

70. Vittoria Colonna to Constanza D'Avalos Piccolomini, 1544 (first letter), quoted in Brundin, *Vittoria Colonna,* 148.

71. Vittoria Colonna to Constanza D'Avalos Piccolomini, 1544 (third letter), quoted in Brundin, *Vittoria Colonna,* 152; Susan Haskins, "Foreword," in Erhardt and Morris, eds., *Mary Magdalene,* xxxiv.

72. Brundin, *Vittoria Colonna,* 134–35; Vittoria Colonna to Cardinal Giovanni Morone, 1544, quoted in Rafanelli, "Michelangelo's *Noli me tangere,*" 245.

73. Rafanelli, "Michelangelo's *Noli me tangere,*" 247.

74. Vittoria Colonna "Spiritual Poem No. 8," in Rafanelli, "Michelangelo's *Noli me tangere,*" 244–45.

75. Colonna was not unique in exploring the Magdalene poetically. Virginia Cox has studied the interpretation of the Magdalene as an ideal of female beauty and penitence in the verse of Moderata Fonte (1555–1592) and Lucrezia Marinella (1579–1653). See Virginia Cox, *The Prodigious Muse: Women's Writing in Counter-Reformation Italy* (Baltimore: Johns Hopkins University Press, 2011), 72–73, 131–37, 149.

76. Elisabeth Gössmann, "Maria Magdalena als Typus der Kirche," in *Maria Magdalena, zu einem Bild der Frau in der christlichen Verkündigung,* ed. Dietmar Bader, Schriftenreihe der Katholischen Akademie der Erzdiözese Freiburg (Munich: Schnell & Steiner, 1990), 60;

Marie de Gournay, *Égalité des hommes et des femmes; Grief des dames, suivi du Proumenoir de Monsieur de Montagne,* ed. Constant Venesoen, Textes littéraires français 433 (Geneva: Librarie Droz, 1993), 52; also quoted in Conley, *The Suspicion of Virtue,* 108.

77. Marie le Jars de Gournay, *The Equality of Men and Women,* in *The Equality of the Sexes: Three Feminist Treatises of the Seventeenth Century,* trans. and ed. Desmond M. Clarke (Oxford: Oxford University Press, 2013), 68, 71.

78. Patricia A. Ward, "Madame Guyon (1648–1717)," in *The Pietist Theologians: An Introduction to Theology in the Seventeenth and Eighteenth Centuries,* ed. Carter Lindberg, The Great Theologians (Malden, MA: Blackwell, 2005), 163, 164; Ronney Mourad and Dianne Guenin-Lelle, "Introduction," in Jeanne Guyon, *The Prison Narratives of Jeanne Guyon,* trans. and ed. Ronney Mourad and Dianne Guenin-Lelle, AAR Religions in Translation (Oxford: Oxford University Press, 2012), 5.

79. Ward, "Madame Guyon," 165.

80. Jeanne Guyon, quoted in Ward, "Madame Guyon," 165.

81. Ward, "Madame Guyon," 161, 166; Mourad and Guenin-Lelle, "Introduction," in *Prison Narratives of Jeanne Guyon,* 7, 9; R. Po-chia Hsia, *The World of Catholic Renewal, 1540–1770,* 2nd ed., New Approaches to European History 30 (New York: Cambridge University Press, 2005), 146.

82. François Rabelais, dedication to Marguerite de Navarre, in *Gargantua and Pantagruel* (1546), book 3, quoted in Gary Ferguson and Mary B. McKinley, "Introduction," in *A Companion to Marguerite de Navarre,* ed. Gary Ferguson and Mary B. McKinley, Brill's Companions to the Christian Tradition 42 (Leiden: Brill, 2013), 13.

83. The description comes from a letter by John Calvin to François Daniel, October 1533, quoted in Ferguson and McKinley, "Introduction," 7–8.

84. Patricia F. Cholakian and Rouben C. Cholakian, *Marguerite de Navarre: Mother of the Renaissance* (New York: Columbia University Press, 2006), 13, 16; Ferguson and McKinley, "Introduction," 3, 7; Jonathan A. Reid, "Marguerite de Navarre and Evangelical Reform," in Ferguson and McKinley, eds., *Companion to Marguerite de Navarre,* 33.

85. Cholakian and Cholakian, *Marguerite de Navarre,* 4; Barbara Stephenson, *The Power and Patronage of Marguerite de Navarre,* Women and Gender in the Early Modern World (Aldershot, England: Ashgate, 2004), 3–5, 9, 11.

86. Stephenson, *The Power and Patronage of Marguerite de Navarre,* 13; Cholakian and Cholakian, *Marguerite de Navarre,* 4, 11.

87. Stephenson, *The Power and Patronage of Marguerite de Navarre,* 7; Reid, "Marguerite de Navarre and Evangelical Reform," 34.

88. Marguerite de Navarre, *Heptaméron,* trans. George Saintsbury, vol. 3 (London: Navarre Society, 1922), 16.

89. François Rigolot, "Magdalen's Skull: Allegory and Iconography in *Heptameron* 32," *Renaissance Quarterly* 47, no. 1 (1994): 59–60, 66–67.

90. Ibid., 63.

91. Patricia Francis Cholakian, *Rape and Writing in the* Heptaméron *of Marguerite de Navarre,* Ad feminam (Carbondale: Southern Illinois University Press, 1991), 9.

92. Marguerite de Navarre, *Poésies chrétiennes,* ed. Nicole Cazauran, Sagesses chrétiennes (Paris: Éditions du Cerf, 1996), 111, 113. I am grateful to Christopher Boyd Brown for assistance with the translation.

93. See Nadia Urbinati, "Half-Toleration: Concordia and the Limits of Dialogue," in *Boundaries of Toleration,* ed. Alfred Stepan and Charles Taylor, Religion, Culture, and Public Life (New York: Columbia University Press, 2014), 132–34.

94. Barbara R. Woshinsky, *Imagining Women's Conventual Spaces in France, 1600–1800: The Cloister Disclosed,* Women and Gender in the Early Modern World (Farnham, England: Ashgate, 2010), 73; Ingrid Maisch, *Mary Magdalene: The Image of a Woman through the Centuries,* trans. Linda M. Maloney (Collegeville, MN: Liturgical Press, 1998), 67.

95. Haskins, "Foreword," xxxiii; *Chroniques de l'ordre des Carmélites de la réforme de Sainte-Thérèse depuis leur introduction en France,* vol. 1 (Troyes, France: Imprimerie d'Anner-André, 1846), 156–57, 236; Philippe de Champaigne, *Le ravissement de Sainte Madeleine: un décor oublié de Philippe de Champaigne (1602–1674): Musée des beaux-arts de Marseille, 27 avril–30 juin 1996* (Marseille: Musées de Marseille, 1996), 32.

96. P. Renee Baernstein, *A Convent Tale: A Century of Sisterhood in Spanish Milan* (New York: Routledge, 2002), 29–30; Christopher Carlsmith, *A Renaissance Education: Schooling in Bergamo and the Venetian Republic, 1500–1650* (Toronto: University of Toronto Press, 2010), 316.

97. Kelley Harness, *Echoes of Women's Voices: Music, Art, and Female Patronage in Early Modern Florence* (Chicago: University of Chicago Press, 2006), 55, 56, 113, fig. 2.3.

98. Ibid., 58.

99. Ibid., 58–61.

100. On the question of ascribing "feminist" projects—such as arguing for the authority to speak in public—to early modern women, see Merry E. Wiesner, "The Early Modern Period: Religion, the Family, and Women's Public Roles," in *Religion, Feminism, and the Family,* ed. Anne Carr and Mary Stewart van Leeuwen, The Family, Religion, and Culture (Louisville, KY: Westminster John Knox, 1996), 149–65.

6. These Magdalens: Diversity in the Reformed Tradition

1. John Calvin, *Commentary on the Gospel According to John,* trans. William Pringle, in *Calvin's Commentaries,* vol. 35 (Grand Rapids, MI: Eerdmans, 1956), 254. See also John Calvin, *Sermons on the Epistles to Timothy and Titus* (1579, repr. Carlisle, PA: Banner of Truth Trust, 1983). On Calvin's treatment of Mary Magdalene in the resurrection narrative, see Jane D. Douglass, *Women, Freedom, and Calvin,* Annie Kinkead Warfield Lectures, 1983 (Philadelphia: Westminster, 1985), 54–59.

2. Susan C. Karant-Nunn, *The Reformation of Feeling: Shaping the Religious Emotions in Early Modern Germany* (New York: Oxford University Press, 2010), 107, 130; John Calvin, *Plusieurs sermons de Iehan Calvin touchant la divinité, humanité, et nativité de nostre Seigneur Iésus Christ* (1558), quoted in Karant-Nunn, *The Reformation of Feeling*, 108. Cf. Jonathan Edwards, "Sinners in the Hands of an Angry God: A Sermon Preached at Enfield, July 8th, 1741," in *The Sermons of Jonathan Edwards: A Reader*, ed. Wilson A. Kimmach, Kenneth P. Minkema, and Douglas A. Sweeney (New Haven, CT: Yale University Press, 1999), 49–65. On Luther's preaching of God's fatherly love, see Paul Althaus, *The Theology of Martin Luther*, trans. Robert C. Schultz (Philadelphia: Fortress, 1966), 183–84. On Calvin's chief aim in preaching, see Karant-Nunn, *The Reformation of Feeling*, 105.

3. Larissa Juliet Taylor, "Apostle to the Apostles: The Complexity of Medieval Preaching about Mary Magdalene," in *Mary Magdalene in Medieval Culture: Conflicted Roles*, ed. Peter V. Loewen and Robin Waugh, Routledge Studies in Medieval Culture 4 (New York: Routledge, 2014), 43; David M. Whitford, "The Moste Folyshe Fable of the Worlde: Preaching the Maudlin," in *Calvinus Pastor Ecclesiae: Papers of the Eleventh International Congress on Calvin Research*, ed. Herman J. Selderhuis and Arnold Huijgen, V&R Academic, Reformed Historical Theology 39 (Göttingen: Vandenhoeck und Ruprecht, 2016), 455, 460–61.

4. Philip Benedict, *Christ's Churches Purely Reformed: A Social History of Calvinism* (New Haven, CT: Yale University Press, 2004), xx–xxi.

5. Whitford agrees that England is "the best place" to assess how influential Calvin's reading was on the Magdalene's subsequent identity for Reformed Protestants. Whitford, "The Moste Folyshe Fable of the Worlde," 457.

6. Wulfert de Greef, *The Writings of John Calvin: An Introductory Guide*, expanded ed., trans. Lyle D. Bierma (Louisville, KY: Westminster John Knox, 2008), 82–83; John Calvin, *Commentaries on the Gospel of John*, in *Calvin's Commentaries*, 35:254.

7. Calvin, *Commentaries on the Gospel of John*, in *Calvin's Commentaries*, 35:254.

8. Calvin, *Commentaries on the Gospel of John*, in *Calvin's Commentaries*, 35:254.

9. Calvin, *Commentaries on the Gospel of John*, in *Calvin's Commentaries*, 35:256, 257, 258. Cf. Martin Luther, *Sermons on the Gospel of St. John, Chapters 18–20* (1528–1529), in *LW*, 69:304–305.

10. John Lee Thompson, *Calvin and the Daughters of Sarah: Women in Regular and Exceptional Roles in the Exegesis of Calvin, His Predecessors, and His Followers*, Travaux d'humanisme et Renaissance 259 (Geneva: Librairie Droz, 1992), 32–33.

11. John Calvin, *Writings on Pastoral Piety*, ed. and trans. Elsie Anne McKee, The Classics of Western Spirituality (New York: Paulist, 2001), 113, 114; Calvin, *Commentaries on the Gospel of John*, vol. 2, chapter 20, sections 16, 17.

12. Calvin, *Commentary on the Gospel of John*, vol. 2, chapter 20, section 17; cf. Johann Spangenberg, *Postilla Deütsch. Fur die jungen Christen / Knaben vnd Meidlein / jnn fragstücke verfasst / Von den fürnemesten Festen / durche gantze Jar* (Wittenberg, 1544), 10r. John Lee Thompson speculates that Calvin's position may have developed in opposition to Dentière's

work, as well as the feminist writing of Henry Cornelius Agrippa; see Thompson, *Calvin and the Daughters of Sarah*, 35–43.

13. John Calvin, *Institutes of the Christian Religion*, chapter 14, section 14, p. 151, Christian Classics Ethereal Library, http://www.ccel.org/ccel/calvin/institutes/Page_151.html.

14. Karant-Nunn, *The Reformation of Feeling*, 108; Cornelis P. Venema, *Accepted and Renewed in Christ: The "Twofold Grace of God" and the Interpretation of Calvin's Theology* (Göttingen: Vandenhoeck und Ruprecht, 2007), 204–7.

15. See Antoinina Bevan Zlatar, *Reformation Fictions: Polemical Protestant Dialogues in Elizabethan England* (Oxford: Oxford University Press, 2011), 64; and Phyllis Mack Crew, *Calvinist Preaching and Iconoclasm in the Netherlands, 1544–1569*, Cambridge Studies in Early Modern History (Cambridge: Cambridge University Press, 1978).

16. "Ceste Marie Magdaleine n'estoit pas soeur de Marthe et de Lazare. . . . Surquoy, nous auons ainsi le tesmoinage de Chrysostom, qui dit clairement, que ceste Marie n'a point esté putain, mais honeste et vertueuse, laquelle auoit soucy de Iesus Christ, et l'aimoit fort avec sa soeur: et que ce n'est point celle putain, de laquelle S. Luc a fait mention. Parquoy c'est une grande impudence aus Caphars d'auoir osé feindre telles fables, et les precher publiquement au peuple." Pierre Viret, *De la vraie et fausse religion* ([Geneva]: Rivery, 1560), 595.

17. Viret, *De la vraie et fausse religion*, 587, 588–89, 590, 595–96; Rachel Geschwind, "The Printed Penitent: Magdalene Imagery and Prostitution Reform in Early Modern Italian Chapbooks and Broadsheets," in *Mary Magdalene: Iconographic Studies from the Medieval to the Baroque*, ed. Michelle A. Erhardt and Amy M. Morris, Studies in Religion and the Arts 7 (Leiden: Brill, 2012), 120–21.

18. Viret, *De la vraie et fausse religion*, 590, 591, 595.

19. Jean-Marie Le Gall, "The Lives of the Saints in the French Renaissance, c.1500–c.1650," in *Sacred History: Uses of the Christian Past in the Renaissance World*, ed. Katherine van Liere, Simon Ditchfield, and Howard Louthan (Oxford: Oxford University Press, 2012), 222; Hugh of Poitiers, *The Vézelay Chronicle: And Other Documents from MS Auxerre 227 and Elsewhere*, trans. and ed. John Scott and John O. Ward (Binghamton, NY: Medieval and Renaissance Texts and Studies, 1992), 13; David A. Hanser, *Architecture of France*, Reference Guides to National Architecture (Westport, CT: Greenwood, 2006), 297; Penny Roberts, *A City in Conflict: Troyes during the French Wars of Religion* (Manchester, England: Manchester University Press, 1996), 140; Kevin D. Murphy, *Memory and Modernity: Viollet-le-Duc at Vézelay* (University Park: Pennsylvania State University Press, 2000), 168; Henry M. Baird, *History of the Rise of the Huguenots of France*, vol. 2 (New York: Scribner's, 1889), 344; Charles Richard Weld, *Notes on Burgundy* (London: Longmans Green, 1849), 181–82. See also Henri de Crignelle, *Le Morvan [A District of France,] Its Wild Sports, Vineyards and Forests with Legends, Antiquities, Rural and Local Sketches*, trans. William Jesse (London: Saunders and Otley, 1851).

20. Theodore Beza, *Sermons sur les trois premiers chapitres du Cantique des Cantiques* ([Geneva]: Jehan le Preux, 1586), 121, cited in Tadataka Maruyama, *The Ecclesiology of Theodore Beza: The Reform of the True Church*, Travaux d'humanisme et Renaissance 166 (Geneva:

Droz, 1978), 206. See also Scott M. Manetsch, *Theodore Beza and the Quest for Peace in France: 1572–1598*, Studies in Medieval and Reformation Thought 79 (Leiden: Brill, 2000), 10.

21. Theodore Beza, *Sermons sur l'histoire de la resurrection de nostre Seigneur Jesus Christ* (Geneva: Jehan le Preux, 1593), 2, 4, 5–6. The second sermon does not contain a specific discussion of Mary Magdalene or the other women at the tomb.

22. "C'est la raison qu'il faut aussi mettre en auant à ceux qui pourroyent trouuer estrange qui'il se soit plustot manifesté à ces femmes qu'a ses Apostres ou quelques autres disciples. Car en toutes choses la volonté de Dieu est la vraie et perpetuelle regle de tout ce qui peut & doit ester dit & droictement faicte. Mais outré cela, l'histoire nous monstre assez claire-ment, qu'encores qu'il y ait eu beaucoup de defauts en ces femmes, comme nous verrons ci après, & que les Apostres . . . auoyent monstré moins de foy et de constance que ces poures femmes, l'ayans accompagné & en la mort & en la sepulture, & maintenant encores l'allant visiter iusque dans le sepulchre, au lieu que les disciples estoyent si esperdus, qu'ils auoyent comme oublié leur Maistre." Beza, *Sermons sur l'histoire*, 67–68.

23. Beza, *Sermons sur l'histoire*, 68.

24. Ibid., 92, 93–94.

25. Ibid., 81, 96–97.

26. Ibid., 103, 108.

27. Ibid., 128–29, 130, 134. See also John Calvin, *Institutes of the Christian Religion*, vol. 1, ed. John T. McNeill, trans. Ford Lewis Battles, Library of Christian Classics (Philadelphia: Westminster John Knox, 1960), 303–4.

28. Beza, *Sermons sur l'histoire*, 148, 152, 153.

29. Ibid., 157, 158–59, 161–62, 166.

30. Ibid., 168, 170.

31. "Commission la plus grande & la plus honorable qu'ait iamais donnee le Seigneur à Proph-ete ni Apostre quelconques, & contenant vne doctrine surmontant la capacité mesmes des Anges. Mais il ne faut pas toutesfois tirer cela en consequence, quant à la personne à laquelle pour ce coup ceste charge a esté donnee: ne portant pas l'ordinaire administration de la maison de Dieu, que les femmes enseignent en l'assemblee, mais au contraire leur estant commandé d'escouter en silence, 1 Cor. 14:34." Beza, *Sermons sur l'histoire*, 173.

32. Beza, *Sermons sur l'histoire*, 182.

33. Karant-Nunn, *The Reformation of Feeling*, 128.

34. Raymond A. Mentzer, "The Huguenot Minority in Early Modern France," in *Religion and the Early Modern State: Views from China, Russia, and the West*, ed. James D. Tracy and Marguerite Ragnow, Studies in Comparative Early Modern History (Cambridge: Cambridge University Press, 2004), 189. The daughter of Philip Gendron, for example, is mentioned in his will as a Mary Magdalen born in 1691; the family lived in the Huguenot settlement on the Santee River in Craven County, South Carolina. *Transactions of the Huguenot Society of South Carolina* 14 (Charleston: Huguenot Society of South Carolina, 1907), 17.

35. G. W. Bernard, *The King's Reformation: Henry VIII and the Remaking of the English Church* (New Haven, CT: Yale University Press, 2005), 442–62; Catharine Davies, *A Religion of the Word: The Defence of the Reformation in the Reign of Edward VI*, Politics, Culture, and Society in Early Modern Britain (Manchester, England: Manchester University Press, 2002), 18–51; Amy M. Froide, "The Religious Lives of Singlewomen in the Anglo-Atlantic World: Quaker Missionaries, Protestant Nuns, and Covert Catholics," in *Women, Religion, and the Atlantic World (1600–1800)*, ed. Daniella Kostroun and Lisa Vollendorf, UCLA Center / Clark Series (Toronto: University of Toronto Press, 2009) 71. For the effect on popular piety, see Eamon Duffy, *The Stripping of the Altars: Traditional Religion in England, 1400–1580* (New Haven, CT: Yale University Press, 1992). *Puritan* was coined as a term of opprobrium in the mid-sixteenth century, for those who were deemed overly concerned with following a biblical way of life and with purging the Church of England of Catholic practices; see Hans J. Hillerbrand, *The Division of Christendom: Christianity in the Sixteenth Century* (Louisville, KY: Westminster John Knox, 2007), 256. It became an informal term adopted by the community as a badge of honor, though never an official designation; see David E. Stannard, *The Puritan Way of Death: A Study in Religion, Culture, and Social Change* (New York: Oxford University Press, 1977), 32.

36. Lisa McClain, "'They Have Taken Away My Lord': Mary Magdalene, Christ's Missing Body, and the Mass in Reformation England," *Sixteenth Century Journal* 38, no. 1 (2007): 92–93; Sarah Carpenter, "Performing the Scriptures: Biblical Drama after the Reformation," in *Staging Scripture: Biblical Drama, 1350–1600*, ed. Peter Happé and Wim Hüsken, Ludus: Medieval and Early Renaissance Theatre and Drama 14 (Boston: Brill-Rodopi, 2016), 29; Patricia Badir, "'To Allure Vnto Their Loue': Iconoclasm and Striptease in Lewis Wager's 'The Life and Repentaunce of Marie Magdalene,'" *Theatre Journal* 51, no. 1 (1999): 2, 4, 12–13.

37. Badir, "'To Allure Vnto Their Loue,'" 5–6, 7. See also Heather Hill Vásquez, *Sacred Players: The Politics of Response in the Middle English Religious Drama* (Washington, DC: Catholic University of America Press, 2007), 172.

38. Lewis Wager, *The Life and Repentaunce of Marie Magdalene* (1567), act 2, lines 1441–56, quoted in Badir, "'To Allure Vnto Their Loue,'" 18–19.

39. Patricia Badir, *The Maudlin Impression: English Literary Images of Mary Magdalene, 1550–1700* (Notre Dame: University of Notre Dame Press, 2009), 83.

40. Ibid., 84.

41. Gervase Markham, *Marie Magdalens Lamentations for the Losse of Her Master Iesus*, quoted in Badir, *The Maudlin Impression*, 88.

42. Gervase Markham, *Marie Magdalens Lamentations for the Losse of Her Master Iesus*, quoted in Patricia Phillippy, *Women, Death, and Literature in Post-Reformation England* (Cambridge: Cambridge University Press, 2002), 66.

43. The difficulty of establishing clear confessional identities for English religious poets may be due to the syncretistic character of elements in that tradition in the seventeenth century; see Benedict, *Christ's Churches Purely Reformed*, xxiv.

44. H. Oskar Sommer, ed., *Thomas Robinson's Life and Death of Mary Magdalene: Ein Legendengedicht in zwei Teilen* (Marburg, Germany: N. G. Elwert'sche, 1887), 21, 25; Götz

Schmitz, *The Fall of Women in Early English Narrative Verse,* European Studies in English Literature (Cambridge: Cambridge University Press, 1990), 180; Christopher Highley, *Catholics Writing the Nation in Early Modern Britain and Ireland* (Oxford: Oxford University Press, 2008), 188; Margaret Hannay, "Mary Magdalene," in *The Gospel of St. John: The Story of the Son of God,* ed. John Drane, The Classic Bible Series (New York: Palgrave Macmillan, 1997), 59; B. Campbell, *Divine Poetry and Drama in Sixteenth-Century England* (Cambridge: Cambridge University Press, 1959), 95. Sommer appeared to posit Robinson as a Reformed pastor, and placed the date of publication at 1621; see Thomas Robinson, *The Life and Death of Mary Magdalene: A Legendary Poem in Two Parts about A. D. 1620,* ed. H. Oskar Sommer, Early English Text Society, Extra Series 78 (London: K. Paul, Trench, Trübner, 1899), xi–xii.

45. For an example of the use of the trope in late medieval preaching, see Anne T. Thayer, *Penitence, Preaching, and the Coming of the Reformation,* St. Andrews Studies in Reformation History (Aldershot, England: Ashgate, 2002), 85.

46. Thomas Robinson, *The Life and Death of Mary Magdalene* (Cambridge: Chadwyck-Healey, 1992), 18.

47. Ibid., 56.

48. Ibid., 30, 34.

49. Ibid., 35–36.

50. Ibid., 41.

51. William J. Bouwsma, *John Calvin: A Sixteenth Century Portrait* (New York: Oxford University Press, 1988), 41; Marijn de Kroon, *The Honor of God and Human Salvation: A Contribution to an Understanding of Calvin's Theology According to His Institutes,* trans. John Vriend and Lyle D. Bierma (Edinburgh: T & T Clark, 2001), 198.

52. John Calvin, quoted in Bouwsma, *John Calvin,* 41.

53. Nick Bunker, *Making Haste from Babylon: The Mayflower Pilgrims and Their World: A New History* (New York: Alfred A. Knopf, 2010), 64.

54. On Protestant depictions of salvation, see Carl C. Christensen, *Art and the Reformation in Germany,* Studies in the Reformation 2 (Athens, OH: Ohio State University Press / Detroit: Wayne State University Press, 1979), 124–30.

55. Robinson, *The Life and Death of Mary Magdalene,* 42.

56. Ibid., 45.

57. Ibid., 51.

58. Ibid., 51, 52–53.

59. Ibid., 65.

60. Ibid., 65.

61. Ibid., 68.

62. Daniel Cudmore, "On Mary Magdalene," in *Rare Poems of the Seventeenth Century,* ed. L. Birkett Marshall (Cambridge: The University Press, 1936), 37; Daniel Cudmore, *Euchodia. Or,*

A prayer-song; being sacred poems on the history of the birth and passion of our blessed Saviour, and several other choice texts of scripture. In two parts (London: J. C. for William Ley in Paul's Chain, 1657), 25–29.

63. Ibid., 28–29.

64. See Nicholas McDowell, *The English Radical Imagination: Culture, Religion, and Revolution, 1630–1660*, Oxford English Monographs (Oxford: Clarendon, 2003).

65. *Religion and Writing in England, 1558–1689: Studies in Community-Making and Cultural Memory*, ed. Roger D. Sell and Anthony W. Johnson (Farnham, England: Ashgate, 2009), 309; Joyce L. Irwin, *Womanhood in Radical Protestantism, 1525–1675*, Studies in Women and Religion 1 (New York: Edwin Mellen, 1979), 174, 175, 176–77.

66. Irwin, *Womanhood in Radical Protestantism*, 117; Tim Cooper, *John Owen, Richard Baxter, and the Formation of Nonconformity* (Farnham, England: Ashgate, 2011), 4; Richard Baxter, *A Christian Directory*, quoted in Irwin, *Womanhood in Radical Protestantism*, 116. See also Richard Schlatter, ed., *Richard Baxter and Puritan Politics* (New Brunswick, NJ: Rutgers University Press, 1957); and N. H. Keeble, *Richard Baxter: Puritan Man of Letters*, Oxford English Monographs (Oxford: Clarendon, 1982).

67. Chrystia Freeland and Mary DeWitt Freeland, *The Records of Oxford, Massachusetts: Including Chapters of Nipmuck, Huguenot, and English History, accompanied with biographical sketches and notes, 1630–1890* (Albany, NY: Munsell's, 1894), 1–2.

68. Jo[hn] Sheffield, "An Epitaph 'Upon the Much-Lamented Death of the Truly Honorable, Very Aged, and Singularly Pious Lady, the Lady Mary Armine, who Dyed Anno Christi 1675,'" quoted in Freeland and Freeland, *The Records of Oxford, Massachusetts*, 4–5.

69. Susan Haskins, *Mary Magdalen: Truth and Myth* (London: Pimlico, 2005), 402.

70. John Donne, "To the Lady Magdalen Herbert, of St. Mary Magdalen," in *The Collected Poems of John Donne*, ed. Roy Booth (Ware, England: Wordsworth Editions, 1994), 243.

71. Susan Wabuda, *Preaching during the English Reformation*, Cambridge Studies in Early Modern British History (Cambridge: Cambridge University Press, 2002), 101, 104.

72. Lancelot Andrewes, *Selected Sermons and Lectures*, ed. Peter McCullough (Oxford: Oxford University Press, 2005), 226; Hannay, "Mary Magdalene," 58.

73. Hannay, "Mary Magdalene," 59.

7. Mark This, Ye Despisers of the Weakness of Women: The Magdalene of the Radical Reformation

1. See Mark U. Edwards, *Luther and the False Brethren* (Stanford, CA: Stanford University Press, 1975). On the Radical Reformation, see R. Emmet McLaughlin, "Radicals," in *Reformation and Early Modern Europe: A Guide to Research*, ed. David M. Whitford, Sixteenth Century Essays and Studies 79 (Kirksville, MO: Truman State University Press, 2008), 80–120.

2. John S. Oyer, *Lutheran Reformers against Anabaptists: Luther, Melanchthon, and Menius, and the Anabaptists of Central Germany,* The Dissent and Nonconformity Series 13 (The Hague: M. Nijhoff, 1964), 159.

3. See, e.g., Martin Luther, *Table Talk* no. 342 (1532), in *LW,* 54:48; and Martin Luther, *A Letter of Dr. Martin Luther Concerning His Book on the Private Mass* (1534), in *LW,* 38:221.

4. See Thomas Müntzer, *Revelation and Revolution: Basic Writings of Thomas Müntzer,* trans. and ed. Michael G. Baylor (Bethlehem, PA: Lehigh University Press, 1993).

5. Religious tolerance arrived in different ways and at different times across the Western world. See Samme Zijlstra, "Anabaptism and Tolerance: Possibilities and Limitations," in *Calvinism and Religious Toleration in the Dutch Golden Age,* ed. R. Po-Chia Hsia and Henk van Nierop (Cambridge: Cambridge University Press, 2004), 112–31; and Ole Peter Grell and Bob Scribner, eds., *Tolerance and Intolerance in the European Reformation* (New York: Cambridge University Press, 1996).

6. Margaret Fell, *Women's Speaking Justified, Proved, and Allowed of by the Scriptures* (London, 1666).

7. The Free Churches that emerged in the early modern period were of the Baptists, Hutterites, Mennonites, and Quakers. For a discussion of the Free Church movement, see Graydon F. Snyder and Doreen M. McFarlane, *The People Are Holy: The History and Theology of Free Church Worship* (Macon, GA: Mercer University Press, 2005), 3–4. I use the term *Free Church* to denote the theological and liturgical connections among the traditions discussed.

8. Thieleman J. van Braght, *The bloody theater: or, Martyrs mirror of the defenseless Christians: who baptized only upon confession of faith, and who suffered and died for the testimony of Jesus, their Saviour, from the time of Christ to the year A.D. 1660* (Scottdale, PA: Herald Press, 1977); Brad S. Gregory, *Salvation at Stake: Christian Martyrdom in Early Modern Europe,* Harvard Historical Studies 134 (Cambridge, MA: Harvard University Press, 2009), 197–231.

9. C. Arnold Snyder and Linda A. Huebert Hecht, eds., *Profiles of Anabaptist Women: Sixteenth Century Reforming Pioneers,* Etudes sur les Femmes et la Religion 3 (Waterloo, ON: Wilfred Laurier University Press, 2010), 2.

10. Snyder and Hecht, eds., *Profiles of Anabaptist Women,* 39; Gregory, *Salvation at Stake,* 202, 228, 246. See also Diarmaid McCulloch, *Silence: A Christian History* (New York: Penguin, 2013), esp. the section "Reformation Radicals: Word and Silence, in chapter 7, ""Silences for Survival," 178–183.

11. Van Braght, *Martyrs mirror,* 549, 569.

12. Soetken van der Houte, "Testament to Her Children," in *Elisabeth's Manly Courage: Testimonials and Songs of Martyred Anabaptist Women in the Low Countries,* ed. Hermina Joldersma and Louis Grijp, Reformation Texts with Translation 1350–1650, Women of the Reformation 3 (Milwaukee, WI: Marquette University Press, 2001), 165. See also Snyder and Hecht, eds., *Profiles of Anabaptist Women,* 4; and Gregory, *Salvation at Stake,* 213.

13. Van Braght, *Martyrs mirror,* 467; Mary van Beckom and Ursel van Werdum, "Martyr Song," in Joldersma and Grijp, eds., *Elisabeth's Manly Courage,* 127; George Huntston Williams, *The Radical Reformation,* 3rd ed., Sixteenth Century Essays and Studies 15 (Kirksville, MO: Truman State University Press, 1992), 779.

14. For a reference to both the Song of Songs and the wise and foolish virgins, see van Braght, *Martyrs mirror,* 908.

15. Van Braght, *Martyrs mirror,* 918; Soetken van der Houte, "Testament," in Joldersma and Grijp, eds., *Elisabeth's Manly Courage,* 167.

16. See William R. Estep, *The Anabaptist Story: An Introduction to Sixteenth-Century Anabaptism,* 3rd ed. (Grand Rapids, MI: Eerdmans, 1996), 190.

17. Jerome Segers to Lijksen Dircks, 1551, quoted in van Braght, *Martyrs mirror,* 517.

18. Charles H. Parker, *The Reformation of Community: Social Welfare and Calvinist Charity in Calvinist Holland, 1572–1620,* Cambridge Studies in Early Modern History (Cambridge: Cambridge University Press, 1998), 175.

19. See Jerome Segers to his sister-in-law, a nun still "among the Papists," in van Braght, *Martyrs mirror,* 918.

20. Van Braght, *Martyrs mirror,* 923.

21. Sigrun Haude, "Gender Roles and Perspectives among Anabaptist and Spiritualist Groups," in *A Companion to Anabaptism and Spiritualism, 1521–1700,* ed. John D. Roth and James M. Stayer, Brill's Companions to the Christian Tradition 6 (Leiden: Brill, 2007), 449. See also Steven Ozment, *When Fathers Ruled: Family Life in Reformation Europe,* Studies in Cultural History (Cambridge, MA: Harvard University Press, 1983).

22. Anna Bijns, quoted in *Sisters: Myth and Reality of Anabaptist, Mennonite, and Doopsgezind Women, ca. 1525–1900,* ed. Mirjam van Veen, Piet Visser, and Gary K. Waite, et al. (Leiden: Brill, 2014), 3; Snyder and Hecht, eds., *Profiles of Anabaptist Women,* 11; Gary K. Waite, *Eradicating the Devil's Minions: Anabaptists and Witches in Reformation Europe, 1525–1600* (Toronto: University of Toronto Press, 2007), 192, 201.

23. Snyder and Hecht, eds., *Profiles of Anabaptist Women,* 19, 21, 49–50, 51, 73, 84.

24. Snyder and Hecht, eds., *Profiles of Anabaptist Women,* 21, 38, 48, 66. Päivi Räisänen-Schröder, "Between Martyrdom and Everyday Pragmatism: Gender, Family, and Anabaptism in Early Modern Germany," in *Gender in Late Medieval and Early Modern Europe,* ed. Marianna G. Muravyeva and Raisa Maria Toivo, Routledge Research in Gender and History 14 (New York: Routledge, 2013), 96.

25. Waite, *Eradicating the Devil's Minions,* 192; Genelle Gertz, *Heresy Trials and English Women Writers, 1400–1670* (Cambridge: Cambridge University Press, 2012), 10; Snyder and Hecht, eds., *Profiles of Anabaptist Women,* 32, 33–34, 35, 47.

26. Räisänen-Schröder, "Between Martyrdom and Everyday Pragmatism," 101; Hans-Jürgen Goertz, *The Anabaptists,* trans. Trevor Johnson, Christianity and Society in the Modern World (New York: Routledge, 1996), 115; Snyder and Hecht, eds., *Profiles of Anabaptist Women,* 39, 49, 65–66.

27. Joyce L. Irwin, *Womanhood in Radical Protestantism, 1525–1675,* Studies in Women and Religion 1 (New York: Edwin Mellen, 1979), 56, 57. On Simons's Catholic career, see Daniel Liechty, "Menno Simons," in *Early Anabaptist Spirituality: Selected Writings,* ed. Daniel Liechty, Classics in Western Spirituality (New York: Paulist, 1994), 247.

28. Harry Loewen, *Luther and the Radicals: Another Look at Some Aspects of the Struggle between Luther and the Radical Reformers* (Waterloo, ON: Wilfred Laurier University Press, 1974), 27; Irwin, *Womanhood in Radical Protestantism,* 58–62.

29. Irwin, *Womanhood in Radical Protestantism,* 62, 63.

30. Caspar Schwenckfeld to Sibilla Eisler, Easter 1561, quoted in Irwin, *Womanhood in Radical Protestantism,* 27–28. See also R. Emmet McLaughlin, *Caspar Schwenckfeld, Reluctant Radical: His Life to 1540,* Yale Historical Publications, Miscellany 134 (New Haven, CT: Yale University Press, 1986); and Robert Emmet McLaughlin, "The Genesis of Schwenckfeld's Eucharistic Doctrine," *Archiv für Reformationsgeschichte* 74 (1983): 94–121.

31. See Williams, *The Radical Reformation,* 553–88. See also Ted Leroy Underwood, *Primitivism, Radicalism, and the Lambs' War: The Baptist-Quaker Conflict in Seventeenth-Century England,* Oxford Studies in Historical Theology (Oxford: Oxford University Press, 1997).

32. Margaret Hope Bacon, *Mothers of Feminism: The Story of Quaker Women in America* (San Francisco: Harper and Row, 1986), 11–12; George Fox to the Duke of Holstein, August 26, 1684, in George Fox, *The Journal of George Fox; Being an Historical Account of His Life, Travels, Sufferings, and Christian Experiences,* vol. 2 (London: Friends Tract Association / Headley, 1901), 407.

33. Some modern scholars accept the family relationship, while others dismiss it as legend; nevertheless the connection was part of Margaret's identity in Quaker lore. See Jane Donawerth, "Margaret Fell, 1614–1702," in *Rhetorical Theory by Women before 1900: An Anthology,* ed. Jane Donawerth (Lanham, MD: Rowman and Littlefield, 2002), 59; and [anonymous], "Thoughts for the Times—No. 20: Margaret Fox," *The Friend: A Religious and Literary Journal* 39.33 (14 April 1866): 258.

34. Margaret Askew Fell, *Women's Speaking Justified, Proved and Allowed by the Scriptures* (1666), quoted in Irwin, *Womanhood in Radical Protestantism,* 182.

35. Carter Lindberg, "Introduction," in *The Pietist Theologians: An Introduction to Theology in the Seventeenth and Eighteenth Centuries,* ed. Carter Lindberg, The Great Theologians (Malden, MA: Blackwell, 2005), 1. For a later example of the same strand of Pietist theology, see the discussion of Nicolaus Zinzendorf in Aaron Spencer Fogleman, *Jesus Is Female: Moravians and the Challenge of Radical Religion in Early America,* Early American Studies (Philadelphia: University of Pennsylvania Press, 2007), 95–96.

36. Fell, *Women's Speaking Justified,* quoted in Irwin, *Womanhood in Radical Protestantism,* 184.

37. Ibid.

38. George Fox, "To the Men and Women's Meetings," quoted in Phyllis Mack, *Visionary Women: Ecstatic Prophecy in Seventeenth-Century England* (Berkeley: University of California Press,

1992), 309; [Sarah Fell], "From our Country Women's meeting in Lancashire to be Dispersed abroad among the Women's meetings everywhere," in *Witnesses for Change: Quaker Women over Three Centuries,* ed. Elisabeth Potts Brown and Susan Mosher Stuard (New Brunswick, NJ: Rutgers University Press, 1989), 25–29, discussed in the editorial "Introduction," 15–16.

39. Milton D. Speizman and Jane C. Kronick, eds., "A Seventeenth-Century Quaker Women's Declaration," *Signs* 1, no. 1 (1975): 239.

40. Speizman and Kronick, eds., "A Seventeenth-Century Quaker Women's Declaration," 240.

41. Loewen, *Luther and the Radicals,* 87; Hans Schneider, ed., *German Radical Pietism,* trans. Gerald T. MacDonald, Revitalization: Explorations in World Christian Movements, Pietist and Wesleyan Studies 22 (Lanham, MD: Scarecrow, 2007), 173; Speizman and Kronick, eds., "A Seventeenth-Century Quaker Women's Declaration," 244; For a contemporary example of Quaker women's attacks on the male clergy culture, see Catie Gill, *Women in the Seventeenth-Century Quaker Community: A Literary Study of Political Identities, 1650–1700,* Women and Gender in the Early Modern World (Aldershot, England: Ashgate, 2005), 95.

42. Lilias Skene, untitled poem, quoted in Gordon Desbrisay, "Lilias Skene: A Quaker Poet and Her 'Cursed Self,'" in *Woman and the Feminine in Medieval and Early Modern Scottish Writing,* ed. Sarah M. Dunnigan, C. Marie Harker, and Evelyn S. Newlyn (Basingstoke: Palgrave Macmillan, 2004), 163–64, 173.

43. Elizabeth Bathurst, *The Sayings of Women, Which were spoken on sundry Occasions, in several places of the Scriptures* (Shoreditch, England: T. Sowle, 1683), 14–15, 18, 20–21, 23.

44. Elizabeth Stirredge, "Strength in Weakness Manifest," in *Autobiographical Writings by Early Quaker Women,* ed. David Booy, The Early Modern Englishwoman 1500–1750: Contemporary Editions (Aldershot, England: Ashgate, 2004), 121.

45. Gill, *Women in the Seventeenth-Century Quaker Community,* 162–63, emphasis in the original.

46. Susanna Blandford, *A Small Treatise Writ by One of the True Christian Faith, Who Believes in God and in His Son Jesus Christ,* quoted in Mack, *Visionary Women,* 393.

47. Quakers certainly underwent persecution for their beliefs, but attacks on Quakers in the British Isles were limited to public shaming, beating, and confiscation of property. See Thomas S. Freeman, "Introduction: Concepts of Martyrdom," in *Martyrs and Martyrdom in England, c. 1400–1700,* ed. Thomas S. Freedman and Thomas F. Mayer, Studies in Modern British Religious History 15 (Woodbridge, England: Boydell, 2007), 28.

Conclusion: An Army of Such Ladies

1. Valerie C. Cooper, *Word, Like Fire: Maria Stewart, the Bible, and the Rights of African Americans,* Carter G. Woodson Institute Series (Charlottesville: University of Virginia Press, 2011), 40.

2. Maria Stewart, "Farewell Address," in *African American Religious History: A Documentary Witness,* ed. Milton C. Sernett, C. Eric Lincoln Series on the Black Experience (Durham, NC: Duke University Press, 1999), 204–6.

3. See Mark A. Noll, "Common Sense Traditions and American Evangelical Thought," *American Quarterly* 37 (1985): 220–25; and Mark A. Noll, *The Rise of Evangelicalism: The Age of Edwards, Whitefield, and the Wesleys*, A History of Evangelicalism 1 (Leicester: InterVarsity, 2003).

4. Mary V. Cook, "The Work for Baptist Women," in *The Negro Baptist Pulpit: A Collection of Sermons and Papers on Baptist Doctrine and Missionary and Educational Work*, ed. E. M. Brawley (Philadelphia: American Baptist Publication Society, 1890), 271.

5. Catharina Regina von Greiffenberg, *Meditations on the Incarnation, Passion, and Death of Jesus Christ*, ed. and trans. Lynne Tatlock, The Other Voice in Early Modern Europe (Chicago: University of Chicago Press, 2009), 129–30.

6. See Richard Marius, *Thomas More: A Biography* (Cambridge, MA: Harvard University Press, 1984), 394.

7. John Lambert, testimony, in John Foxe, *The Acts and Monuments of the Church*, 1563 ed., book 3, 610, The Acts and Monuments Online, https://www.johnfoxe.org/index.php?realm =text&gototype=&edition=1563&pageid=610.

8. Joyce L. Irwin, *Womanhood in Radical Protestantism, 1525–1675*, Studies in Women and Religion 1 (New York: Edwin Mellen, 1979), 184.

Acknowledgments

I AM GRATEFUL to Barbara Diefendorf and Phillip Haberkern of Boston University's History Department, and to Virginia Reinburg of Boston College for their insightful reading and comments on the work through many stages of revision. Steven Ozment was a generous and enthusiastic mentor. They have all provided inspiring examples of the fellowship of the scholarly life. Many thanks are also due to the Boston University School of Theology librarians, especially Stacey Battles de Ramos and James Skypeck, for assistance in obtaining—and patience in renewing—materials. Participants at the 2012 International Luther Congress in Helsinki offered invaluable responses to an early draft. Deeana Klepper's reading suggestions first led me to the subject of this study. I am indebted to the support of my editor at Harvard University Press, Kathleen McDermott, and the suggestions of those who read for the Press. All of these long-suffering persons are excused from responsibility for any errors within, which are entirely my own.

This work was possible because of the love of my family: my parents, John and Kathryn Arnold, my daughters, Rose and Clara, and my sister, Mary Kate. My friend Sarah Emsley has always been the best of conversation partners. The people of Grace Episcopal Church in Medford, Massachusetts, responded with kindness and encouragement to countless presentations on Mary Magdalene.

The book is for Christopher: a very base sort of coin, for the gold that I have received.

Index

Absolution: Catholic theology of, 100, 110, 135, 230, 242; Christ pronouncing, 24–25; Protestant theology of, 48–50, 64, 71, 87, 192, 229, 242

Acarie, Barbe, 145

Agustin de la Madre de Dios, 124–125

Aix-en-Provence, 20–21

Albrecht von Brandenburg, 25

Amsdorf, Nicholas von, 54

Anabaptists, 15, 201–214, 217, 220, 222, 228, 232, 235, 238

Andrewes, Lancelot, 198–199

Anna (the Prophetess), 237

Anne de Vesvres, 144

Anne of Austria, 161

Anointing at Bethany, 84–87, 153, 192, 196, 226, 232

Antwerp, 206–7, 236

Apostola apostolorum title: rejected by authors, 2, 168, 237, 240; used by authors, 21, 31–32, 100, 123, 153, 178–180, 182, 199, 240

Argula von Grumbach, 75–77, 228, 237

Armine, Lady Mary, 195–196

Asceticism: of female saints, 26, 129, 138–142, 241; of Mary Magdalene, 23, 32, 38, 113, 161, 211, 230; Protestant forms of, 86, 91

Ashe, George, 84, 232

Askew, Anne, 72, 81–83, 214, 235

Attaingnant, Pierre, 119

Augsburg, 49, 55, 98

Augustine of Hippo, 27, 47, 55, 121, 131, 150

Aurelia Maria, 147–148

Badir, Patricia, 3, 16, 122, 184

Bale, John, 72, 81–82, 235

Baptism, 38, 47, 64, 66, 172, 201, 208, 214

Barbier, Marie, 145

Bathurst, Elizabeth, 219

Baxter, Richard, 194–195, 199

Beckum, Maria and Ursula van, 204

Bellarmine, Cardinal Robert, 121

Bentley, Thomas, 84

Bernard of Clairvaux, 22

Bérulle, Pierre de, 139

Beza, Theodore, 176–183, 199, 224, 227–28, 232, 242

Bible, 187; interpretation by Catholics, 148; interpretation by Protestants, 81, 201, 207–209, 213–214, 237–238, 240; reading in the vernacular, 1, 11, 88, 211, 219–220, 223, 227–228, 231; restrictions on reading, 97, 108, 127, 165, 198, 205–206; translation, 12, 75, 157

Bijns, Anna, 207

Blandford, Susannah, 221

Blessed Battista, 30

Bols, Elizabeth, 221

Bonaventure, 24

Book of Common Prayer, 184

Borromeo, Carlo, 103, 105

Borromeo, Federico, 97, 146–148, 224, 233

Bourgeoys, Marguerite, 141–142

Bouts, Dieric, 25

Bozon, Nicholas, 23, 33

Braght, Thieleman van, 203–204

Breton, Nicholas, 198

Briçonnet, Guillaume, 157

Broickwy von Königstein, Antonius, 101

Brome, Richard, 199

Brown, Christopher Boyd, 51

Bugenhagen, Johann, 48–49

Bunyan, John, 199

Burgundy, House of, 27

Cajetan, Cardinal Tommaso de Vio, 47, 98

Calvin, John, 15, 167–172, 176, 178–182, 197–199, 227–228; and English Reformation, 184, 188–194, 216; and Marguerite de Navarre, 157, 160; and Marie Dentière, 79–81

Campbell, Lily, 187

Cana, wedding, 20, 23, 45, 175–176

Canaanite woman, 101, 132, 140, 194, 217

Canisius, Peter, 98

Capuchin Order, 114

Caracciolo, Robert, 25

Caravaggio, 116–117

Carmelite Order, 112, 124–125, 129–141, 145, 161, 228, 235

Cathars, 174

Catherine de St-Augustin, 144

Catherine of Alexandria, 150

Catherine of Siena, 26

Cefalu, Paul, 122

Champaigne, Philippe de, 161

Chantal, Jeanne Françoise de, 110, 142–143

Charles IX, 176

Christine de Pizan, 13, 36, 156

Chrysostom, John, 174

Cistercian Order, 22, 31–32, 111, 125

Clement of Alexandria, 55

Clerical authority: attacks on, 12, 61–65, 81–82, 209, 218, 237, 241; defenses of, 7, 25, 28, 49

Clothing, 25, 31, 81, 115, 149, 184, 210–211

Colette of Corbie, 26–27

Coletti, Teresa, 40

Colonna, Vittoria, 149–150, 152

Confession: of faith, 67, 76, 102, 104, 108, 111, 201–202, 206–209, 224, 235, 240; of sins, 24–25, 49–50, 87, 100, 109–110, 112, 135

Confessionalization, 4, 102

Confraternities, 23

Conscience, 46, 77, 188–190, 194, 230

Constable, Henry, 121

Contemplation, 230–231; Catholic expressions of, 112, 162–63; conflict with the active life, 22–23, 82, 124–125, 127–129, 134–135, 141–142, 145; integration with the active life, 32, 55–57, 68, 74, 76, 122–124, 130–132, 143, 197, 241; Mary of Bethany as model for, 40, 106, 108, 160; nuns practicing, 96, 147, 165, 213; Protestant expressions of, 94, 219

Conversion: of Catholics to Protestantism, 49, 79, 85, 157, 184, 206; expressions in holiness of life, 31, 113, 201–202, 210–211, 214; Mary Magdalene converting others, 20, 35, 38, 54, 98, 122, 144, 150, 161, 168; Mary Magdalene's own, 21, 23, 26–27, 87, 109–110, 133, 162, 239; of pagans, 5, 181; from prostitution or promiscuity, 14, 96, 108–109, 114–119, 139–40, 174, 187–188; of Protestants to Catholicism, 67, 101; produced by preaching, 13, 23, 207, 175, 242; swift vs. gradual, 136, 190, 230; women converting others, 208–209

Cook, Mary V., 226–227

Corinthians, Paul's First Epistle to the (1 Cor. 14:34–40), 63–65, 106, 153, 178, 181, 194, 214, 226, 236

Corvinus, Anton, 45, 66–68

Cozzolani, Chiara Margarita, 148

Cranach, Lucas the Elder, 53, 190

Cudmore, Daniel, 192–193

Cyril of Alexandria, 55

Dancing, 118–119

Daughters of Charity, 103–104, 144

David (King), 52, 82

David and Levina, 204

Davis, Natalie Zemon, 6–7, 10, 224

Deborah, 77, 80, 194, 217, 225

De' Medici, Marie, 161

Dentière, Marie, 14, 71–72, 78–81, 90, 157, 172, 237

Devotional writing, 109–111, 154, 157, 161; in poetry, 121–124, 185–193, 197–198, 218–219

Digby Mysteries, 28–29

Dircks, Lijksen, 205–206

Dolnikowski, Edith Wilks, 82

Dominic, Saint, 129

Dominican Order, 21, 32–33, 124, 237

Donne, John, 197–199

Dowerman, Hendrik, 25

Eade, Jane, 83

Education: in the home, 68; and nuns, 8, 141; in reform programs, 95, 98–99; in sermons, 49–51; of women, 90–91, 105–108; women as patrons of, 72, 84–85, 162, 195; women teaching, 76–77, 103–104, 144–146, 172, 207–209, 226

Edward VI, 183, 198

Elisabeth von Braunschweig-Lüneburg, 67

Elizabeth I, 72, 83–85, 94, 138, 160, 183, 232

Erasmus, Desiderius, 40, 105–106

Esther, 225

Eucharist, 37, 62–63, 81, 112–113, 133, 155, 201, 212, 214

Eve, 26, 37, 43, 100, 120, 219

Eyck, Jan van, 29

Faith: and domestic responsibilities, 204, 220–221, 240; and emotion, 159–160, 169, 178, 180–82; fruits of, 52, 54, 86, 230; praise for Mary Magdalene's, 171, 199, 211; praise for women's, 195, 197–198; salvation by, 47–48, 50–51, 66; and works, 55–57, 98–100, 173, 229. See also Confession

Fanwiler, Winbrat, 208

Fasting, 26, 91, 129, 138, 221

Fayet, Geneviève, 144

Feast of St. Mary Magdalene (July 22), 154, 174, 183–184, 197; in drama, 146–147, 162; in journals and letters, 78, 134, 147; sermons for, 24, 44–45, 49–51, 99–100

Fell, Margaret Askew, 15, 152, 202, 214–218, 224, 237

Fell, Sarah, 217–218

Feucht, Jakob, 99–100

First Great Awakening, 226

Fisher, John, 40

Flagellants, 23

Florence, 23, 34

Fox, George, 15, 202, 214, 217, 224, 237

Foxe, John, 82–83, 224, 235–236

Francis of Assisi, 23, 129

Franciscan Order, 23–24, 33, 101

François de Sales, 109–110, 125, 143, 154, 190, 230

Franco y Ortega, Alonso, 114

Gallo, Giuseppe, 148

Garth, Helen Meredith, 19

Gender, 26–28, 93, 96, 231–234, 239, 241

Geneva, 79, 109, 173, 176, 240

Gentileschi, Artemisia, 149, 151, 162

Geschwind, Rachel, 109

Giovanni da San Gemingnano, 32

Gnosticism, 19

Golden Legend, 31, 33–34, 123

Gonzaga, Federico, 116

Gospel of Mary, 19

Gournay, Marie le Jars de, 91, 153

Gregory IX, 26

Gregory X, 32

Gregory the Great, 19, 54, 184

Greiffenberg, Catharina Regina von, 74, 85–89, 94, 216, 228, 234

Guyon, Jeanne, 154–155, 233

Habermann, Johann, 45, 52, 54–55

Halliwell, Luci, 28

Hannah, 65, 67

Hannay, Margaret, 187
Haskins, Susan, 2
Hassenstein, Margarethe von, 52
Hellwart, Margaret, 208–209
Hendricks, Elizabeth, 214
Henry III, 111
Henry VIII, 183
Herbert, Lady Magdalen, 197
Heresy, 28, 154, 174
Herman, Nicolaus, 17, 45, 50–51, 235
Herolt, Johannes, 25
Hoffmeister, Johann, 98–100
Holy Spirit, 63, 66, 88–89, 214, 218–219, 234, 236–237
Hosias, S., 104
Hottinger, Margaret, 208–209
Humanism, 5, 9, 36, 40, 94, 107, 149, 156–158, 233–234, 238–239
Humility, 142, 147, 181, 191, 231; lack of, 131; Mary Magdalene's, 25, 47–48, 56, 61, 152, 210–211; posture of, 18, 27, 72, 77, 82, 88, 90, 144–145, 163–164
Hymns, 17, 50–51, 204, 207, 235. *See also* Music

Iconoclasm, 173, 176, 199, 203, 223–224
Ignatius of Loyola, 112–113, 125, 134, 137
Ingolstadt, University of, 75–76, 99
Inquisition, 10, 130, 134, 156
Intimacy with Christ: evangelical theology of, 75–76, 91; Mary Magdalene's, 21, 30, 93, 111, 124, 132–133, 146, 150, 161, 167, 182, 204–205, 227–229, 240; and preaching, 33, 35, 72, 94; women's, 86, 92, 138, 154, 158, 163, 215–216, 220

Jack, Belinda, 127
Jansen, Katherine, 1–2, 233
Jansz, Anneken, 207
Jerome, Saint, 75, 101
Jesuit Order, 112, 121–125, 129, 138, 237
Joachimsthal, 50–52
Johann Friedrich, Elector of Saxony, 54
John the Baptist, 32, 38, 66, 145

John 20:1–18, 15, 58–60, 65–66, 122, 133, 147–148, 169–172, 179–181, 188, 198, 212, 219
Judith, 205
Justification, 105, 168, 173, 234, 241–242; by faith, 3, 46–52, 54–55, 89, 101, 179, 182, 184, 224, 229; by works, 98–100, 110, 230

Karant-Nunn, Susan, 8–9, 167
Karlstadt, Andreas Bodenstein von, 52, 201
Kelly, Joan, 3
Kempe, Margery, 30–31
Kessler, Johannes, 77
Kienzle, Beverly Mayne, 28
Kneller, Sir Godfrey, 118

Lambert, John, 236
La Vallière, Louise Françoise de la Baume Le Blanc, duchesse de, 139–140, 235
Law / Gospel, 55, 89, 190, 213
Lazarus, 28–29, 36, 100, 193
Le Ber, Jeanne, 142
Lefèvre d'Étaples, Jacques, 2, 15, 40–41, 45, 80, 107, 156–157, 167, 176, 238–239
Lely, Peter, 118
Le Picart, François, 80, 237
Letters, 79, 83, 110, 146–147, 150, 203–207, 212, 214, 217–218, 233
Leyden, Lucas van, 119
Linck, Agnes, 208–209
Liturgy, 11–12, 17, 37–38, 45, 50–51, 66, 149, 153, 184, 214
Locke, John, 226
Longueval, Marie de, 123
Louise of Savoy, 156, 158, 161
Love, 186; Christ's, 21, 27, 86, 88, 92, 94, 112, 133, 214, 224; criticism of, 159–60; disciples' compared to the Magdalene's, 22, 111, 212; human, 9, 119–120; Mary Magdalene's, 24, 30, 124–125, 147–148, 152, 181, 192–193, 228; and preaching, 44, 60, 100, 123, 150; salvation caused by, 46, 110, 121; salvation producing, 51–52;

sinful, 119; women's, 87, 131, 138–139, 177–179, 204, 215–217, 226; works of, 48–49, 50, 54, 98–99, 191

Luke 7:36–50, 229–230, 241–242; Baptist interpretations, 210–211, 226; Catholic interpretations, 98–99, 110–111, 116, 125, 130, 135–136, 139, 147, 158–159; Lutheran interpretations, 46–52, 54–55, 87; Quaker interpretations, 217; Reformed interpretations, 174, 176–177, 179, 182, 191, 196, 198

Luke 10:38–42: Baptist interpretations, 204–207, 209, 211–212, 227–231; Catholic interpretations, 106–108, 124–125, 129–132, 134–136, 143–145, 157, 163; Lutheran interpretations, 55–57, 76; Quaker interpretations, 219–222; Reformed interpretations, 83, 90–91, 179–180, 195, 198

Lüneburg, 49

Luther, Martin, 43–46, 71, 89, 121–122, 131; preaching on John, 18–20, 13, 57–62, 234; preaching on Luke 7, 46–49, 136, 229, 239; preaching on Luke 10, 55–57, 98–99; and women, 9, 62–65, 75, 236

Lux-Sterritt, Laurence, 141

Lydia, 81, 181, 194

Magdalene houses, 2, 14, 26, 114, 143, 149, 174, 183, 230

Maisch, Ingrid, 113

Marguerite de Navarre, 14, 71, 79, 83, 155–161, 178

Mària de San José (Salazar), 136–137, 235

Maria Maddalena, Archduchess of Florence, 149, 162, 164

Maria Maddalena de' Pazzi, 137–139, 239

Marie de l'Incarnation, 145

Marie de St-Joseph, 144

Markham, Gervase, 185–186

Marriage, 8–9, 29, 45, 57, 74, 102, 106–108, 124, 194–195, 206–207, 210–212; clerical, 78–79; mystical, 22, 92, 138, 147, 154, 196, 204–205, 228, 231–233, 238–239

Marseilles, 2, 20, 29, 33–34, 38, 54, 144, 153, 156

Marsin, M., 74, 90

Martha, 22–24, 107–108, 123, 175, 230–231, 241; and nuns' vocation, 129–132, 134–135, 139–143, 145, 163–164, 241; and Protestant vocation, 55–57, 68, 194–195. See also Luke 10:38–42

Martyrs, 72, 81–83, 201–211, 222, 232, 235–236, 238. See also Persecution

Mary (Mother of God), 30–31, 35, 80, 100, 107, 111, 138–139, 141, 195–196, 230, 236–237; Assumption of, 44–45, 55–56, 66, 83, 85–86, 161, 164

Mary I, 81, 105, 160, 187

Master of the Female Half-Lengths, 119

Master of the Magdalene Legend, 118

Mathesius, Johannes, 51–52, 123

Melanchthon, Philipp, 62

Merici, Angela, 141

Michel, Jean, 28, 119

Michelangelo, 150, 152

Mission work, 241–242; of the Catholic Counter-Reformation, 124–125, 134–135, 138, 141–144, 235; of Mary Magdalene, 100, 153, 181; in the nineteenth century, 226, 235

Monasticism: and cult of the Magdalene, 21, 112; Mary Magdalene as exemplar for, 22, 32, 96, 124, 127, 129–132, 135–142, 145–146, 158, 230–231, 235, 239; reforms of, 9, 55, 57, 102–103, 164–165, 183, 241. See also Contemplation; Luke 10:38–42; Magdalene houses

Morality, 238; and Counter-Reformation, 95–96, 102, 108–109, 164, 230; and education, 106, 233; and Luke 7, 23, 116, 184; and Radical Reformation, 202, 209–214, 218

More, Thomas, 40, 105

Moser, Lucas, 38–39

Motherhood, 206–207, 211–212, 220–221, 231, 240

Moulins de Rochefort, François de, 156

Münster, 210, 214

Münzer, Thomas, 61, 201

Music, 11–12, 20, 114–115, 118–119, 146–148, 163, 209. *See also* Hymns

Mycoff, David, 22

Mysticism, 30–31, 91–92, 129, 132, 138, 154, 199, 201, 227

Nadal, Jerome

Nausea, Friedrich, 99–100

Neoplatonism, 121

Nervèze, Antoine de, 161

Nicodemites, 150

Noli me tangere: Catholic interpretations of, 36–37, 112, 122, 137, 152, 235; Protestant interpretations of, 60, 83, 170–171, 180–181, 212

Ochino, Bernardino, 114, 150, 152

Odo of Cluny, 27

Origen, 55

Pamphlet war, 75–77

Panigarola, Francesco, 116

Paratus, 24

Paris, University of, 156–157

Passion of Christ, 204; compassion for, 87, 120, 125; disciples' role in, 109, 111; Mary Magdalene's role in, 17, 20, 22, 43–44, 196; piety of, 24, 30, 132–133, 138, 154; plays, 13, 28–29, 58, 80, 119; Virgin Mary's role in, 107

Patronage: of art, 116, 146, 150, 162–164; of the church by Protestant women, 52, 84, 123, 195, 210, 224, 226, 232; Mary Magdalene's, 72, 81, 217

Paul, Saint: and justification, 48; and love for God, 130, 136; as ordinary sinner, 52, 58, 110, 135; as preacher, 145, 181; and prohibition on women's speech, 27–28, 63, 65, 79, 100–101, 104, 106, 153, 194, 225–226; and spiritual equality, 62

Peasants' War, 61, 75

Pedro y Urrutia, 114

Penitence, 229–230, 235; Catholic interpretations, 95–96, 99, 101–102, 109–110, 113–114, 116, 135–136, 138–141, 158, 160, 162–163; Protestant interpretations, 86–89, 168, 184, 187, 191, 198–199, 211; and sacrament of Penance, 2, 24–25, 46–47, 97–98, 100, 229, 242

Perrette de Bermond, 145

Persecution, 10, 123, 125, 136, 212, 214, 228, 232, 234; resisting, 68, 72, 219; violent, 9, 78, 201–210, 222, 238

Peter, Saint: authority of, 71, 176; conflict with Mary Magdalene, 28, 34–36, 58–59, 154, 169–170, 179, 192; equated with Mary Magdalene, 63, 78, 82–83, 135; sins of, 86, 109, 124

Philip: daughters of, 63–65, 67, 77

Phoebe, 153, 214

Pierre de Vaux, 27

Pietism, 61, 91, 154, 215

Pietro de' Natali, 38

Pifaro, Marc'Antonio del, 119

Pope, 34, 58, 62, 101

Porrer, Sheila, 40

Prayer: books, 114, 154; Mary Magdalene as exemplar of, 78, 231; practice of, 110, 132, 134–135, 145, 163, 190, 195, 221, 235

Preaching, 11, 23–24, 26, 31–33; alternate modes of, 207–210; Counter-Reformation, 96–100, 114, 124, 230; Lutheran, 44, 48–49, 51, 54, 94; of Mary Magdalene, 12, 34–37, 59–62, 83, 95–97, 125–126, 150, 194, 234–238; Radical Reformation, 213; Reformed, 122–123, 167–168, 177–182, 190, 192, 198–199; of women defended, 27, 62–69, 71–74, 77–79, 90–91, 93, 145–146, 153, 202, 214, 216–219, 224–225; of women denied, 100, 167, 172, 176, 178, 181

Priesthood of all believers, 61–64, 66, 68, 71, 77, 197, 206, 221–222, 229–231, 240–241

Prostitution: and Mary Magdalene, 168, 174, 176, 202, 232; reforms of, 26, 96,

108–109, 114, 140, 143, 149; as term of libel, 76, 184
Purgatory, 25
Puritans, 190, 193–196, 198

Quakers, 15, 201, 213–222, 237–238, 240
querelle des femmes, 36, 80, 171, 214

Rabanus Maurus, 20–22
Rabelais, François, 155–157
Rabus, Ludwig, 77
Raymond of Capua, 26
Reason, 169–170, 179
Regents, 155, 161–164
Relics, 20–21, 158, 176
Rémi de Beauvais, 122
Resurrection of Christ: Catholic interpretations of, 100–101, 111–112, 122, 125, 132–133, 137, 152–153, 157, 159; Lutheran interpretations of, 51–52, 57–60, 65–67, 78, 88; Radical Reformation interpretations of, 202, 207, 212, 214, 216–219, 222–223, 225; Reformed interpretations of, 82–84, 92–93, 169–173, 177–182, 187–188, 192, 194, 196–199
Rhegius, Urbanus, 49
Riccardi, Ricardo, 162
Righteousness, 47–48, 57, 121, 132, 190, 206
Robinson, Thomas, 186–292
Rogers, John, 194
Roper, Lyndal, 7
Rubens, Peter Paul, 118
Rupert of Deutz, 27

Sacraments, 47, 112, 122–123, 168, 178, 185, 201, 208, 212–214, 235–237. *See also* Baptism; Eucharist
Saint Bartholomew's Day Massacre, 176
Sainte-Baume, 118, 138, 150, 153, 156, 174
Samaritan woman, 79–80, 132, 137, 140, 194, 217
Schleitheim Confession, 208
Schmalkaldic War, 54
Schmitz, Götz, 187

Schurman, Anna Maria van, 74, 90–91, 94, 220
Schwartz, Adelheit, 209
Schwenckfeld, Caspar, 201, 212
Scuola di San Rocco, 114
Segers, Jerome, 205–206, 211
Silence: as strategy, 203–204, 209; women instructed to keep, 64–67, 77, 79, 81, 106–107, 181, 194, 214, 221
Simons, Menno, 210–212
Simon the Pharisee / Leper, 20, 24, 46–47, 51–52, 54, 110
Simul iustus et peccator, 47, 87, 180, 190
Sins, 18, 40, 47, 58–59, 86, 124, 170, 172–173, 180, 182, 222; contrition for, 33, 36, 78, 98, 102, 110, 124–125, 135, 193, 240; forgiveness of, 24–25, 48–52, 54, 87–89, 98–101, 158–159, 229; Mary Magdalene's sexual, 2, 20, 26, 88, 93, 95–96, 113–121, 168, 184, 187–189, 238–239; original, 89, 120; seven deadly, 83, 184; women's sexual, 23, 31, 109, 139–140, 164–65, 174, 210–211, 234–235
Sixtus V, 136
Skene, Lilias, 219
Soderini, Agostino, 148
Sola Scriptura, 40, 205
Sommer, Heinrich Oskar, 187
Song of Songs: Catholic interpretations, 21–22, 24, 124, 138, 147–149, 154, 233; Protestant interpretations, 78, 92, 130, 177, 190, 194, 204–205, 232, 238
Southwell, Robert, 97, 121–123, 185–187, 192, 232–233
Spangenberg, Johann, 45, 49–50, 56–57, 65–68
Spee, Friedrich, 123–124, 233
Spindler, Georg, 182–183
Stewart, Maria, 225–227
Stirredge, Elizabeth, 219–220
Stjerna, Kirsi, 11
Strasbourg, 77, 79
Susannah, 205
Sustermans, Justus, 162

Taylor, Larissa, 2, 168
Teresa of Avila, 129–136, 163, 190, 224, 228, 230–231, 235, 239
Thompson, John Lee, 171
Timothy, Paul's First Letter to (1 Timothy 2), 79, 81, 106, 194, 214, 226
Titian, 115–116, 118
Torelli, Ludovica, 162
Tour d'Auvergne, Madeleine de la, 120
Trapnel, Anna, 91–92
Trent, Council of, 95–97, 102, 105, 127–128, 146

Ursulines, 103, 141, 144–145, 154

Vézelay, 21, 27, 176
Vialart, Charles, 110, 125, 228
Viret, Pierre, 173–176
Visitandines, 103, 110, 142–143
Visual art, 11–12, 25, 29–30, 37–38, 83, 112–120, 149, 151–152, 161–164, 233
Vives, Juan Luis, 105–108
Vocation, 239, 241–242; for Catholics, 125–131, 134–135, 139–143, 146, 155, 163–165, 223–224, 230, 233–236; for Protestants, 56–57, 89–92, 195, 197, 220, 222–224, 227, 229, 231, 234, 240
Vulgate, 97

Wager, Lewis, 184–185, 188, 232
Wakefield / Towneley Mysteries, 28
Waldensians, 80, 90
Watson, Mary, 221

Weeping: and contrition, 78, 113, 116, 184, 186, 191; criticism of, 159–160, 167, 169–170, 173, 188, 199; and grief, 120–122, 124, 152; praise for, 13, 24, 26, 36, 87, 101, 180, 182, 192–193, 211; and preaching, 21; women's, 27, 31, 133, 139, 147–148, 217, 240
Wengert, Timothy, 61–62
Werden, Johannes von, 24
Weyden, Rogier van der, 30
Whitford, David, 3, 168
Widows, 108
Wiesner-Hanks, Merry, 8–9
Wintour, Helena, 149
Wintrow, Joan and Susannah, 220–221
Witzel, Georg, 101
Word of God: and hearing, 122; and Mary of Bethany, 56–57, 68, 76, 195–196, 205, 207, 211, 213, 227, 230; and ordinary believers, 64, 66, 91, 94, 163, 209, 222–223, 228–229, 231; persevering in, 182, 235; power of, 185, 235
Works: of charity, 132, 142; salvation by, 24–26, 46, 98–101, 190, 230; salvation not achieved by, 48, 50, 68, 86, 186, 229
Wouters, Jan, 206

Xavier, Francis, 138

Zell, Katharina Schütz, 72, 76–78, 94, 227–228, 231–232, 237
Zurich, 209
Zwingli, Ulrich, 201